Contents

List of Plates

Introduction

THE MOST POPULAR LITERATURE in Britain during the late eighteenth and early nineteenth centuries was not Romantic poetry, but 'the latest trash of the day': the Gothic novel. By the end of 1794 the critical reviewers were unable to keep up with 'the present daily increasing rage for novels addressed to the strong passions of wonder and terrour' (*British Critic*, August 1794). This was the earliest genuinely popular literature, appealing to all classes of readers rather than just to an élite literary culture, and producing the first 'bestseller' in Ann Radcliffe's *The Mysteries of Udolpho* (1794). Though first editions were relatively expensive, a wide readership was assured by the existence of cheap reprints and numerous circulating libraries from which they could be borrowed, well stocked by specialist publishers such as William Lane's Minerva Press in Leadenhall Street in the City of London. The novels written by Radcliffe's colleagues were regarded as 'sofa companions', never destined to find a place on the shelves of a gentleman's library. Most of the novelists were women, working in a self-aware feminine literary tradition; they were dismissed by most male critics and refused canonical status. But by all contemporary accounts, these novels effected a revolution in popular taste and, in Sir Walter Scott's words, 'flew from hand to hand' among middle-class tradespeople and their daughters, working-class men, ladies' maids, university students and professors, earls and gentlewomen.

In this selection of readings I have endeavoured to provide representative samples of the major Gothic genres (Historical Gothic, the Radcliffe School of Terror, the Lewis or 'German' School of Horror, tragic melodrama, comic parody, chapbooks, supernatural poetry and ballads, literary criticism and theory, book reviews and polemic), supplemented by private letters and diaries, and contemporary anecdotes about dramatic performances and the design of theatre sets. My major aim has been to establish the literary-cultural context of the Gothic. The selections illustrate the major Gothic issues (e.g. the aesthetics of the Sublime, religion and the supernatural, the influence of ancient Romance, the discourse of Enlightenment reason versus Romantic imagination), as well as the genre's conventions or 'hobgoblin machinery' (e.g. vampires, spectres, orphans, the Inquisition, banditti, nuns, storms, ruined castles, phantasmagoric labyrinths and mystic forests) and important social themes (e.g. prison reform, revolutionary politics, mother–daughter relationships, illicit sexuality, sensibility, madness). All of the major writers are represented, as well as the authors of the seven 'horrid' novels listed in Jane Austen's parody *Northanger Abbey*.

The Gothic novel is not easily encompassed during a single educational term: Radcliffe's *The Mysteries of Udolpho* is nearly 300,000 words long, and Maturin's *Melmoth the Wanderer* is not much shorter. Mary Shelley's *Frankenstein* is often chosen for study because of its relative shortness as well as intrinsic interest. There have been many anthologies of Gothic tales or short stories, but the characteristic form of the genre was the long novel. Unfortunately, if one reads a whole novel by each of the major writers – Horace Walpole, Ann Radcliffe, Matthew Gregory Lewis, Charles Robert Maturin, Mary Shelley (possibly also Charlotte Smith, William Godwin, Charlotte Dacre) – little time is left for studying the minor writers – writers who represent the genre just as much as those in the canon. For the sake of both these minor writers and overworked students, this reader contains many short extracts from long novels – following the precedent set by their contemporary reviewers.

I have chosen 1764 – the publication date of Horace Walpole's *The Castle of Otranto* – as the starting date. Many works earlier than this influenced the Gothic tradition – Edmund Burke's *On the Sublime* (1756), the poetry of James Thomson, Thomas Gray, James Macpherson's 'Ossian', Edward Young and the graveyard poets, and revivals of 'Celtic' or 'Saxon' or 'Bardic' poetry by antiquarians – but if all influential work were included, we would have to go back to the ghost scene in Shakespeare's *Hamlet* and the witches' scene in *Macbeth*. My touchstone has been whether or not a work was 'part of' rather than 'an influence on' the Gothic tradition.

The original or 'first wave' of the Gothic tradition peaked around 1810 and then fell out of fashion very quickly. Maturin's *Melmoth the Wanderer* in 1820 was regarded as a revival of a dying tradition. Gothic novels appeared at the rate of more than a dozen every year from 1794 through 1797, and increased to nearly two dozen per year for 1798 through 1810, before subsiding to little more than half a dozen per year for 1811 through 1820, then to only three or four per year for 1821 to 1830 (F. S. Frank, *The First Gothics*, 1987). I have selected material up to about 1840 so as to include a few items from the turning-point at which the Gothic was felt to be in need of revival (as in the case of Ainsworth's *Rookwood*), and to include retrospective criticism that sums up the achievements and failures of the tradition. I have refrained from including items which properly form part of the regeneration or 'second wave' of the tradition, during the Victorian era, by which time it had lost much of its original focus on 'dreadful pleasure' and been superseded by a new emphasis on abnormal psychological states deriving from Maturin and Poe rather than from Radcliffe and Lewis.

I have divided the two main streams of the Gothic novel into Radcliffe and the School of Terror, and Lewis and the 'German' School of Horror. These two schools are often portrayed as emphasizing, respectively, sensibility versus sensationalism. Although the 'machinery' of the Radcliffe School is often mocked, the agents and incidents of terror in this stream are usually *internal*, whereas the agents and incidents of horror in the Lewis School are usually *external*. The former is characterized by mystery and corner-of-the-eye creepiness, whereas the latter is characterized by violence and raw-head-and-bloody-bones. In the former we are often invited to wonder if the events are not really in the mind of the narrator, whereas in the latter our focus is often directed to political agents of oppression. In the former a common theme is sensibility; in the latter a common theme is sadomasochism. Nevertheless I would not push this personal/public dichotomy too far. Both schools exploit the resources of the subconscious, taboo, trauma and nightmare, sexuality, mental disorientation and madness, and both schools portray social injustice, prisons, and the brutalizing effect of poverty. Both schools are, in other words, equally 'Gothic'.

For the past generation it has been fashionable to distinguish between 'the female Gothic' and 'the male Gothic'. Ellen Moers coined the term 'female Gothic' in *Literary Women* (1976), and much of the feminist approach of the mid-1980s focused on the 'gendered' discourse of sensibility and how that relates to the dichotomy of 'female' supernaturalism versus 'male' reason; the historical position of women in 'patriarchal' society and how that relates to questions of female authorship; contested sites of female sexuality such as the castle and the home; and the villain's use of the male gaze to police female sexuality. A feminist awareness is undoubtedly fruitful for analysing the Gothic – most of whose authors were women – but the conception of 'the female Gothic' risks falling into sexist stereotypes about women being best at portraying emotions while men are best at recounting action. This rather ignores the high number of murders that occur in novels by women. A supposed dichotomy between 'the female Gothic' and 'the male Gothic' can be hard to maintain along historical principles. For example, the *Lady's Magazine* is undoubtedly a site for 'the female Gothic', yet major contributors to the magazine were men, such as George Moore whose *Grasville Abbey* was serialized in it under the perhaps gender-ambiguous initials 'G. M.' Coleridge's 'Christabel' can be fruitfully analysed as part of 'the female Gothic', especially in its depiction of the relationship between Christabel and Geraldine, but in this poem Coleridge borrowed from *The Castle Spectre* by Lewis, head of 'the male Gothic' tradition. Minor male writers such as Isaac Crookenden and T. J. Horsley Curties were thoroughly Radcliffean, while two of the leading women writers, Mary Shelley and Charlotte Dacre, were thoroughly Lewisian. A rigid categorization by gender generates too many cross-dressers.

The psychoanalytical approach was popular throughout the 1980s, especially in the use of Freudian theory and Freud's concept of 'the uncanny'. Much attention has been given to the analysis of repressed sexuality and how this is reflected by Gothic compositional devices such as premonitory dreams and the projection or displacement of fear, and Gothic images such as the spectre or monster (representing 'the other'). During the 1990s the psychoanalytical approach focused specifically on female sexual issues, such as female masochism, and theories about the 'pre-Oedipal' stage in which the female infant fears being absorbed into the mother (who certainly haunts many novels). Lacanian theory is sometimes employed in an amalgam of psychoanalytical, feminist and post-structuralist approaches, and Kristeva's theory of 'abjection' has been used to analyse Gothic melancholia.

There is a general consensus that the terror at the heart of the Gothic reflects pent-up desire. Some Gothic plots are seen as narratives of emergent female sexuality, in terms of the heroine's relation both with her mother and with the patriarchal villain. The heroines of Gothic novels never quite grow up, but remain fixed at some childhood or 'pregenital' stage. Fear of being raped is often cited as being fundamental to 'the female Gothic', while actual rape is fundamental to 'the male Gothic'. But prurient rape imagery is found not only in Lewis's *The Monk*, but also in many examples of 'the female Gothic'. Incest is a frequent theme in the genre, often explicitly, as in Lewis's *The Monk* and Walpole's *The Mysterious Mother*, sometimes implicitly, as in the strong bonds expressed between brother and sister in Joanna Baillie's play *De Monfort*.

Sometimes the Gothic is seen as a kind of cover for subversive or illicit sexuality. An interest in 'unspeakable' and 'unnatural' desires and crimes in works by Walpole, Lewis and Beckford (and sometimes Maturin) is often perceived as a reflection of the writer's own homosexuality, with suppression and secrecy being linked to the homophobia of contemporary English society. Very strong bonds between women, and between daughters and mothers, are also sometimes perceived as reflecting (suppressed) lesbian desire. Undoubtedly there are sexually subversive themes in much Gothic literature, but we must guard against identifying the entire genre with these themes. The reductive claim that they are all grounded in homosexual fantasy founders on the fact that most Gothic novels were written by married women in order to support their large families.

Modern and postmodern criticism have increasingly moved away from a focus on individual psychology to a focus on social, political, economic and ideological issues. The 'female Gothic' is often informed by an awareness of the economic dependency – or powerlessness – of women. The feminist/Marxist approach has pointed out how often issues of money and property dominate Gothic novels by women. It is unfair and male-chauvinist, for example, to accuse Emily in *The Mysteries of Udolpho* of secretly harbouring erotic desire for the man whom she clearly despises for murdering her aunt to get her property. But money, power and sex all employ the same set of tropes.

The political ferment that paralleled the rise of the Gothic novel – the Revolution and the Terror in France – has always been recognized. Gothic novels often attack the prevailing rule of class, church, and patriarchal society – summed up in the figure of an aristocratic Roman Catholic tyrant. But this is not a simple matter of attacking a male 'patriarchy', for such tyrants are not always princes or monks: some wicked Marchesas and cold Mother Superiors also fit the bill. The attack on Roman Catholicism, usually very explicit, derives mainly from the xenophobic enmity of British Anglicanism (and Protestantism) towards European Roman Catholicism. The upheavals of the old political order mirror the attacks on the *ancien régime* in Gothic novels, but though the rigidity of feudalism is explicitly attacked, the broad class structure is usually retained. These novels draw their potent imagery from the fall of the Bastille in 1789, but by the end of the last volume, after the wicked are punished and the just are married, the new social order that replaces feudal tyranny might best be termed upper-middle-class benevolence. All romantic novels, Gothic or sentimental, toy with the subversive possibility of inter-class love, but the heroines rarely marry into the class beneath them, a fate prevented by the discovery of a strawberry birthmark that proves that their peasant lover is, after all, of noble (or at least gentle) birth, the same as they.

The long-running argument about whether the Gothic novel is genuinely subversive or genuinely reactionary has not been resolved. Contemporary critics complained (accurately) that many Gothic novels tended to undermine social, religious and moral conventions, but we are less sure about how far they tended to be politically subversive. Most post-structuralists will probably contend that the Gothic novel reinscribes rather than deconstructs bourgeois ideology. A long and predominantly Socialist tradition generally condemns the Gothic novel for being reactionary. It is argued that the genre tends to make readers feel helpless to effect progressive social change. It is difficult to combine within a single genre both romance and realism or, more specifically, intense individual psychology with a broad social critique. It is perhaps mainly in depictions of prisons and the Inquisition (as in novels by Godwin and Maturin) that social realism works happily hand in hand with imaginative Gothicism. My own feeling is that many Gothic novels are indeed subversive, but primarily upon the individual rather than the social level.

It is less difficult to recognize that the attack on Gothic novels in the contemporary press was informed by a conservative political ideology. As the Revolution in France degenerated into the wholesale slaughter of the Terror, which seemed to bury the ideals of liberty, equality and fraternity, much of the reactionary ruling class in England condemned such democratic ideals as leading inevitably to the complete collapse of society. Gothic novels were politically censured as 'the terrorist system of writing', and their authors denounced as Jacobins set on destroying England. Gothic novels were un-English – and un-manly. Even the less demonstrative women novelists were branded as belonging to 'the Wollstonecraft school' of early feminism.

The approaches I have been discussing deal mainly with substance, whereas another fruitful approach – the aesthetic – deals mainly with form, structure, motifs and conventions. We can enjoy the Gothic as a literary construct, whatever its cultural, psychological or political significance. There has been a tendency to overpraise works such as Walpole's *The Castle of Otranto* for their psychological drama; this novella might better be appreciated as a highly artificial 'amusing fiction' by a sophisticated connoisseur of things medieval. Similarly, the economic themes in novels by women are too often seen as occupying centre stage, when in most cases such themes are subsidiary. By 'fore-grounding' ideology, we risk forgetting that the Gothic is grounded in the desire to entertain the reader through the use of literary devices. Even the most disgusting passage in Lewis –

> Sometimes I felt the bloated toad, hideous and pampered with the poisonous vapours of the dungeon, dragging his loathsome length along my bosom. Sometimes the quick cold lizard roused me, leaving his slimy track upon my face, and entangling itself in the tresses of my wild and matted hair. Often have I at waking found my fingers ringed with the long worms which bred in the corrupted flesh of my infant.

– can be analysed in terms of its poetics: rhythm, rhyme, alliteration, assonance, acrostic scrambling, chiasmus.

The primary motivation for most Gothic writers was the joy of literary creation. The Gothic novel creates, above all, a very literary world. Novels and poetry are read and discussed by the heroines, and libraries are often found in castles, convents or mansions, from Charlotte Smith's *Emmeline* (1788) to Edgar Allan Poe's 'The Fall of the House of Usher' (1839). Books and manuscripts are important physical objects in Gothic fiction – even Frankenstein's monster studies books. Gothic heroines frequently compose their own poems, and Radcliffe's *The Romance of the Forest* (1791) could well be seen as 'A Portrait of the Artist as a Gothic Heroine'. Literary consumption was important in the increasingly constrained lives of women during this period, and the writing of fiction was a way for them to escape some of the limitations placed upon them by an increasingly male-dominated culture.

The Gothic is a paradoxical genre, and many writers took delight in its paradoxes. Much of its content streams forth from the unconscious, but is carefully channelled by the hyperconscious. Irony and satire play across the surface of a stormy sea, calming the subversive currents that threaten to wreck the ship. The 'spirits from the vasty deep' are kept well in check by the aesthetic reins of 'the Sublime', 'the Beautiful' and 'the Picturesque' – and by a fourth aesthetic category which has not been sufficiently appreciated, 'the Ridiculous', for example, the deliberate use of lower-class characters to contrast with and subtly satirize the Sublimity of the villains and the Beauty of the heroines. Gothic literature was written to delight as well as to terrify, as demonstrated by its oft-repeated paradoxes of 'dreadful pleasure', 'delightful horror' and 'fearful joy'.

Note on the Texts

Most of the selections use the first editions, and follow the spelling and punctuation of the original texts, with some modernization of printing conventions: titles of books are put in italics rather than quotation marks; quotation marks appear only at beginnings and ends of quotations, rather than repeatedly along the left margin; errors in the placing of quotation marks are silently corrected to avoid confusion; apostrophes are silently inserted in possessives (but not removed from the very common use of 'it's' as a possessive). Errors obviously due to the printer rather than the author have been silently corrected. But unusual or no-longer-current spellings are retained, usually without an intrusive [*sic*] to indicate that the 'error' is not mine.

Short List of Resources

Barron, N. (ed.), *Fantasy and Horror*, Metuchen, NJ: Scarecrow/UPA, 1998.

Birkhead, E., *The Tale of Terror*, London: Constable, 1921.

Blain, V., Clements, P. and Grundy, I. (eds), *The Feminist Companion to Literature in English*, London: B. T. Batsford, 1990.

Blakey, D., *The Minerva Press 1790–1820*, Bibliographical Society, 1939.

Botting, F., *Gothic*, London: Routledge, 1996.

Butler, M., *Romantics, Rebels, and Reactionaries*, Oxford University Press, 1981.

Clery, E. J., *The Rise of Supernatural Fiction, 1762–1800*, Cambridge University Press, 1995.

Fleenor, J. E. (ed.), *The Female Gothic*, Montreal: Eden Press, 1983.

Frank, F. S., *The First Gothics*, New York: Garland, 1987.

Frank, F. S., *Gothic Fiction*, Westport, CT: Meckler, 1988.

Frank, F. S., *Guide to the Gothic: An Annotated Bibliography of Criticism*, Metuchen, NJ: Scarecrow, 1984.

Frank, F. S., *Guide to the Gothic II*, Metuchen, NJ: Scarecrow, 1995.

Frank, F. S. (comp.) *Guide to the Gothic III*, updated 21 January 2000, <http://www.toolcity.net/~ffrank/GOTHICIII.html>.

Geary, R. F., *The Supernatural in Gothic Fiction*, Lewiston, NY: Edwin Mellen Press, 1992.

The Gothic: Materials for Study, accessed 21 January 2000, <http://www.engl.virginia.edu/~enec981/Group/title.html>.

Gothic Literature, comp. D. Thomson, accessed 21 January 2000, <http://www2.gasou.edu/facstaff/dougt/gothic.html>.

The Gothic Literature Page, comp. F. Potter, updated 18 September 1999, <http://members.aol.com/iamudolpho/basic.html>.

Graham, K. W. (ed.), *Gothic Fictions*, New York: AMS, 1989.

Hoeveler, D. L., *Gothic Feminism*, Pennsylvania State University Press, 1998.

Howard, J., *Reading Gothic Fiction*, Oxford: Clarendon Press, 1994.

Howells, C. A., *Love, Mystery and Misery*, London: Athlone Press, 1978.

Images from the Gothic Chapbooks, comp. F. S. Frank, accessed 21 January 2000, <http://www.toolcity.net/~ffrank/Figure-01.gif.html>.

Kilgour, M., *The Rise of the Gothic Novel*, London: Routledge, 1995.

The Literary Gothic, comp. J. G. Voller, updated 9 January 2000, <http://www.siue.edu/~jvoller/gothic.html>.

McNutt, D. J., *The Eighteenth-Century Gothic Novel*, New York, Garland, 1975.

Mayo, R. D., *The English Novel in the Magazines 1740–1815*, Oxford University Press, 1962.

Miles, R., *Gothic Writing 1750–1820*, London: Routledge, 1993.

Moers, E., *Literary Women*, New York, Doubleday, 1976.

Mulvey-Roberts, M. (ed.), *The Handbook to Gothic Literature*, New York University Press, 1998.

Napier, E. R., *The Failure of Gothic*, Oxford: Clarendon Press, 1987.

Punter, D., *The Gothic Tradition*, London: Longman, 1996.

The Sadleir–Black Gothic Collection, comp. F. S. Frank, accessed 21 January 2000, <http://www.lib.virginia.edu/speccol/colls/gold.html>.

Sage, V. (ed.), *The Gothick Novel*, London: Macmillan, 1990.

The Sickly Taper, comp. F. S. Frank, updated 21 January 2000, <http://www.toolcity.net/~ffrank/>.

Spector, R. D., *The English Gothic*, Westport, CT: Greenwood Press, 1984.

Sublime Anxiety, University of Virginia Exhibition, modified 17 August 1999, <http://www.lib.virginia.edu/exhibits/gothic/index.html>.

Summers, M., *A Gothic Bibliography*, 1941, rprt. 1964.

Summers, M., *The Gothic Quest*, 1938, rprt. 1964.

Todd, J. (ed.), *Dictionary of British Women Writers*, London: Routledge, 1989.

Tracy, A. B., *The Gothic Novel 1790–1830*, University of Kentucky Press, 1981.

Varma, D. P., *The Gothic Flame*, 1957.

Voller, J. G., *The Supernatural Sublime*, Northern Illinois University Press, 1994.

— 1 —

Historical Gothic

HORACE WALPOLE is generally credited with – and claimed for himself – the creation of 'a new species of romance' with *The Castle of Otranto* (1764), which he subtitled 'A Gothic Story'. Some would trace the roots of the tradition to the terrifying scenes in Tobias Smollett's *Adventures of Ferdinand Count Fathom* (1753) and some would argue that Thomas Leland's *Longsword, Earl of Salisbury* (1762) – subtitled 'An Historical Romance' – is really the 'first' Gothic novel. *Longsword* does indeed have the medievalism typical of the early works in the genre – which of course is why the form is called 'Gothic' – but it lacks the defining sense of the supernatural or the marvellous. Another early example of the genre is William Hutchinson's *The Hermitage* (1772), which is full of supernatural machinery. But Walpole's invention did not find many imitators until Clara Reeve set out to improve upon his technique in *The Old English Baron* (1777/1778), which she also subtitled 'A Gothic Story' to establish its pedigree. The tradition developed slowly: the next date was 1783 with the publication of *Edwy and Edilda: A Gothic Tale* by Thomas Sedgwick Whalley.

The distinguishing feature of the subdivision termed 'Historical Gothic' is the provision of historical details that root the story in 'ancient', 'medieval' or simply 'olden' times. The attempt to recreate the authentic manners and settings of the feudal age (the fourteenth century was often chosen) was seldom believable and sometimes laughable. Ann Radcliffe's first novel, *The Castles of Athlin and Dunbayne* (1789), relates the conflict between rival feudal Scottish clans, but is typical of many Historical Gothic novels in having only the slightest grasp of history. In her novel *A Sicilian Romance*, supposedly contemporary with the poetry of Tasso, a sumptuous Renaissance ball is followed by a private musical trio, in which Ferdinand plays the violoncello, Verezzi plays the German flute, and Julia accompanies her singing on the pianoforte. The more successful Historical Gothic novels drew their inspiration from antiquarian studies of English medieval Romance literature popular in the mid-1700s, notably Richard Hurd's *Letters on Chivalry and Romance* (1762), Bishop Thomas Percy's *Reliques of Ancient English Poetry* (1765), Thomas Warton's *History of English Poetry* (1774–81) and Clara Reeve's *The Progress of Romance* (1785): 'Romance may not improperly be called the polite literature of early ages, and they have been the favourite amusements of later times.'

The heightened romantic colouring given to historical times and events may be part of the escapism with which the Gothic novel is sometimes charged. Walpole, for example, secure in his 'Gothick' villa at Strawberry Hill with its bookcases modelled on medieval tombs, felt that 'there is no wisdom comparable to that of exchanging what is called the realities of life for dreams. Old castles, old pictures, old histories, and the babble of old people make one live back into centuries that cannot disappoint one' (letter, 5 January 1766). But the central flaw of Historical Gothic is that the impulse towards historicism ultimately runs counter to the impulse towards romanticism; erudition and idealism do not sit happily together. The dream-like obscurity that is so important to the terror of the Gothic is repeatedly undermined by the requirements of antiquarian accuracy.

Historical romance survived throughout the entire period, and is remembered today primarily by the rise of the regional novel. Subtitles easily identify Historical Gothic novels: for example, an anonymous author's *Mortimore Castle: A Cambrian Tale* (1793), George Walker's *Haunted Castle: A Norman Romance* (1794), Palmer's *Haunted Cavern: A Caledonian Tale* (1796) – one among many Scottish novels which ring with the adventures of the Highland chieftains. Sydney Owensen, Lady Morgan, was a fervent Irish nationalist, and the Irish novelist Regina Maria Roche, author of *The Children of the Abbey* (1796), also wrote Historical Gothic novels set in Yorkshire and Ireland (*The Monastery of St Colombe*, 1813), Cornwall (*Trecothick Bower; or, The Lady of the West Country*, 1814), and six novels set in Ireland; her *The Tradition of the Castle; or, Scenes in the Emerald Isle* (1824) is a convincing treatment of absentee landlords, religious freedom and Irish national pride. Regional Historical Gothics laid the ground for the work of Sir Walter Scott and Maria Edgeworth, in which supernaturalism is replaced by nationalism.

The Castle of Otranto (1764)*

HORACE WALPOLE (1717–97)

The Castle of Otranto *was published anonymously on 24 December 1764 in 500 copies and was an immediate success. The poet Thomas Gray wrote to Walpole that it made 'some of us cry a little, and all in general afraid to go to bed o' nights' (letter, 30 December 1764). In the second edition, also of 500 copies in April 1765, Walpole included a sonnet to Lady Mary Coke signed with his initials and thereby revealed his identity. By the time of his death, his novella had been translated into several languages and had appeared in several illustrated editions. With its five*

---

* Horace Walpole, *The Castle of Otranto, A Gothic Story*, 2nd edn (London: William Bathoe and Thomas Lownds, 1765), pp. v–xi, xv–xvi.

PLATE 1

The staircase at Strawberry Hill, from *A Description of the Villa of Horace Walpole . . . at Strawberry Hill* (1774). The first Gothic novel, *The Castle of Otranto* (1764), grew from a dream in which Walpole saw a gigantic hand in armour on the uppermost bannister of a great staircase. Engraving by J. Newton after E. Edwards. By permission of the London Borough of Richmond upon Thames.

chapters, it resembles a five-act drama, closely observing the 'dramatic unities' and employing dialogue more than description. Its reasonably accurate thirteenth-century setting encloses a fantastical tale about a tyrant who tries to seduce the fiancée of his dead son and who murders his own daughter before he is revealed as a usurper by a giant ghost. Although the diction and characters of Walpole's novella are as highly polished as any Augustan could require, the work nevertheless had its roots in the world of the irrational: 'I waked one morning in the beginning of last June from a dream, of which all I could recover was, that I had thought myself in an ancient castle (a very natural dream for a head filled like mine with Gothic story) and that on the uppermost bannister of a great staircase I saw a gigantic hand in armour' (letter to William Cole, 9 March 1765). Many of the issues common to subsequent discourse about the Gothic novel are raised in Walpole's Preface to his story: the characteriza-tion of the Gothic novel as the union of the marvels of medieval romance with the realism of modern novels, exploitation of the Aristotelian categories of pity and terror, the increase of sublime themes through contrast with lower-class humorous characters, and the appeal to the authority of Shakespeare to justify one's own extravagant style (indeed, the novel contains echoes of Macbeth, Cymbeline *and* Romeo and Juliet*). (See also Sir Walter Scott's critique of the novel, pp. 323ff.; and excerpts from Walpole's* Mysterious Mother, *pp. 176ff.)*

Preface to the First Edition (1764)

The following work was found in the library of an ancient Catholic family in the north of England. It was printed at Naples, in the black letter, in the year 1529. How much sooner it was written does not appear. The principal incidents are such as were believed in the darkest ages of christianity; but the language and conduct have nothing that savours of barbarism. The style is purest Italian. If the story was written near the time when it is supposed to have happened, it must have been between 1095, the era of the first crusade, and 1243, the date of the last, or not long afterwards. There is no other circumstance in the work, that can lead us to guess at the period in which the scene is laid. The names of the actors are evidently fictitious, and probably disguised on purpose: yet the Spanish names of the domestics seem to indicate that this work was not composed until the establishment of the Arragonian kings in Naples had made Spanish appellations familiar in that country. The beauty of the diction, and the zeal of the author (moder-ated, however, by singular judgment), concur to make me think, that the date of the composition was little antecedent to that of the impression. Letters were then in their most flourishing state in Italy, and contributed to dispel the empire of superstition, at that time so forcibly attacked by the reformers. . . .

Miracles, visions, necromancy, dreams, and other preternatural events, are exploded now even from romances. That was not the case when our author wrote; much less when the story itself is supposed to have happened. Belief in every kind of prodigy was so established in those dark ages, that an author would not be faithful to the manners of the times, who should omit all mention of them. He is not bound to believe them himself, but he must represent his actors as believing them.

If this air of the miraculous is excused, the reader will find nothing else unworthy of his perusal. Allow the possibility of the facts, and all the actors comport themselves as persons would do in their situation. There is no bombast, no similes, flowers, digressions, or unnecessary descriptions. Every thing tends directly to the catastrophe. Never is the reader's attention relaxed. The rules of the drama are almost observed throughout the conduct of the piece. The characters are well drawn, and still better maintained. Terror, the author's principal engine, prevents the story from ever languishing; and it is so often contrasted by pity, that the mind is kept up in a constant vicissitude of interesting passions.

Some persons may, perhaps, think the characters of the domestics too little serious for the general cast of the story; but, besides their opposition to the principal personages, the art of the author is very observable in his conduct of the subalterns. They discover many passages essential to the story, which could not be well brought to light but by their naiveté and simplicity: in particular, the womanish terror and foibles of Bianca, in the last chapter, conduce essentially towards advancing the catastrophe. . . .

Preface to the Second Edition (1765)

The favourable manner in which this little piece has been received by the public, calls upon the author to explain the grounds on which he composed it. But before he opens those motives, it is fit that he should ask pardon of his readers for having offered his work to them under the borrowed personage of a translator. As diffidence of his own abilities, and the novelty of the attempt, were the sole inducements to assume that disguise, he flatters himself he shall appear excusable. He resigned his performance to the impartial judgment of the public; determined to let it perish in obscurity, if disapproved; nor meaning to avow such a trifle, unless better judges should pronounce that he might own it without a blush.

It was an attempt to blend the two kinds of Romance, the ancient and the modern. In the former, all was imagination and improbability: in the latter, nature is always intended to be, and sometimes has been, copied with success. Invention has not been wanting; but the great resources of fancy have been dammed up, by a strict adherence to common life. But if in the latter species Nature has cramped imagination, she did but take her revenge, having been totally excluded from old Romances. The actions, sentiments, conversations, of the heroes and heroines of ancient days were as unnatural as the machines employed to put them in motion.

The author of the following pages thought it possible to reconcile the two kinds. Desirous of leaving the powers of fancy at liberty to expatiate through the boundless realms of invention, and thence of creating more interesting situations, he wished to conduct the mortal agents in his drama according to the rules of probability; in short, to make them think, speak and act, as it might be supposed mere men and women would do in extra-ordinary positions. He had observed, that in all inspired writings, the personages under the dispensation of miracles and witnesses of the most stupendous phenomena, never lose sight of their human character: whereas in the productions of romantic story, an improbable event never fails to be attended by an absurd dialogue. The actors seem to lose their senses, the moment the laws of nature have lost their tone. As the public have applauded the attempt, the author must not say he was entirely unequal to the task he had undertaken: yet if the new route he has struck out shall have paved a road for men of brighter talents, he shall own with pleasure and modesty, that he was sensible the plan was capable of receiving greater embellishments than his imagination or conduct of the passions could bestow on it.

With regard to the deportment of the domestics, on which I have touched in the former preface, I will beg leave to add a few words. The simplicity of their behaviour, almost tending to excite smiles, which at first seems not consonant to the serious cast of the work, appeared to me not only not improper, but was marked designedly in that manner. My rule was Nature. However grave, important, or even melancholy, the sensations of Princes and heroes may be, they do not stamp the same affections on their domestics: at least the latter do not, or should not be made to express their passions in the same dignified tone. In my humble opinion, the contrast between the sublime of the one and the *naiveté* of the others, sets the pathetic of the former in a stronger light. The very impatience which a reader feels, while delayed by the coarse pleasantries of vulgar actors from arriving at the knowledge of the important catastrophe he expects, perhaps heightens, certainly proves, that he has been artfully interested in the depending event. But I had higher authority than my own opinion for this conduct. The great master of nature, SHAKESPEARE, was the model I copied. Let me ask, if his tragedies of *Hamlet* and *Julius Caesar* would not lose a considerable share of their spirit and wonderful beauties, if the humour of the grave-diggers, the fooleries of Polonius, and the clumsy jests of the Roman citizens, were omitted, or vested in heroics? Is not the elo-quence of *Antony*, the nobler and affectedly-unaffected oration of *Brutus*, artificially exalted by the rude bursts of nature from the mouths of their auditors? These touches remind one of the *Grecian* sculptor, who to convey the idea of a Colossus within the dimensions of a seal, inserted a little boy measuring his thumb.

No, says *Voltaire* in his edition of *Corneille*, this mixture of buffoonery and solemnity is intolerable. − *Voltaire* is a genius − but not of *Shakespeare*'s magnitude. Without recurring to disputable authority, I appeal from *Voltaire* to himself. I shall not availl myself of his former encomiums on our mighty poet; though the *French* critic has twice translated the same speech in *Hamlet*, some years ago in admiration, latterly in derision; and I am sorry to find that his judgment grows weaker when it ought to be farther matured. . . .

The result of all I have said, is, to shelter my own daring under the canon of the brightest genius this country, at least, has produced. I might have pleaded, that having created a new species of romance, I was at liberty to lay down what rules I thought fit for the conduct of it: But I should be more proud of having imitated, however faintly, weakly, and at a distance, so masterly a pattern, than to enjoy the entire merit of invention, unless I could have marked my work with genius as well as with originality. Such as it is, the Public have honoured it sufficiently, whatever rank their suffrages allot to it.

Sir Bertrand, a Fragment (1773)*

JOHN AIKIN (1747–1822)

John Aikin's important 'Fragment' is often wrongly ascribed to his more famous sister Anna Laetitia Aikin (later Mrs Barbauld), because it appeared in their joint collection of Miscellaneous Pieces *(1773). (The correct attribution is given in the* Analytical Review *for December 1798, and confirmed by their niece Lucy Aikin in her Memoir prefixed to* The Works of Anna Laetitia Barbauld, *1825.) It was a literary exercise designed to illustrate the principles in his sister's prefatory essay 'On the Pleasure Derived from Objects of Terror' (see pp. 281ff.). Aikin made no other contribution to the Gothic tradition, but many of the images in his Fragment were copied in later Gothic novels: the progression through a series of stairways and vaulted halls in an ancient mansion, the massy door creaking on its hinges, the mysterious blue flame, the touch of a cold dead hand, a deep hollow groan, and of course the protagonist's sensation of terror.*

—— AFTER this adventure, Sir Bertrand turned his steed towards the woulds, hoping to cross these dreary moors before the curfew. But ere he had proceeded half his journey, he was bewildered by the different tracks; and not being able, as far as the eye could reach, to espy any object but the brown heath surrounding him, he was at length quite uncertain which way he should direct his course. Night overtook him in this situation. It was one

---

* J. and A. L. Aikin, *Miscellaneous Pieces, in Prose* (London: J. Johnson, 1773), pp. 127–37.

of those nights when the moon gives a faint glimmering of light through the thick black clouds of a lowering sky. Now and then she suddenly emerged in full splendour from her veil; and then instantly retired behind it, having just served to give the forlorn Sir Bertrand a wide extended prospect over the desolate waste. Hope and native courage a while urged him to push forwards, but at length the increasing darkness and fatigue of body and mind overcame him; he dreaded moving from the ground he stood on, for fear of unknown pits and bogs, and alighting from his horse in despair, he threw himself on the ground. He had not long continued in that posture when the sullen toll of a distant bell struck his ears – he started up, and turning towards the sound, discerned a dim twinkling light. Instantly he seized his horse's bridle, and with cautious steps advanced towards it. After a painful march he was stopt by a moated ditch surrounding the place from whence the light proceeded; and by a momentary glimpse of moon-light he had a full view of a large antique mansion, with turrets at the corners, and an ample porch in the centre. The injuries of time were strongly marked on everything about it. The roof in various places was fallen in, the battlements were half demolished, and the windows broken and dismantled. A draw-bridge, with a ruinous gate-way at each end, led to the court before the building – He entered; and instantly the light, which proceeded from a window in one of the turrets, glided along and vanished; at the same moment the moon sunk beneath a black cloud, and the night was darker than ever. All was silent – Sir Bertrand fastened his steed under a shed, and approaching the house, traversed its whole front with light and slow footsteps. – All was still as death. – He looked in at the lower windows, but could not distinguish a single object through the impenetrable gloom. After a short parley with himself, he entered the porch, and seizing a massy iron knocker at the gate, lifted it up, and hesitating, at length struck a loud stroke. The noise resounded through the whole mansion with hollow echoes. All was still again – He repeated the strokes more boldly and louder – another interval ensued – A third time he knocked, and a third time all was still. He then fell back to some distance that he might discern whether any light could be seen in the whole front – It again appeared in the same place, and quickly glided away as before – at the same instant a deep sullen toll sounded from the turret. Sir Bertrand's heart made a fearful stop – He was awhile motionless; then terror impelled him to make some hasty steps towards his steed – but shame stopt his flight; and urged by honour, and a resistless desire of finishing the adventure, he returned to the porch; and working up his soul to a full steadiness of resolution, he drew forth his sword with one hand, and with the other lifted up the latch of the gate. The heavy door, creaking upon its hinges, reluctantly yielded to his hand – he applied his shoulder to it and forced it open – he quitted it, and stept forward – the door instantly shut with a thundering clap. Sir Bertrand's blood was chilled – he turned back to find the door, and it was long ere his trembling hands could seize it – but his utmost strength could not open it again. After several ineffectual attempts, he looked behind him, and beheld, across a hall, upon a large staircase, a pale bluish flame which cast a dismal gleam of light around. He again summoned forth his courage and advanced towards it – It retired. He came to the foot of the stairs, and after a moment's deliberation ascended. He went slowly up, the flame retiring before him, till he came to a wide gallery – The flame proceeded along it, and he followed in silent horror, treading lightly, for the echoes of his footsteps startled him. It led him to the foot of another staircase, and then vanished – At the same instant another toll sounded from the turret – Sir Bertrand felt it strike upon his heart. He was now in total darkness, and with his arms extended, began to ascend the second staircase. A dead cold hand met his left hand and firmly grasped it, drawing him forcibly forwards – he endeavoured to disengage himself, but could not – he made a furious blow with his sword, and instantly a loud shriek pierced his ears, and the dead hand was left powerless in his – He dropt it, and rushed forwards with a desperate valour. The stairs were narrow and winding, and interrupted by frequent breaches, and loose fragments of stone. The stair-case grew narrower and narrower, and at length terminated in a low iron grate. Sir Bertrand pushed it open – it led to an intricate winding passage, just large enough to admit a person upon his hands and knees. A faint glimmering of light served to show the nature of the place. Sir Bertrand entered – A deep hollow groan resounded from a distance through the vault – He went forwards, and proceeding beyond the first turning, he discerned the same blue flame which had before conducted him. He followed it. The vault, at length, suddenly opened into a lofty gallery, in the midst of which a figure appeared, compleately armed, thrusting forwards the bloody stump of an arm, with a terrible frown and menacing gesture, and brandishing a sword in his hand. Sir Bertrand undauntedly sprang forwards; and aiming a fierce blow at the figure, it instantly vanished, letting fall a massy iron key. The flame now rested upon a pair of ample folding doors at the end of the gallery. Sir Bertrand went up to it, and applied the key to a brazen lock – with difficulty he turned the bolt – instantly the doors flew open, and discovered a large apartment, at the end of which was a coffin rested upon a bier, with a taper burning on each side of it. Along the room on both sides were gigantic statues of black marble, attired in the Moorish habits, and holding enormous sabres in their right hands. Each of them reared his arm, and advanced one leg forwards, as the knight entered; at the same moment the lid of the coffin flew open, and the bell tolled. The flame still glided forwards, and Sir Bertrand resolutely followed, till he arrived within six paces of the coffin. Suddenly, a lady in a shroud and black veil rose up in it, and stretched out her arms towards him – at the same time the statues clashed their sabres and advanced. Sir Bertrand flew to the lady and clasped her in his arms – she threw up her veil and kissed his lips; and instantly the whole building shook as with an earthquake, and fell asunder with a horrible crash. Sir Bertrand was thrown into a sudden trance, and on recovering, found himself seated on a velvet sofa, in the most magnificent room he had ever seen, lighted with innumerable tapers, in lustres of pure crystal. A sumptuous banquet was set in the middle. The doors opening to soft music, a lady of incomparable beauty, attired with amazing splendour, entered, surrounded by a troop of gay nymphs more fair than the Graces – She advanced to the knight, and falling on her knees thanked him as her deliverer. The nymphs placed a garland of laurel upon his head, and the lady led him by the hand to the banquet, and sat beside him. The nymphs placed themselves at the table, and a numerous train of servants entering, served up the feast; delicious music playing all the time. Sir Bertrand could not speak for astonishment – he could only return their honours by courteous looks and gestures. After the banquet was finished, all retired but the lady, who leading back the knight to the sofa, addressed him in these words: ———

The Old English Baron (1778)*

Clara Reeve (1729–1807)

Clara Reeve was very well read (in foreign literature as well as in English literature), and her book The Progress of Romance *(1785) is a useful history of romance and the novel. She wrote several other historical romances (such as* The Exiles; or Memoirs of the Count de Cronstadt, *1788, and* Memoirs of Sir Roger de Clarendon, *1793) and translations from the French. Most of her work is too obviously didactic and scholarly – and too domestic – to be imaginatively satisfying. The* Old English Baron: A Gothic Story *was first published anonymously in 1777, in Colchester, as* The Champion of Virtue. A Gothic Story, *and republished with its new title, and revisions, in 1778. As Reeve states in her introduction, she was endeavouring to improve upon Walpole's model by giving her story a greater sense of probability, even while retaining supernatural elements. Many of her setpieces found their way into later novels, notably secret doors behind tapestries, a haunted apartment with decaying furniture, dismal hollow groans, a ghost who reveals a secret murder, and themes of guilt and retribution.*

---

* Clara Reeve, *The Old English Baron: A Gothic Story*, 2nd edn (London: Edward and Charles Dilly, 1778), pp. iii–viii.

Preface to the Second Edition

As this Story is of a species which, tho' not new, is out of the common track, it has been thought necessary to point out some circumstances to the reader, which will elucidate the design, and, it is hoped, will induce him to form a favourable, as well as a right judgment of the work before him.

This Story is the literary offspring of the *Castle of Otranto*, written upon the same plan, with a design to unite the most attractive and interesting circumstances of the ancient Romance and modern Novel, at the same time it assumes a character and manner of its own, that differs from both; it is distinguished by the appellation of a Gothic Story, being a picture of Gothic times and manners. Fictitious Stories have been the delight of all times and all countries, by oral tradition in barbarous, by writing in more civilized ones; and altho' some persons of wit and learning have condemned them indiscriminately, I would venture to affirm, that even those who so much affect to despise them under one form, will receive and embrace them under another.

Thus, for instance, a man shall admire and almost adore the Epic poems of the Ancients, and yet despise and execrate the ancient Romances, which are only Epics in prose.

History represents human nature as it is in real life; – alas, too often a melancholy retrospect! – Romance displays only the amiable side of the picture; it shews the pleasing features, and throws a veil over the blemishes: Mankind are naturally pleased with what gratifies their vanity; and vanity, like all other passions of the human heart, may be rendered subservient to good and useful purposes.

I confess that it may be abused, and become an instrument to corrupt the manners and morals of mankind; so may poetry, so may plays, so may every kind of composition; but that will prove nothing more than the old saying lately revived by the philosophers the most in fashion, 'that every earthly thing has two handles.'

The business of Romance is, first, to excite the attention; and, secondly, to direct it to some useful, or at least innocent, end; Happy the writer who attains both these points, like Richardson! and not unfortunate, or undeserving praise, he who gains only the latter, and furnishes out an entertainment for the reader!

Having, in some degree, opened my design, I beg leave to conduct my reader again, till he comes within view of the *Castle of Otranto*; a work which, as already has been observed, is an attempt to unite the various merits and graces of the ancient Romance and modern Novel. To attain this end, there is required a sufficient degree of the marvellous, to excite the attention; enough of the manners of real life, to give an air of probability to the work; and enough of the pathetic, to engage the heart in its behalf.

The book we have mentioned is excellent in the two last points, but has a redundancy in the first; the opening excites the attention very strongly;

the conduct of the story is artful and judicious; the characters are admirably drawn and supported; the diction polished and elegant; yet, with all these brilliant advantages, it palls upon the mind (though it does not upon the ear); and the reason is obvious, the machinery is so violent, that it destroys the effect it is intended to excite. Had the story been kept within the utmost *verge* of probability, the effect had been preserved, without losing the least circumstance that excites or detains the attention.

For instance; we can conceive, and allow of, the appearance of a ghost; we can even dispense with an enchanted sword and helmet; but then they must keep within certain limits of credibility: A sword so large as to require an hundred men to lift it; a helmet that by its own weight forces a passage through a court-yard into an arched vault, big enough for a man to go through; a picture that walks out of its frame; a skeleton ghost in a hermit's cowl: – When your expectation is wound up to the highest pitch, these circumstances take it down with a witness, destroy the work of imagination, and, instead of attention, excite laughter. I was both surprised and vexed to find the enchantment dissolved, which I wished might continue to the end of the book; and several of its readers have confessed the same disappointment to me: The beauties are so numerous, that we cannot bear the defects, but want it to be perfect in all respects.

In the course of my observations upon this singular book, it seemed to me that it was possible to compose a work upon the same plan, wherein these defects might be avoided; and the *keeping*, as in *painting*, might be preserved.

But then I began to fear it might happen to me as to certain translators, and imitators of Shakespeare; the unities may be preserved, while the spirit is evaporated. However, I ventured to attempt it; I read the beginning to a circle of friends of approved judgment, and by their approbation was encouraged to proceed, and to finish it.

By the advice of the same friends I printed the first Edition in the country, where it circulated chiefly, very few copies being sent to London, and being thus encouraged, I have determined to offer a second Edition to that public which has so often rewarded the efforts of those, who have endeavoured to contribute to its entertainment.

The work has lately undergone a revision and correction, the former Edition being very incorrect; and by the earnest solicitation of several friends, for whose judgment I have the greatest deference, I have consented to a change of the title from the *Champion of Virtue* to the *Old English Baron*: – as that character is thought to be the principal one in the story.

I have also been prevailed upon, though with extreme reluctance, to suffer my name to appear in the title-page; as I do now, with the utmost respect and diffidence, submit the whole to the candour of the Public.

The Recess (1785)*

Sophia Lee (1750–1824)

The sisters Harriet, Sophia and Ann Lee, following their father's death in 1781, opened a school at Bath for some 70 daughters of the gentry. To supplement their income, Sophia and Harriet Lee each wrote several novels, dramas, and translations from French and German. Their Canterbury Tales *(1796 onwards), a very popular collection of short stories inspired by German sources, dealt with such Gothic subjects as the relationship between science and the supernatural, and figures such as banditti and the Wandering Jew. The* Recess *was said to be one of Ann Radcliffe's favourite novels. Historical authenticity is a key feature of the work, whose action is motivated by Queen Elizabeth's persecution of Mary Queen of Scots, and the seclusion of her two daughters by a secret marriage. The tyranny that Sophia Lee portrays is social and political rather than familial or supernatural, although her use of two sisters as joint heroines, and their concern over their separation from their mother, are themes common to what has been called 'the female Gothic'. Sophia Lee's major contribution to the Gothic was the striking surrealistic image of 'the Recess', a place of concealment which is simultaneously a sanctuary and a prison, a place of refuge and a den of horror – the ambivalent 'sequestered spot' that is central to the (female) Gothic imagination.*

My life commenced with an incident so extraordinary as the following facts alone could incline any one to credit. As soon as capable of reflection, I found myself and a sister of my own age, in an apartment with a lady, and a maid older than herself. – Every day furnished us with whatever was necessary for subsistence or improvement, supplied as it seemed by some invisible hand; for I rarely missed either of the few who commonly surrounded me. This Recess could not be called a cave, because it was composed of various rooms; and the stones were obviously united by labor; yet every room was distinct, and divided from the rest by a vaulted passage with many stairs, while our light proceeded from small casements of painted glass, so infinitely above our reach that we could never seek a world beyond; and so dim, that the beams of the sun were almost a new object to us when we quitted this retirement. These remarks occurred as our minds unfolded; for at first we were content, through habit and ignorance, nor once bestowed a thought on surrounding objects. The lady I have mentioned called us her children, and caressed us both with parental fondness. – Blest with every charm, it is not wonderful she fully possessed the affections of those who had no one else to idolize. Every morning we met in a

* Sophia Lee, *The Recess; or, A Tale of Other Times*, 3 vols (London: T. Cadell, 1785), vol. 1, pp. 2–5, 7–9, 22–4, 43–8.

larger room than the rest, where a very venerable man performed mass, and concluded with a discourse calculated to endear retirement. From him we learnt there was a terrible large place called the world, where a few haughty individuals commanded miserable millions, whom a few artful ones made so; that Providence had graciously rescued us from both, nor could we ever be sufficiently grateful. Young hearts teem with unformed ideas, and are but too susceptible of elevated and enthusiastic impressions. Time gave this man insensibly an influence over us, as a superior being, to which his appearance greatly contributed. Imagine a tall and robust figure habited in black, and marked by a commanding austerity of manners. – His features bore the traces of many sorrows, and a kind of early old age, which interested every observer. The fire and nobility of his eye, the gracefulness of his decay, and the heart-affecting solemnity of his voice,

> *While on his reverend temples grew*
> *The blossoms of the grave,*

gave an authority almost irresistible to Father Anthony, as we called him from hearing our mamma, to whom we understood he was brother. . . .

Being deprived of my customary resource, books, to amuse a part of our melancholy leisure, we mutually agreed to invent tales from the many whole-length pictures, which ornamented the best room, and to take them as they came alternately. Ellinor readily invented a ludicrous story upon the portrait of an old man, which made us both laugh heartily. I turned my eyes to consider what I should say about the next; they rested on the figure of a man of noble mien, his dress I then knew no name for, but have since found to be armour; a page held his helmet and his hair, of a pale brown, fell over his shoulders. He was surrounded with many emblems of martial merit, and his eyes, which seemed bent on me, were full of a tender sweetness. A sentiment of veneration, mingled with a surprising softness, pierced my soul at once; my tongue faltered with a nameless idea, and I rested my head against the shoulder of my sister. That dear girl turned to me with quickness, and the beam of her eye was like that of the picture. I surveyed her over and over, and found in every feature the strongest resemblance; when she frowned, she had all his dignity; when she smiled, all his sweetness. An awe, I could not conquer, made me unable to form any tale on that subject, and I directed my attention toward the next. It represented a lady in the flower of youth, drest in mourning, and seeming in every feature to be marked by sorrow; a black veil half shaded a coronet she wept over. If the last picture awakened veneration, this seemed to call forth a thousand melting sensations; the tears rushed involuntarily into our eyes, and, clasping, we wept upon the bosoms of each other. 'Ah! who can these be? cried we both together. Why do our hearts thus throb before inanimate canvas? surely every thing we behold is but part of one great mystery;

when, will the day come, destined to clear it up.' We walked arm in arm round, and moralized on every portrait, but none interested us like these; we were never weary of surveying or talking about them; a young heart is frequently engrossed by a favorite idea, amid all the glare of the great world; nor is it then wonderful ours were thus possessed when entombed alive in such a narrow boundary. . . .

'My children,' said Mrs. Marlow, faintly, 'an unforeseen event obliges us once more to retire to the Recess. Every thing is at this moment preparing for our reception. You are now at years to judge of the importance of its concealment, nor will I longer make it a mystery. – But why thus afflict yourselves for a temporary restraint? If I am willing, for your sakes, to be carried thither, like a corpse into a tomb, surely you will not be so ungenerous as to vent one selfish lamentation?'

Effectually silenced by this noble reproof, we collected, in confusion and grief, our clothes and ornaments; when, returning to her room, we found there Father Anthony, an old domestick called James, Alice, and the Housekeeper; who, having dispersed the other servants, preceded us to a store-room on the ground floor, and opening a press, unfastened a false back, which conducted us into a closet, dark, but for our torches. She then lifted a part of the floor, fitted very neatly, and discovered a narrow pair of stairs, down which we went, leaving her behind, and effectually secured ourselves, by bolting it firmly on the inside. We past through several subterraneous passages built on arches, and preserved from damps by cavities which passed through every statue that ornamented the garden, 'till at last we reached our prison. But judge of my astonishment, when I found the so often-sought entrance was a door of the size of that portrait which first gave me such singular sensations, and which I perceived was made to fall together, with a spring almost imperceptible.

Father Anthony silenced the exclamations I would have made, and drew me at once to Mrs. Marlow; who, pale and lifeless with the fatigue of this removal, gave additional terrors to the moment. Whether the agitation of her mind increased her malady, or it was originally beyond cure, I know not; but I saw, with speechless affliction, from the moment of our return to the Recess, she would never leave it alive. Enclosed in a spot without sufficient air, attendance, or advice, we saw her finish her generous attachment to us, by resolutely resisting our intreaties. . . .

[Mrs. Marlow tells of her activity after the departure of Matilda Howard, now Lady Scroope.] In the time of her absence, I spent many hours in reviewing the ruins [of St Vincent's Abbey] with which this place abounded; the gloomy magnificence of those great remains of art, was more suited to my sadness of soul than the softer and more varied scenes of nature; the liking I had conceived for these places, doubtless first caused the housekeeper to shew me the Recess. She had lived in the family a vast number of years, and knew the secret. How often had I walked through its ruined aisles, without suspecting it could possibly contain one habitable spot! I will now, my dear children, explain its situation and structure: – It was once inhabited by nuns of the order of St. Winifred, but deserted before the abolition of Convents, from its ruinous condition; in this situation it remained many years, shunned by the country people, and devoutly visited by those travellers whom chance or curiosity brought this way. When the Reformation, in the time of Henry, robbed the monks of their vast domains, the ancestor of Lord Scroope obtained this land of the King; he pulled down the monastery to erect a convenient mansion in the same taste, and discovered a secret passage from thence to the Convent; it was blocked up without being generally known, and the ruins left as an addition to the prospect; nor till chance gave the communication a value, was it remembered. The nobleman who could obtain so vast a favor, 'tis needless to mention, professed the reformed religion, but not able to forget that in which he had been brought up, his house became the asylum of many of the unrevenued fathers; this circumstance being noticed, he found his views in the world depended on his expelling them, when the secret passage occurred to his remembrance. He had the stones removed cautiously by the holy fathers, and found the place well arched and paved, and free from damps; it terminated in a room they supposed to have been the refectory, and which still remained entire. They removed, by degrees, such accommodations as were necessary into it, and thither the refugees retired, being supplied with food from the Abbey; but finding themselves shut up in too small a place, and in total want of employment, they began working under ground, and by degrees formed two other passages from the Recess, one of which ends in the Hermit's cave, where the eldest of them lived, and the other in the midst of the ruins. Thus providing against discovery, or rather securing their escape if that should happen. In surveying the ruins, they found several places enclosed, and yet undemolished; from among those, they selected the few we have lived in, chusing them always separated to prevent suspicion. Thus, in a few years, each father had his own cell, and a monastery was hid among the ruins of the convent. At length, the severity of government abating, several of the monks ventured again into the world, and of the eight who made it their asylum, two only ended their days here. Lord Scroope, sensible of the value of such a retirement, carefully kept the secret when its inhabitants were gone; two servants alone knew it, and they were faithful; nor till the house-keeper told me the story, had I an idea of such a place.

This account appeared almost fabulous to me; – the ruin was at least half a mile from the mansion, which then had a view of its rising plantations daily diminished, till the wood became frequented, or indeed passable only on the side near the Hermit's cave: I impatiently desired to explore the whole romantic secret.

The house-keeper did not delay a moment to gratify my curiosity; she summoned an old servant who knew the way, with torches, to lead me through the windings. The arched roof which was by some contrivance in the building, kept astonishingly free from damps, echoed to our very feet. The gloominess of the scene accorded with my ideas, and suggested a scheme which I have since thought a providential one, to my mind. The division of the rooms, the bare walls, and holes in the roof for air, displeased me; but since my affection for Lord and Lady Scroope debarred me from devoting myself to a convent, I resolved to fit this place up, and retire to it whenever the owners, with their guests, made St. Vincent's Abbey too gay for me. Three times I visited it, and each time found my desire greater. I discoursed with the old man, who, from a considerable reward I offered him, agreed, with the assistance of his son, who was a builder, to render this a comfortable habitation. I was unwilling to admit a third person into the secret, but soon discovered his son James was already acquainted with it. They directly began lodging their implements in the cave, which was altered to give a face to the whole. Three months made it what it now is . . .

Vathek (1786)*

WILLIAM BECKFORD (1760–1844)

William Beckford, whom Byron dubbed 'England's wealthiest son', devoted his enormous fortune to building an enormous Gothic mansion, Fonthill Abbey, which he filled with one of England's finest private collections of paintings, books, and exquisite objets d'art. *Ostracized by society because of his homosexuality, he became a kind of Gothic type, noted for his decadence, extravagance and perversity. As reported by an American traveller in the 1820s, 'notwithstanding the curiosity which the building of it [Fonthill Abbey] excited in the country around, the proprietor has chosen to keep it entirely concealed from the public; and according to report, he lives a solitary and a depraved life; taking no pains to secure the esteem of his neighbours, and being despised by most of them' (John Griscom,* A Year in Europe, *1823).* Vathek *(originally written in French), his best and most famous work, is part of the Oriental/Arabic tradition that includes Walter Savage Landor's* Gebir *(1798), Robert Southey's* Thalaba the Destroyer *(1801) and* The Curse of Kehama *(1810), Shelley's 'Zeinab and Kathema' (1811–12), Byron's* The Giaour *(1813) and other Turkish tales, and a large body of Middle Eastern travel writing from which Beckford drew his inspiration. I have included it in this section on the Historical Gothic partly to avoid the inconvenience of having a small isolated section on the Oriental Gothic, and partly because it has as much antiquarian underpinning as the medieval feudalism of the other works in this section (though I have*

---

* William Beckford, *Vathek*. Translated from the Original French. Fourth Edition, Revised and Corrected (London: W. Clarke, 1823), pp. 57–72.

omitted its superabundance of footnotes about Arabic religion and culture). The Oriental despot is an easy parallel to the feudal tyrant. Beckford read and translated Arabic originals, and a series of Oriental 'Episodes' meant to accompany Vathek *were never published during Beckford's lifetime. Despite* Vathek's *surrealism, the work is also a* roman à clef, *for the Princess Carathis is a satiric portrait of Beckford's Methodist mother, Gulchenrouz is his boyfriend William Courtenay, Nouronihar is his cousin Louisa, and the Caliph is Beckford's fantastic portrait of himself. Beckford was also probably the anonymous author rather than translator of* Popular Tales of the Germans *(1791), a collection of German-inspired tales such as the fine 'The Nymph of the Fountain', and two novels parodying the Gothic genre (see pp. 261ff.).*

Prayer at break of day was announced, when Carathis and Vathek ascended the steps, which led to the summit of the tower; where they remained for some time though the weather was lowering and wet. This impending gloom corresponded with their malignant dispositions; but when the sun began to break through the clouds, they ordered a pavilion to be raised, as a screen against the intrusion of his beams. The Caliph, overcome with fatigue, sought refreshment from repose; at the same time, hoping that significant dreams might attend on his slumbers; whilst the indefatigable Carathis, followed by a part of her mutes, descended to prepare whatever she judged proper, for the oblation of the approaching night.

By secret stairs, contrived within the thickness of the wall, and known only to herself and her son, she first repaired to the mysterious recesses in which were deposited the mummies that had been wrested from the catacombs of the ancient Pharaohs. Of these she ordered several to be taken. From thence, she resorted to a gallery; where, under the guard of fifty female negroes mute and blind of the right eye, were preserved the oil of the most venomous serpents; rhinoceros' horns; and woods of a subtile and penetrating odour, procured from the interior of the Indies, together with a thousand other horrible rarities. This collection had been formed for a pupose like the present, by Carathis herself; from a presentiment, that she might one day, enjoy some intercourse with the infernal powers: to whom she had ever been passionately attached, and to whose taste she was no stranger.

To familiarize herself the better with the horrors in view, the Princess remained in the company of her negresses, who squinted in the most amiable manner from the only eye they had; and leered with exquisite delight, at the sculls and skeletons which Carathis had drawn forth from her cabinets; all of them making the most frightful contortions and uttering such shrill chatterings, that the Princess stunned by them and suffocated by the potency of the exhalations, was forced to quit the gallery, after stripping it of a part of its abominable treasures.

Whilst she was thus occupied, the Caliph, who instead of the visions he expected, had acquired in these unsubstantial regions a voracious appetite, was greatly provoked at the mutes. For having totally forgotten their deafness, he had impatiently asked them for food; and seeing them regardless of his demand, he began to cuff, pinch, and bite them, till Carathis arrived to terminate a scene so indecent, to the great content of these miserable creatures: 'Son! what means all this?' said she, panting for breath. 'I thought I heard as I came up, the shrieks of a thousand bats, torn from their crannies in the recesses of a cavern; and it was the outcry only of these poor mutes, whom you were so unmercifully abusing. In truth, you but ill deserve the admirable provision I have brought you.' – 'Give it me instantly,' exclaimed the Caliph; 'I am perishing for hunger!' – 'As to that,' answered she, 'you must have an excellent stomach if it can digest what I have brought.' – 'Be quick,' replied the Caliph; – 'but, oh heavens! what horrors! what do you intend?' 'Come; come;' returned Carathis, 'be not so squeamish; but help me to arrange every thing properly; and you shall see that, what you reject with such symptoms of disgust, will soon complete your felicity. Let us get ready the pile, for the sacrifice of to-night; and think not of eating, till that is performed: know you not, that all solemn rites ought to be preceded by a rigorous abstinence?'

The Caliph, not daring to object, abandoned himself to grief and the wind that ravaged his entrails, whilst his mother went forward with the requisite operations. Phials of serpents' oil, mummies, and bones, were soon set in order on the balustrade of the tower. The pile began to rise; and in three hours was twenty cubits high. At length darkness approached, and Carathis, having stripped herself to her inmost garment, clapped her hands in an impulse of ecstacy; the mutes followed her example; but Vathek, extenuated with hunger and impatience, was unable to support himself, and fell down in a swoon. The sparks had already kindled the dry wood; the venomous oil burst into a thousand blue flames; the mummies, dissolving, emitted a thick dun vapour; and the rhinoceros' horns, beginning to consume; all together diffused such a stench, that the Caliph, recovering, started from his trance, and gazed wildly on the scene in full blaze around him. The oil gushed forth in a plenitude of streams; and the negresses, who supplied it without intermission, united their cries to those of the Princess. At last, the fire became so violent, and the flames reflected from the polished marble so dazzling, that the Caliph, unable to withstand the heat and the blaze, effected his escape; and took shelter under the imperial standard.

In the mean time, the inhabitants of Samarah, scared at the light which shone over the city, arose in haste; ascended their roofs; beheld the tower on fire, and hurried, half naked to the square. Their love for their sovereign immediately awoke; and, apprehending him in danger of perishing in his tower, their whole thoughts were occupied with the means of his safety. Morakanabad flew from his retirement, wiped away his tears, and cried out for water like the rest. Bababalouk, whose olfactory nerves were more familiarized to magical odours, readily conjecturing, that Carathis was engaged in her favourite amusements, strenuously exhorted them not to be alarmed. Him, however, they treated as an old poltroon, and styled him a rascally traitor. The camels and dromedaries were advancing with water; but, no one knew by which way to enter the tower. Whilst the populace was obstinate in forcing the doors, a violent north-east wind drove an immense volume of flame against them. At first, they recoiled, but soon came back with redoubled zeal. At the same time, the stench of the horns and mummies increasing, most of the crowd fell backward in a state of suffocation. Those that kept their feet, mutually wondered at the cause of the smell; and admonished each other to retire. Morakanabad, more sick than the rest, remained in a piteous condition. Holding his nose with one hand, every one persisted in his efforts with the other to burst open the doors and obtain admission. A hundred and forty of the strongest and most resolute, at length accomplished their purpose. Having gained the stair-case, by their violent exertions, they attained a great height in a quarter of an hour.

Carathis, alarmed at the signs of her mutes, advanced to the stair-case; went down a few steps, and heard several voices calling out from below: 'You shall, in a moment have water!' Being rather alert, considering her age, she presently regained the top of the tower; and bade her son suspend the sacrifice for some minutes; adding, – 'We shall soon be enabled to render it more grateful. Certain dolts of your subjects, imagining no doubt that we were on fire, have been rash enough to break through those doors, which had hitherto remained inviolate; for the sake of bringing up water. They are very kind, you must allow, so soon to forget the wrongs you have done them; but that is of little moment. Let us offer them to the Giaour [i.e. 'infidel', the agent of Eblis, Prince of Darkness], – let them come up; our mutes, who neither want strength nor experience, will soon dispatch them; exhausted as they are, with fatigue.' – 'Be it so,' answered the Caliph, 'provided we finish, and I dine.' In fact, these good people, out of breath from ascending fifteen hundred stairs in such haste; and chagrined, at having spilt by the way, the water they had taken, were no sooner arrived at the top, than the blaze of the flames, and the fumes of the mummies, at once overpowered their senses. It was a pity! for they beheld not the agreeable smile, with which the mutes and negresses adjusted the cord to their necks: these amiable personages rejoiced, however, no less at the scene. Never before had the ceremony of strangling been performed with so much facility. They all fell, without the least resistance or struggle: so that Vathek, in the space of a few moments, found himself surrounded by the dead bodies of the most faithful of his subjects; all which were thrown on the top of the pile. Carathis, whose presence of mind never forsook her, perceiving that she had carcasses sufficient to complete her oblation, commanded the chains to be stretched across the stair-case, and the iron doors barricadoed, that no more might come up.

No sooner were these orders obeyed, than the tower shook; the dead bodics vanishcd in the flames; which, at once, changed from a swarthy crimson, to a bright rose colour: an ambient vapour emitted the most exquisite fragrance; the marble columns rang with harmonious sounds, and the liquified horns diffused a delicious perfume. Carathis, in transports, anticipated the success of her enterprize; whilst her mutes and negresses, to whom these sweets had given the cholic, retired grumbling to their cells.

Scarcely were they gone, when, instead of the pile, horns, mummies and ashes, the Caliph both saw and felt, with a degree of pleasure which he could not express, a table, covered with the most magnificent repast: flaggons of wine, and vases of exquisite sherbet reposing on snow. He availed himself, without scruple, of such an entertainment; and had already laid hands on a lamb stuffed with pistachios, whilst Carathis was privately drawing from a fillagreen urn, a parchment that seemed to be endless; and which had escaped the notice of her son. Totally occupied in gratifying an importunate appetite, he left her to peruse it without interruption; which having finished, she said to him, in an authoritative tone, 'Put an end to your gluttony, and hear the splendid promises with which you are favoured!' She then read, as follows: 'Vathek, my well-beloved, thou has surpassed my hopes: my nostrils have been regaled by the savour of thy mummies, thy horns; and, still more by the lives, devoted on the pile. At the full of the moon, cause the bands of thy musicians, and thy tymbals, to be heard; depart from thy palace, surrounded by all the pageants of majesty; thy most faithful slaves; thy best beloved wives; thy most magnificent litters; thy richest loaded camels; and set forward on thy way to Istakhar. There, I await thy coming: that is the region of wonders: there shalt thou receive the diadem of Gian Ben Gian; the talismans of Soliman; and the treasures of the pre-adamite sultans: there shalt thou be solaced with all kinds of delight. – But beware how thou enterest any dwelling on thy route; or thou shalt feel the effects of my anger.'

The Caliph, notwithstanding his habitual luxury, had never before dined with so much satisfaction. He gave full scope to the joy of these golden tidings; and betook himself to drinking anew. Carathis, whose antipathy to wine was by no means insuperable, failed not to pledge him at every bumper he ironically quaffed to the health of Mahomet. This infernal liquor completed their impious temerity, and prompted them to utter a profusion of blasphemies. They gave a loose to their wit, at the expense of the ass of Balaam, the dog of the seven sleepers, and the other animals admitted into the paradise of Mahomet. In this sprightly humour, they descended the fifteen hundred stairs, diverting themselves as they went, at the anxious faces they saw on the square, through the barbacans [*sic*] and loop-holes of the tower; and, at length, arrived at the royal apartments, by the subterranean passage. Bababalouk was parading to and fro, and issuing his mandates, with great pomp to the eunuchs; who were snuffing the lights and painting the eyes of the Circassians. No sooner did he catch sight of the Caliph and his mother, than he exclaimed, 'Hah! you have, then, I perceive, escaped from the flames: I was not, however, altogether out of doubt.' – 'Of what moment is it to us what you thought, or think?' cried Carathis: 'go; speed; tell Morakanabad that we immediately want him: and take care, not to stop by the way, to make your insipid reflections.'

Morakanabad delayed not to obey the summons; and was received by Vathek and his mother, with great solemnity. They told him, with an air of composure and commiseration, that the fire at the top of the tower was extinguished; but that it had cost the lives of the brave people who sought to assist them.

'Still more misfortunes!' cried Morakanabad, with a sigh. 'Ah, commander of the faithful, our holy prophet is certainly irritated against us! it behoves you to appease him.' – 'We will appease him, hereafter!' replied the Caliph, with a smile that augured nothing of good. 'You will have leisure sufficient for your supplications, during my absence: for this country is the bane of my health. I am disgusted with the mountain of the four fountains, and am resolved to go and drink of the stream of Rocnabad. I long to refresh myself, in the delightful valleys which it waters. Do you, with the advice of my mother, govern my dominions, and take care to supply whatever her experiments may demand; for, you well know, that our tower abounds in materials for the advancement of science.'

The tower but ill suited Morakanabad's taste. Immense treasures had been lavished upon it; and nothing had he ever seen carried thither but female negroes, mutes and abominable drugs. Nor did he know well what to think of Carathis, who, like a cameleon, could assume all possible colours. Her cursed eloquence had often driven the poor mussulman to his last shifts. He considered, however, that if she possessed but few good qualities, her son had still fewer; and that the alternative, on the whole, would be in her favour. Consoled, therefore, with this reflection; he went, in good spirits, to soothe the populace, and make the proper arrangements for his master's journey.

Review of White's *John of Gaunt* (1790)*

The Adventures of John of Gaunt, Duke of Lancaster. By James White, Esq. Author of Earl Strongbow, Conway Castle, &c. 12mo. 3 Vols. About 250 Pages in each. 9s. sewed. Crowder, &c. 1790

We collect that the foregoing narrative of Earl Strongbow has attracted considerable attention, as the author of these adventures now declares

---

* Review of James White's *The Adventures of John of Gaunt*, *Monthly Review*, **2** (August 1790), pp. 416–21.

himself, on the credit of being the writer of that work. In a preface, the style of which reminds us of the proeme to Gay's Pastorals, we are conducted to the ruins of another ancient castle, said to have been a residence of Geoffrey Chaucer; where, in an old cupboard that had been plastered over, the author professes to have found a roll of vellum, on which these adventures were recorded in Latin. We are, moreover, prepared for farther publications of a like kind, by his declaring himself in possession of a small ancient MS. account of books of English chivalry, hidden in various places by the monks, and others, at the Reformation: so that, he adds, he is empowered, as it were by patent, to make discoveries of this nature. It is, indeed, a patent, the extent of which depends on the curiosity of the public; and if this curiosity does not tire, we may, in due time, be supplied with the whole history of England, loaded with fiction from his prolific imagination, into an enormous romance, that may turn the less amusing details of Rapin and Hume out of doors!

These adventures of John of Gaunt, are confined to those which happened in *one* journey that he took in company with his three brothers, Edward the heroic Black Prince of Wales, and the Dukes of York and Gloucester, to whom the adventures were common. They are, indeed, more properly, the adventures of the Black Prince, since the journey was his, to the castle of Beauchamp Earl of Warwick, stimulated by his love to the fair Erminilda. In their way, they overtook Owen Glendour the Cambrian hero, who was posting to Caernarvon castle, to a grand tournament, at which, he added, the lady Erminilda was expected to appear; an article of intelligence that determined all their steps to that exhibition. They called on Chaucer at Woodstock, and the visit is thus described: [omitted] . . .

The adventures are all in the style of heroic errantry, and consist of tilting, suffering from cruel beauties, succouring distressed damsels, punishing lawless caitiffs, and other events, of course, in the records of chivalry. Like Gil Blas, this illustrious company fell into the hands of a community of banditti, among whom they were detained until we are informed of their way of life and adventures; and then the princes and their friends recover their liberty, disperse the gang, and release their prisoners.

As novelty seems to be the author's aim, and will indeed prove the best recommendation to a revival of this species of composition, the following adventure is undoubtedly calculated both to surprize and amuse:

About half way between Aber and the foot of Pen Maen Mawr, we espied a knight upon the strand, who appeared to be in profound meditation. At a little distance from the beach lay a fishing-boat, in which were some sailors sleeping. At our approach the stranger discontinued his reverie, and, perceiving that we were knights, saluted us very courteously. We enquired whence he came, and what adventures had befallen him. That vessel, replied he, that lies at anchor, conveyed me from an island, which, if your eyes be faithful, ye may discern right before ye, extending its ridgy back from north to south. That, Sirs, is the isle of Man. To Britain am I come, in quest of knightly succours, against a cruel monster, (for, though of human form, he is in mind a monster,) who inhabits a prodigious fortress to the east of yonder island, where he enslaves and bitterly torments many dames and damsels of dignified condition, many knights and potent barons, and even some of princely station. For, know, valorous warriors, that this tyrant keeps armed vessels, in which his retainers scour the seas, and often make descents upon the neighbouring shores, carrying off whomsoever they meet, that is of honourable dignity, but sparing the meaner sort. For it is the atrocious maxim of the caitiff whom they serve, to collect, and confine within his castle the high-born and magnificent, and compel them to submit to the most ignominious drudgery: intending, as he saith, thereby to humble the pride of human kind, instruct them in the varieties of life, and season them with that philosophy which is the offspring of woe.

This audacious invader of the rights of men hath, at this instant, in his power five barons of England, and seven Scottish lairds, a king of Kerry, three abbots, two bishops, and divers knights renowned, with a cousin of the king of Norway, (a beauteous princess) many damsels also of the noblest lineage, and of transcendent charms, and (what grieves my heart full sorely) the daughter of Mac Sweyno, prince of the Orkney islands. I, gallant knights, am named Sir Allen Mac Fergus, heir of the Mac Fergus laird of Annandale, and was on the point of espousing this accomplished princess, when the rovers of that unknightly barbarian seized her as she walked upon the shores of her paternal island, and bore her away in triumph to the fortress already mentioned.

No sooner had the news of this disaster reached mine ears, than I took shipping for the isle of Man, and, having landed safely, disguised myself as a peasant who had fruit to sell, and straightway repaired to the castle. I readily found admittance, and was conducted by the domestics to the kitchen. I availed myself of the ill-breeding that was suitable to my feigned character, and, as clowns are always inquisitive, asked many questions concerning those whom I saw in various departments of this numerous household. There (sad vicissitude!) two damsels of an august house, and of incomparable beauty, were salting a rump of beef; the king of Kerry was gutting a turkey, the lord abbot of Conway, with a bib under his chin, composing a plumb pudding, and the bishop of St. Asaph's spitting a neck of mutton.

At this cruel spectacle I trembled for the fate of the fair princess of the Orkneys. I enquired with faultering accents if such a person was in the castle. But oh! what was my chagrin, when they replied, that they believed she was washing in the scullery! My knees knocked together, and the power of vision very nearly forsook my eyes. At length I recovered myself sufficiently to approach the place which contained the beloved of my soul. There, valiant warriors, (I can scarce refrain from weeping as I tell it,) did I behold the unhappy princess, with an aged prioress, wringing a pair of sheets, which but a little while before she had taken out of the wash-tub. She, who from her infant years had never known what it was to labour, but, on the contrary, had flourished in that delicate composure befitting an illustrious maiden, was now in a deplorable perspiration; her unparalleled elbows were befrothed with suds, her night-cap tucked up from her ears, her apparel loose and sordid.

As I knew that the sight of me would but afflict the princess, and render her situation the more intolerable, I forbore to discover myself to her; contenting my eyes with such a mournful perspective of her injured beauty, as the place of my concealment, which was behind some drying garments, would admit of. In another part of the scullery was the cousin of the king of Norway, scouring some greasy trenchers, and mingling, ever and anon, her briny tears (which dropt like orient pearls) with the dish-water that steamed beneath her.

From this melancholy scene I repaired to the court-yard, where the abbot of St. Alban's was wheeling out manure. As for the laird of Glenco, and the chief of the Mac Intoshes, they were sweeping the stable, while two English barons were rubbing down the palfreys. I vow to the very heavens it grieved my heart to behold them: I was utterly overcome: I could not stand it, but retreated precipitately to the castle, where, as I passed by one of the rooms, I beheld a company of majestic and angelic damsels, some of whom were darning stockings, some clapping cloaths, some ironing; while a beldame of a hideous aspect stood over them, as task-mistress, and with inhuman taunts, and terrifying menaces, constrained them to attend to their respective occupations.

My bosom burned with fury for the wrongs of these noble virgins, but more especially for the indignities of the fair princess of the Orkneys. I quitted the castle with a firm resolution to attempt their delivery, or perish. But reflecting that the prowess of no single arm could atchieve an enterprize so arduous, I determined to set out in quest of succours, from the valiant knights and barons of this neighbouring isle of Britain. Having, therefore, hired a fishing-boat, I crossed over to these parts, hoping here to meet some warrior who was in search of high adventures.

Here ended Sir Allen Mac Fergus. Though Scotland and the Hebrides were our object for the present, an expedition to the isle of Man, for the relief of illustrious personages, was in all respects congenial to our ideas of knightly glory. The discomfiture of that caitiff was an exploit which no son of chivalry could despise. Accordingly we prof fered to the Scottish chief our services, who esteemed himself most fortunate in having met with such auxiliaries. We alighted, and sat down upon the pebbled beach, expecting the ebb-tide with impatience. At length the water turns: we awake the sailors, and embark on board the fishing-boat. Luckily the wind proved as favourable to us as the tide; so that in a few hours we landed on the island.

Our first care was to consult concerning the method of attack. It was the opinion of Chaucer that we should borrow the jackets and trowsers of the seamen, and wear them over our armour; that, in this disguise, we should present ourselves at the castle, as seafaring persons arrived from foreign lands, and whose vessel was laden with choice productions of the Indies. For thus, continued Geoffrey, we shall gain admittance into a fortress, which to any forcible attempt will doubtless prove impregnable.

This counsel was adopted: we forthwith arrayed ourselves in the habits of the sailors, which concealed our coats of mail, and our weapons. This done, we proceeded to the castle of the caitiff, Sir Allen Mac Fergus being our guide. When arrived at the gates, we affected the jargon of voyagers, and were suffered to pass in. We marched forward to the great hall, where the tyrant himself was seated; then, scorning our disguise, astonished him with the sight of warriors clad in refulgent steel, and waving over his head their tremendous faulchions. Dismayed as he was, he yet shouted to his retainers, who rushed into the hall with such weapons as they could find. And now, my lord of Marche, a horrid combat ensued. The enemy, who out-numbered us, disputed the day with obstinacy, their caitiff lord encouraging them by his lion-like example. But a sudden reinforcement of abbots, bishops, lairds, and barons armed with their flesh-forks, spits, and brooms, appearing on our side, the impetuosity of the felons abated. At length a fatal blow from the faulchion of the Black Prince severed from his shoulders the head of the barbarian. Their captain slain, the rabble sued for mercy, which was readily granted to them, on their laying down their arms, and surrendering the keys to the fortress.

A general muster of the captives (those high-born cooks and scullions, whose condition Sir Allen so lamented) was the consequence of this victory, and liberty was proclaimed through every chamber of the castle.

Were a taste for knight-errantry still prevalent, and were the other adventures here related of the same extravagant cast with that which we have just produced, we should have received this work as the production of another Cervantes: but to raise up dead writers from oblivion, for the sole purpose of killing them again, might suit the pretensions of Falstaffe, but was a motive certainly beneath the views of this writer. Sterne was credited with profundity, till the public were profoundly tired with the investigation of his hidden meanings; and whatever may be the drift of this composition, such of our readers as may have condescended to amuse themselves with the humour of Tom Brown, will, on reading the above extract, unavoidably recollect the droll letters of Joe Haines and Beau Norton, describing the old vicissitudes of rank that took place on changing this world for that beyond the river Styx. . . .

Mysteries Elucidated (1795)★

ANNA MARIA MACKENZIE (d. after 1816)

Anna Maria Mackenzie married twice and after the death of her first husband supported her four children by writing, sometimes using the pseudonym Ellen of Exeter. Between 1784 and 1811 she wrote 16 or 18 novels, many 'based on Historical Fact' and most of them published by William Lane at the Minerva Press. Mysteries Elucidated *is an example of Historical Gothic, set in the reign of Edward II, the heroine being persecuted by the historical figures of Mortimer and Isabella. It is also one of the first novels to be directly influenced by Radcliffe's* Mysteries of Udolpho, *with standard features such as a hollow voice, apartments of gloomy grandeur, a discovered manuscript, an obscuring fog — all rather ineptly designed to cater for a fashion, though the characterization is good. In her Preface, Mackenzie pointedly alludes to Ann Radcliffe and argues that historical romances are better than supernatural romances.*

To the Readers of Modern Romance

As many opinions have lately been promulgated, respecting the innovations upon (I would rather say, *amendment of*) ANCIENT ROMANCE, blaming, on the one hand, every attempt to reduce the monster to a more reasonable standard; and on the other, depriving him of the most necessary traits of his former dignity; a few remarks upon the subject may perhaps be admitted, without the imputation of officiousness, as they will neither be embittered by impertinent reflection, nor malevolent satire: but as it is a cause made really important to the female world, by its influence and effects, I shall venture to give my own sense of it, as adopted through long

★ Anna Maria Mackenzie, *Mysteries Elucidated, A Novel*, 3 vols (London: William Lane, Minerva Press, 1795), vol. 1, pp. i–xvi.

and frequent consideration, and in this place I must beg leave to observe the progression and perversion of such alterations. . . .

The princess too, who once held her beautiful and sacred person at an awful distance, 'till her gallant defender had cut his way to her fortified prison, through the whole phallanx of horrible beings, brought into existence by the heated brain, and distorted fancy of mistaken writers; either not knowing him under the mighty change, or finding she must give up every hope of future celebrity, unless, trying her chance in a new situation, she weighs the difference, and quietly consents to enter the same road, substituting *cross guardians* for *cruel dragons* – *travelling chaises* for *flying chariots* – and vulgar *post boys* for *rosy cupids* – the *massy gates*, *grated windows*, and *impervious walls* vanish from the disenchanted eye, and the lady finds herself obliged to accept the common assistance of a *waiting maid*, to effect her escape, happy if she can retain so much of her former consequence, as to leap from the open sash to the arms of her expecting lover. . . .

That the general run of novels have this sort of tendency, I believe every subscriber to a Circulating Library can witness; (but with the sincerest admiration of their talents, let me exclude the names of Burney, Bennet, Parsons, &c. from a share in the censure, whose elegant performances will, I trust, remove much of the contempt which has fallen upon works of this denomination;) and though the following observation may possibly be deemed an anachronism, yet I will venture to remark, that as it was not in the power comparatively of a few individuals to destroy, or even successfully oppose, such a formidable body, it was thought expedient to attempt a middle kind of writing, founded too upon historical facts, neither so improbable (*impossible* might sound as well) as the one, nor so dangerous to the young and indiscriminating as the other.

The success of the *Recess*, *Warbeck*, *Monmouth*, the *Danish Massacre*, *Duke of Clarence* [*Monmouth* and the *Danish Massacre* are her own], founded on particular periods in the history of this country, and one or two more, have proved the utility of the undertaking, and ladies are contented to be interested and improved, without being terrified.

But another modern genius has lately out-soared them all, and scorning the track of more moderate predecessors, has contrived to give her story the highest colouring of unfettered invention, by a choice of fictious [*sic*] subjects, which naturally affords a greater latitude to the excentricities [*sic*] of a brilliant imagination, spurning the trammels of sober reason, and forcing, as it were, the willing slave of terror, to adopt the enthusiasm of ideas, which, like the description they are cloath'd in, are all wild, vast, and terrific.

But while I would give all due praise to the merit of these designs, some objection seems to obtain against the general tenor of them: that they are really wonderful, I readily grant, but if the spirit of description can only be kept up by a succession of bold and horrible images, there is some reason to fear unhappy effects on the young and ductile mind. Indeed, were I possessed of powers equal to that truly ingenious author, I should be cautious of giving them that unbounded licence. Let every mystery thicken in the progress of the story, 'till the whole is elucidated, but let it be without the intervention of super, or preternatural appearances. Dreams and apparitions savour too much of the superstition which ought never to be encouraged; and indeed I was happy to see, in that author's last voluminous publication, an amendment of this error.

As it may be deemed presumptuous in one, whose powers of imagination are certainly inferior to those of this writer, to cavil at what has given such works much of their celebrity, I will endeavour to obviate the charge, by remarking, that as in every performance there must be a *sombre* tint, so it will be but a fair and common conclusion to observe, that nothing can be absolutely perfect.

In historical traits, the objection before hinted, appears yet stronger, and though I am well aware, that the superstition of former times, may give an air of plausibility to descriptions of this nature, yet its effects will not be less impressive on the tender mind, perhaps the more so, from the supposition of its being founded upon facts, though I think it does not set them many degrees above *Baker's Chronicle*, or *God's Revenge against Murder*.

It is extremely clear, from what I have formerly attempted, and what I have now ventured to lay before the public, that in my idea, historical anecdotes are the most proper vehicles for the elucidation of mysteries; but it clearly behoves an author to be careful in the choice of subjects, always premising, for instruction's sake, that they shall be chosen from such as offer a description of vice in her proper garb, punished by the success of her detestable operations, while virtue, if it triumph not in the rewards of merit here, shall be painted in colours soft enough to allure the attention, and, if possible, inspire the emulation of young and well disposed readers: and here, another observation or two arises from the use made of the present mode of amusement, though I shall first observe, that to the combination of mysterious and perplexed events, the following sheets will witness; but I thought it a duty absolutely owing to those who may honour them with a perusal, to avoid even the supposition of visionary figures; and though, in so doing, it may appear as an open reflection upon the many, who following the masterly hints already thrown out by their great original, (Walpole, in his *Castle of Otranto*) have died their walls in blood – given life to pictures – disturbed the inhabitants of the silent grave – drag'd from his peaceful bed the airy form, to appear against the monsters who had destroyed an innocent family – nay, the enchanted glade – the ruined chapel, with all the perturbed elements which are brought in, to complete the horrid scene; yet I shall be better satisfied to escape the censure of the prudent, than to derive fame by my success, in alarming the timid: to excite wonder is one thing, to incur contempt another; nor can it reflect any credit upon an author, who prostitutes his own reason, and his reader's judgment, to the profits of his pen.

A licentious novel may sully the purity of a lady's ideas, while the unnatural performances of the petty modern romance, claims almost equal power of doing mischief; so that between both, the head and the heart must be in a dangerous state.

And that this important consideration may affect every one, who possessing the writing influenza, have yet their materials to select, is the sincere and earnest wish of,

Ladies and Gentlemen,

Your grateful and obedient servant,

ANNA MARIA MACKENZIE.

The Haunted Cavern (1796)⋆

JOHN PALMER (1742?–1798)

Eldred crossed the draw-bridge without the least suspicion, and had scarce entered the court-yard, when his ear was saluted by the jocund sound of festivity. He entered the building, and making his way to that part whence the noise proceeded, he came to a hall which was decorated by the arms and banners of its various possessors. Here he found a goodly company sacrificing largely to Bacchus: swiftly was the mantling goblet passed around, while the warlike deeds of the Scottish Chieftains rung through the stately edifice!

Eldred, darting a look around, saw at the farther end his rival, and Jane seated by him, over whose spirits, neither the juice of the grape, nor the voice of the bard, had the least influence. Pale melancholy was pictured in her features; her face was averted from the hated society wherein she was compelled to mix, while the briny moisture from her eye fell in the sparkling cup, and diluted the potent beverage.

The sight of his mistress fired the soul of Glencairn [i.e. Eldred]: hardly could he restrain from sacrificing the ravisher in the midst of his adherents; but policy prevented him, and he determined to counteract the villainy of Donald by stratagem.

Long did he continue at the castle, without the happiness of communicating a word to the loved object who had brought him thither; when, as he stood reclining against his beachen [*sic*] spear in painful rumination, the Highland Chief passed near him, and fixed his eyes steadfastly on him; then, suddenly withdrawing them, left the court-yard. Our hero was in

---

⋆ John Palmer, Jun., *The Haunted Cavern: A Caledonian Tale* (London: B. Crosby, 1796), pp. 115–25.

amazement, he naturally conjectured he was known; still he determined not to abandon the place without making Jane his companion.

His suspicions, however, were soon evaporated, by the Baron taking no farther notice of him, and fortune soon after favored his wishes. As his mistress was enjoying the cool evening breeze upon the terrace, he found means to convey a letter, unperceived, into her hand, imparting the danger he encountered for her sake, and with every tender argument, soliciting an interview that night, near the western tower, as his friend Edric would have charge of the draw-bridge, who would enable him to snatch her from the captivity in which she languished.

Eldred waited with anxiety the inseparable companion of love, till he thought the inhabitants of the castle buried in sleep, then flew upon the wings of impatience to the appointed spot. Long did he tarry, but no Jane appeared. Furious at his disappointment, he was about to retire, when the distant view of a female, again rekindled his hopes, and in a minute he held the daughter of Wallace in his arms. Fain would he have chid, but joy restrained his tongue from any language, save what love inspired. With rapture he strained her to his breast, apprehensive he should be once more deprived of her.

Thus does the shipwrecked mariner – when wan despair forbids the thought of ever regaining land, by chance some friendly billow wafts him towards a rock, where close he clings, and fears the impetuous surge will tear him from his only hope!

With eagerness did Glencairn hurry cross the draw-bridge, where he was joined by his Squire, who had received from Edric intimation of his master's design.

'These excursions,' said Andrew, 'may be vastly entertaining to you, my Lord and Lady, who are lovers, who can banquet on each other's words and warm yourselves with the breath of mutual protestations. But, for my part, I would rather have been employed in feasting on a well-fed capon, and a flaggon of wine. Here have I tarried, till I am perfectly a walking piece of ice; my body is now in as cold a state as the summit of Arthur's seat [the large hill in Edinburgh] on a winter's night. Our horses too are stolen, and by the beard of St. Andrew, which way they went, I know not: however 'tis for your service I suffer this inconvenience, and that thought softens my sufferings.'

Already they were at a distance from the hostile place, and safe, they thought, from the persecution of their enemies. The transition from a situation so deplorable, to one directly opposite, produced such a revolution in their tender minds, as lovers only can imagine.

They were fondly entertaining each other with mutual protestations, when the harsh din of footsteps fast advancing, caused them to mend their pace. Taking Jane's trembling hand, Eldred hurried on, but their pursuers gained upon them, and he distinguished the voice of Donald.

'Stop, villain!' he cried, 'yield up your prize, or this moment you breathe your last.'

They were now so close, that all escape was hopeless. Eldred, therefore, like to the forest lion when at bay, placed himself before his fair companion, and drawing his sword, prepared to meet his foes. Andrew followed his example; exclaiming, '*It's a hard battle where none escape!*'

The Lord of the Isles, whose impatience quickened his steps, first came up and attacked his rival. They fought with valor, and Glencairn was on the point of gaining the victory, when he received a wound in the back, that brought him drowned in gore upon the earth, at which Jane uttered a piercing cry, and sunk lifeless on his body, while the follower of our unfortunate hero being disarmed, was fast bound and gagged, and with the lady, whom they forced from her lover, conveyed to the Castle.

Eldred recovering from the swoon, wherein loss of blood had cast him, found himself deprived of his adored Jane, and manacled in chains; at which rage and indignation renewed his strength.

'Cowardly assassin!' he cried, 'thou disgrace to knighthood, who canst not rely on the strength of thine own arm, but causest these, thy myrmidonian crew, basely to lend thee aid! Free me from this hated bondage, restore my arms, renew the combat, and let the victor be rewarded with the charms of Jane.'

'Fool!' retorted Donald, 'thinkest thou I will play for that, which is my own already? No! the female thou dost mention is within my power, even now she enters my mansion, never to retrace her steps, till by the holy forge of matrimony she is linked to me. For thee, rash stripling, in a deep dungeon shalt thou expiate thy audacity. Could thy presumption prompt thee to imagine thy shallow brain could defeat the schemes of Donald?'

Hubert de Sevrac (1796)★

MARY ROBINSON (1758–1800)

Actress, dramatist, poet, victim of a debt-ridden husband, mistress (briefly) of the Prince of Wales, among others, and author of numerous, and profitable, novels of sensibility, Mary Robinson was one of those independent 'viragos' who upset so many conventional men at the end of the eighteenth century. She was admired by Mary Wollstonecraft, Godwin, and Coleridge, and her poems and novels found a wide readership among all classes despite her notoriety. Mathias (see pp. 292ff.) classified her together with those 'ingenious ladies' through whose novels young women were sometimes 'tainted with democracy'. Her novel Hubert de Sevrac *shows a*

★ Mary Robinson, *Hubert de Sevrac, A Romance of the Eighteenth Century*, 3 vols (London: Hookham and Carpenter, 1796), vol. 1, pp. 5–15.

greater political awareness than most, and is set in the present, during the beginning of the reign of Terror in France. Some of her Gothic trappings were borrowed from Radcliffe and Lewis, and were in turn borrowed by Coleridge (for 'Christabel'). (For Coleridge's remarks on her, see p. 354.)

Chapter 1

O how portentous is prosperity!
How, comet-like, it threatens while it shines.
YOUNG.

The ancient chateau of Montnoir, situated on the confines of Lombardy, was the melancholy asylum of Hubert de Sevrac and his unfortunate family. Born to an elevated rank in society, and educated amidst the splendours of a court, he shrunk from the approach of poverty, because it was accompanied by the menace of disgrace, and embraced the moment which presented an opportunity for flight, under the dreadful apprehension, that the next might conduct him to a scaffold.

He commenced his wandering journey, as one, who had relinquished every thing of his original consequence, except an exquisitely feeling heart, and a dignified sense of honour, which could not be subdued by the severity of fortune. Monsieur de Sevrac, previous to an epoch, the most important in the annals of Europe, enjoyed many dignified and lucrative appointments in the political affairs of France, with the hereditary rank of Marquis, and a private fortune, which had been bequeathed to his wife shortly after his marriage.

Gifted by nature, not only with every exterior grace, but with a mind, generous and benevolent, his popularity had kept pace with his good fortune; and even in the mazes of a court, where the rank weed of envy spreads its most baleful influence, he was beloved by his equals; while those who were placed beneath him revered his virtues, and felt the effects of his munificence.

But, at that dreadful period, when the tumult of discontent perverted the cause of universal liberty; when vast multitudes were destined to expiate the crimes of individuals, indiscriminate vengeance swept all before it, and like an overwhelming torrent engulphed every object that attempted to resist its force. It was at that momentous crisis, that the wise, the virtuous, and the unoffending, were led forth to the scene of slaughter; while in the glorious effort for the emancipation of millions, justice and humanity were for a time unheard, or unregarded.

In the summer of 1792, the Marquis, and Madame de Sevrac, with their only daughter, and the venerable Abbé Le Blanc, quitted their habitation in the Place de Vendome, and, disguised as peasants, passed the barrier of

Paris: From the heights of Chaillot, they frequently heard the distant sound of the tocsin [alarm bell], while the shouts of the populace filled their minds with augmented agitation.

It was at that awful hour, that de Sevrac examined the retrospect of his prosperous days. All the phantoms of delight purchased by the sufferings of the people, all the irritated tribes of wretchedness, whose wants had hitherto been unregarded, now conspired to taunt his imagination. He probed his lacerated bosom; and he found, that though no act of oppression, immediately proceeding from himself, had contaminated its feelings, he had been accessory to crimes, and deserved to participate in their punishment. The scene of delusive grandeur was at an end; the splendid pageantry viewed through the medium of reflection, faded into nothing, all of the deceptive had vanished; and the prospect before him and his companions, was cold, desolate, melancholy and forlorn.

Six hundred louis d'ors, and the jewels of Madame de Sevrac, now composed the whole of their diminished fortune; an old *cabriolet*, which they purchased on their second day's route, served to convey them; Madame de Sevrac and Sabina occupied the vehicle, while the Marquis and the Abbé Le Blanc walked by turns, and by turns undertook the arrangement of each day's journey. The court had been the only sphere in which they had hitherto moved with *eclat*; driven from their native circle, without a glimpse of hope, friendless, and unknown, all the corners of the earth presented, with an equal portion of attraction, an asylum, where sorrow might repose, but where memory never could be obliterated.

The first twenty-four hours stole slowly on, marked with that silence which is the effect of deep and melancholy musing. Scarcely accustomed to the disguise which was become necessary for their safety, and fearful of betraying their real situation to those, whom chance might throw in their way, and whose minds had leisure to scrutinize the sorrows of others, they agreed to speak but little; and they were cautious not to utter a syllable more than was absolutely requisite for the convenience of travelling. The Abbé was a native of Languedoc, and perfectly knew the provincial dialect of the country; on him devolved the task of conversing with the inhabitants of the different places through which they were obliged to pass, until they were more at liberty to resume their names, and throw off the disguise that concealed them.

Sabina, who was the darling of her parents, frequently watched her mother's eyes, where tears of sympathy often marked the attention she paid to the varying emotions, which agitated the mind of Monsieur de Sevrac. During the third day a tempest overtook them; the thunder rolled in successive peals above their heads, and the vivid flashes of lightning played round their carriage. As they were at some distance from any house, they hastened for shelter to the skirts of a thick wood; where in a few minutes they found a safe retreat from the fury of the elements.

'I remember the time,' said Madame de Sevrac, 'when my heart would have shuddered, and my blood have been chilled, at the sight of the dreadfully embattled clouds, that are now bursting over us! Is it thus that calamity makes its worst scenes familiar? thus can the mind become insensible of danger by the repetition of perillous [*sic*] events? I have often listened to the storms of winter, when I was sheltered in the abode of prosperity; and as often sighed in pity for the poor villager, whose little dwelling was exposed to their destructive fury!'

'And yet,' said Monsieur de Sevrac, 'that villager was happier than yourself, cherished in obscurity, the deceptions of a court, and the clamours of an oppressed multitude, were alike unknown to him: as he knew no guile, he dreaded no punishment; secure, amidst those of an equal station, he laboured cheerfully, and lived unenvied.'

'But did the labours of the villager at all times ensure him the comforts of life?' said Sabina.

'The necessaries of life they did,' replied Monsieur de Sevrac; 'nature required no more.'

'Then' said Sabina, 'if the nobles had relinquished their superfluous luxuries, and by a more equal participation, afforded the peasantry something, beyond the bare necessaries of life, would not the world have been more at peace?'

'The human mind is never satisfied. It is restless, irritable, and ever awake to misery:' answered the Marquis.

'Have not the poor, *minds*, as well as the rich?' continued Sabina: 'Surely they have; and as they are less cultivated, they are more liable to all the defects which you have described. Is it not barbarous then to drive that being to despair, who has not acquired the means of guarding against its approaches?'

'I always pitied the unhappy' said the Marquis. 'I never oppressed them, Heaven knows!'

'And yet we lived amongst such as never felt for those, whose hard fortune placed them in poverty: all our friends, all our associates, were the enemies of the people,' cried Sabina.

'Not all I hope,' answered the Marquis, shuddering at the reflection.

Madame de Sevrac, endeavoured to change the subject of conversation.

'The storm will soon pass over,' said she 'and the journey will be more pleasant after the refreshing torrents have ceased to fall.'

'This,' replied de Sevrac, 'is but a transient tempest; when will the storm subside that pours its crimson torrents over my distracted country, that strikes her children to the dust, or scatters them over the earth to beg for mercy? what is to become of her laws? who will afford an asylum to her exiled nobles?'

'Why cannot they live like those happy villagers, whom you described just now?' cried Sabina. 'You say, that they labour cheerfully, and dread no punishment: that they have the necessaries of life; and, that Nature requires no more.'

The simplicity with which Sabina uttered the most penetrating reproofs, silenced Monsieur de Sevrac, the storm passed on, the evening closed, and the remainder of that day was marked by mournful rumination.

The Novice of Saint Dominick (1806)*

SYDNEY OWENSON (LADY MORGAN) (1776–1859)

Sydney Owenson (Lady Morgan), daughter of an Irish comedian, wrote many popular Irish novels, her best-selling novel being The Wild Irish Girl *(1806). She was active in Dublin high society, combining fashionable living with patriotic Irish nationalism. She also wrote poetry, travel books, and a comprehensive biography and catalogue raisonée of Salvator Rosa, the Gothic novelists' favourite artist. She and her husband (Sir Charles Morgan, physician to the Marquis and Marchioness of Abercorn) moved to London in 1834, where she held brilliant receptions. She was dubbed 'The Irish de Staël'. Owenson's first novel* St Clair *(1802), written in imitation of* Werther, *was translated into German with a Preface asserting that 'the authoress had strangled herself with an embroidered cambric handkerchief, in a fit of despair and disappointed love'. Maturin, author of* Melmoth the Wanderer, *became a good friend; when failure followed his initial success, he required Lady Morgan's influence with publishers and producers to get his later works published.*

~❧~

Chapter 1

The sharp reproof of the pious and learned lady Magdelaine de Montmorell still shone on her keen eye, though it had ceased to murmur on her lip. The little amanuensis received it in silence, hung her head, and sighed – she dared not weep. One solitary intrusive tear alone had escaped from her eye; and glittered on the glowing surface of her cheek, like the dewdrop which the power of repulsion scarcely suffers to embalm the bosom of the rose it spangles. The little amanuensis brushed it lightly off with the feather of her pen, and waited in patient silence till the inspirations of the lady Magdelaine should again command its efforts.

The lady Magdelaine had already spent four years in composing a voluminous History of the Crusades, whether foreign or domestic, against infidel or apostate, from the first instigation of Peter the Hermit in 1104 to the massacre of St. Bartholomew in 1572; of the latter she had herself been a witness. She had retired from Paris to the chateau de Montmorell, which rose on the northern skirts of the forest of Champagne, as a residence more

---

* Sydney Owenson, *The Novice of Saint Dominick*, 4 vols (London: Richard Phillips, 1806), vol. 1, pp. 1–12.

appropriate to the pursuits of one who expected to unite the heathen reputation of an Anna de Commines with the holy fame of a Saint Geneviève: and solitude and a total sequestration from the world, together with the convent-library of the Dominican sisters (then rich in legendary lore and pious tradition), gave boundless scope to the profound meditations of philosophy, and favoured the deep researches of history; and while, with kindling ardour, fanaticism traced the recorded horrors of religious frenzy in the gloomy 'deeds of other times,' France still groaned under the struggling efforts of religious prejudice, or bled beneath the uplifted sword of civil dissension.

It was on the eve of St. Theodora the Martyr, and a few days after Henry the Fourth had invested Neufchatel, that a later hour than usual still found the lady Magdelaine in her study, dictating to her young secretary the most remarkable circumstances of the siege of Beziers, where six thousand obstinate heretics were put to the sword in cold blood, and four hundred committed to the flames, for the *love of God*. It was a note panegyrical and elucidatory on this instance of religious ardour, which had drawn from the horror-struck amanuensis (a young novice of the order of St. Dominick) such animadversions as seldom failed to elicit the disapprobation of her patroness, and rouse every feeling of pious zeal into action. It was some time ere the lady Magdelaine could rally back that abstracted attention which the unanswerable, but not unreproved, comments of the little secretary had put to flight. A glance into the page of the seraphic doctor, St. Bonaventure, restored the train of her dissipated ideas; and, determined to finish her note with an animated apostrophe, she exultingly exclaimed: 'Oh! fortunate though deluded creatures, who by the pious zeal of your holy persecutors were forced to return to the fold from whence you strayed!' 'And did they return, madam?' interrupted the novice, 'to the faith they had abjured?' 'They were all put to death without distinction,' said the lady Magdelaine. 'Kill away, cried the bishop of Citeaux, God will take care of his own!' 'Then what became of the bishop of Citeaux?' demanded the secretary.

The lady Magdelaine, again immersed in a learned puzzle; made no reply, but cast up her eye, pinched the folds of her ruff, and bit her nails, in vain endeavours to lure back the truant and felicitous thought which was to round the period of her apostrophe: and while the brain of learned dullness in vain gave the torture to exhausted memory, the vivid thought of genius darted through regions of impossibility, and pursued with ardour the glowing phantoms of fancy's creation. And thine was a genius, young Novice of St. Dominick, that soared far beyond the occupation allotted thee: and thine was an age when the mastery of the attention is seldom obtained; when the mind will admit an image or embrace an idea wholly foreign from the pursuit in which it is engaged, because it steals on its apprehension under the glowing form of joys anticipated, or wears the pensive, grateful semblance of joys elapsed: happy age!

The brain of the lady Magdelaine still pursued with unwearied diligence the learned trifle that distracted it, while the vagrant fancy of the little amanuensis wandered through scenes of fairy reflection. And never did a strain breathe in stronger unison to a soft and fanciful idea than that which stole on the rapt attention of the young secretary, as, tracing viewless characters with the feather of her pen, she

> 'gave to airy nothing
> A local habitation and a name.'

The storm raged loud, yet in every intervening pause the melodious tones of a harp were more distinctly heard. Panting and breathless, the Novice arose, crept softly to the casement, raised herself on a small stool, and flung an inquiring glance through its painted sash; but the stained and narrow panes, lit up by the watery beams of a declining moon, gave no form to her eager eye, except that of an ancient dame of the family de Montmorell praying with sympathetic piety before the faded figure of her lord in armour.

Yet if her eye was ungratified by the sight of the musician, her ear more distinctly caught the strain, which at first faintly breathed at a distance, now lingered on every passing breeze, now directly ascended from the terrace beneath the casement, and now, gradually fading away, became lost amid the loud howling of the wind.

Rapt, entranced, the little amanuensis still remained at the casement, even long after the magic spell which had lured her thither was dissolved; while fancy still fed her ear with those tones which distance or the storm had lulled into silence, and amazement was busied in assigning a cause for an effect so singular, so delightful. But even fancy at last ceased to delude; and Imogen, with a sigh of disappointment, returned to her seat at the moment when the lady Magdelaine, starting from hers, exclaimed, 'I must consult the bishop of Beauvais.'

'Did you not hear the sound of music, madam?' demanded Imogen. – 'Music!' said the lady Magdelaine, mechanically speaking the word with a tone and air of abstraction that denoted her absence of mind and her inattention to the demand.

'To me it breathed no human sound,' said the amanuensis, 'but such as fancy gives to those aërial strains which waft the souls of dying saints to heaven. In good sooth, it thrilled upon my heart: e'en now methinks I hear it.' – 'What?' demanded the lady Magdelaine, awakening. – 'Hush! I am not deceived. Yet methinks 'tis in the castle: it steals along the corridor; do you not hear it, madam?'

The lady Magdelaine (whose auricular faculties were somewhat less acute that those of her companion) now for the first time heard those strains which had awakened raptures beneath the steady tenor of her philosophic mind: they had indeed awakened emotions of a very different nature; and, advancing to a distant part of the chamber, she drew back a sliding door, which opened on the corridor that surrounded the servants' hall. The grand-dame of the present lady de Montmorell had constructed this door for the purpose of obtaining secret information of all the politics of her domestic system. The lady Magdelaine, whose imagination was less on the *qui vive?* than that of her young secretary, readily believed that these mysterious strains were not only of human sound, but that they proceeded from some unlicensed merriment in her domestics; and now appropriated the sliding-door to a purpose it had served, for two generations back, to the ladies de Montmorell. Instantly the tones of a harp, accompanied by a fine voice, interrupted by repeated and loud bursts of laughter, arose from the great hall below. Imogen, followed by the lady Magdelaine, sprung forward; and, hanging over the balustrade, with a heart beating in unison to the lively air which had awakened its palpitation, observed the musician surrounded by a group who paid the tribute of boisterous applause to the talents he exerted for their entertainment. Followed by the reluctant and delighted Imogen, the lady Magdelaine, with noiseless step, returned in silence to her study, closed the slide, and rung with some violence the little silver bell which lay on her table; but no ready page obeyed the summons. . . . 'For twenty years,' said the lady Magdelaine, throwing herself into her chair, 'for twenty years the sound of ill-managed mirth, or rude entertainment, has not been heard till this night within the walls of de Montmorell!' – 'I can well believe it,' sighed Imogen.

The Radcliffe School of Terror

IF HORACE WALPOLE WAS THE FATHER of the Gothic novel, Ann Radcliffe was certainly its mother. The publication of her novel *A Sicilian Romance* in 1790 marks the real beginning of the full-fledged Gothic novel. Very few Gothic novels were published before then, but a flood of them appeared afterwards. The medieval trappings used by Walpole acted as a constraint upon creativity, but once writers jettisoned antiquarian authenticity in favour of vaguely late-medieval or Renaissance exoticism, they felt freer to follow their imagination. Sir Walter Scott in 1824 recalled that when *A Sicilian Romance* appeared, it 'attracted in no ordinary degree the attention of the public', and it was on the basis of its poetic imagery and scenery – 'like those of a splendid oriental tale' – that Scott awarded Radcliffe the title of 'the first poetess of romantic fiction'.

The publication of Radcliffe's *The Romance of the Forest* the following year (1791) established the rage for the Gothic novel. It immediately became a classic of 'modern romance', and was plundered by imitators. For example, the *Critical Review* in May 1794 noted that George Walker's *The Romance of the Cavern; or, the History of Fitz-Henry and James* (1792) was 'copied from various popular novels. *The Romance of the Forest* gave it the name; the *Recess* its heroes; and *Ferdinand Count Fathom* has supplied some of its most interesting events'. Jane Austen's aunt Cassandra Cooke in the preface to her *Battleridge: An Historical Tale* (1799), makes the point: 'She is the Queen of the *tremenduous* [*sic*]; and alas! is most copiously, most inadequately imitated by almost every writer since her *Romance of the Forest* appeared.' This 'romance' played a significant role in spreading the popularity of the very genre of 'romance'. The *Critical Review*, which for years had published a Monthly Catalogue of 'Novels', for the first time in March 1794 expanded the heading to 'Novels and Romances'. We sometimes fail to appreciate that in the 1790s, Gothic novels were 'modern' novels.

Most of the novels in the Radcliffe School bear the imprint of their progenitor. About a third of all the novels published between 1796 and 1806, and many serials in ladies' magazines, had scenes inspired by *A Sicilian Romance* and *The Romance of the Forest*. Radcliffe's earliest works were imitated in *The Mysteries of the Forest*, a Minerva novel by Mary Houghton (1810); Ann Ker's *Adeline St Julian* (1799); and *The Mysteries of the Castle* by

Miles Peter Andrews (1795), though, as the *Critical Review* remarked, 'we fear that lady will not feel herself flattered by the relationship'. John Palmer Jr was said to have had *The Romance of the Forest* beside him as he wrote *The Haunted Cavern* (1796). Radcliffe's Marquis de Montalt and his abbey of St Clair fathered *Montaldo* (no date); *Montalva* by Mary Ann Hamilton (1811); *The Mysteries of St Clair* by Catherine Ward (1824); and *The Convent of St Clair* by Mary Martha Sherwood (1833). Adeline, in *Romance of the Forest*, gave birth to *Adeline de Courcy* (1797); *Adeline St Julian* by Mrs Ann Ker (1799); and *Adeline; or, The Grave of the Forsaken* (1841). The 'hideous progeny' of Radcliffe's *The Mysteries of Udolpho* (1794) included *The Monk of Udolpho* by T. J. Horsley Curties (1807); *Montoni; or, The Confessions of the Monk of Saint Benedict* by Edward Mortimer (1808); and *St Aubin; or, The Infidel* (1821). And the offspring of Radcliffe's *The Italian* (1797) boasted *Vivonio; or, The Hour of Retribution* by Sophia Francis (1806); *Italian Marauders* (1807); *The Castle of Vivaldi; or, The Mysterious Injunction* by Catherine Harwood (1810); *Italian Banditti* (1811); *Italian Mysteries* (1820); *The Mysterious Novice; or, Convent of the Grey Penitents* by Mrs Sarah S. Wilkinson (1809); *The Convent of Grey Penitents; or, The Apostate Nun* (1810), again by Mrs Wilkinson. The prolific Mrs Wilkinson, who knew when she was on to a good thing, also imitated 'Monk' Lewis in *The Castle Spectre* (1820) and *The Mysteries of the Castle Del Carino* (no date), and she imitated both Radcliffe and Lewis together in *The Priory of St Clair; or, Spectre of the Murdered Nun* (1811). The list goes on and on.

Imitations, derivative adaptations, plagiarisms, borrowings and inspirations drew upon Radcliffe's works to an unprecedented degree. Innumerable chapbooks stripped away Radcliffe's sentiment and aesthetic taste and transformed Radcliffean terror into Lewisian horror. The four-volume *The Mysteries of Udolpho* was reduced to a 72-page shilling shocker called *Lewis Tyrrel; or, The Depraved Count* (1804). In Isaac Crookenden's chapbook *The Vindictive Monk; or The Fatal Ring* (1802) Sceloni is obviously modelled on Schedoni and the plot abbreviates that of Radcliffe's *The Italian*, except that Sceloni now works for a lascivious nobleman rather than a wicked Marchesa, and the scene in which Sceloni is about to plunge a dagger into the sleeping hero is plagiarized from Schedoni's forestalled murder of Ellena. Thus, by the simple means of changing the gender of the key characters, the 'female Gothic' is transformed into the 'male Gothic'. In the pages of the *Marvellous Magazine* in 1802–3, *The Italian* became *The Midnight Assassin, or Confessions of the Monk Rinaldi*; *A Sicilian Romance* became *The Southern Tower, or Conjugal Sacrifice and Retribution*; *The Romance of the Forest* became *The Secret Oath; or Blood-Stained Dagger*; *Udolpho* became *The Veiled Picture, or the Mysteries of Gorgono*; and *The Castles of Athlin and Dunbayne* became *Highland Heroism, or the Castles of Glencoe and Balloch*.

Whereas Historical Gothic novels were set mainly in medieval England, the novels of the Radcliffe School were set mainly in sixteenth-century France and Italy; by moving from the domestic or native scene to foreign places, these novelists evoked an exotic sense of the past which was more appealing to their readers' imaginations. Travel literature, particularly records of travels to Italy such as Henry Swinburne's *Travels in the Two Sicilies* (1783, 1785) and John Smith's *Select Views of Italy* (1792), and also William Coxe's *Travels in Switzerland* (1789), was mined for romantic settings. Allusions to old English ballads were replaced by the refined poetry of Tasso or the fantasies of Ariosto. By setting their tales in an idealized late-medieval transitional period, novelists could raise images of splendour, mystery, high passions and exquisite taste. At the same time this justified portraying less feudal, more egalitarian manners, which permitted greater identification by the modern young women and men reading such novels in the revolutionary 1790s.

Beautiful and 'romantic' descriptions of nature were important features of the Radcliffean tradition. Evocations of the paintings of Claude Gelée (Lorrain), Salvator Rosa, Nicholas Poussin – whose works represented respectively the Beautiful, the Sublime and the Grand – became almost a cliché, and the five elements of a proper 'landskip' were consciously employed: foreground, middle ground, background, flanking sides, and the obscure distant view. Theories of the Sublime in Edmund Burke's *A Philosophical Enquiry into the Origin of our Ideas of the Sublime and Beautiful* (1756) and theories of the Picturesque in William Gilpin's *Observations on the River Wye, and Several Parts of South Wales, &c. Relative Chiefly to Picturesque Beauty* (dated 1782 but published 1783) informed Radcliffe's writing, and hence that of her imitators. The juxtaposition of opposite extremes, particularly soft Beauty and hard Sublimity, creates a chiaroscuro of effects whose ultimate aim is illustrated by an evocative phrase in *The Mysteries of Udolpho* – 'The landscape, with the surrounding Alps, did indeed present a perfect picture of the lovely and the sublime, of "beauty sleeping in the lap of horror".' Obscurity – a world of terrible shadows – was an especially powerful aesthetic technique for stimulating the reader's imagination. Gilpin in *Remarks on Forest Scenery* (1791) calls this process 'sublimication', by which the skilful writer throws out vague hints that are taken up by the readers and worked into sublime images in their own minds, thereby becoming all the more powerful for being the joint creation of writer and reader. The anticipation of terror, rather than the full face of horror, became the hallmark of this school.

Other key features of the Radcliffe School include the use of the explained supernatural, in which apparently supernatural occurrences are eventually found to have natural causes (sometimes involving deliberate trickery); a heroine of preternatural sensibility and suggestibility, a kind of tasteful reflection of the superstitious gullibility of her maidservant; the haunting image of the sequestered mother; abandoned apartments in castles

PLATE 2

William Gilpin's watercolour of Furness Abbey near Lancaster, an archetype of romantic beauty frequently visited by travellers in search of the picturesque. From Gilpin's *Observations, Relative Chiefly to Picturesque Beauty, Made in the Year 1772, On several Parts of England; Particularly the Mountains, and Lakes of Cumberland, and Westmoreland* (1786). By permission of the British Library 979.h.6.

or mansions, previously occupied by the mother of the heroine, presumed murdered, a trope often symbolizing a lost birthright; the heroine's resolute determination in the face of patriarchal tyranny; and the use of premonitory dreams, as illustrated in the first excerpt in this collection, from the anonymous *Fate of Velina de Guidova*.

The Fate of Velina de Guidova (1790)*

Henrique Aldovido to Velina de Guidova

With a mind distracted by all the torments of suspense, and with all the horrors of apprehension, I rise from a sleepless couch to call once more upon your pity. Velina! this is the third letter I have sent to entreat you will tell me you exist and that you remember me. I conjure you by humanity – by the tenderness of love – and by all that is most sacred – to write. If it is only one line – one word – write. Let me know that you live, and, if it must be so! let me know that you have forgot to love me. Relieve me from this dreadful incertitude, any state is more tolerable than this. Oh! if it were possible you could understand the extent of my sufferings – cold and altered as you are, you would pity and relieve them! Sleep gives no momentary respite to my sorrows. My imagination is incessantly haunted with the most terrific images. I see you, Velina, forgetful of my vows, I see you cold and indifferent to me. I see you married to another – to another, whom your father has chosen and you have approved. I see you bestow those smiles on him which were once my own – and my heart swells almost to breaking. I fly from recollection to the most rude and savage scenes – I fly to the deep recesses of the forest, or to the frightful precipice of the mountain – I fly to lose the horrors of my own mind in the horrors of nature – but alas! your image still pursues me – still torments me in the most tremendous solitudes.

My heart sickens at the light of day, and I retreat to the thickest shades. There do I spend the lonely hours in musing misery – there does fancy call up all her train of hideous forms to agonize my soul. In vain I endeavour to escape from her influence – in vain I endeavour to dissolve her enchantments. Every effort recoils upon my heart in tenfold misery.

Oh! Velina, if ever I was dear to you, and I once believed I was, if ever your heart melted to the woes of another, compassionate and relieve mine. If – oh! if – your heart no longer acknowledges me – if I have a rival more fortunate than myself, yet – yet tell me so. Ah! what do I say? – Rather conceal what will destroy me – rather deceive me with false hopes than tell

----

* *The Fate of Velina de Guidova*, 3 vols (London: William Lane, 1790), vol. 2, pp. 158–67.

me you are another's. All – all but this I can endure! – this – But let me not dwell on the thought. I am not doomed to such excess of misery! Yet write. Pardon the inconsistencies of a distracted brain. . . .

Worn out with agitation, nature yielded to sleep but not, alas! to repose. The most terrifying visions haunted my fancy. Methought, Velina, methought I was in the aisle of a large and gloomy church. The obscurity of the place was dimly shewn by the reflection of torches that gleamed from a remote part of the fabric. A few people passed at a distance between the pillars and disappeared in the darkness of the pile. All was lonely and vast: as I stood musing in melancholy silence the solemn notes of an organ swelled at a distance and gradually stole upon my ear till the sounds rose at length to the most full and ravishing harmony. I stood entranced, and seemed as if in those celestial abodes, where such sounds are said to flow. While I yet listened, the notes died away at distance, and were lost in the silence of the place.

Suddenly the torches which glimmered from afar blazed with new brightness. I heard the echoes of footsteps in the aisles and presently saw some people hurrying towards the choir. The light encreased, and at length the whole church was iluminated. As I gazed in wonder on the scene, the people dispersed, and the lights gradually declined, till the place was left in it's first obscurity.

A hollow voice from the altar called me. I endeavoured to approach down the aisles, but my feet faultered, as they do in dreams. I several times fell to the ground and vainly tried to proceed. The voice called again – my feet now favoured me, and opening the iron gates which separated the aisles from the choir, I beheld an old and ghastly man in the habit of a priest standing at the foot of the altar. From him the voice had come. He beckoned me towards him. He held in his hand a glimmering taper, which threw a feeble light over the place, and discovered you, Velina, at some distance. Your look was pensive, and your eyes had all that mournful sweetness in them which they expressed in our last interview. You saw me, and, while I vainly endeavoured to approach, you sunk into the earth, waving your hands to me and seeming to implore me to save you. I struggled to fly to your assistance, but my feet again forsook me, and, without having the power to help you, I saw you gradually sink from my view and disappear. The ground closed, and I was left in total darkness. The horror of the scene awakened me.

Surely, oh! surely there is some mystery in this dream which is to destroy me. My torments are, if possible, heightened by this vision. Velina, if you do not write immediately on the receipt of this, I shall set out for Spain. No power on earth shall hold me.

Henrique

The Castle of Wolfenbach (1793)*

ELIZA PARSONS (d. 1811)

Eliza Parsons wrote about twenty novels, including The Castle of Wolfenbach
and The Mysterious Warning *(see pp. 290ff.) – two of the 'horrid' novels listed
in Austen's* Northanger Abbey. *According to a contemporary account, 'It was
imperious necessity, not inclination, or vanity, that led Mrs. Parsons to take up the
pen.' Her husband was a turpentine merchant whose business was destroyed when
his warehouses had to be pulled down to prevent the spread of a fire in Bow, London,
in 1782. A few months earlier their eldest son had died in Jamaica, and Mr Parsons'
health broke. He had a heart attack and survived in a paralytic affliction for three
years before he died, leaving his wife and seven children unprovided for (the remaining two sons and one daughter were to die in unhappy circumstances). 'The liberal
indulgence she met with from her friends and public encouraged her to proceed in her
employment, while struggling with many sorrows and heavy afflictions.' Many
elements in* The Castle of Wolfenbach *are derived from Radcliffe's early novels,
especially the exploitation of the explained supernatural. The* British Critic *for
February 1794 noted: 'This novel is opened with all the romantic spirit of the*
Castle of Otranto, *and the reader is led to expect a tale of other times, fraught
with enchantments, and spells impending from every page. As the plot thickens, they*
vanish into air – into thin air, *and the whole turn out to be a company of well-
educated and well-bred people of fashion.' The sequestered mother, one of the
archetypes of 'the female Gothic', in the following extract explains how she was
forced to play the role of a ghost.*

I had been in the castle about three weeks, when, one evening, as I was
sitting in my room, at the close of the day I heard a little noise at the
window. I was startled, but recovering myself, I took a chair and got upon
the window seat; I saw the figure of a man, I shrunk down; again the
window rattled, I recovered and looked up; presently I distinctly perceived
a man, who, with a diamond, was cutting a small strip out of a pane of glass;
he accomplished his work, thrust a letter in, and disappeared behind the
battlements in a moment; I secured the letter, with a beating heart, and on
opening it, found it came from the Chevalier De Montreville. I was surprised and agitated; I perused this fatal letter; it was filled with the tenderest
expressions of regret at my unhappy fate. His own misery he could have
borne, he said, had I been happy; but to see the woman he adored treated
so unworthily, was more pain than he had philosophy to support; he
entreated I would write a few lines, to tell him in what manner my husband

---

* Eliza Parsons, *The Castle of Wolfenbach; A German Story*, 2 vols (London: William Lane at
the Minerva Press, 1793).

behaved to me, and if there was a possibility of his doing me either service or pleasure. I shed floods of tears over this epistle: I found, though I had suppressed, I had not subdued my affection for him; yet what would it avail to encourage a correspondence I felt was improper: I hesitated, – I considered for some time whether I should write or not; at length I took up my pen. I acknowledged myself obliged for the interest he took in my happiness, but at the same time assured him any attentions of his never could do me service; on the contrary, I had reason to believe the Marquis was very jealous of him, and that possibly all his motions might be watched, I therefore besought him to return to Vienna, and leave me to my destiny. The following day, nearly at the same hour, I heard the noise at the window repeated; trembling for fear of interruption, I hastily got up, and slid my answer through, resolved at the same time to run no such risks, nor receive any more letters, – happy had it been could I have kept my resolution. The next evening I did not go to my room till accompanied by Margarite. I trembled every moment, lest the signal should be repeated, but I heard nothing. The next day I was peevish and dissatisfied; the Count gloomy and sullen. After dinner, as usual, he went out among the people he had at work in the wood: involuntarily I hastened to my apartment; I will own the truth, I wished, though I dreaded hearing the signal. Towards the close of the day the sounds at the window were repeated: scarce knowing what I did, I got on the window-seat, and secured the letter: fancying I heard footsteps coming up stairs, I too hastily stept back on the chair, which gave way, and I came with violence to the ground; at the same instant my door opened: I had received a dreadful blow on the side of my head, though it did not altogether deprive me of life, yet I was unable to speak. The Count ran to me, he snatched the fatal paper from my hand, and then rang for assistance; Margarite came up. With his help I was placed on the bed; she bathed my head, gave me drops and water, and I was soon restored to sense and misery. He ordered the nurse out of the room, and then coming up to me, 'Wretch!' cried he, furiously, 'behold a proof of thy guilt and falsehood: I could sacrifice thee to my vengeance, but I will have more exquisite satisfaction, and complete revenge, such as shall strike thee with remorse and endless sorrow.' I besought him to hear me; I repeated what I have told you, and added it was the last I ever intended to receive. He smiled with disdain, 'Doubtless it was, and I take upon me to say it will be the last you shall ever receive from him.' He never left me the whole evening, but used every cruel malicious expression it was possible to conceive. I continued very ill and agitated that night and great part of the day. In the afternoon my persecutor left me, but Margarite remained; I got up, and was under the most dreadful apprehensions of what might happen; my eyes were continually turned to the window; I suffered the most agonizing terrors, when in a moment they were realized beyond whatever I could conceive of horror. A violent noise was heard on the stairs, like persons struggling, and in a moment the door was burst open; the Count and his man appeared, dragging in the Chevalier, with his mouth bound, his hands tied, and every mark of cruel treatment; I screamed, and clasped my hands, but could not speak; he made several desperate efforts to free himself – alas! to little purpose. Let me hasten over the dreadful catastrophe. 'Now,' said the cruel Count, 'you have your minion where you wished him to be, in your bed-chamber, nor shall he ever quit it alive.' I tried to speak, I threw myself on my knees, 'Spare, O spare!' was all I could say, and fell senseless, but I was soon recovered by the officious Margarite, to still greater horror. 'We have waited your recovery,' said the barbarian; 'I would not deprive you of so great a pleasure as seeing your lover's last breath expire for you.' He was then dragged into the closet opposite to where I sat, and immediately repeated stabs were given with a short dagger, by the Count, through several parts of his body; his blood flowed in torrents, and with groans he fell on his face and expired. Great God! cried he, here the scene never will be absent from my remembrance. I sat like one petrified; I neither spoke, shrieked, or groaned, but with my eyes fixed on the closet I appeared insensible to every thing. The inhuman Count was not satisfied; he came and dragged me to the closet, and seated me by the side of the body, the blood flowing round me. 'Now,' said he, 'clasp your beloved Chevalier – now despise the old and cross looking Count,' – words I had once said in his hearing, long before I was married – 'and now enjoy the company of him for whom you despised your husband.' Saying this, he ordered Margarite and Peter to leave the room; and finding I was still unable to speak or move, he pushed me farther into the closet, locked the door, and left me. How long I continued in this state, I know not; I believe I swooned, for it was day-light when I found myself on the floor, my clothes covered with blood, and the unhappy murdered Chevalier dead before me. 'Tis impossible to describe the horror of that moment; I found myself seized with violent pains; I began to think the monster had poisoned me – the idea gave me pleasure, and I endeavoured to bear my pangs without a groan; nature however asserted its claims; I became so very ill, I could be silent no longer, I groaned, I cried aloud. Presently the door was unlocked, – the Count and Margarite appeared; they saw me in agonies; 'I am dying, barbarian; you will be satisfied, you have murdered a worthy man who never injured you – you have killed an innocent wife.' I could say no more. Margarite cried out, 'My Lord, my dear mistress is in labour, for God's sake assist her to her apartment.' He seemed to hesitate, but she urging her request, between them I was conveyed to the bed, and without any other assistance than hers delivered of a boy. When a little recovered, the Count entered the room, Peter with him. 'I do not design to destroy you; no, you may live a life of horror, but dead to all the world; yet your infant shall be sacrificed.' I screamed, I cried for mercy to my child and instant death to me. He paused and I expected the welcome stroke at last;

'On one condition your child may live.' 'Oh! name it,' I said; 'any conditions.' 'Remember what you say: you shall join with these two persons, in taking a solemn oath, with the sacrament, that without my permission, you will never reveal the transactions of this night and day – never mention the Chevalier's name, nor ever presume to contradict the report I shall make of your death to the world.' I shuddered, but alas! there was no alternative; he fetched a prayer-book, and making the two poor creatures kneel, we all joined in the solemn oath, and received the sacrament from his polluted hands. Methinks at this moment I tremble at the impiety of that horrid wretch. My child was delivered to me; Peter was ordered to assist Margarite in making a fire and getting necessaries for me. How I survived such horrors is astonishing! The curtains were drawn, and that night the body was removed, but where it was carried to, heaven only knows, for Margarite never was informed. A coffin and every necessary for a funeral was bespoke and brought home. It was given out I had died in child-bed, and therefore in decency my own women only could attend me. A figure or bundle, wrapt in a sheet, was placed in the coffin (Margarite used to think it was the Chevalier's body) and the whole ceremony took place without any one's presuming to doubt the truth. Judge what must have been my feelings, and what an excellent constitution I must have had, to bear such dreadful scenes without dying of distraction. In a few days I was removed to another room, and, as I heard, the fatal closet was cleaned out by Peter; the rooms locked up, and orders given no one should enter them. The Count never appeared before me until I was up, and able to walk about the room; one morning he entered, just as I had done breakfast. I forgot to tell you I had no sustenance for my poor babe, consequently it was brought up by hand. The dear infant was laying on my lap; I started with surprise and terror. 'Come, madam,' said he, with a look that made me tremble, 'come and view your former apartment.' 'God God!' I cried, 'why must I return there?' ''Tis my pleasure,' answered he; then bidding Margarite take the child, he ordered me to follow him. I tottered across the gallery, and on entering the room saw the windows barricaded with iron bars, the pictures and toilet taken away, and the whole appearance gloomy to excess. 'This is once more your bed chamber; no more Chevaliers,' said he, with horrid grin, 'can convey letters here – here you are to reside for ever.' 'Oh! kill me!' I cried, 'rather than shut me up here – death is far more desirable.' 'That is the reason I chuse you shall live, to repent every hour of your life the wrongs you have done me: and now hear me – your child you will see no more.' At these words, overcome with the unexpected shock, I dropped senseless on the floor; I was soon recalled to life. 'Your oath,' I cried; 'O, spare my child!' 'I do not mean to hurt its life; I will have it properly taken care of, but the indulgence is too great for you to enjoy. I here swear, that as long as you remain confined in this castle, and observe your oath, never to reveal the Chevalier's murder, nor undeceive the world respecting your fate, so long your boy's life is safe; I will take care of him, and one day or other, there is a possibility, you may see him again; but if you ever escape from hence, or divulge these particulars, without my permission, instant death awaits you both, for I shall have a constant spy.' To these conditions, dreadful as they were, I was compelled to subscribe. Margarite was ordered into confinement with me, for he found she was my friend. That night the child was conveyed away: dear and precious boy! alas, heaven only knows whether I shall ever see him more; unconscious he has a mother, if he lives, we may remain strangers to each other! We were locked in, and for three days the Count himself brought our scanty fare; the fourth, he entered with Joseph, who was the under gardener. I was startled to see a stranger, – he appeared equally shocked at seeing me. 'Here you both are, remember your oath, madam, for on it more than one life depends. And you,' said he, turning to Joseph, 'tremble, if you dare break your solemn vow, never to let any person know this woman is alive, never to suffer her to pass from these apartments, without my permission, to hold no conversation with her, but when you bring her food, and in fine, to obey every command of mine and not hers.' 'I will obey your Lordship,' cried the man, trembling. ''Tis well, then you will preserve her life, and gain my favor. No strangers must be permitted to remain here, should chance or inclination engage any one to visit this castle. Remember this side of it must never be seen, 'tis haunted – do you understand me?' 'I do, my Lord,' answered Joseph, 'and I promise you, these apartments shall never be looked into.' 'On that depends her existence and yours.' They now quitted my room, and left me scarcely able to breathe. The following day the Count and Peter left the castle. Every other day Joseph came with necessaries, and Margarite was permitted to go down, accompanied by Joseph, to carry up and down water and other conveniences. In this state I lived two years, if living it could be called, having no other consolation than now and then hearing from my sister; for I had so far gained upon Joseph to permit Margarite's letters, after shewing them to him, to pass under cover to him, and as he found I carefully preserved my secret from others, the poor fellow granted me that indulgence. At the expiration of two years, the Count unexpectedly made his appearance. I shrunk from his sight; he viewed me some time with great emotion; 'I am satisfied with your conduct,' said he, 'and am come to extend my indulgence to you.' 'O, my child!' I cried out. 'No,' answered he, 'that cannot be granted; but you shall have permission to live in the rooms below, and if you swear to enter the garden only at night, the door into it shall be opened.' I joyfully agreed to this, and was once more led to the rooms below. Peter was still with him; a bed was brought from another room, and placed in a small parlour, also one for Margarite. The apartments above were again locked up. I tried to soften the Count; he sometimes appeared moved and affected, then again stern and cruel; he staid near a week – the day he left the castle he came to visit me. 'Once more I leave you, but as there is some danger that strangers may come here, I charge you, by every thing that is sacred, by your child's life and your own, should any person sleep in this castle, that you go to the gallery or next apartments, rattle a chain I shall leave for that purpose, groan, and make such kind of noises as may appal those who come here, and drive them hence, under an idea of the castle's being haunted: I have already sworn Joseph, do you promise the same.' 'Ah! Sir,' cried I, 'why all these oaths. Why all these persecutions, which must give you a world of pains, to punish an innocent woman?' 'Because,' said he, furiously, 'because I prefer revenge to my own quiet; because I will be feared, and make your destiny hang on my pleasure.' I could say no more, I wept bitterly, but nothing could soften his heart; he made me renew my vows, still threatening the life of my child, if I failed – he told me it was well, and carefully attended. I was compelled to acquiesce with his request, or rather command, and he once more left me. He regularly came once in two years, for some time, but latterly it was above four years since I had seen him, till the fatal night he carried me off.

The Mysteries of Udolpho (1794)[*]

ANN RADCLIFFE (1764–1823)

The life of Ann Radcliffe is as much a mystery as anything hidden behind the black veil in her novels. An archetypal reclusive celebrity, she did not even deny the rumours that she had gone insane, or premature announcements in the journals that she had died. Since she led an ordinary middle-class life, walking her beloved dogs and taking seaside holidays in Dover, it may be suspected that she deliberately sequestered herself in order to ensure her reputation as the greatest novelist of her age. On the other hand, she exhibited intense shyness even as a child, and her domestic seclusion may reflect her melancholia and the probability that she suffered two nervous breakdowns. She was seven years old when her parents moved to Bath and sent her to live with her uncle Thomas Bentley (partner of the famous ceramic manufacturer Josiah Wedgwood). The manic-depressive mother figures and petty-tyrannical father figures in her novels, and heroines exhibiting pessimism, repressive self-control, and acute anxiety, seem likely to reflect the child's sense of having been abandoned by her parents.

An important marker of Radcliffe's cultural achievement was the £500 royalty she received from the publisher George Robinson for The Mysteries of Udolpho*: this sum was double her husband's annual income as a newspaper proprietor, and aston-ishing when compared to the £10 or £20 paid to authors of three-volume Minerva*

---

[*] Ann Radcliffe, *The Mysteries of Udolpho*, 4 vols (London: G. G. and J. Robinson, 1794), vol. 2, pp. 164–73.

novels. The publishers Cadell paid £800 for her next novel, The Italian. *Never before had so much money been paid for a novel, and Ann Radcliffe thereby played a pivotal role in the professional marketing of fiction by women. Her novel was recognized by all the critics as a work of genius, and many of her contemporaries joined in one breath the names of Shakespeare, Milton, Ariosto, Radcliffe. Radcliffe was praised as the Great Enchantress, and the general public bought* The Mysteries of Udolpho *so eagerly that it has been called the first 'best-seller'. Radcliffe's hallmark is a mysterious unseen terror, which seems to have three sources: the aesthetic sensibility of Radcliffe its creator; the 'distempered imagination' of her heroine; and patriarchal oppression. The objectification of this terror in the castello di Udolpho has been often anthologized, but rightly so.*

A Castle in the Apennines

At length, the travellers began to ascend among the Apennines. The immense pine-forests, which, at that period, overhung these mountains, and between which the road wound, excluded all view but of the cliffs aspiring above, except that, now and then, an opening through the dark woods allowed the eye a momentary glimpse of the country below. The gloom of these shades, their solitary silence, except when the breeze swept over their summits, the tremendous precipices of the mountains, that came partially to the eye, each assisted to raise the solemnity of Emily's feelings into awe; she saw only images of gloomy grandeur, or of dreadful sublimity, around her; other images, equally gloomy and equally terrible, gleamed on her imagination. She was going she scarcely knew whither, under the dominion of a person, from whose arbitrary disposition she had already suffered so much, to marry, perhaps, a man who possessed neither her affection, or esteem; or to endure, beyond the hope of succour, whatever punishment revenge, and that Italian revenge, might dictate. – The more she considered what might be the motive of the journey, the more she became convinced, that it was for the purpose of concluding her nuptials with Count Morano, with that secrecy which her resolute resistance had made necessary to the honour, if not to the safety, of Montoni. From the deep solitudes, into which she was immerging [*sic*], and from the gloomy castle, of which she had heard some mysterious hints, her sick heart recoiled in despair, and she experienced, that, though her mind was already occupied by peculiar distress, it was still alive to the influence of new and local circumstance; why else did she shudder at the idea of this desolate castle?

As the travellers still ascended among the pine forests, steep rose over steep, the mountains seemed to multiply, as they went, and what was the summit of one eminence proved to be only the base of another. At length, they reached a little plain, where the drivers stopped to rest the mules, whence a scene of such extent and magnificence opened below, as drew even from Madame Montoni a note of admiration. Emily lost, for a moment, her sorrows, in the immensity of nature. Beyond the amphitheatre of mountains, that stretched below, whose tops appeared as numerous almost, as the waves of the sea, and whose feet were concealed by the forests – extended the *Campagna* of Italy, where cities and rivers, and woods and all the glow of cultivation were mingled in gay confusion. The Adriatic bounded the horizon, into which the Po and the Brenta, after winding through the whole extent of the landscape, poured their fruitful waves. Emily gazed long on the splendours of the world she was quitting, of which the whole magnificence seemed thus given to her sight only to increase her regret on leaving it; for her, Valancourt alone was in that world; to him alone her heart turned, and for him alone fell her bitter tears.

From this sublime scene the travellers continued to ascend among the pines, till they entered a narrow pass of the mountains, which shut out every feature of the distant country, and, in its stead, exhibited only tremendous crags, impending over the road, where no vestige of humanity, or even of vegetation, appeared, except here and there the trunk and scathed branches of an oak, that hung nearly headlong from the rock, into which its strong roots had fastened. This pass, which led into the heart of the Apennine, at length opened to day, and a scene of mountains stretched in long perspective, as wild as any the travellers had yet passed. Still vast pine-forests hung upon their base, and crowned the ridgy precipice, that rose perpendicularly from the vale, while, above, the rolling mists caught the sun-beams, and touched their cliffs with all the magical colouring of light and shade. The scene seemed perpetually changing, and its features to assume new forms, as the winding road brought them to the eye in different attitudes; while the shifting vapours, now partially concealing their minuter beauties and now illuminating them with splendid tints, assisted the illusions of the sight.

Though the deep vallies between these mountains were, for the most part, clothed with pines, sometimes an abrupt opening presented a perspective of only barren rocks, with a cataract flashing from their summit among broken cliffs, till its waters, reaching the bottom, foamed along with unceasing fury; and sometimes pastoral scenes exhibited their 'green delights' in the narrow vales, smiling amid surrounding horror. There herds and flocks of goats and sheep, browsing under the shade of hanging woods, and the shepherd's little cabin, reared on the margin of a clear stream, presented a sweet picture of repose.

Wild and romantic as were these scenes, their character had far less of the sublime, than had those of the Alps, which guard the entrance of Italy. Emily was often elevated, but seldom felt those emotions of indescribable awe which she had so continually experienced, in her passage over the Alps.

Towards the close of day, the road wound into a deep valley. Mountains, whose shaggy steeps appeared to be inaccessible, almost surrounded it. To the east, a vista opened, that exhibited the Apennines in their darkest horrors; and the long perspective of retiring summits, rising over each other, their ridges clothed with pines, exhibited a stronger image of grandeur, than any that Emily had yet seen. The sun had just sunk below the top of the mountains she was descending, whose long shadow stretched athwart the valley, but his sloping rays, shooting through an opening of the cliffs, touched with a yellow gleam the summits of the forest, that hung upon the opposite steeps, and streamed in full splendour upon the towers and battlements of a castle, that spread its extensive ramparts along the brow of a precipice above. The splendour of these illumined objects was heightened by the contrasted shade, which involved the valley below.

'There,' said Montoni, speaking for the first time in several hours, 'is Udolpho.'

Emily gazed with melancholy awe upon the castle, which she understood to be Montoni's; for, though it was now lighted up by the setting sun, the gothic greatness of its features, and its mouldering walls of dark grey stone, rendered it a gloomy and sublime object. As she gazed, the light died away on its walls, leaving a melancholy purple tint, which spread deeper and deeper, as the thin vapour crept up the mountain, while the battlements above were still tipped with splendour. From those too, the rays soon faded, and the whole edifice was invested with the solemn duskiness of evening. Silent, lonely and sublime, it seemed to stand the sovereign of the scene, and to frown defiance on all, who dared to invade its solitary reign. As the twilight deepened, its features became more awful in obscurity, and Emily continued to gaze, till its clustering towers were alone seen, rising over the tops of the woods, beneath whose thick shade the carriages soon after began to ascend.

The extent and darkness of these tall woods awakened terrific images in her mind, and she almost expected to see banditti start up from under the trees. At length, the carriages emerged upon a heathy rock, and, soon after, reached the castle gates, where the deep tone of the portal bell, which was struck upon to give notice of their arrival, increased the fearful emotions, that had assailed Emily. While they waited till the servant within should come to open the gates, she anxiously surveyed the edifice: but the gloom, that overspread it, allowed her to distinguish little more than a part of its outline, with the massy walls of the ramparts, and to know, that it was vast, ancient and dreary. From the parts she saw, she judged of the heavy strength and extent of the whole. The gateway before her, leading into the courts, was of gigantic size, and was defended by two round towers, crowned by overhanging turrets, embattled, where, instead of banners, now waved long grass and wild plants, that had taken root among the mouldering stones, and which seemed to sigh, as the breeze rolled past, over the desolation around them. The towers were united by a curtain, pierced and embattled also, below which appeared the pointed arch of an huge portcullis, surmounting the gates: from these, the walls of the ramparts extended to other towers, overlooking the precipice, whose shattered outline, appearing on a gleam, that lingered in the west, told of the ravages of war. – Beyond these all was lost in the obscurity of evening.

While Emily gazed with awe upon the scene, footsteps were heard within the gates, and the undrawing of bolts; after which an ancient servant of the castle appeared, forcing back the huge folds of the portal, to admit his lord. As the carriage-wheels rolled heavily under the portcullis, Emily's heart sunk, and she seemed, as if she was going into her prison; the gloomy court, into which she passed, served to confirm the idea, and her imagination, ever awake to circumstance, suggested even more terrors, than her reason could justify.

Grasville Abbey (1793–7)*

GEORGE MOORE (fl. 1793–1811)

Grasville Abbey; A Romance 'by G. M.' was serialized in 47 instalments in The Lady's Magazine *from March 1793 through August 1797. The magazine was published by G. G. and J. Robinson, who would publish Radcliffe's* The Mysteries of Udolpho *and other Gothic novels, and was a rich source of Radcliffean Gothic. By means of serialization the expectation of terror was prolonged from month to month – for more than four years in the case of* Grasville Abbey*! Matilda, like many Gothic heroines, is a prototypical detective, carefully observing strange events and small details and speculating on their import. Moore also wrote* Theodosius De Zulvin, The Monk of Madrid *(1802),* Montbar; or The Buccaneer *(1804), and* Tales of the Passions *(1808 and 1811).*

Agnes was astonished, when she awoke in the morning, to perceive Matilda was not undressed, and immediately enquired the cause: the latter, who had already determined on an answer, told her that having sat up longer than usual to finish a book, she fell asleep for the night. Agnes doubted not her veracity, and cheerfully went to prepare breakfast.

Matilda was perplexed to know in what manner to act, concerning the light in the west tower. The strange circumstances which seemed to encompass this abbey with a mist of doubtful horror, every day became more uncomfortable and disagreeable. It was true, the good sense and instructions of her mother had brought her up to despise superstition, and

---

* George Moore, 'Grasville Abbey', *The Lady's Magazine*, **26** (September 1795), pp. 402–6.

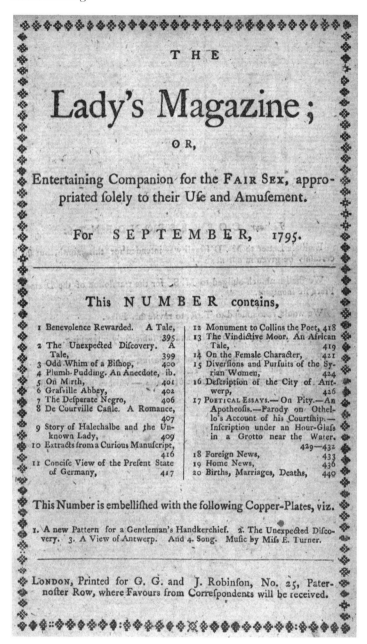

PLATE 3

The Lady's Magazine provided an outlet for sentimental Gothic literature for many years. This issue for September 1795 contained, among other things, serialized instalments from *Grasville Abbey* and *De Courville Castle*, and a 'Concise View of the Present State of Germany' extracted from Ann Radcliffe's *A Journey made in the Summer of 1794*. Author's collection.

laugh at the folly of those who listened to uncommon reports. But the occurrences she had lately been witness to gave her strong reasons to believe in supernatural existences. The crash and groans in the apartment, she had herself heard distinctly, and was certain both her brother and Leonard must have seen something more than common, to have uttered such exclamations of surprise and horror. Her aunt's manuscript gave a particular account of a light being seen in the west tower, not only by her father and his servant, but by more than one of the villagers. An interval from that time had now passed of near one-and-twenty years, yet she had again seen a light in the same building, which had most probably never been inhabited even when the late count Maserini resided in the abbey. Such strange and mysterious events staggered all the fortitude she had derived from the lessons of her parent, and both alarmed and terrified her. She resolved however to keep the knowledge of the light to herself for the present, and watch again at the same hour, when she might possibly make some further discovery.

With these resolutions she descended to the parlour. Her brother was already up, and the breakfast waited for her. In about two hours, they were ready to walk to the hermit, and left the abbey accordingly. Father Peter received them at the entrance of his cell, and conducted them to the inner part, where he begged they would be seated. They discoursed on several subjects; Father Peter shewed himself to be a man of great understanding and quick imagination; these gifts of nature seemed also to have been cherished by an excellent education. His manners were elegant and polished, while his whole deportment commanded respect and admiration. There was however a settled gloom which overspread his countenance, that shewed he had a heavy sorrow at heart, which he was unable to overcome. Alfred, at the latter part of their visit, mentioned the terror which people in general suffered concerning Grasville Abbey.

''Tis a misfortune from birth, my son,' replied the hermit, 'which is greatly increased by the errors of education.'

'Yet surely, such terrors are natural,' said Matilda; 'and in every situation, we should be subject to their influence.'

'True,' answered Father Peter: 'yet they are greatly encouraged by tales of horror, and terrific recitals, which curiosity prompts us to listen to, and which so far win on our fancy, as to make us anxious after such entertainment.'

'Your observations, father, are just,' said Alfred: 'yet there may, sometimes, circumstances of a strange nature happen to us, that to all human probability would confirm the appearance of supernatural beings.'

Here he looked at Leonard, whose countenance changed, while he seemed to shudder at the ideas his master's words had occasioned. None, except Matilda, observed it; but she had lately watched every look of both her brother and Leonard. – Father Peter appeared also disturbed; he hesitated some time before he answered; at length, however, he gave a short reply, and the conversation took another turn.

After a little time, they took their leave, and again walked to the abbey. Alfred, when dinner was finished, had a conference of some time with Leonard; and the latter immediately after walked out. Matilda, with surprise, asked where he was gone; Alfred answered her with some confusion, that he had sent him to try if he could, by any stratagem, find if there were letters directed to him at the post-house. This she knew to be entirely evasive: but she said no more; and her brother soon after retired to his chamber.

Agnes, the moment he was gone, began talking, as usual, of the room that was next that they were now in, and declared she expected every instant some hobgoblin would start through the large heavy folding doors before them. Matilda asked if she knew whether her brother or Leonard had examined the apartment.

'Oh yes, mademoiselle, the other morning before you was up.'

'And, pray, did they see any thing particular?'

'Nothing then,' answered Agnes: 'but they did that dreadful night; for you must know I had the curiosity to listen to their discourse while they were searching the place; and though they spoke very low, I could just make out mademoiselle, they had seen a ghost.'

'I am determined to have a view of this room,' said Matilda, walking to that end of the parlour.

'Oh, for heaven's sake, mademoiselle, do not enter for the world.'

'Ridiculous!' replied Matilda, and immediately pushed against the doors with all her strength, when they immediately flew open.

The apartment was spacious, and one of those they had examined at their first coming to the abbey. The furniture was in better order than most of the others; but the shutters being closed, the only light came from an opening at the top. She walked entirely round, and could perceive no alteration whatever. Agnes stood at the door, and at intervals attempted to peep in, but directly shrunk back, and retired. Matilda, having satisfied herself, closed the doors, while Agnes impatiently inquired if she had seen any thing extraordinary. Matilda smiled at the earnestness with which she asked the question, and told her she had nothing to fear. Agnes, however, was by no means divested of her terrors; and after the strange occurrences that had already happened, and those which followed, it is not to be wondered at that they greatly increased.

In about two hours, Alfred descended to the parlour, and shortly after Leonard returned; he brought some articles with him, but they were carried to the chambers above, and Matilda had no opportunity of knowing what they were. Supper-time arrived; when both Leonard and his master seemed, in some measure, to have regained their usual spirits: yet Alfred was impatient to retire to rest; at an early hour they therefore parted for the night, Matilda took up a book: Agnes, after being undressed, wished her, good repose, and was presently in a profound sleep.

Matilda now seated herself in the window, impatiently waiting the hour of midnight, yet dreading a repetition of the circumstance she had already seen. Her brother and Leonard, she could hear, continued in close discourse for some time; the purport of it, however, it was impossible for her to make out, as they spoke in a low tone of voice. At length the expected time arrived, and she kept watching with a palpitating heart the casement in the west tower. The night was extremely gloomy, the moon at intervals gave a light, but heavy clouds continued frequently to eclipse it, and thunder rolled at a distance, while flashes of strong lightning darted from an illumined part of the heavens, which seemed to form a mountain of fire. Matilda still kept her eye fixed on the tower; but no light appeared, except that from above, which fell on its grey decayed walls, o'ergrown with ivy, and slowly tumbling to the ground through the ravages of time.

She was just going to quit her situation, when she thought she perceived something move in the court below. A few minutes before, she had heard, as she supposed, her brother's chamber-door open softly, and a step cautiously descend the stair-case to the hall. At the time she conceived it to be a fancy, but her ideas were now different. A strong flash of lightning gave her an opportunity to discover a figure walk slowly with a dark lanthorn across the court towards the outer-gates. It was closely wrapped up; but by the height it seemed like Leonard.

He now disappeared among some trees, but she still saw the light through the foliage. Matilda, more and more agitated, remained at the window. In about five minutes, the light again moved towards the abbey, and the moon at that moment suddenly appearing from a heavy cloud, she could plainly perceive two men follow the person who held the lanthorn. Both, by their dress, seemed Italians; but their cloaks were entirely fastened round them, and their hats flapped over their faces so as to conceal the countenance.

Astonished at such an unexpected sight, and ready to sink with terror, she knew not in what manner to act. Leonard might be a villain! She checked herself at so uncharitable a supposition: yet, why should he leave his bed at such an hour, and admit two strangers into the abbey, where her brother had, in all probability, preserved his life through the secrecy of his habitation?

This unaccountable adventure had so strange and dreadful an appearance, that she resolved to apprise him of the visitors, as she had every reason to believe he was asleep when Leonard left the chamber: at the moment, however, she was going to execute this resolution, she heard the latter enter, and softly accost Alfred in a low voice, saying, 'They are come, sir:' and immediately they both descended as she supposed, to the parlour.

The idea of the light in the west tower now vanished from her mind, and she was entirely taken up with the occurrence that had just past.

It was plain to her that Alfred had expected these men, as he could not be even undressed by his directly leaving the room when Leonard came up with the information of their arrival: yet what business he could have with them, was an entire mystery: and the most tormenting suspicions, which she blushed to encourage, at different intervals agitated her mind. She resolved, at all events, to watch their departure, which did not happen for nearly an hour and a half; when Leonard, with his lanthorn, again conducted them across the court. Soon after Alfred and himself entered their chamber, and, as she supposed, retired to rest. Matilda, harassed out and perplexed with the scene she had been witness to, undressed herself, and lay down on the sleepless pillow.

The conduct of her brother was so equivocal and secret, that she was greatly at a loss to assign even one single reason for his late behaviour, since that period when Leonard returned from his first journey to the market, and desired to speak with him alone. The intelligence he received that day was certainly the cause of his strange manner of conduct since, let it be of what nature it would. Though she had laughed at Agnes's fears concerning the apartment next the parlour, yet something had been seen to cause alarm and terror: for the countenances both of Leonard and his master, which she even then took notice of, confirmed her they had been greatly shocked.

The light in the west tower had not appeared again as she expected; and she might have been rather doubtful of being deceived by the lightning, had she not seen an arm move within it at the same time. At length, wearied with reflection, she strove to compose herself to rest, and fell into a disturbed slumber.

They assembled to breakfast at a very late hour the next day, and all (except Agnes) by no means refreshed from the little rest they had enjoyed. They deferred visiting the hermit till the afternoon. Matilda took particular notice of her brother, but could perceive no alteration in his manner from the day before.

Having walked to Father Peter's cave, he received them at the entrance with his usual cordiality, and set before them some fruits for refreshment.

'I had them,' said the old man, 'from a peasant in the village, whom I often visit, and have known for many years, but never could persuade him to come near my habitation: for being once frightened at passing Grasville Abbey, he has never dared venture near it since, not even in the day-time!'

All laughed at the man's simplicity as they called it, yet were all conscious they were a prey to similar fears.

'Indeed, father,' said Alfred, 'I have heard so much talk of this abbey, that I intend to enter it myself, and satisfy that curiosity which has been raised by the different stories I have heard concerning it.'

The hermit's countenance changed at Alfred's words, and he, in vain, strove to conceal that agitation which worked in his heart.

'By no means fulfil such a resolution, my son: the attempt may be dangerous. – I am an old man, and know more of that abbey than you do. – You must promise you will give up all idea of it.'

Alfred fixed his eyes on Father Peter; – Leonard looked chagrined; Matilda listened with attention; and Agnes trembled with emotion.

'Excuse me,' said Alfred, who was the first that broke silence: 'but you forget yourself, father, and in a great degree contradict the usual tenor of your discourse.'

The hermit raised his eyes, and was offended at the remark.

'I did but warn you, signor,' answered he: 'but follow your own inclination: do not, however accuse me of dissimulation.'

Alfred felt the rebuke, and made an apology.

Soon after they took their leave, and returned to the abbey.

Father Peter's behaviour appeared now more strange than ever; and Alfred determined not yet to trust him with the history of his affairs. They took an early supper, and retired soon after.

(To be continued.)

Camilla (1796)*

FANNY BURNEY (1752–1840)

Although Fanny Burney writes solidly within the mainstream of fictional realism, her third novel Camilla *is notable for incorporating elements of Gothic romanticism fashionable in the 1790s. Burney had read Radcliffe's* Mysteries of Udolpho, *and* Camilla *was partly designed to replicate its commercial success. During May 1794 she and her father, the musicologist Dr Charles Burney, discussed the phenomenal £500 royalty that Mrs Radcliffe was paid for her novel. Even the size of Burney's novel was calculated to imitate that of her predecessor (which was 1,800 pages): 'I wish to know whether, if I part with the Copy right, it would not be rather an advantage to the Publisher to have 5 volumes instead of 4, or else 4 large as Udolpho, as he may then raise to non-subscribers' (letter to her brother Charles Burney, 5 July 1795); 'I entreat, with whomsoever you deal, you will enquire whether it will be better or worse to curtail the Work. If we print ultimately for ourselves, according to our original plan, we always meant to make 4 Udolphoish volumes, & reprint the Edition that succeeds the subscription in 6 volumes duod^{mo} common, for a raised price' (letter to Charles Burney, 15 July 1795). Burney's deliberate exploitation of pathos – she realized that 'crying novels' were now earning more than comic novels – also paid off, and* Camilla *sold out quickly, despite censures from some of the critical reviews.*

---

* Fanny Burney, *Camilla: or, A Picture of Youth*, 5 vols (London: T. Payne; T. Cadell Jun. and W. Davies, 1796), vol. 5, pp. 457–63.

A Vision

When the first violence of this paroxysm of sorrow abated, Camilla again strove to pray, and found that nothing so much stilled her. Yet, her faculties confused, hurried, and in anguish, permitted little more than incoherent ejaculations. Again she sighed for her Father; again the spirit of his instructions recurred, and she enquired who was the clergyman of the parish, and if he would be humane enough to come and pray by one who had no claim upon him as a parishioner.

Peggy said he was a very good gentleman, and never refused even the poorest person, that begged his attendance.

'O go to him, then,' cried she, 'directly! Tell him a sick and helpless stranger implores that he will read to her the prayers for the dying! – Should I yet live – they will compose and make me better; – if not – they will give me courage for my quick exit.'

Peggy went forth, and she lay her beating head upon the pillow, and endeavoured to quiet her nerves for the sacred ceremony she demanded.

It was dark, and she was alone; the corpse she had just quitted seemed still bleeding in full view. She closed her eyes, but still saw it; she opened them, but it was always there. She felt nearly stiff with horrour, chilled, frozen, with speechless apprehension.

A slumber, feverish nearly to delirium, at length surprised her harassed faculties; but not to afford them rest. Death, in a visible figure, ghastly, pallid, severe, appeared before her, and with its hand, sharp and forked, struck abruptly upon her breast. She screamed – but it was heavy as cold, and she could not remove it. She trembled; she shrunk from its touch; but it had iced her heart-strings. Every vein was congealed; every stiffened limb stretched to its full length, was hard as marble: and when again she made a feeble effort to rid her oppressed lungs of the dire weight that had fallen upon them, a voice hollow, deep, and distant, dreadfully pierced her ear, calling out: 'Thou hast but thy own wish! Rejoice, thou murmurer, for thou diest!' Clearer, shriller, another voice quick vibrated in the air: 'Whither goest thou,' it cried, 'and whence comest thou?'

A voice from within, over which she thought she had no controul, though it seemed issuing from her vitals, low, hoarse, and tremulous, answered, 'Whither I go, let me rest! Whence I come from let me not look back! Those who gave me birth, I have deserted; my life, my vital powers I have rejected.' Quick then another voice assailed her, so near, so loud, so terrible – she shrieked at his horrible sound. 'Prematurely,' it cried, 'thou art come, uncalled, unbidden; thy task unfulfilled, thy peace unearned. Follow, follow me! the Records of Eternity are opened. Come! write with thy own hand thy claims, thy merits to mercy!' A repelling self-accusation instantaneously overwhelmed her. 'O, no! no! no!' she exclaimed, 'let me not sign my own miserable insufficiency!' In vain was her appeal. A force unseen, yet irresistible, impelled her forward. She saw the immense volumes of Eternity, and her own hand involuntarily grasped a pen of iron, and with a velocity uncontroulable wrote these words: 'Without resignation, I have prayed for death: from impatience of displeasure, I have desired annihilation: to dry my own eyes, I have left – pitiless, selfish, unnatural! – a Father the most indulgent, a Mother almost idolizing, to weep out their's!' Her head would have sunk upon the guilty characters; but her eyelids refused to close, and kept them glaring before her. They became, then, illuminated with burning sulphur. She looked another way; but they partook of the same motion; she cast her eyes upwards, but she saw the characters still; she turned from side to side; but they were always her object. Loud again sounded the same direful voice: 'These are thy deserts; write now thy claims: – and next, – and quick, – turn over the immortal leaves, and read thy doom.' – 'Oh, no!' she cried, 'Oh, no!' – 'O, let me yet return! O, Earth, with all thy sorrows, take, take me once again, that better I may learn to work my way to that last harbour, which rejecting the criminal repiner, opens its soft bosom to the firm though supplicating sufferer!' In vain again she called; – pleaded, knelt, wept in vain. The time, she found, was past; she had slighted it while in her power; it would return to her no more; and a thousand voices at once, with awful vibration, answered aloud to every prayer, 'Death was thy own desire!' Again, un-licensed by her will, her hand seized the iron instrument. The book was open that demanded her claims. She wrote with difficulty – but saw that her pen made no mark! She looked upon the page, when she thought she had finished, – but the paper was blank! – Voices then, by hundreds, by thousands, by millions, from side to side, above, below, around, called out, echoed and re-echoed, 'Turn over, turn over – and read thy eternal doom!' In the same instant, the leaf, untouched, burst open – and – she awoke. But in a trepidation so violent, the bed shook under her, the cold sweat, in large drops, fell from her forehead, and her heart still seemed labouring under the adamantine pressure of the inflexibly cold grasp of death. So exalted was her imagination, so confused were all her thinking faculties, that she stared with wild doubt whether then, or whether now, what she experienced was a dream.

In this suspensive state, fearing to call, to move, or almost to breathe, she remained, in perfect stillness, and in the dark, till little Peggy crept softly into the chamber.

Certain then of her situation, 'This has been,' she cried,'only a vision – but my conscience has abetted it, and I cannot shake it off.'

The Children of the Abbey (1796)*

REGINA MARIA ROCHE (1764–1845)

Mrs Regina Maria Roche was born in Co. Waterford, Munster, Ireland, and brought up in Dublin. She later recalled that 'Books were my early passion.' Her third novel The Children of the Abbey *(1796) was an immediate best-seller, and became one of the most popular novels of the nineteenth century, going through at least 14 editions during her lifetime, and French and Spanish editions. Her novel* Clermont *(1798) was one of the 'horrid' novels satirized in Austen's* Northanger Abbey. *Her works were ignored by the critics: the circulating library was her market. Eleven of her novels were published by Lane and Newman's Minerva Press, and four by Newman after the demise of Minerva. She worked in all modes of Gothic: Sentimental Gothic (borrowing directly from Radcliffe), Terror Gothic (borrowing directly from Lewis), Historical Gothic, as well as five regional Irish novels. Her husband's bankruptcy, and a ten-year Chancery suit attempting to regain her father's property (a solicitor fraudulently persuaded her to transfer her rights to him) left her destitute in old age.*

Vol. III. Chap. XI

My list'ning pow'rs
Were awed, and every thought in silence hung,
And wond'ring expectation.

AKENSIDE.

'My dear Fanny,' said Mrs. Duncan, addressing our heroine by her borrowed name, 'if at all inclined to superstition, you are now going to a place which will call it forth. Dunreath-Abbey is gothic and gloomy in the extreme, and recalls to one's mind all the stories they ever heard of haunted houses and apparitions; the desertion of the native inhabitants has hastened the depredations of time, whose ravages are unrepaired, except in the part immediately occupied by the domestics; yet what is the change in the building compared to the revolution which took place in the fortunes of her who once beheld a prospect of being its mistress; the Earl of Dunreath's eldest daughter, as I have often heard from many, was a celebrated beauty, and as good as she was handsome; but a malignant step-mother thwarted her happiness, and forced her to take shelter in the arms of a man who had every thing but fortune to recommend him; but in wanting that, he wanted every thing to please her family.

---

* Regina Maria Roche, *The Children of the Abbey, A Tale*, 4 vols (London: William Lane, Minerva Press, 1796), vol. 3, pp. 218–29.

'After some years of distress she found means to soften the heart of her father; but here the invidious step-mother again interfered, and prevented her experiencing any good effects from his returning tenderness, and it was rumoured, by a deep and iniquitous scheme, deprived her of her birth-right. Like other rumours, however, it gradually died away, perhaps from Lady Malvina and her husband never hearing of it, and none but them had a right to inquire into its truth; but if such a scheme was really contrived, woe be to its fabricator; the pride and pomp of wealth can neither alleviate or recompence the stings of conscience, much rather,' continued Mrs. Duncan, laying her hands upon her children's heads as they sat at her feet, 'much rather would I have my babes wander from door to door, to beg the dole of charity than live upon the birth-right of the orphan.

'If Lady Dunreath in reality committed the crime she was accused of, she met, in some degree, a punishment for it. Soon after the Earl's death she betrayed a partiality for a man every way inferior to her, which partiality, people have not scrupled to say, commenced, and was indulged to a criminal degree during the life-time of her husband. She would have married him had not her daughter, the Marchioness of Rosline, interfered. Proud and ambitious, her rage, at the prospect of such an alliance, knew no bounds, and seconded by the Marquis, whose disposition was congenial to her own, they got the unfortunate mother into their power, and hurried her off to a Convent in France. I know not whether she is yet living; indeed I believe there are few either know or care, she was so much disliked for her haughty disposition. I have sometimes asked my aunt about her, but she would never gratify my curiosity. She has been brought up in the family, and no doubt thinks herself bound to conceal whatever they choose.

'She lives in ease and plenty, and is absolute mistress of the few domestics that reside at the Abbey; but of those domestics I caution you in time, or they will be apt to fill your head with frightful stories of the Abbey, which sometimes, if one's spirits are weak, in spite of reason, will make an impression on the mind. They pretend that the Earl of Dunreath's first wife haunts the Abbey, venting the most piteous moans, which they ascribe to grief for the unfortunate fate of her daughter, and that daughter's children being deprived of their rightful patrimony.

'I honestly confess, when at the Abbey a few years ago, during some distresses of my husband's, I heard strange noises one evening at twilight as I walked in a gallery. I told my aunt of them, and she was quite angry at the involuntary terror I expressed, and said it was nothing but the wind whistling through some adjoining galleries which I heard. But this, my dear Fanny,' said Mrs. Duncan, who on account of her children had continued the latter part of her discourse, in a low voice, 'is all between ourselves; for my aunt declared she would never pardon my mentioning my ridiculous fears, or the yet more ridiculous fears of the servants to any human being.'

Amanda listened in silence to Mrs. Duncan's discourse, fearful that if she spoke she should betray the emotions it excited.

They at last entered between the mountains that enclosed the valley on which the Abbey stood. The scene was solemn and solitary; every prospect, except one of the sea, seen through an aperture in one of the mountains, was excluded. Some of these mountains were bare, craggy, and projecting; others were skirted with trees, robed with vivid green, and crowned with white and yellow furze; some were all a wood of intermingled shades, and others covered with long and purple heath, various streams flowed from them into the valley, some stole gently down their sides in silver rills, giving beauty and vigour wherever they meandered, others tumbled from fragment to fragment with a noise not undelightful to the ear, and formed for themselves a deep bed in the valley, over which trees, that appeared coeval with the building, bent their old and leavy heads.

At the foot, of what to the rest was called a gently swelling hill, lay the remains of the extensive gardens, which had once given the luxuries of the vegetable world to the banquets of the Abbey; but the buildings which had nursed those luxuries were all gone to decay, and the gay plantations were over-run with the progeny of neglect and sloth.

The Abbey was one of the most venerable looking buildings Amanda had ever beheld; but it was in melancholy grandeur she now saw it. In the wane of its days, when its glory was passed away, and the whole pile proclaimed desertion and decay, she saw it, when, to use the beautiful language of Hutchinson, its pride was brought low, when its magnificence was sinking in the dust, when tribulation had taken the seat of hospitality, and solitude reigned, where once the jocund guest had laughed over the sparkling bowl, whilst the owls sung nightly their strains of melancholy to the moon-shine that slept upon its mouldering battlements.

The heart of Amanda was full of the fond idea of her parents, and the sigh of tender remembrance stole from it. 'How little room,' thought she, should there be in the human heart for the worldly pride, which so often dilates it, liable as all things are to change, the distress in which the descendants of noble families are so often seen, the decline of such families themselves should check that arrogant presumption with which so many look forward to having their greatness and prosperity perpetuated through every branch of their posterity.

The proud possessors of this Abbey, surrounded with affluence, and living in its full enjoyment, never perhaps admitted the idea as at all probable, that one of their descendants should ever approach the seat of her ancestors without that pomp and elegance which heretofore distinguished its daughters. Alas! one now approaches it neither to display or contemplate the pageantry of wealth; but meek and lowly, not to receive the smile of love, or the embrace of relatives, but afflicted and unknown, glad to find a shelter, and procure the bread of dependance beneath its decaying roof.

Mrs. Duncan happily marked not Amanda's emotion as she gazed upon the Abbey; she was busily employed in answering her children's questions, who wanted to know whether she thought they would be able to climb up the great big hills they saw.

The carriage at last stopped before the Abbey. Mrs. Bruce was already at the door to receive them; she was a little smart old woman, and welcomed her niece and the children with an appearance of the greatest pleasure. On Amanda's being presented to her she gazed stedfastly in her face a few minutes, and then exclaimed, 'Well, this is very strange, though I know I could never have seen this young Lady before, her face is quite familiar to me.'

The hall into which they entered was large and gloomy, paved with black marble, and supported by pillars, through which the arched doors that led to various apartments were seen, rude implements, such as the Caledonians had formerly used in war and hunting, were ranged along the walls. Mrs. Bruce conducted them into a spacious parlour, terminated by an elegant saloon; this she told them had once been the banquetting-room; the furniture, though faded, was still magnificent, and the windows, though still in the gothic stile, from being enlarged considerably beyond their original dimensions, afforded a most delightful view of the domain.

'Do you know,' said Mrs. Duncan, 'this apartment, though one of the pleasantest in the Abbey in point of situation, always makes me melancholy; the moment I enter it I think of the entertainments once given in it, and then its present vacancy and stillness almost instantly reminds me, that those who partook of these entertainments are now almost all humbled with the dust.' – Her aunt laughed, and said, 'she was very romantic.'

The solemnity of the Abbey was well calculated to heighten the awe which stole upon the spirit of Amanda from her first view of it; no noise was heard throughout it, except the hoarse creeking of the massy door, as the servants passed from one room to another adjusting Mrs. Duncan's things, and preparing for dinner. Mrs. Duncan was drawn into a corner of the room by her aunt, to converse, in a low voice, about family affairs, and the children were rambling about the hall, wondering and inquiring about every thing they saw.

Thus left to herself, a soft languor gradually stole over the mind of Amanda, which was almost exhausted from the emotions it had experienced. – The murmuring sound of waterfalls, and the buzzing of the flies, that basked in the sunny rays which darted through the casements, lulled her into a kind of pensive tranquillity.

'Am I really,' she asked herself, 'in the seat of my ancestors? Am I really in the habitation where my mother was born, where her irrevocable vows were plighted to my father? I am, and, oh! within it. May I at last find an asylum from the vices and dangers of the world; within it may my sorrowing spirit lose its agitation, and subdue, if not its affections, at least its murmurs, at the disappointment of those affections.'

The appearance of dinner interrupted her. She made exertions to overcome any appearance of dejection, and the conversation, if not lively, was at least cheerful. After dinner Mrs. Duncan, who had been informed by Amanda of her predilection for old buildings, asked her aunt's permission to shew her the Abbey. Mrs. Bruce immediately arose, and said she would have that pleasure herself. She accordingly led the way; many of the apartments yet displayed the sumptuous taste of those who had furnished them. 'It is astonishing to me,' said Mrs. Duncan, 'that so magnificent a pile as this should be abandoned, as I may say, by its possessors.'

'The Marquis of Rosline's Castle is a more modern structure than this,' said Mrs. Bruce, 'and preferred by them on that account.'

'So like the family monument,' rejoined Mrs. Duncan, 'they are merely satisfied with permitting this to stand, as it may help to transmit the Marchioness's name to posterity.'

'How far does the Marquis live from this?' asked Amanda.

'About twelve miles,' replied Mrs. Bruce, who did not appear pleased with her niece's conversation, and led the way to a long gallery, ornamented with portraits of the family. This gallery Amanda knew well by description; this was the gallery in which her father had stopped to contemplate the picture of her mother, and her heart throbbed with impatience and anxiety to see that picture.

Mrs. Bruce, as she went before her, told her the names of the different portraits. She suddenly stopped before one; – 'that,' cried she, 'is the Marchioness of Rosline's, drawn for her when Lady Augusta Dunreath.' Amanda cast her eyes upon it, and perceived in the countenance the same haughtiness as still distinguished the Marchioness. She looked at the next pannel, and found it empty.

'The picture of Lady Malvina Dunreath hung there,' said Mrs. Bruce; 'but after her unfortunate marriage it was taken down.'

'And destroyed,' exclaimed Amanda, mournfully.

'No; but it was thrown into the old Chapel, where, with the rest of the lumber' (the soul of Amanda was struck at these words) – 'it has been locked up for years.'

'And is it impossible to see it?' asked Amanda.

'Impossible indeed,' replied Mrs. Bruce; 'the Chapel, and the whole eastern part of the Abbey, have long been in a ruinous situation, on which account it has been locked up.'

'This is the gallery,' whispered Mrs. Duncan, 'in which I heard the strange noises; but not a word of them to my aunt.'

Amanda could scarcely conceal the disappointment she felt at finding she could not see her mother's picture. She would have entreated the

Chapel might be opened for that purpose, had she not feared exciting suspicions by doing so.

They returned from the gallery to the parlour, and in the course of conversation Amanda heard many interesting anecdotes of her ancestors from Mrs. Bruce. Her mother was also mentioned, and Mrs. Bruce, by dwelling on her worth, made amends, in some degree, to Amanda for having called her picture lumber. She retired to her chamber with her mind at once softened and elevated by hearing of her mother's virtues. – She called upon her, upon her father's spirit, upon them whose kindred souls were reunited in Heaven, to bless their child, to strengthen, to support her in the thorny path marked out for her to take; nor to cease their tutelary care till she was joined to them by Providence.

The Italian; or, The Confessional of the Black Penitents (1797)*

ANN RADCLIFFE (1764–1823)

The Italian, *though less magical than* The Mysteries of Udolpho, *is a technical tour de force, and many critics believe that Radcliffe profited from a reading of Lewis. But whereas we know for certain that Lewis read and was deeply influenced by* The Mysteries of Udolpho, *there is no clear proof that Radcliffe read anything more of Lewis's* The Monk *than what was excerpted in the critical reviews. Schiller's tragedy* The Robbers *(English trans. 1792), one of Radcliffe's favourite works, may have been a more direct source, especially its theme of anguish of mind and remorse. In* The Italian *the sublimation for which Radcliffe is famous is replaced by sensationalist references to the 'sickening anguish' of torture in the cells of the Inquisition, and much of her romantic atmosphere (e.g. landscape and poetry) has been curtailed, giving a tighter concentration on plot and action. Also, centre stage is taken by a male, the villain Schedoni whose shadow lay behind 'the Byronic Hero'. The differences between Radcliffe and Lewis are fundamental: for Radcliffe, good characters ultimately cannot be deceived by demons, and guilt and depravity are constructed upon the desire for absolute power rather than repressed sexuality. In the selection I have chosen, Radcliffe's wicked characters express a Lewisian cynical disdain for mere goodness, and the Marchesa's rationalist-philosophical depiction of her husband could have been spoken by a character in a novel by the Marquis de Sade. After* The Italian, *Radcliffe inexplicably ceased writing for publication, though she was at the height of her powers, and would live for another 26 years.*

* Ann Radcliffe, *The Italian*, 3 vols (London: T. Cadell Jun. and W. Davies, 1797), vol. 2, pp. 118–38.

Vol. II, Chap. IV

Along the roofs sounds the low peal of Death,
And Conscience trembles to the boding note;
She views his dim form floating o'er the aisle,
She hears mysterious murmurs in the air,
And voices, strange and potent, hint the crime
That dwells in thought, within her secret soul.

The Marchesa repaired, according to her appointment, to the church of San Nicolo, and, ordering her servants to remain with the carriage at a side-door, entered the choir, attended only by her woman.

When vespers had concluded, she lingered till nearly every person had quitted the choir, and then walked through the solitary aisles to the north cloister. Her heart was as heavy as her step; for when is it that peace and evil passions dwell together? As she slowly paced the cloisters, she perceived a monk passing between the pillars, who, as he approached, lifted his cowl, and she knew him to be Schedoni.

He instantly observed the agitation of her spirits, and that her purpose was not yet determined, according to his hope. But, though his mind became clouded, his countenance remained unaltered; it was grave and thoughtful. The sternness of his vulture-eye was, however, somewhat softened, and its lids were contracted by subtlety.

The Marchesa bade her woman walk apart, while she conferred with her Confessor.

'This unhappy boy [i.e. her son Vivaldi],' said she, when the attendant was at some distance, 'How much suffering does his folly [i.e. his love for Ellena] inflict upon his family! My good father, I have need of all your advice and consolation. My mind is perpetually haunted by a sense of my misfortune; it has no respite; awake or in my dream, this ungrateful son alike pursues me! The only relief my heart receives is when conversing with you – my only counsellor, my only disinterested friend.'

The Confessor bowed. 'The Marchese is, no doubt, equally afflicted with yourself,' said he; 'but he is, notwithstanding, much more competent to advise you on this delicate subject than I am.'

'The Marchese has prejudices, father, as you well know; he is a sensible man, but he is sometimes mistaken, and he is incorrigible in error. He has the faults of a mind that is merely well disposed; he is destitute of the discernment and the energy which would make it great. If it is necessary to adopt a conduct, that departs in the smallest degree from those common rules of morality which he has cherished, without examining them, from his infancy, he is shocked, and shrinks from action. He cannot discriminate the circumstances, that render the same action virtuous or vicious. How then, father, are we to suppose he would approve of the bold inflictions we meditate?'

PLATE 4

Frontispiece to *The Midnight Assassin, or Confessions of the Monk Rinaldi*, the chapbook version of Ann Radcliffe's *The Italian* (1797), published on 1 May 1802 in the *Marvellous Magazine*. A generation was thrilled by the famous scene in which the monk is about to plunge his dagger into the breast of the sleeping heroine, just before he notices the locket at her throat which suggests that she is his own daughter. By permission of the British Library 1578/2144(2).

'Most true!' said the artful Schedoni, with an air of admiration.

'We, therefore, must not consult him,' continued the Marchesa, 'lest he should now, as formerly, advance and maintain objections, to which we cannot yield. What passes in conversation with you, father, is sacred, it goes no farther.'

'Sacred as a confession!' said Schedoni, crossing himself.

'I know not,' – resumed the Marchesa, and hesitated; 'I know not' – she repeated in a yet lower voice, 'how this girl [i.e. Ellena, whom Vivaldi loves] may be disposed of; and this it is which distracts my mind.'

'I marvel much at that,' said Schedoni. 'With opinions so singularly just, with a mind so accurate, yet so bold as you have displayed, is it possible that you can hesitate as to what is to be done! You, my daughter, will not prove yourself one of those ineffectual declaimers, who can think vigorously, but cannot act so! One way, only, remains for you to pursue, in the present instance; it is the same which your superior sagacity pointed out, and taught me to approve. Is it necessary for me to persuade *her*, by whom I am convinced! There is only one way.' . . .

The Marchesa was for some time silent and thoughtful, and then repeated deliberately, 'I have not the shield of the law to protect me.'

'But you have the shield of the church,' replied Schedoni; 'you should not only have protection, but absolution.'

'Absolution! – Does virtue – justice, require absolution, father?'

'When I mentioned absolution for the action which you perceive to be so just and necessary,' replied Schedoni, 'I accommodated my speech to vulgar prejudice, and to vulgar weakness. And, forgive me, that since you, my daughter, descended from the loftiness of your spirit to regret the shield of the law, I endeavoured to console you, by offering a shield to conscience. But enough of this; let us return to argument. This girl is put out of the way of committing more mischief, of injuring the peace and dignity of a distinguished family; she is sent to an eternal sleep, before her time. – Where is the crime, where is the evil of this? On the contrary, you perceive, and you have convinced me, that it is only strict justice, only self-defence.'

The Marchesa was attentive, and the Confessor added, 'She is not immortal; and the few years more, that might have been allotted her, she deserves to forfeit, since she would have employed them in cankering the honour of an illustrious house.'

'Speak low, father,' said the Marchesa, though he spoke almost in a whisper; 'the cloister appears solitary, yet some person may lurk behind those pillars. Advise me how this business may be managed; I am ignorant of the particular means.'

'There is some hazard in the accomplishment of it, I grant,' replied Schedoni; 'I know not whom you may confide in. – The men who make a trade of blood' ——

'Hush!' said the Marchesa, looking round through the twilight – 'a step!'

'It is the Friar's, yonder, who crosses to the choir,' replied Schedoni.

They were watchful for a few moments, and then he resumed the subject. 'Mercenaries ought not to be trusted,' –

'Yet who but mercenaries' – interrupted the Marchesa, and instantly checked herself. But the question thus implied, did not escape the Confessor.

'Pardon my astonishment,' said he, 'at the inconsistency, or, what shall I venture to call it? of your opinions! After the acuteness you have displayed on some points, is it possible you can doubt, that principle may both prompt and perform the deed? Why should we hesitate to do what we judge to be right?'

'Ah! reverend father,' said the Marchesa, with emotion, 'but where shall we find another like yourself – another, who not only can perceive with justness, but will act with energy.'

Schedoni was silent.

'Such a friend is above all estimation; but where shall we seek him?'

'Daughter!' said the Monk, emphatically, 'my zeal for your family is also above all calculation.'

'Good father,' replied the Marchesa, comprehending his full meaning, 'I know not how to thank you.'

'Silence is sometimes eloquence,' said Schedoni, significantly.

The Marchesa mused; for her conscience also was eloquent. She tried to overcome its voice, but it would be heard; and sometimes such starts of horrible conviction came over her mind, that she felt as one who, awaking from a dream, opens his eyes only to measure the depth of the precipice on which he totters. In such moments she was astonished, that she had paused for an instant upon a subject so terrible as that of murder. The sophistry of the Confessor, together with the inconsistencies which he had betrayed, and which had not escaped the notice of the Marchesa, even at the time they were uttered, though she had been unconscious of her own, then became more strongly apparent, and she almost determined to suffer the poor Ellena to live. But returning passion, like a wave that has recoiled from the shore, afterwards came with recollected energy, and swept from her feeble mind the barriers, which reason and conscience had begun to rear.

'This confidence with which you have thought proper to honour me,' said Schedoni, at length, and paused; 'This affair, so momentous' –

'Ay, this affair,' interrupted the Marchesa, in a hurried manner, – 'but when, and where, good father? Being once convinced, I am anxious to have it settled.'

'That must be as occasion offers,' replied the Monk, thoughtfully. – 'On the shore of the Adriatic, in the province of Apulia, not far from

Manfredonia, is a house that might suit the purpose. It is a lone dwelling on the beach, and concealed from travellers, among the forests, which spread for many miles along the coast.'

'And the people?' said the Marchesa.

'Ay, daughter, or why travel so far as Apulia? It is inhabited by one poor man, who sustains a miserable existence by fishing. I know him, and could unfold the reasons of his solitary life; – but no matter, it is sufficient that *I know him.*'

'And would trust him, father?'

'Ay, lady, with the life of this girl – though scarcely with my own.'

'How! If he is such a villain he may not be trusted! think further. But now, you objected to a mercenary, yet this man is one!'

'Daughter, he may be trusted, when it is in such a case; he is safe and sure. I have reason to know him.'

'Name your reasons, father.'

The Confessor was silent, and his countenance assumed a very peculiar character; it was more terrible than usual, and overspread with a dark, cadaverous hue of mingled anger and guilt. The Marchesa started involuntarily as, passing by a window, the evening gleam that fell there, discovered it; and for the first time she wished, that she had not committed herself so wholly to his power. But the die was now cast; it was too late to be prudent; and she again demanded his reasons.

'No matter,' said Schedoni, in a stifled voice – 'she dies!'

'By his hands?' asked the Marchesa, with strong emotion. 'Think, once more, father.'

They were both again silent and thoughtful. The Marchesa, at length, said, 'Father, I rely upon your integrity and prudence;' and she laid a very flattering emphasis upon the word integrity. 'But I conjure you to let this business be finished quickly, suspense is to me the purgatory of this world, and not to trust the accomplishment of it to a second person.' She paused, and then added, 'I would not willingly owe so vast a debt of obligation to any other than yourself.'

'Your request, daughter, that I would not confide this business to a second person,' said Schedoni, with displeasure, 'cannot be accorded to. Can you suppose, that I, myself' –

'Can I doubt that principle may both prompt and perform the deed,' interrupted the Marchesa with quickness, and anticipating his meaning, while she retorted upon him his former words. 'Why should we hesitate to do what we judge to be right?'

The silence of Schedoni alone indicated his displeasure, which the Marchesa immediately understood.

'Consider, good father,' she added significantly, 'how painful it must be to me, to owe so infinite an obligation to a stranger, or to any other than so highly valued a friend as yourself.'

Schedoni, while he detected her meaning, and persuaded himself that he despised the flattery, with which she so thinly veiled it, unconsciously suffered his self-love to be soothed by the compliment. He bowed his head, in signal of consent to her wish.

'Avoid violence, if that be possible,' she added, immediately comprehending him, 'but let her die quickly! The punishment is due to the crime.'

The Marchesa happened, as she said this, to cast her eyes upon the inscription over a Confessional, where appeared, in black letters, these awful words, '*God hears thee!*' It appeared an awful warning. Her countenance changed; it had struck upon her heart. Schedoni was too much engaged by his own thoughts to observe, or understand her silence. She soon recovered herself; and considering that this was a common inscription for Confessionals, disregarded what she had at first considered as a peculiar admonition; yet some moments elapsed, before she could renew the subject.

'You was speaking of a place, father,' resumed the Marchesa – 'you mentioned a' –

'Ay,' muttered the Confessor, still musing, 'in a chamber of that house there is' –

'What noise is that?' said the Marchesa, interrupting him. They listened. A few low and querulous notes of the organ sounded at a distance, and stopped again.

'What mournful music is that?' said the Marchesa in a faultering voice, 'It was touched by a fearful hand! Vespers were over long ago!'

'Daughter,' said Schedoni, somewhat sternly, 'you said you had a man's courage. Alas! you have a woman's heart.' . . .

'Hark!' interrupted the Marchesa, starting, 'that note again!'

The organ sounded faintly from the choir, and paused, as before. In the next moment, a slow chaunting of voices was heard, mingling with the rising peal, in a strain particularly melancholy and solemn.

'Who is dead?' said the Marchesa, changing countenance; 'it is a requiem!'

'Peace be with the departed!' exclaimed Schedoni, and crossed himself; 'Peace rest with his soul!'

'Hark! to that chaunt!' said the Marchesa, in a trembling voice; 'it is a first requiem; the soul has but just quitted the body!'

They listened in silence. The Marchesa was much affected; her complexion varied at every instant; her breathings were short and interrupted, and she even shed a few tears, but they were those of despair, rather than of sorrow. 'That body is now cold,' said she to herself, 'which but an hour ago was warm and animated! Those fine senses are closed in death! And to this condition would I reduce a being like myself! Oh, wretched, wretched mother! to what has the folly of a son reduced thee!'

She turned from the Confessor, and walked alone in the cloister. Her agitation encreased; she wept without restraint, for her veil and the evening gloom concealed her, and her sighs were lost amidst the music of the choir.

Schedoni was scarcely less disturbed, but his were emotions of apprehension and contempt. 'Behold, what is woman!' said he – 'The slave of her passions, the dupe of her senses! When pride and revenge speak in her breast, she defies obstacles, and laughs at crimes! Assail but her senses, let music, for instance, touch some feeble chord of her heart, and echo to her fancy, and lo! all her perceptions change: – she shrinks from the act she had but an instant before believed meritorious, yields to some new emotion, and sinks – the victim of a sound! O, weak and contemptible being!'

The Marchesa, at least, seemed to justify his observations. The desperate passions, which had resisted every remonstrance of reason and humanity, were vanquished only by other passions; and, her senses touched by the mournful melody of music, and her superstitious fears awakened by the occurrence of a requiem for the dead, at the very moment when she was planning murder, she yielded, for a while, to the united influence of pity and terror. Her agitation did not subside; but she returned to the Confessor.

'We will converse on this business at some future time,' said she; 'at present, my spirits are disordered. Good night, father! Remember me in your orisons.'

'Peace be with you, lady!' said the Confessor, bowing gravely, 'You shall not be forgotten. Be resolute, and yourself.'

The Marchesa beckoned her woman to approach, when, drawing her veil closer, and leaning upon the attendant's arm, she left the cloister. Schedoni remained for a moment on the spot, looking after her, till her figure was lost in the gloom of the long perspective; he then, with thoughtful steps, quitted the cloister by another door. He was disappointed, but he did not despair.

The Orphan of the Rhine (1798)*

ELEANOR SLEATH (fl. 1798–1810)

Virtually nothing is known about Eleanor Sleath beyond her six novels, which include Who's the Murderer? or, The Mysteries of the Forest *(1802),* The Bristol Heiress; or, The Errors of Education *(1809) (which combines a serious discussion of women's education and a haunted castle) and* The Nocturnal Minstrel; or, The Spirit of the Wood *(1810), all published by the Minerva Press. Her first novel,* The Orphan of the Rhine *(1798) is one of the seven*

* Eleanor Sleath, *The Orphan of the Rhine*, 4 vols (London: William Lane at the Minerva Press, 1798).

'horrid' novels listed in Austen's Northanger Abbey. *Mrs Sleath competently works her way through the major set pieces of each of Ann Radcliffe's novels, sometimes plagiarizing whole passages. Even the numerous poems that the heroine composes are imitations of her mentor's, and every chapter is headed by a verse epigraph. Several inset tales seem to be expanded versions of half-told tales alluded to by Radcliffe. The novel has a dual heroine: Julie de Rubine (whose name is a transparent reference to Henry Mackenzie's popular sentimental novel* Julia de Roubigné *(1777)) and Laurette, the 'orphan' of the title, whom she has adopted in mysterious circumstances. Julie is tricked into a 'marriage' performed by a pretended priest, then abandoned by her 'husband' after he tires of her. She takes on the name 'Madame Chamont' and decides on a life of seclusion with her child Enrico and another child whom she has been asked to adopt, for which she receives payments from a mysterious benefactor.*

> Now o'er the braid from fancy's loom,
> The rich tints breathe a deeper gloom,
> While consecrated domes beneath,
> Midst hoary shrines and caves of death,
> Secluded from the eye of day,
> She bids her pensive vot'ry stray;
> Brooding o'er monumental cells,
> Where awe diffusing silence dwells,
> Save when along the lofty fane,
> Devotion wakes her hallow'd strain.
>
> SALMAGUNDI

La Roque, having concluded his narration, was conducted by Madame Chamont, agreeable to the appointment of the Monk, to the end of the eastern rampart.

Though she had ill succeeded in the endeavour of concealing her emotions during this pathetic recital; yet that Madame Chamont, by which name only she was known to him, was Julie de Rubine, that unfortunate beauty who was the innocent cause of the death of Signor Vescolini, was a suspicion that never occurred to the agitated mind of La Roque. And as she prudently avoided mentioning any thing relative to her knowledge of the Marchese, he had no reason to suppose, even had his mind been sufficiently tranquillized to have reflected, that her story was in the least connected with his own.

Father Benedicta, who was faithful to the hour he had proposed, was in readiness to receive them; and, the better to disguise the object of his compassion from the gaze of curiosity, had conveyed a habit of his order.

As La Roque advanced towards the Monk, with a mournful yet dignified air, the benevolent Father sprung forward to receive him, who, after regarding him for a moment with a look of silent interrogation, threw back his hood upon his shoulders; whilst La Roque, who instantly recognized a long lost friend disguised under the habit of a Carthusian, rushed into his arms.

Surprise and joy for some time deprived them of utterance, till the name of De Pietro escaping the lips of La Roque, convinced Madame Chamont that the penitent Father, who was now become eminent for that meekness, piety, and virtuous resignation which dignify the Christian character, was no other than the once brilliant Italian, whose dangerous example and seductive accomplishments had ensnared the affectionate, the once noble Della Croisse, and had finally annihilated his happiness.

When the first transports of joy, grief, and astonishment, which were alternately expressed in the countenances of La Roque and the Monk, were in some degree subsided, the former was arrayed in the holy vestment of a Carthusian; and after taking an affectionate adieu of Madame Chamont, which was accompanied with an expression of gratitude which words could not have conveyed, he put himself under the protection of his newly discovered friend, and repaired to the monastery.

Pensive, thoughtful, and dejected, Madame Chamont continued on her way towards the castle; musing as she went upon this singular adventure, which now engrossed all her attention.

Having entered the gate leading into the outer court, she missed a bracelet from her arm. It was one which contained the portrait of her father, and she felt distressed and chagrined at the loss.

Thinking it probable that she might have dropped it in her way from the tower, with hurried steps and a perturbed air she returned again towards the forest.

After walking along the whole extent of the battlements, and through the deep recesses of the wood which secreted the turret, without success, she began to lose all hopes of recovering it, till recollecting that she might have lost it when liberating La Roque from his fetters, she descended once more into the dungeon.

The dim and nearly extinguished lamp that glimmered from a remote corner of the abyss, throwing a melancholy gleam upon the dark and mouldering walls, just served as a guide for her steps; having raised it from the ground, she looked carefully around, but not discovering the object of her search, she replaced the light, meaning to examine those parts of the castle where she remembered to have been in the morning.

When passing by the door of the chapel, it occurred to her that she might have dropped it on assembling with the rest of the family at matins; and that the surprising incidents of the day, which had so strangely affected her mind, had prevented her from discovering her loss before. But afraid lest Laurette should be alarmed at her long absence, she determined first to partake of some refreshment with her, and to endeavour at least to revive her deeply depressed spirits, and then to explore the chapel.

The ill-assumed appearance of serenity with which Madame Chamont attempted to conceal the grief La Roque's adventures had revived, and which the recent loss of the picture had increased, appeared too unnatural to escape the notice of Laurette, who watched every movement of her countenance with an earnest anxiety.

The inexorable cruelty of the Marchese, the heart-rending sorrows of La Roque, the murder of Vescolini, herself the primary cause, flashed upon her mind in spite of every effort to the contrary, and heaved her bosom with convulsive throbbings.

As soon as dinner was removed, she repaired to her apartment; and, as was her custom when any new griefs or misfortunes assailed her, bowed her knee before a small altar that was erected for the purpose, and addressed herself to Heaven, in the hope that, with the divine assistance, she might be enabled to triumph over the severest attacks of human misery.

With spirits somewhat more composed she descended the stairs, and proceeded, with a slow and measured step, towards the chapel.

It was a fine and cloudless evening, and no sound but the sighing of the wind amongst the trees, broke the stillness that prevailed. The sun was just quitting the hemisphere; its appearance was at once sublime and beautiful, which induced her to pause for a moment to survey it: now richly illuminating the western canopy with a crimson glow, and then trembling awhile at the extremity of the horizon, and at last sinking from the sight beyond the summits of the mountains.

Having opened the door of the chapel, she fixed her eyes upon the ground, and walked slowly through the aisles, in hopes of discovering the bracelet; but being still unsuccessful in the pursuit, and believing it to be irrecoverably gone, she began to reconcile herself to the loss.

At the corner of the chapel was a door which she had before frequently observed, but without any hopes of being able to ascertain whither it led, as it was always fastened whenever she had attempted to open it; from which circumstance it appeared probable that it belonged to the burial vault, in which the ancient inhabitants of the castle were entombed.

As she passed this door, which terminated one of the eastern aisles, she perceived that it was not entirely closed, and curiosity induced her to examine it.

Having opened it without difficulty, she descended a winding flight of steps, and proceeding through a stone arch, whose strength seemed to defy the arm of Time, entered a spacious building, which, instead of being merely a receptacle for coffins, as her imagination had suggested, appeared to have been originally used as a chapel; as the monuments which it contained were more costly and ornamented than those in the place which had latterly been appropriated to purposes of devotion, and were evidently much more ancient. This surmise seemed still more probable, when she considered that the part of the edifice which was used as a chapel, was more modern than the rest of the structure; and that neither the doors nor the windows were strictly gothic, like those belonging to the other parts of the castle. A small grated window at the farther end of the place, which dimly admitted the light, discovered to her the last abode of man, and spoke of the vanity of human greatness.

It was dreary and of vast extent; the walls, which were once white, were now discoloured with the damps, and were mouldering fast into decay.

At the upper end of the abyss were erected two statues, now headless, which though not sufficiently entire to betray the original design, gave additional melancholy to the scene.

Having lingered for some time amid the graves, whose proud arches contained all that remained of former greatness, and whose inscriptions were too much effaced to convey the intended lesson to mortality; she felt herself impressed with a solemn awe, and an emotion of fear, which she could neither account for, nor subdue, directed towards the grated aperture.

The sky was clear and serene, and nothing but the light trembling of the leaves, heard at intervals in the breeze, disturbed the silence of the place. It was a moment sacred to meditation, and wrapped in sublime contemplations, she beheld the deepening veil of the twilight, which had just shaded the meek blue of the heavens, stealing upon the surrounding scenery. As she gazed, the first pale star trembled in the eastern sky, and the moon rising slowly above the tops of the trees, sailed majestically through the concave; all lower objects the height of the window had excluded, except the foliage of the trees that waved mournfully over the place, and replied to the moaning of the rising blast.

Unwilling to quit a scene so congenial to her feelings, and anxious to examine the stately monuments that arose above the remains of former greatness, she determined to convey a light to the place, since it was now too dark to distinguish them, and another opportunity of satisfying her curiosity she considered might not speedily occur.

This design was no sooner formed than executed; having procured a lamp, unobserved by any of the family she again returned to the chapel, and descending the stairs, as before, entered the vaulted building.

Having observed with the most earnest attention the stately busts that adorned the niches, the heavy gloom of the impending monuments, and the cross-bones, saints, crucifixes, and various other devices suitable to the nature of the place, which were once painted on the walls, but which time had now nearly obliterated, she felt an uneasy sensation stealing upon her mind; and, as the partial gleam of the lamp fell upon the ghastly countenances of the marble figures before her, she started involuntarily from the view. Ashamed of having given way to this moment of weakness, she seated herself upon a fallen stone near the entrance, and, setting down the lamp by her side, cast her eyes calmly around, as if determined to conquer the fears that assailed her, and then taking her pencil from her pocket, wrote the following lines:

To Melancholy

Oh! thou, the maid, in sable weeds array'd,
Who haunt'st the darksome caverns, dreary shade,
Or wrapp'd in musing deep, mid charnels pale,
Meet'st in thy sunless realms the humid gale,
That sullen murmurs, and then loudly blows,
Disturbing Silence from her deep repose;
Whilst in the mournful, dreaded midnight hour,
The hermit owl screams from yon mould'ring tower,
Or flaps his boding wing, the death room nigh,
Waking grim Horror with his funeral cry.
Hence, horrid dame, with all thy spectre train,
And let Hope's star illume this breast again;
Not with that dazzling, that delusive ray,
Which oft misleads the youthful Pilgrim's way;
But that pure beam that burns serenely bright,
And leads to visions of eternal light.

Having raised the lamp from the steps, she arose, and perceiving that it was nearly extinguished, was retiring in haste; when casting her eyes over this extensive and gloomy abode, to take a last survey of the whole, she thought she distinguished, by the expiring gleam of the lamp, a tall white figure, who having emerged slowly from behind one of the gigantic statues at the remotest part of the building, glided into an obscure corner.

The alarm that this strange appearance, whether real or imaginary, occasioned, was so great that Madame Chamont was for some moments unable to move; but in a short time again collecting her spirits, yet at the same time not daring to turn her eyes to that part of the chapel where the phantom had appeared, she gained the steps she had descended; willing to persuade herself it was only an illusion, yet not daring to be convinced, when she thought she heard a faint rustling, as of garments, which was succeeded by the sound of distant footsteps. Fear added swiftness to her flight, but before she could reach the top of the stairs, the lamp, which had been some time glimmering in the socket, expired and left her in total darkness.

Having with much difficulty reached the door leading into the chapel, exhausted and almost sinking with terror, she paused for breath, and was for some moments unable to proceed, however dreadful her present situation.

The aspect being an eastern one, the moon shining full into the window partly dissipated her fears, and she again stopped to listen if all was still. In the same minute the rustling sound which she had heard upon the stairs returned; and, without closing the door which she had entered, with the swiftness of an arrow she darted through the aisles, not slackening her pace till she had reached that part of the building communicating with the chapel; then turning once more to be assured that no one was following her, she saw, by the partial beam of the moon, a tall stately figure moving slowly by the window without the chapel.

Having reached a door which was open to admit her, she stopped at the entrance, and following the phantom with her eyes, saw it sweep mournfully along the corner of the edifice, and then glide into the deep recesses of the wood.

This strange occurrence so much alarmed Madame Chamont, that it was some time before she could recompose her spirits; and being too much fatigued to endure conversation, she excused herself to Laurette, whose looks anxiously enquired the cause of these emotions, and retired to her bed. But her mind was not sufficiently tranquillized to admit of rest; the strange appearance she had seen, continually occurred to her memory, and when she sunk into forgetfulness, her dreams were confused, wild, and horrible. Sometimes the image of Vescolini would present itself to her fancy, covered with blood, and gasping in the agonies of death; at others, the ill-fated La Roque loaded with chains, weak, pale, and emaciated, torn from his tenderest connections, and consigned to a dungeon as to his grave.

These terrible imaginations and dreadful realities worked too powerfully upon her mind not to occasion indisposition, and she awoke in the morning weak and unrefreshed. Her griefs were not of a nature to be softened by friendly participation; for prudence forbidding her to reveal them, condemned her to suffer in silence.

Laurette discovering that some hidden sorrow was preying upon the spirits of her revered protectress, exerted every effort she was mistress of to remove it; these gentle attentions were usually rewarded with a smile, but it was a smile that expressed more of melancholy than of pleasure, and which was frequently followed with a tear.

Wieland; or, The Transformation (1798)*

CHARLES BROCKDEN BROWN (1771–1810)

Charles Brockden Brown is sometimes called America's first professional writer and first Gothic novelist. His first work Alcuin *(1798) was 'A Dialogue on the Rights of Women' explicitly supporting Mary Wollstonecraft's famous* Vindication. *He*

---

* Charles Brockden Brown, *Wieland; or The Transformation. An American Tale* (New York: Printed by T. & J. Swords, for H. Caritat, 1798), pp. 176–84.

wrote half a dozen Gothic romances under the combined influence of William Godwin and Ann Radcliffe, and the London editions of his novels were published by the Minerva Press. His works are noted for the exploitation of the explained supernatural, somnambulism in the case of Edgar Huntly; or, Memoirs of a Sleep-Walker *(1799) and ventriloquism in the cases of* Wieland *(1798) and* Memoirs of Carwin, the Biloquist *(1803–5). Brown was fascinated by pathological mental states (like his compatriot Poe) and America's Puritan fanaticism (like his compatriot Hawthorne). His novels tend to fall apart in contradictions, either because he did not take enough care over his compositions, or because he could not resolve some kind of identity conflict (reflected in his novels in constant 'transformations' between 'inner' and 'outer' selves,* doppelgängers, *multiple motivations and the unreliability of one's own perceptions). After marrying in 1804, he abandoned fiction in favour of journalism and translating.*

～⚹✦～

Chapter XVI

As soon as I arrived in sight of the front of the house [writes Clara Wieland], my attention was excited by a light from the window of my own chamber. No appearance could be less explicable. A meeting was expected with Carwin, but that he pre-occupied my chamber, and had supplied himself with light, was not to be believed. What motive could influence him to adopt this conduct? Could I proceed until this was explained? Perhaps, if I should proceed to a distance in front, some one would be visible. A sidelong but feeble beam from the window, fell upon the piny copse which skirted the bank. As I eyed it, it suddenly became mutable, and after flitting to and fro, for a short time, it vanished. I turned my eye again toward the window, and perceived that the light was still there; but the change which I had noticed was occasioned by a change in the position of the lamp or candle within. Hence, that some person was there was an unavoidable inference.

I paused to deliberate on the propriety of advancing. Might I not advance cautiously, and, therefore, without danger? Might I not knock at the door, or call, and be apprized of the nature of my visitant before I entered? I approached and listened at the door, but could hear nothing. I knocked at first timidly, but afterwards with loudness. My signals were unnoticed. I stepped back and looked, but the light was no longer discernible. Was it suddenly extinguished by a human agent? What purpose but concealment was intended? Why was the illumination produced, to be thus suddenly brought to an end? And why, since someone was there, had silence been observed?

The[s]e were questions, the solution of which may be readily supposed to be entangled with danger. Would not this danger, when measured by a woman's fears, expand into gigantic dimensions? Menaces of death; the stunning exertions of a warning voice; the known and unknown attributes of Carwin; our recent interview in this chamber; the pre-appointment of a meeting at this place and hour, all thronged into my memory. What was to be done?

Courage is no definite or steadfast principle. Let that man who shall purpose to assign motives to the actions of another, blush at his folly and forbear. Not more presumptuous would it be to attempt the classification of all nature, and the scanning of supreme intelligence. I gazed for a minute at the window, and fixed my eyes, for a second minute, on the ground. I drew forth from my pocket, and opened, a penknife. This, said I, be my safeguard and avenger. The assailant shall perish, or I myself shall fall.

I had locked up the house in the morning, but had the key of the kitchen door in my pocket. I, therefore, determined to gain access behind. Thither I hastened, unlocked and entered. All was lonely, darksome, and waste. Familiar as I was with every part of my dwelling, I easily found my way to a closet, drew forth a taper, a flint, tinder, and steel, and, in a moment as it were, gave myself the guidance and protection of light.

What purpose did I meditate? Should I explore my way to my chamber, and confront the being who had dared to intrude into this recess, and had laboured for concealment? By putting out the light did he seek to hide himself, or mean only to circumvent my incautious steps? Yet was it not more probable that he desired my absence by thus encouraging the supposition that the house was unoccupied? I would see this man in spite of all impediments; ere I died, I would see his face, and summon him to penitence and retribution; no matter at what cost an interview was purchased. Reputation and life might be wrested from me by another, but my rectitude and honor were in my own keeping, and were safe.

I proceeded to the foot of the stair. At such a crisis my thoughts may be supposed at no liberty to range; yet vague images rushed into my mind, of the mysterious interposition which had been experienced on the last night. My case, at present, was not dissimilar; and, if my angel were not weary of fruitless exertions to save, might not a new warning be expected? Who could say whether his silence were ascribable to the absence of danger, or to his own absence?

In this state of mind, no wonder that a shivering cold crept through my veins; that my pause was prolonged; and, that a fearful glance was thrown backward.

Alas! my heart droops, and my fingers are enervated; my ideas are vivid, but my language is faint; now know I what it is to entertain incommunicable sentiments. The chain of subsequent incidents is drawn through my mind, and being linked with those which forewent, by turns rouse up agonies and sink me into hopelessness.

Yet I will persist to the end. My narrative may be invaded by inaccuracy and confusion; but if I live no longer, I will, at least, live to complete it.

What but ambiguities, abruptnesses, and dark transitions, can be expected from the heroine who is, at the same time, the sufferer of these disasters?

I have said that I cast a look behind. Some object was expected to be seen, or why should I have gazed in that direction? Two senses were at once assailed. The same piercing exclamation of *hold! hold!* was uttered within the same distance of my ear. This it was that I heard. The airy undulation, and the shock given to my nerves, were real. Whether the spectacle which I beheld existed in my fancy or without, might be doubted.

I had not closed the door of the apartment I had just left. The staircase at the foot of which I stood, was eight or ten feet from the door, and attached to the wall through which the door led. My view, therefore, was sidelong, and took in no part of the room.

Through this aperture was an head thrust and drawn back with so much swiftness, that the immediate conviction was, that thus much of a form, ordinarily invisible, had been unshrouded. The face was turned towards me. Every muscle was tense; the forehead and brows were drawn into vehement expression; the lips were stretched as in the act of shrieking, and the eyes emitted sparks, which, no doubt, if I had been unattended by a light, would have illuminated like the corruscations of a meteor. The sound and the vision were present, and departed together at the same instant; but the cry was blown into my ear, while the face was many paces distant.

This face was well suited to a being whose performances exceeded the standard of humanity, and yet its features were akin to those I had before seen. The image of Carwin was blended in a thousand ways with the stream of my thoughts. This visage was, perhaps, portrayed by my fancy. If so, it will excite no surprise that some of his lineaments were now discovered. Yet affinities were few and unconspicuous, and were lost amidst the blaze of opposite qualities.

What conclusion could I form? Be the face human or not, the intimation was imparted from above. Experience had evinced the benignity of that being who gave it. Once he had interposed to shield me from harm, and subsequent events demonstrated the usefulness of that interposition. Now was I again warned to forbear. I was hurrying to the verge of the same gulf, and the same power was exerted to recall my steps. Was it possible for me not to obey? Was I capable of holding on in the same perilous career? Yes. Even of this I was capable!

The intimation was imperfect: it gave no form to my danger, and prescribed no limits to my caution. I had formerly neglected it, and yet escaped. Might I not trust to the same issue? This idea might possess, though imperceptibly, some influence. I persisted; but it was not merely on this account. I cannot delineate the motives that led me on. I now speak as if no remnant of doubt existed in my mind as to the supernal origin of these sounds; but this is owing to the imperfection of my language, for I only mean that the belief was more permanent, and visited more frequently my sober meditations than its opposite. The immediate effects served only to undermine the foundations of my judgment and precipitate my resolutions.

I must either advance or return. I chose the former, and began to ascend the stairs. The silence underwent no second interruption. My chamber door was closed, but unlocked, and aided by vehement efforts of my courage, I opened and looked in.

No hideous or uncommon object was discernible. The danger, indeed, might easily have lurked out of sight, have sprung upon me as I entered, and have rent me with his iron talons; but I was blind to this fate, and advanced, though cautiously, into the room.

Still everything wore its accustomed aspect. Neither lamp nor candle was to be found. Now, for the first time, suspicions were suggested as to the nature of the light which I had seen. Was it possible to have been the companion of that supernatural visage; a meteorous refulgence producible at the will of him to whom that visage belonged, and partaking of the nature of that which accompanied my father's death?

The closet was near, and I remembered the complicated horrors of which it had been productive. Here, perhaps, was enclosed the source of my peril, and the gratification of my curiosity. Should I adventure once more to explore its recesses? This was a resolution not easily formed. I was suspended in thought: when glancing my eye on a table, I perceived a written paper. Carwin's hand was instantly recognized, and snatching up the paper, I read as follows:–

'There was folly in expecting your compliance with my invitation. Judge how I was disappointed in finding another in your place. I have waited, but to wait any longer would be perilous. I shall still seek an interview, but it must be at a different time and place: meanwhile, I will write this – How will you bear – How inexplicable will be this transaction! – An event so unexpected – a sight so horrible!'

Such was this abrupt and unsatisfactory script. The ink was yet moist, the hand was that of Carwin. Hence it was to be inferred that he had this moment left the apartment, or was still in it. I looked back, on the sudden expectation of seeing him behind me.

What other did he mean? What transaction had taken place adverse to my expectations? What sight was about to be exhibited? I looked around me once more, but saw nothing which indicated strangeness. Again I remembered the closet, and was resolved to seek in that the solution of these mysteries. Here, perhaps, was enclosed the scene destined to awaken my horrors and baffle my foresight.

I have already said, that the entrance into this closet was beside my bed, which, on two sides, was closely shrouded by curtains. On that side nearest the closet, the curtain was raised. As I passed along I cast my eye thither. I started, and looked again. I bore a light in my hand, and brought it nearer my eyes, in order to dispel any illusive mists that might have hovered before them. Once more I fixed my eyes upon the bed, in hopes that this more steadfast scrutiny would annihilate the object which before seemed to be there.

This then was the sight which Carwin had predicted! This was the event which my understanding was to find inexplicable! This was the fate which had been reserved for me, but which, by some untoward chance, had befallen on another!

I had not been terrified by empty menaces. Violation and death awaited my entrance into this chamber. Some inscrutable chance had led *her* hither before me, and the merciless fangs of which I was designed to be the prey, had mistaken their victim, and had fixed themselves in *her* heart. But where was my safety? Was the mischief exhausted or flown? The steps of the assassin had just been here; they could not be far off; in a moment he would rush into my presence, and I should perish under the same polluting and suffocating grasp!

My frame shook, and my knees were unable to support me. I gazed alternately at the closet door and at the door of my room. At one of these avenues would enter the exterminator of my honor and my life. I was prepared to defence; but now that danger was imminent, my means of defence, and my power to use them were gone. I was not qualified, by education and experience, to encounter perils like these: or, perhaps, I was powerless because I was again assaulted by surprise and had not fortified my mind by foresight and previous reflection against a scene like this.

Fears for my own safety again yielded place to reflections on the scene before me. I fixed my eyes upon her countenance. My sister's well-known and beloved features could not be concealed by convulsion or lividness. What direful illusion led thee hither? Bereft of thee, what hold on happiness remains to thy offspring and thy spouse? To lose thee by a common fate would have been sufficiently hard; but thus suddenly to perish – to become the prey of this ghastly death! How will a spectacle like this be endured by Wieland? To die beneath his grasp would not satisfy thy enemy. This was mercy to the evils which he previously made thee suffer! After these evils death was a boon which thou besoughtest him to grant. He entertained no enmity against thee: I was the object of his treason; but by some tremendous mistake his fury was misplaced. But how comest thou hither? and where was Wieland in thy hour of distress?

I approached the corpse: I lifted the still flexible hand, and kissed the lips which were breathless. Her flowing drapery was discomposed. I restored it to order, and seating myself on the bed, again fixed steadfast eyes upon her countenance. I cannot distinctly recollect the ruminations of that moment. I saw confusedly, but forcibly, that every hope was extinguished with the life of *Catharine*. All happiness and dignity must henceforth be banished from the house and name of Wieland: all that remained was to linger out in agonies a short existence; and leave to the world a monument of blasted hopes and changeable fortune. Pleyel was already lost to me; yet, while Catharine lived life was not a detestable possession: but now, severed from the companion of my infancy, the partaker of all my thoughts, my cares, and my wishes, I was like one set afloat upon a stormy sea, and hanging his safety upon a plank; night was closing upon him, and an unexpected surge had torn him from his hold and overwhelmed him forever.

Romance of the Pyrenees (1803)*

Catherine Cuthbertson

Catherine Cuthbertson was one of the best of the Radcliffe imitators, but nothing is known about her other than her novels: Santo Sebastiano *(1806),* Forest of Montalbano *(1810),* Adelaide; or, The Counter-charm *(1813),* Rosabella *(1817),* The Hut and the Castle *(1823),* Sir Ethelbert *(1830), and her earliest novel,* Romance of the Pyrenees *(1803). This was published anonymously in 1803 by G. and J. Robinson, the publishers of Radcliffe's* Mysteries of Udolpho, *and was understand-ably attributed to Radcliffe. It skilfully draws upon Walpole, Lewis and Radcliffe, and uses most of the techniques of the Radcliffe School, even to the extent of explaining the supernatural by the natural – the phantom in this instance is revealed to be a parrot. Some misfortune caused the destruction of the stock of the first edition before it was removed from the warehouse for dis-tribution, but the novel became famous in a serialized reprint and in subsequent editions, and was translated into French and German.*

The barren appearance of the country as they descended the mountains gave birth to many gloomy apprehensions which they had not experienced in France; but these fears were in some measure lulled by the out-riders assuring signora Octavia that they were sufficiently armed and prepared to repel the attack of any banditti that could molest them. It was past sun-set, and the dusk of evening was gliding fast into the darker shades of night, when, having entered an extensive valley at the foot of the Pyrenees, the carriage suddenly struck out of the main road into a winding path through a thick and gloomy forest. Victoria and Hero felt new alarms; whilst Octavia, more accustomed to travelling, appeared perfectly composed, until the rising of the moon, which in some degree becalmed the fears of

---

* Catherine Cuthbertson, *Romance of the Pyrenees*, 4 vols, 3rd edn (London: G. Robinson, 1807), vol. 1, pp. 202–9, 216–17.

her companions, first awakened hers, by its bright beams, which now and then penetrated through the thick foliage of the wood, discovering to her that the road they were slowly passing over was an unbeaten turf, that bore not the vestige of a single wheel, or any trace whatever of being frequented. Instantly concluding the drivers had mistaken the way, she hastened to inform them of her supposition. For some time they obstinately asserted they were in the right road to Bascara, and Victoria thought all contention with them vain; but signora Bernini now convinced that there was some collusion between the postillions and a banditti [*sic*], roused at once all the spirit she was mistress of, declared she would not be trifled with, and commanded the attendants immediately to compel the drivers to turn back to the last inn they had stopped at near the foot of the Pyrenees.

Murmuring at an order which they considered so unreasonable, the attendants were proceeding slowly to obey, when the sound of many horses' feet against the rocky soil suddenly assailed their ears. Victoria was alarmed, and Octavia by no means devoid of serious apprehension; but Hero was almost frantic with joy, as she had no doubt of its being conte Urbino and attendants coming to conduct them back to France.

The horses drew nearer and still nearer, when the out-riders in consternation declared the approach of a numerous banditti, which they instantly prepared to engage with. In one moment more the coach was surrounded by a band of armed ruffians; and the loud clashing of swords, and the continued discharge of carabines, announced to the trembling and terror-struck females the imminence and magnitude of their danger; and scarcely had they time to offer up prayers to heaven for succour, when the coach door was thrown open by the victorious banditti, and they, almost expiring with well-grounded apprehensions, dragged from the carriage, and each tied to the back of a ruffian on horseback, the appearance alone of whom, without the aid of other circumstances, would have proved sufficient to extinguish the flame of courage in more heroic minds.

Hero's wild shrieks were soon silenced by her grim conductor, who coolly informed her he should shoot her through the head if she did not instantly cease. Resistance Victoria and Octavia were without power of offering, even could resistance avail. Devoutly they consigned themselves to the care of heaven; but even their pious reliance upon that Being who is the protector of the friendless was scarcely sufficient to support their fainting spirits when the ruffians rode off with them into the most intricate part of the forest.

The moon was now completely obscured, and scarcely a ray of light could penetrate through the surrounding gloom. Along narrow, winding, and uneven paths, these ruffians rode, until cautiously descending a sudden and steep declivity, our three dismayed females found themselves at the brink of a rapid stream, where a boat and some more ruffians were waiting; into the boat were they hurried, and six oars plied by those ruffians glided them swiftly along.

Again the moon broke forth in all her splendour, displaying in full force the gloomy horrors of the scenery. For about half a quarter of a league, rocks of an astonishing height bounded the stream on one side, and on the other a lofty and almost impenetrable wood. At length the wood was suddenly lost, and they were enveloped by stupendous black rocks, which seemed to threaten every moment to fall in heavy vengeance upon them, often almost closing at top for a length of way together, precluding every ray of light, save what a lantern in the boat afforded; and very frequently the helmsman seemed to encounter no trifling share of difficulty in navigating the boat with safety through this most perplexed labyrinth of rocks.

At length, after an intricate and dangerous navigation, they approached the mouth of an immense and hideous cavern; the external of which, on the instant it was beheld, annihilating every idea in the mind of the dismayed spectator but that of its leading to immediate destruction. Into it the boat now glided, with only the feeble rays of a lantern to light them through this dark and apparently illimitable place; and where the mournful echo of the lofty vaulted roof, made clearer by the influence of the water beneath, resounded the strokes of the oars terrifically upon the beating hearts of our fear-chilled captives.

For about half an hour the boat proceeded slowly: an awfully horrid silence prevailed, interrupted only by the convulsive sobs and half stifled cries of Hero. At length a distant ray of light glanced feebly on the water: it was not the light of heaven; it seemed like reflected fire, and, brightening and increasing as they advanced, added horror to horror by discovering all the terrors of the place. The eye now reaching the boundary of the cavern, beheld in its concave architecture figures of fantastic formation, which, seen in light and shade, and varying their appearances as the boat moved on, seemed like grim spectres floating in the air; whilst the water, left in one mass of shadow, was seen as a black unfathomable gulf, on the surface of which the light now played in sanguinary rays, like flames of liquid fire.

Hero, casting her eyes around in wild dismay, fell at once into a swoon. Bernini, with a soul harrowed up by terror, sat motionless in the sad stupor of horrid amazement and despair; while Victoria, shuddering and appalled by what she saw and all she apprehended, sunk upon her knees, and, as the only hope she had left, in defiance of the stern interdict from speaking, fervently and audibly consigned herself and two hapless companions to the protection of heaven, imploring from its mercy fortitude to bear, as she ought, those trials it might judge proper to inflict upon her.

Benefiting by the light, the boat passed more swiftly on, and at last they entered a recess which formed a kind of harbour, that seemed the termination of the cavern. Its roof was low, and a winding staircase met the edge of the water, where half a dozen more ruffians, bearing each a torch (which emitted the light that guided the helmsman and terrified the captives), were waiting the arrival of the boat, which they soon hauled close to the steps.

Victoria and Octavia were first lifted out of the boat; but both, subdued by agonising terrors, were unable to support themselves, and sunk against some of the projections of the rock; when the boatmen, seeing they were unable to walk, bore them, as well as Hero, in their arms, preceded by the torch-bearers, up winding ascents, through narrow passages, trap-doors, and strange-formed iron works, into an immense kitchen of Gothic or rather Saracen architecture, where a deformed and melancholy-looking old woman was employed, as they entered, in washing the stain of blood from a table and the floor.

Victoria and Bernini were placed in arm chairs; – Hero on a table, being still insensible.

'Why,' said the old woman petulantly, 'Why do you bring your dead bodies littering here, Juan?'

'We left all the game we killed to-night behind us in the forest,' replied one of the men; 'so put on your spectacles, mistress Teresa, and you will then see, that this, is not a corse yet.'

'More is the pity!' returned Teresa: 'Poor young woman! was she my child, I should pray to heaven to close her eyes for ever.'

'You would, would you!' answered the man, grinning: 'that is a good one, d—m me; and the young woman would be much obliged to you for your kind prayers: but if I mistake not, if the wench could speak, she would not cry amen to it.' . . .

'I wonder,' said Teresa, 'that my master has any stomach for food to-night: I should have thought the dish of blood he has already had, would have been supper enough for him.'

'Pish,' replied Juan, 'you think like what you are – an old fool. Blood is no new sight to him; and I shall eat my supper with a good appetite I warrant, although I have sent more than one soul post to hell this night. There was warm work in the forest. Your attendants fought hard, ladies, and died bravely.'

This shocking intelligence, and the depravity of the boasting murderer, harrowed up the very souls of Victoria and Octavia; while Hero, now deprived of all reason, in fancy beheld the weapon of death levelled at her, and upon her knees vehemently implored Juan to spare her life.

'Is the wench mad?' said he, staring at her: then, familiarly patting her cheek, continued, 'Do you think that we don't know better than to put a pretty young woman to death? No, no; they are treasures so seldom seen in this castle, that we know how to prize them.'

The few remaining particles of Victoria's firmness now fled at once; she fainted, and fell back in her chair unobserved.

Secrets of the Castle (1806)*

DAVID CAREY (1782–1824)

Flowers of Literature was a kind of Regency Reader's Digest, containing extracts from the most interesting literature to appear in the preceding twelve months: belles lettres, *biography, travel, the fine arts, poetry – and Gothic novels. The volume for 1806 contains, for example, extracts from T. J. Horsley-Curties's* The Monk of Udolpho *and Carey's* Secrets of the Castle; or, The Adventures of Charles D'Almaine, *which is reproduced here.*

The Prisoners of Banditti
or, The Vault of the Castle

Hitherto no violence had been offered to the person of our captive hero, and his thoughts were not a little employed to find out the cause: for the threats and the savage looks of the banditti were still in his remembrance, and gave him no room to doubt but that, however delayed by confinement and other means of oppression, the gloomy fate that seemed to await him was not the less certain.

It was about the eleventh hour of the night, when his thoughts were occupied by reflections on his forlorn condition, that the entrance of Jerome was announced by a low whisper from the adjoining vault. Jerome approached with a shade of concern visibly marked on his countenance. 'I am sorry to be the messenger of bad news,' said he; 'your fate is at last determined upon.' The frame of our hero, at these words, shook with violent emotion. For some time he dared not enquire the extent of his fears; he read it too plainly in the sympathising features of the faithful Jerome. At last, mustering sufficient courage to propose the question, Jerome informed him, that he had been privy to a consultation held by his companions, wherein it was determined to sacrifice him to their revenge; adding, that so long as their captain was averse, as he declared himself, to their determination, there were yet hopes of escaping the impending catastrophe. Notwithstanding, Jerome could not conceal his apprehension of foul play from those to whom he alluded, who were inflamed against our hero for the loss of their companions. Is it not they alone who are conscious of guilt that are capable of fear? Charles, who a moment before was on the point of resigning himself to the agony of mind that the thoughts of certain destruction must inspire, felt the most grateful consolation from the assurance that there were still hopes of life from a quarter he could least expect it.

---

* *Flowers of Literature, for 1806*, ed. Francis William Blagdon (London: R. Crosby, 1807), pp. 114–25.

Yet he could not help shuddering at a recollection of the dangers to which he was exposed; for treachery and revenge seldom stop short of their aim, when once they have entered into the thoughts of man. 'You are a young man,' said Jerome, 'and may have a parent who vainly sorrows for your loss —' Charles sighed at the mention of the name of parent, and Jerome went on, suddenly exclaiming, as if recollecting himself, and looking in Charles's face, 'Have you courage to venture into the family vault of the castle at midnight? have you also the resolution to trust yourself in any other unfrequented part of the castle?' Charles imagining that this was said with a view to facilitate his escape by some means or other, eagerly answered that conscious innocence had nothing to fear, and that he was ready to convince him how much it was superior to guilt in this particular; but his impatience at that moment made him forget that, however courageous human nature may be in the midst of visible danger, it always shrinks back, affrighted and appalled, at supernatural power, or that which is invisible. A pause succeeded, and Jerome seemed lost in profound reverie, as if labouring with a secret which he was unwilling to trust beyond the limits of his own bosom. Suddenly they heard a gentle noise, as if proceeding from the vault, and soon after their attention was rivetted to the spot by the clanking of chains, heard at a distance, and growing more indistinct, till the sound was lost in seeming distance. Charles, in spite of his boasted courage, felt an uncommon sensation of apprehension, and even awe, rush on his mind, and Jerome started with visible emotion. 'From whence can it proceed?' said he, not daring to go in search of the cause. – 'I have been often in this place, and the places adjoining, and never heard any sounds similar to these before.' Charles was apprehensive of a discovery, and hinted his fears for his visitor's safety on his account. But Jerome was of opinion that this was unlikely, as he had some reasons to suppose that no one but himself was privy to the communication leading thereto.

'It is true,' said he, 'that there are strange appearances seen in that part of the castle, to which the direction of the sound tended, which made me ask you if you were afraid of such things, or willing to hazard your person in that wing of the building.' 'What appearances?' said Charles; 'and what inducement is held out to such attempt?' 'To explain my meaning for such a proposition,' replied the friendly Jerome, endeavouring to appear tranquil in the course of his narration, 'it will be necessary to recount to you some particulars with which few but myself are acquainted.' Charles expressed himself grateful for his confidence, and Jerome proceeded to this effect: 'It was shortly after our arrival at the castle, one stormy night, (I shall never forget that night of horror, and the sensations it occasioned in my mind, and I think in the minds of the most hardened of our troop,) the wind roared among the ancient oaks that surrounded the castle; the rain fell in torrents; the lightning darted at intervals through the gloom, illuminating the woods; whilst the tremendous peals of thunder that re-echoed over our heads alarmed the consciences of the guilty, and I am afraid,' said Jerome wildly, 'gave them but a faint idea of what they have to fear hereafter. As for myself, who was then abroad with a party of our companions, exposed to the fury of the elements, I thought all the sins which I had committed in the whole course of my life, were then present to my mind.

'In the midst of this storm, as I was afterwards informed, a gentleman and lady, who had lost their way, had arrived at the castle, drenched in the rain, in hopes of finding lodging for the night. The drawbridge was up, and they found themselves prevented from going any farther by the deep moat with which it is encircled. All arround [*sic*] appeared dark and profoundly silent.

'They went wandering about the castle in search of some light, in hopes that some one of the inhabitants would be up, and grant them shelter from so tempestuous a night. But not a glimmering of light could be discovered. They shouted as loud as they could, but no one answered. Supposing that the inhabitants were buried in sleep, or that perhaps the noise of the storm prevented their being heard, they again returned to the front, and stood observing it through the flashes of lightning that at intervals rendered it visible. They advanced as near as possible, and suddenly beheld a light to wind along the battlements of the castle, by which they could plainly perceive the person who carried it to be a being of a most terrific appearance, giving them the idea of something supernatural. The light and the figure again disappeared, and the place was totally dark. They waited some time, and the light once more appeared on the turret, but the figure was invisible. "These strange appearances astonish me," said the man, and turned to his partner; but the exertion and fatigue, joined to the thoughts of some horrible murder having been committed there, and the castle being haunted, were too much for her to sustain, and she fainted on the re-appearance of the lights. At that moment, our party coming up, heard the man again shouting for assistance. Recovered from the momentary insensibility, and the drawbridge in the meantime being let down at the summons, the unfortunate strangers were conducted into the castle. Apprehensive lest their retreat might be discovered, should the travellers be allowed to proceed in search of a habitation, it was previously determined that they should suffer death; but this sentence was soon afterwards overruled by a majority of the troop. As their appearance denoted them to be persons of rank, notwithstanding their forlorn condition, they were led into a spacious saloon, on the east wing of the castle, unconscious of the misery that awaited them. It is true, we could plainly perceive that the strangers were struck, at first sight, with the desolate state of the room through which they passed, and the warlike appearance of those who surrounded them. But they were not allowed to remain long in ignorance of their situation. They were both young and handsome, and appeared destined for each other. To be permitted to remain in the same place of confinement together, enjoying the free interchange of thought, and the sight of each other, would have been too happy a lot; and that apparent happy destiny was changed into the bitterest of fates, that of tormenting uncertainty, and separation from the object beloved.' Charles sighed at this part of the story, so much resembling his own situation, and Jerome continued: – 'I shall never forget the parting of these two lovers, when four armed men burst into the place where they were sitting, and disarmed the youth, who had snatched a weapon of defence from one of my companions, as he attempted to approach him, and stood, with the spirit of a lion in his countenance, resolving to defend his lovely charge, who had thrown herself into his arms for protection. But he was soon overpowered by numbers; not, however, before he had killed one of my companions, who attempted to drag the lady from under his protection, which so enraged the rest, that one of them plunged his poniard into the bosom of the faithful youth, and he fell bleeding by the side of my companion. One last embrace was permitted to his fair partner before they were separated for ever, and she was torn from his grasp, frantic, and confined to a separate chamber. Her defender survived but to be immured in one of the dungeons of that part of the castle which is said to be haunted, where, it is reported, he soon afterwards died of his wound.'

Manfroné; or, The One-Handed Monk (1809)★

MARY ANNE RADCLIFFE (b. *c.* 1746, d. after 1810)

Manfroné *was one of the most popular Gothic novels of the early nineteenth century (fondly remembered, for example, by Thackeray). It was frequently attributed to Mrs Ann Radcliffe (of* Mysteries of Udolpho *fame), though it is generally assumed that the real author was another Mrs Radcliffe: Mrs Mary Anne Radcliffe. Very little is known about her, though she is presumably the same person as Mary Anne Radcliffe who wrote the feminist tract* The Female Advocate; or, An Attempt to Recover the Rights of Women from Male Usurpation *(written in 1792, but not published until 1799).* The Memoirs of Mrs Mary Anne Radcliffe; in Familiar Letters to Her Female Friend *(1810) complicates matters by referring to neither the novels nor the tract. Other novels attributed to Mary Anne Radcliffe are* Radzivil *and* The Fate of Velina de Guidova *(see pp. 44ff.), both published in 1790 by William Lane at the Minerva Press.* Radclife's [sic] New Novelist's Pocket Magazine *appeared in 1802, a chapbook collection of tales compiled 'By Mrs Mary Anne Radclife, of Wimbledon in Surrey'; this was published in Edinburgh, where Mary Anne Radcliffe of* The Memoirs *spent her last years, so it*

★ Mary Anne Radcliffe, *Manfroné; or, The One-Handed Monk. A Romance* (London: Milner, n.d.), pp. 5–8.

seems likely there was only one Gothic novelist by the name of Mrs Mary Anne Rad-
cliffe. However, her authorship of Manfroné *may still be incorrect: Mrs Ann Louisa*
Belinda Ker listed this title among her novels in several letters applying for assistance
to the Royal Literary Fund in 1822 and later (Ker's novels include The Heiress di
Montalde *(1799),* Adeline St. Julian; or, The Midnight Hour *(1799) and*
other Radcliffe imitations). The 1893 edition of Manfroné *was retitled* Manfred *in*
order to cash in on the success of Byron's poetic drama of that name. Novels such as
these are in a sense the property of their publishers rather than their authors.

Chapter I

Rosaline, for some time lost in thought, rested her head on her white arm,
till the increasing gloom of her chamber made her look to her expiring
lamp; hastily she arose to trim it, for she feared to be left in the shades of
darkness, as her thoughts were sorrowful, and sleep seemed not inclined to
'steep her senses in forgetfulness.' Her apartment was spacious and lofty, the
wainscoting was of dark cedar, and the ceiling was formed of the same. The
uncertain flicker of the lamp, which doubtfully fluttered the wick, scarcely
shed its faint light further than the table on which it was placed. An almost
nameless sensation, but in which terror held a share, disturbed Rosaline;
for, as she gazed around, she almost fancied the distant shades as the shrouds
of spectral forms, gliding along with noiseless pace; and fancy made her
listen in idea to the hollow tones of their sepulchral voices. She had some
time dismissed her servant, who had retired to her bed; and whether it was
the effect of the tale she had been perusing, or some presentiment of ill
which arose in her breast, and which filled her bosom with a secret dread,
is uncertain; but she was going to summon her domestic to remain with her
during the night, when a noise at the further extremity of her chamber
fixed her, trembling, to her seat.

The sounds seemed to be occasioned by the sliding of a panel through
its groves [*sic*], and which appeared to move with difficulty, as if long
disused. Terror deprived Rosaline of the power of action and speech; her
lamp grew every moment more dim, and the gloomy shades which filled
her apartment more dense. The noise, however, soon ceased, and Rosaline
began slowly to recover from her terrors. She was not naturally of a fearful
disposition; but her imagination, heated by her disturbed ideas, made her
that night somewhat timid; true it was, that the apartment she was in was
solitary, and the light of her lamp served rather to make the darkness visible,
than to chase away its solemn shades.

Rosaline, after some time spent in endeavouring to penetrate through
the gloom, and listening for the renewal of the noise that had so much disturbed her, summoned up sufficient courage to advance to the lamp to trim
it; having so done, she held it up, in order to examine the remote parts of

the chamber, when, to her terror-struck vision, appeared a tall figure in a sable mantle, advancing towards her with a noiseless tread, whose features were not perceptible, for they were shaded by the dark plumage he wore in his barette. Rosaline started back, for at the first glance she imagined the form before her was that of some supernatural visitant; her senses were fast congealing with horror, and the lamp dropped from her trembling hand; but, in a moment after she was terribly convinced to the contrary, for she felt herself seized by a firm grasp, from which she was unable to disengage herself. The lamp, when it fell to the floor was extinguished; and thus, in utter darkness, Rosaline was at the mercy of some unknown assailant, whose base purpose soon became no matter of doubt.

Her piercing shrieks re-echoed through the vaulted corridors of the castle, and soon were heard by the Duke Rodolpho, her father, who, hastily taking his sword, rushed towards her chamber, the portal of which he burst open, and beheld his daughter in the arms of the daring intruder, her strength nearly exhausted, and her voice becoming every moment more faint.

Without laying down his lamp, he rushed on the unknown, who, leaving the trembling Rosaline, defended himself against the furious attack of the duke.

The lamp which the duke held was soon struck out of his hold, and they fought in utter darkness, till at length the stranger was disarmed, and, groaning deeply, fled; the duke would have pursued him but could not discover what way he had gone, for his footsteps became suddenly silent, and nothing was now heard but poor Rosaline, who lay on the floor, gasping for breath, and unable to speak. The servants, alarmed at the clashing of swords, and the screams of Rosaline, at length rushed into the chamber, where stood the duke, resting against the table, covered with blood, for he had been wounded in the violent contest; the sight of her father in that situation completely roused Rosaline from her insensibility, and she tottered forward to support him.

'My father!' she exclaimed, 'my dear father, you are wounded. – Oh, Pietro, Gulieno, hasten away to procure assistance.'

'There is no occasion for your alarms, Rosaline,' said the duke, 'my hurts are, I trust, not dangerous; but where could the villain have escaped? Search instantly this chamber, for I am certain he did not go out at the portal.'

The servants instantly obeyed the command, but nowhere could they discover any trace of the person they sought, but Rosaline, who by this time was perfectly returned to her recollection, mentioned the circumstance of the noise she had heard; from which they concluded that there was a private entrance into the chamber, and on examining in the direction she pointed out, a loose panel was found, which, being forced from its holds, disclosed a small passage which terminated in a flight of steps; the drops of blood on the floor shewed that the unexpected visitant had gone that way, and the servants were ordered to descend the stairs, and to trace his steps. In this however, they did not succeed; for after descending them, they found that they led into the subterraneous apartments of the castle, whose intricate turnings and windings they followed for a long time, till at last, satisfied that the object of their pursuit must have left the precincts of the castle by some concealed entrance to the vaults, they returned to Rosaline's chamber, to report their ill success to the duke.

After the departure of the servants, Rodolpho, faint with loss of blood had retired, and Rosaline was left with her favourite servant Carletta. Though repeatedly assured by him and father Augustino, confessor to the castle, who was greatly skilled in surgical knowledge, that none of his hurts were dangerous, yet she was not able to dismiss her fears on her parent's account, and sat in tears by the side of her couch, till a violent scream from Carletta, who was arranging the furniture of the apartment which had been thrown into confusion during the late mysterious occurrence, made her start from her seat to inquire into the cause, when she beheld her attendant standing with her eyes fixed on some object on the floor, and her hands clasped together, while her trembling frame bespoke the agitation she endured.

'What is the matter, Carletta?' said she, advancing – 'what alarms you so much?'

Scarcely had she concluded her question, when her eyes rested on the object that had caused the exclamation of affright from her attendant, and which, with horror, she perceived to be a human hand, blood-stained, and apparently but lately severed from its limb. She sickened and turned pale at the sight, and, sinking into a chair, covered her eyes with her hands, lest she should again behold so unpleasant an object; while Carletta, whose fears were still greater than those of her mistress, fainted away, and lay inanimate on the floor, close to the cause of her alarm. In this situation they were found by the domestics, on their return from their fruitless search. Lupo, the castellain, entered first, and Rosaline, when she beheld him, gathered sufficient courage to point out to him the bleeding hand, which he immediately took up and examined; it was large and muscular, but no rings being on the fingers, they were at a loss to conceive who the owner could be.

'At any rate,' said Lupo, 'it will be easy to recognize again, should he be anyone belonging to the castle, and which I should almost conceive to be the case, by his being so well acquainted with the private passages of it. As to his hand, lady,' continued he, 'it shall no longer alarm you.'

Thus having said, the castellian [*sic*], opening a case[ment window] which overlooked the wide waters of the lake Abruzzo, threw out the hand of the mysterious intruder, and having fastened the pannel, departed with his followers to the apartment of the duke, to acquaint him with the circumstances.

Rookwood (1834)*

WILLIAM HARRISON AINSWORTH (1805–82)

Ainsworth's first novel Rookwood *opens phantasmagorically in a mausoleum piled high with coffins, and its first line is pure Gothic: 'Within the gloomy precincts of a vault – by the feeble light of a candle stuck in a sconce against its walls – and at midnight's witching hour, two figures might be discovered, seated on an old oaken coffin-lid, and wrapped in silence as deep as that of the dead around them.' The novel was deliberately constructed in the Radcliffean mode, in an effort to revive a fading tradition. Ainsworth's formula was very successful, and sales were good. Ainsworth believed that the structure of romance which had been created by Walpole, Radcliffe, Lewis and Maturin, had been left in an imperfect state; in Germany and France, Hoffman, Tieck, Hugo, Dumas, Balzac, and Paul Lacroix had modified the genre, but it still awaited a skilful architect for its full renovation: presumably in his own hands. However, he subsequently gave less attention to the blending of the natural with the supernatural, and went on to write numerous historical novels. His second novel, about the highwayman* Jack Sheppard *(1839), is part of 'the Newgate school' of crime fiction. The revival of romance that he foresaw was left to his competitor Edward Bulwer-Lytton, who renovated the full-blooded supernatural, notably in his novels* Falkland *(1827) and* Zanoni *(1842) and his short tale 'The Haunted and the Haunters' (1859). Ainsworth stands at the juncture where the first wave of the Gothic has subsided and the second wave is gathering strength.*

Preface

During a visit to Chesterfield, in the autumn of the year 1831, I first conceived the notion of writing this Tale. Wishing to describe, somewhat minutely, the trim gardens, the picturesque domains, the rook-haunted groves, the gloomy chambers, and gloomier galleries of an ancient hall, with which I was acquainted; I resolved to attempt a story in the by-gone style of Mrs Radcliffe (which had always inexpressible charms for me), substituting an old English squire, an old English manorial residence, and an old English highwayman, for the Italian marchese, the castle, and the brigand of that great mistress of Romance.

While revolving this subject, I happened, one evening, to enter the spacious cemetery, attached to the church with the queer, twisted steeple, which, like the uplifted tail of the renowned Dragon of Watley, to whom 'houses and churches were as capons and turkies,' seems to menace the before-mentioned town of Chesterfield and its environs with destruction.

* William Harrison Ainsworth, Prefaces to *Rookwood: A Romance*, Standard Novels No. 60 (London: Richard Bentley, 1837), pp. xiii–xiv, xxiv–xxv, xxxviii–xxxix.

Here, an incident occurred, on the opening of a vault, which it is needless to relate, but which supplied me with a hint for the commencement of my Tale, as well as for the ballad, entitled 'The Coffin,' introduced in the course of the narrative. Upon this hint I immediately acted; and the earlier chapters of the book, together with the description of the ancestral mansion of the Rookwoods, were completed before I quitted Chesterfield.

Written at intervals, printed as it was written, and composed without a fixed scheme being previously laid down for the structure of the story, the work had, no doubt, a disjointed effect, on its first appearance, – a fault, which I have endeavoured to remedy in subsequent editions. But, having imagined the outline of a grim, Bluebeard-like legend (the hero of which was to play the part of a Henry the Eighth in private life), I gave myself little concern as to details; leaving the disposition of my characters, and the solution of my mysteries, entirely to chance. . . . I have been charged by the *Edinburgh Review* with extravagance. This extravagance was intentional. My object was to blend the natural with the supernatural; the sober realities of every-day life, and the calm colouring of rural scenery, with the startling situations, the wild grouping and fantastic delineations of romance, in a degree, that could not be accomplished without some appearance of irregularity and exaggeration. . . .

The supernatural occurrence, which forms the groundwork of one of these ballads ('The Lime Tree'), and which I have made the harbinger of doom to the house of Rookwood, is ascribed, by popular superstition, to a family resident in one of our southern counties; upon whose estate the fatal tree (a gigantic lime, with mighty arms, and huge girth of trunk, as described in the song,) is still carefully preserved.

The ancient mansion, to which this singular piece of timber is attached, is, I may state, for the benefit of the curious, the real Rookwood Place; for I have not drawn upon imagination, but upon memory, in describing the seat and domains of that fated family. The general features of the venerable structure, several of its chambers, the old garden, and, in particular, the noble park, with its spreading prospects, its picturesque views of the hall, 'like bits of Mrs Radcliffe' (as the poet Shelley once observed of the same scene), its deep glades, through which the deer come lightly tripping down, its uplands, lopes, brooks, brakes, coverts, and groves, are delineated with, I think, entire accuracy. These sylvan retreats rise to my recollection, as I now, in fancy, retrace them, with the vividness and distinctness of reality. How fresh is even the *thought* of such a scene! The fern is crushed beneath our feet; the rooks are cawing overhead; the lordly stag gazes proudly at us from yon steep acclivity; that umbrageous thicket invites us to its shade. – But alas! I am rambling from my subject all this while, and must return to my preface, instead of dreamingly wandering into the 'good greenwood.'

To come back to the point whence I have strayed: − The superstition that a falling branch afforded a presage of approaching death, is not peculiar to the family I have mentioned. Many other old houses have been equally favoured: in fact, there is scarcely an ancient family without its boding sign. . . .

If the design of Romance be, what it has been held, the exposition of an useful truth, by means of an interesting story, I fear I have but imperfectly fulfilled the office I have imposed upon myself; having, as I will freely confess, had, throughout, an eye, rather to the reader's amusement, than his edification. One wholesome moral, however, may, I trust, be gathered from its perusal; namely, that, without due governance of the passions, high aspirations and generous emotions will little avail their possessor. The impersonations of the Tempter, the Tempted, and the Better Influence, may be respectively discovered, by those who care to cull the honey from the flower, in Alan Rookwood, in Luke, and in Sybil.

The chief object I had in view, in making the present essay, was to see how far the infusion of a warmer, and more genial current into the veins of Old Romance would succeed in reviving her fluttering and feeble pulses. The attempt has succeeded beyond my most sanguine expectation. The ancient lady has arisen from her couch, taken the air, and succeeded in attracting a crowd of youthful admirers. Let me hope that, in more able hands, her restoration will be complete.

Romance, if I am not mistaken, is destined shortly to undergo an important change. Modified by the German and French writers, − by Hoffman, Tieck, Hugo, Dumas, Balzac, and Paul Lacroix (*le Bibliophile Jacob*) − the structure, commenced in our own land by Horace Walpole, Monk Lewis, Mrs Radcliffe, and Maturin, but left imperfect and inharmonious, requires, now that the rubbish, which choked up its approach, is removed, only the hand of the skilful architect to its entire renovation and perfection. I have not included the great name of WALTER SCOTT in this list, because, in the sense to which I would confine the term, he is not a *Romancer*. But I cannot help echoing the wish of the French aspirant (Victor Hugo. − *Littérature et Philosophie Mêlées*), that we may yet see the only romance, which could surpass the creations of our, as yet, unrivalled novelist; − 'le Roman, à la fois, drame et épopée; pittoresque, mais poétique; réel, mais idéal; vrais, mais grand; qui enchâssera Walter Scott dans Homère!'

'The Fall of the House of Usher' (1839)⋆

EDGAR ALLAN POE (1809–49)

*Like most American writers during the early nineteenth century, Edgar Allan Poe
was deeply indebted to the British Romantic tradition, though Americans followed
about one generation behind European literary fashions. Coming in at the moribund
end of the first wave of the Gothic tradition, Poe pretended to distance himself from
the school to which he was the obvious heir: 'If in many of my productions terror has
been the thesis, I maintain that terror is not of Germany, but of the soul' (Preface to*
Tales of the Grotesque and Arabesque*, 1839–40). Despite Poe's fixation on
the mind haunted by its own demons, his Gothic poems and tales reveal a studious
reading of Radcliffe, Lewis, Beckford, Byron, Shelley, Scott and the German
ballads. On the one hand he revived the Gothic tradition by pioneering detective
fiction and science fiction, and on the other hand he turned it towards the dead end of
morbid psychology. The following excerpt from the opening pages of Poe's most
famous story (originally published in* Graham's Magazine*) demonstrates his technique for refocusing Radcliffe's imagery in order to achieve a sense of pathological
sickness rather than the sublime. Although some critics would place Poe in the same
line as Lewis and Maturin, much of his inspiration comes from Radcliffe, both in his
exploitation of literary (poetic) devices and in his exploration of the 'distempered
imagination'.*

During the whole of a dull, dark, and soundless day in the autumn of the
year, when the clouds hung oppressively low in the heavens, I had been
passing alone, on horseback, through a singularly dreary tract of country;
and at length found myself, as the shades of the evening drew on, within
view of the melancholy House of Usher. I know not how it was – but, with
the first glimpse of the building, a sense of insufferable gloom pervaded my
spirit. I say insufferable; for the feeling was unrelieved by any of that half-
pleasureable, because poetic, sentiment, with which the mind usually
receives even the sternest natural images of the desolate or terrible. I looked
upon the scene before me – upon the mere house, and the simple landscape
features of the domain – upon the bleak walls – upon the vacant eye-like
windows – upon a few rank sedges – and upon a few white trunks of
decayed trees – with an utter depression of soul which I can compare to no
earthly sensation more properly than to the after-dream of the reveller
upon opium – the bitter lapse into everyday life – the hideous dropping off
of the veil. There was an iciness, a sinking, a sickening of the heart – an
unredeemed dreariness of thought which no goading of the imagination
could torture into aught of the sublime. What was it – I paused to think –

⋆ *Tales by Edgar A. Poe* (London: Wiley and Putnam, 1845), pp. 64–8.

what was it that so unnerved me in the contemplation of the House of Usher? It was a mystery all insoluble; nor could I grapple with the shadowy fancies that crowded upon me as I pondered. I was forced to fall back upon the unsatisfactory conclusion, that while, beyond doubt, there *are* combinations of very simple natural objects which have the power of thus affecting us, still the analysis of this power lies among considerations beyond our depth. It was possible, I reflected, that a mere arrangement of the particulars of the scene, of the details of the picture, would be sufficient to modify, or perhaps to annihilate its capacity for sorrowful impression; and, acting upon this idea, I reined my horse to the precipitous brink of a black and lurid tarn that lay in unruffled lustre by the dwelling, and gazed down − but with a shudder even more thrilling than before − upon the remodelled and inverted images of the grey sedge, and the ghastly tree-stems, and the vacant and eye-like windows.

Nevertheless, in this mansion of gloom I now proposed to myself a sojourn of some weeks. Its proprietor, Roderick Usher, had been one of my boon companions in boyhood; but many years had elapsed since our last meeting. A letter, however, had lately reached me in a distant part of the country − a letter from him − which, in its wildly importunate nature, had admitted of no other than a personal reply. The MS. gave evidence of nervous agitation. The writer spoke of acute bodily illness − of a mental disorder which oppressed him − and of an earnest desire to see me, as his best, and indeed his only personal friend, with a view of attempting, by the cheerfulness of my society, some alleviation of his malady. It was the manner in which all this, and much more, was said − it was the apparent *heart* that went with his request − which allowed me no room for hesitation; and I accordingly obeyed forthwith what I still considered a very singular summons.

Although, as boys, we had been even intimate associates, yet I really knew little of my friend. His reserve had been always excessive and habitual. I was aware, however, that his very ancient family had been noted, time out of mind, for a peculiar sensibility of temperament, displaying itself, through long ages, in many works of exalted art, and manifested, of late, in repeated deeds of munificent yet unobtrusive charity, as well as in a passionate devotion to the intricacies, perhaps even more than to the orthodox and easily recognisable beauties, of musical science. I had learned, too, the very remarkable fact, that the stem of the Usher race, all time-honoured as it was, had put forth, at no period, any enduring branch; in other words, that the entire family lay in the direct line of descent, and had always, with very trifling and very temporary variation, so lain. It was this deficiency, I considered, while running over in thought the perfect keeping of the character of the premises with the accredited character of the people, and while speculating upon the possible influence which the one, in the long lapse of centuries, might have exercised upon the other −

it was this deficiency, perhaps, of collateral issue, and the consequent undeviating transmission, from sire to son, of the patrimony with the name, which had, at length, so identified the two as to merge the original title of the estate in the quaint and equivocal appellation of the 'House of Usher' – an appellation which seemed to include, in the minds of the peasantry who used it, both the family and the family mansion.

I have said that the sole effect of my somewhat childish experiment – that of looking down within the tarn – had been to deepen the first singular impression. There can be no doubt that the consciousness of the rapid increase of my superstition – for why should I not so term it? – served mainly to accelerate the increase itself. Such, I have long known, is the paradoxical law of all sentiments having terror as a basis. And it might have been for this reason only, that, when I again uplifted my eyes to the house itself, from its image in the pool, there grew in my mind a strange fancy – a fancy so ridiculous, indeed, that I but mention it to show the vivid force of the sensations which oppressed me. I had so worked upon my imagination as really to believe that about the whole mansion and domain there hung an atmosphere peculiar to themselves and their immediate vicinity – an atmosphere which had no affinity with the air of heaven, but which had reeked up from the decayed trees, and the grey wall, and the silent tarn – a pestilent and mystic vapor, dull, sluggish, faintly discernible, and leaden-hued.

Shaking off from my spirit what *must* have been a dream, I scanned more narrowly the real aspect of the building. Its principal feature seemed to be that of an excessive antiquity. The discoloration of ages had been great. Minute fungi overspread the whole exterior, hanging in a fine tangled web-work from the eaves. Yet all this was apart from any extraordinary dilapidation. No portion of the masonry had fallen; and there appeared to be a wild inconsistency between its still perfect adaptation of parts, and the crumbling condition of the individual stones. In this there was much that reminded me of the specious totality of old woodwork which has rotted for long years in some neglected vault, with no disturbance from the breath of the external air. Beyond this indication of extensive decay, however, the fabric gave little token of instability. Perhaps the eye of a scrutinising observer might have discovered a barely perceptible fissure, which, extending from the roof of the building in front, made its way down the wall in a zigzag direction, until it became lost in the sullen waters of the tarn.

Noticing these things, I rode over a short causeway to the house. A servant in waiting took my horse, and I entered the Gothic archway of the hall. A valet, of stealthy step, thence conducted me, in silence, through many dark and intricate passages in my progress to the *studio* of his master. Much that I encountered on the way contributed, I know not how, to heighten the vague sentiments of which I have already spoken. While the objects around me – while the carvings of the ceilings, the sombre tapestries of the walls, the ebon blackness of the floors, and the phantasmagoric armorial trophies which rattled as I strode, were but matters to which, or to such as which, I had been accustomed from my infancy – while I hesitated not to acknowledge how familiar was all this – I still wondered to find how unfamiliar were the fancies which ordinary images were stirring up. On one of the staircases, I met the physician of the family. His countenance, I thought, wore a mingled expression of low cunning and perplexity. He accosted me with trepidation and passed on. The valet now threw open a door and ushered me into the presence of his master.

The room in which I found myself was very large and lofty. The windows were long, narrow, and pointed, and at so vast a distance from the black oaken floor as to be altogether inaccessible from within. Feeble gleams of encrimsoned light made their way through the trellised panes, and served to render sufficiently distinct the more prominent objects around; the eye, however, struggled in vain to reach the remoter angles of the chamber, or the recesses of the vaulted and fretted ceiling. Dark draperies hung upon the walls. The general furniture was profuse, comfortless, antique, and tattered. Many books and musical instruments lay scattered about, but failed to give any vitality to the scene. I felt that I breathed an atmosphere of sorrow. An air of stern, deep, and irredeemable gloom hung over and pervaded all. . . .

— 3 —

The 'German' School of Horror

ANNA LAETITIA BARBAULD, trying to account for why Ann Radcliffe wrote no more novels after *The Italian* (1797), observed (in Preface to *The British Novelists*, 1810): 'if she wishes to rise in the horrors of her next, she must place her scene in the infernal regions' – this was left to the School of Horror.

Novels of sensibility (such as Goethe's *Werther*) flowed into the channel of terror earlier in Germany than in England, and developed into the well-defined sub-genres *Ritter-, Räuber- und Schauerroman* (novels about knights or robbers, and shudder-novels). Schiller's tragedy *Die Räuber* (1781, translated into English in 1792 as *The Robbers*) and short novel *Der Geisterseher* (1784, partly translated into English in 1795 as *The Ghost-Seer, or Apparitionist*) were very influential on English works, and some of the Gothic novelists, especially Matthew Gregory Lewis, were well versed in German folk tales and ballads of the supernatural. It is especially useful to distinguish the Lewis School from the Radcliffe School by calling it the German School. The sources and settings are often German, sometimes Spanish, sometimes English, whereas Radcliffean novels of terror are often set in Italy or France.

Nearly everyone who attacked the School of Horror defined it as 'the German school', though as Coleridge pointed out, this was partly a false *English* construction (see pp. 213ff.). Montague Summers in his Introduction to a modern edition of *Horrid Mysteries* (1797) observes that Gothic novels frequently declared themselves on the title page to be 'Translated from the German', 'Taken from the German', 'A tale adapted from the German': 'but it seems that in some instances the German ascription was made solely to enhance the popularity and give a fashionable cachet to the work'. By the beginning of the nineteenth century, many critics echoed the sentiments of the editors of *Flowers of Literature; for 1803*: 'We would wish to see banished from our literature those *hobgobliana*, which the German school first suggested, and which Mrs. Ratcliffe [*sic*], by her superior talents, rendered popular.'

Sensationalistic 'raw head and bloody bones' are more characteristic of the School of Horror, and partly help to define it. Full-bodied demons have replaced the filmy spectres of the School of Terror. Incest and rape

become almost commonplace, and scenes of torture and death are portrayed in lurid physical detail. Chapbook condensations helped to intensify
such horrors, for they spared no room for the niceties of landscape description or character development. But even long, leisurely novels such as
M.   *Melmoth* achieve an almost unbearable pitch of intensity and are
ful   ʒhic images such as descriptions of being burned alive and eyes
me   ι their sockets. With Maturin and Poe, 'the intense school'
acl   level of horror that would characterize the development of the
ʒɛc   ve of the Gothic.
          ×ically, Horror Gothic is also characterized by having more
me   :al or philosophical interests than the sentimental Terror Gothic.
Ag   may be partly due to its roots in German literature; hence the
freꞑ   of novels about the Illuminati, black magic and Satanic ritual,
and t.   pseudo-sciences of astrology and alchemy. Radical politics and
demonic metaphysics often worked hand-in-hand in this tradition, as in
Mary Shelley's *Frankenstein*.

Another woman, Charlotte Dacre, was also a leading practitioner in the
School of Horror, which some critics classify too reductively as the 'male
Gothic'. The central defining feature of this tradition was the influence of
Matthew Gregory Lewis's novel *The Monk*, his play *The Castle Spectre*, and
his ballad *Alonzo the Brave and Fair Imogine*. Most horror novels, dramas and
ballads contain passages inspired, if not borrowed directly, from Lewis. In
the work of Lewis and his followers, evil becomes an attractive force, and
story and character are constructed in such a way that the reader is tempted
to identify with the 'Hero Villain', a brooding social outcast. In these
novels, morality is debunked as mere prejudice, or what today might be
called a social construct; clear moral standards are undermined by moral
ambivalence: hence the genuine subversiveness of these works.

The Necromancer
or The Tale of the Black Forest (1794)*

PETER TEUTHOLD (trans.)

The Necromancer was printed for William Lane at the Minerva Press 'translated
from the German of Lawrence Flammenberg'. Montague Summers identified the
source as Der Geisterbanner, eine Wundergeschichte aus mündlichen und
schriftlichen Traditionen gesammelt *(1792), by Karl Friedrick Kahlert using*
the pseudonym Lorenz Flammenberg. However, like all 'translators' of German

---

* *The Necromancer: or The Tale of the Black Forest*. Translated from the German of Lawrence
Flammenberg, by Peter Teuthold. 2 vols (London: William Lane, at the Minerva Press,
1794), vol. 1, pp. 86–94.

Gothic tales, Peter Teuthold seems to have handled his material very freely. It is one of the 'horrid' novels listed in Austen's Northanger Abbey. *The 'icy fangs of horror' are its* raison d'être.

At ten o'clock we stole silently to the castle without a light, the Lieutenant's servant lighted our lamp in the court-yard, and we went to the hall, where we had spent the first night, waiting with impatience for the last quarter before midnight. The Lieutenant did not believe the old man would be as good as his word, I joyfully seconded his opinion, and would have been glad if we had not waited for him; but the Baron, who, from his juvenile days, had been fond of every thing bearing the aspect of mysteriousness, was quite charmed with the reverend appearance of the old man, and maintained, upon his honor, that he certainly would stick to his appointment.

The Lieutenant began to discourse with the Baron on apparitions and necromancers, maintaining by experience and reasoning, that all was either deceit or the effects of a deluded fancy; yet the Baron would not relinquish his opinion, adding, that one ought not to speak lightly of those matters, and that the old man certainly would prove the truth of his assertion: We were still conjecturing who that strange wanderer might be, when we saw by our watches, that there were but sixteen minutes wanting to twelve; as soon as it was three quarters after eleven, we heard the sound of gentle steps in the passage.

'Our greybeard,' said the Lieutenant, 'is a man of honor,' and took up the lamp to meet the old man.

Now he entered the hall, his black wallet on his back, and beckoned in a solemn manner to follow him. We did so, and he led us through the apartments and the vaulted passage down stairs: We followed him thro' the court-yard to the iron gate of the cellar, without uttering a word; there he stopped, turning towards us, and eyeing us awhile, with a ghastly look; after an awful pause of expectation, he said with a low trembling voice, 'Don't utter a word as you value your lives.' Then he went down the two first steps, taking from his bosom an enormous key, which had been suspended round his neck by an iron chain, and opened, without the least difficulty, the monstrous padlock, the door flew open, and the old man took the lamp from the Lieutenant, leading us down a large staircase of stone; we descended into a spacious cellar, vaulted with hewn stone, and beheld all around large iron doors, secured by strong padlocks; our hoary leader went slowly towards an iron folding door, opposite to the staircase, and opened it likewise with his key; it flew suddenly open, and we beheld with horror a black vault, which received a faint light from a lamp suspended to the ceiling by an iron chain.

The old man entered, uncovering his reverend head, and we did the same, standing by his side in trembling expectation, awed by the solemnity that reigned around us; a dreadful chillness seized us, we felt the grasp of the icy fangs of horror, being in a burying vault surrounded with rotten coffins: Skulls and mouldered bones rattled beneath our feet, the grisly phantom of death stared in our faces from every side, with a grim ghastly aspect. In the centre of the vault we beheld a black marble coffin, supported by a pedestal of stone, over it was suspended to the ceiling a lamp spreading a dismal dying glimmering around. The air was heavy and of a musty smell, we hardly could respire, the objects around seemed to be wrapped in a bluish mist. The hollow sound of our footsteps re-echoed through the dreary abode of horror as we walked nigher.

The old man stopped at a small distance from the marble coffin, beckoning to us to come nigher; we moved slowly on, and he made a sign not to advance farther than he could reach with extended arms. The Lieutenant placed himself at his right, I took my station at his left, and the Baron opposite him.

Now he put the lamp on the ground before him, taking his book, an ebony wand, and a box of white plate, out of his wallet: – Out of the latter he strewed a reddish sand around him, drew a circle with his wand, and folded his hands across his breast, then he pronounced amid terrible convulsions, some mysterious words, opened the book and began to read, whilst his face was distorted in a grisly manner; his convulsions grew more horrible as he went on reading; all his limbs seemed to be contracted by a convulsive fit. His eyebrows shrunk up, his forehead was covered with wrinkles, and large drops of sweat were running down his cheeks – at once he threw down his book, gazing with a staring look, and his hands lifted up at the marble coffin.

We soon perceived that midnight had set in; the trampling of horses and the sound of horns was heard; the Necromancer did not move a limb, still staring at the coffin with a haggard look. Now the noise was on the staircase of the cellar and still he was motionless, his eyes being immoveably directed towards the coffin: But now the noise was in the cellar; he brandished his wand, and all around was buried in awful silence. He pronounced again three times an unintelligible word with a horrible thundering voice. A flash of lightning hissed suddenly through the dreary vault, licking the damp walls, and a hollow clap of thunder roared through the subterraneous abode of chilly horror. The light in the lamp was now extinguished, silence and darkness swayed all around; soon after we heard a gentle rustling just before us, and a faint glimmering was spreading through the gloomy vault. It grew lighter and lighter, and we soon perceived rays of dazzling light shooting from the marble coffin, the lid of which began to rise higher and higher – at once the whole vault was illuminated, and a grisly human figure rose slow and awful from the coffin. The phantom, which was wrapped up in a shroud, bore a dying aspect, it trembled violently as it rose, and emitted an hollow groan, looking around with chilly horror. Now the spectre descended from the pedestal, and moved with trembling steps and haggard looks towards the circle where we were standing.

'Who dares,' groaned it, in a faltering hollow accent, 'who dares to disturb the rest of the dead.'

'And who art thou?' replied our leader, with a threatening frowning aspect, 'who art thou, that thou darest to disturb the stillness of this castle, and the nocturnal slumber of those that inhabit its environs?'

The phantom shuddered back, groaning in a most lamentable accent, 'Not I, not I, my cursed husband disturbs the peace around and mine.'

Old man. 'For what reason?'

Ghost. 'I have been assassinated, and he who judges men has thrown my sins upon the murderer.'

Old man. 'I comprehend thee, unhappy spirit, betake thyself again to rest; by my power, which every spirit dreads, he shall disturb thee no more – be gone.'

The phantom bowed respectfully, staggered towards the pedestal, climbed up, got into the coffin, and disappeared; the lid sunk slowly down, and the light which had illuminated the dismal mansion of mortality died away by degrees. A flash of lightning hissed again through the vault, licking the damp walls; the hollow sound of thunder roared through the subterraneous abode of horror; the lamp began again to burn, and awful silence of the grave swayed all around.

Things as They Are; or, The Adventures of Caleb Williams (1794)*

WILLIAM GODWIN (1756–1836)

William Godwin married Mary Wollstonecraft, author of A Vindication of the Rights of Woman *(1792), who died a few days after the birth of their daughter Mary (Shelley), author of* Frankenstein *(1818, see pp. 157ff.). The political philosophy in Godwin's* Enquiry Concerning Political Justice *(1793) influenced many intellectuals of his generation, and his ideas were given a wider appeal through his novel* Caleb Williams. *This is the best of those radical political novels which contemporaries called 'philosophical romances'. Many examples employed Gothic melodrama to heighten their social realism, such as Thomas Holcroft's* Anna St. Ives *(1792) and Hugh Trevor (1794) and Robert Bage's* Hermsprong; or, Man as he is not *(1796). The genre included contributions to the ideology of*

---

* William Godwin, *Things as They Are; or, The Adventures of Caleb Williams*, 3 vols (London: B. Crosby, 1794), vol. 2, chap. 11, pp. 204–24.

women's rights such as Mary Hays's Memoirs of Emma Courtney *(1796), in the Preface to which she specifically mentioned the link between Radcliffe and Godwin in their focus upon passion, and linked psychology to political purpose: 'The most interesting, and the most useful, fictions, are perhaps, such, as delineating the progress, and tracing the consequences, of one strong, indulged, passion, or prejudice, afford materials, by which the philosopher may calculate the powers of the human mind, and learn the springs which set it in motion.' Godwin's critique of society, as in the selection describing Caleb's response to his imprisonment, draws upon descriptions of the horrors of the Inquisition, feudal tyranny, criminal biographies or 'Tyburn chronicles', and works on prison reform. He attacked the complacency of the English who thought that fortresses like the Bastille – and all it represented – existed only in France. Godwin was keen to emphasize the realism of his portraits: a footnote asserts that the incident of the man with the knife 'really occurred, and was witnessed by a friend of the author a few years since in Newgate'; another footnote asserts that 'A story extremely similar to this [about the highway robber] is to be found in the Newgate Calendar.' Much of the criticism directed against Godwin in the press was that his knowledge of the law and prisons was limited and erroneous. Godwin's radical circle selected their material to support their view that no imaginative terrors could exceed the horrors of injustice found in contemporary society. Godwin's later novel* St. Leon *(1799), set in the sixteenth century and more specifically Gothic, drew heavily upon Radcliffe and Lewis (for contemporary comments see pp. 329ff. and 348ff.).*

For my own part I had never seen a prison, and like the majority of my brethren had given myself little concern to enquire what was the condition of those who committed offence against, or became obnoxious to suspicion from the community. Oh, how enviable is the most tottering shed under which the labourer retires to rest, compared with the residence of these walls!

To me every thing was new, the massy doors, the resounding locks, the gloomy passages, the grated windows, and the characteristic looks of the keepers, accustomed to reject every petition, and to steel their hearts against feeling and pity. Curiosity and a sense of my situation induced me to fix my eyes on the faces of these men, but in a few minutes I drew them away with unconquerable loathing. It is impossible to describe the sort of squalidness and filth with which these mansions are distinguished. I have seen dirty faces in dirty apartments, which have nevertheless borne the impression of health, and spoke carelessness and levity rather than distress. But the dirt of a prison speaks sadness to the heart, and appears to be already in a state of putridity and infection.

I was detained for more than an hour in the apartment of the keeper, one turnkey after another coming in, that they might make themselves familiar with my person. As I was already considered as guilty of felony to a considerable amount, I underwent a rigorous search, and they took from me a penknife, a pair of scissars and that part of my money which was in gold. It was debated whether or not these should be sealed up, to be returned to me, as they said, as soon as I should be acquitted; and had I not displayed an unexpected firmness of manner and vigour of expostulation, such was probably the conduct that would have been pursued. Having undergone these ceremonies, I was thrust into a day room in which all the persons then under confinement for felony were assembled, to the number of eleven. Each of them was too much engaged in his own reflections to take notice of me. Of these two were imprisoned for horse-stealing, and three for having stolen a sheep, one for shop lifting, one for coining, two for highway robbery, and two for burglary.

The horse stealers were engaged in a game at cards, which was presently interrupted by a difference of opinion, attended with great vociferation, they calling upon one and another to decide it to no purpose; one paying no attention to their summons, and another leaving them in the midst of their story, being no longer able to endure his own internal anguish in the midst of their mummery.

It is a custom among thieves to constitute a sort of mock tribunal of their own body, from whose decision every one is informed whether he shall be acquitted, respited or pardoned, as well as respecting the supposed most skilful way of conducting his defence. One of the housebreakers who had already passed this ordeal was stalking up and down the room with a forced bravery, exclaimed to his companion that he was as rich as the Duke of Bedford himself. He had five guineas and a half, which was as much as he could possibly spend in the course of the ensuing month, and what happened after that, it was Jack Ketch's [i.e. the hangman's] business to see to, not his. As he uttered these words he threw himself abruptly upon a bench that was near him, and seemed to be asleep in a moment. But his sleep was uneasy and disturbed, his breathing was hard, and at intervals had rather the nature of a groan. A young fellow from the other side of the room came softly to the place where he lay with a large knife in his hand, and pressed the back of it with such violence upon his neck, the head hanging over the side of the bench, that it was not till after several efforts that he was able to rise. 'Oh, Jack!' cried this manual jester, 'I had almost done your business for you!' The other expressed no marks of resentment, but sullenly answered, 'Damn you, why did not you take the edge? It would have been the best thing you have done this many a day!'

The case of one of the persons committed for highway robbery was not a little extraordinary. He was a common soldier, of a most engaging physiognomy, and two and twenty years of age. The prosecutor, who had been robbed one evening, as he returned late from the alehouse, of the sum of three shillings, swore positively to his person. The character of the prisoner was such as has seldom been equalled. He had been ardent in the pursuit of intellectual cultivation; and he drew his favourite amusement from the works of Virgil and Horace. His integrity had been proverbially great. In one instance he had been instructed by a lady to convey a sum of a thousand pounds to a person at some miles distance: in another he was employed by a gentleman during his absence with the care of his house and furniture to the value of at least five times that sum. His habits of thinking were strictly his own, full of justice, simplicity and wisdom. He from time to time earned money of his officers by his peculiar excellence in furbishing arms; but he declined offers that had been made him to become a serjeant or a corporal, saying, that he did not want money, and that in a new situation he should have less leisure for study. He was equally constant in refusing presents that were offered him by persons who had been struck with his merit: not that he was under the influence of false delicacy and pride, but that he had no inclination to accept that, the want of which he did not feel to be an evil. This man died while I was in prison. I received his last breath.

The whole day I was obliged to spend in the company of these men, some of them having really committed the actions laid to their charge, others whom their ill fortune had rendered the victims of suspicion. The whole was a scene of misery, such as nothing short of actual observation can suggest to the mind. Some were noisy and obstreperous, endeavouring by a false bravery to keep at bay the remembrance of their condition; while others, incapable even of this effort, had the torment of their thoughts aggravated by the perpetual noise and confusion that prevailed around them. In the faces of those who assumed the most courage, you might trace the furrows of anxious care, and in the midst of their laboured hilarity dreadful ideas would ever and anon intrude, convulsing their features, and working every line into an expression of the keenest agony. To these men the sun brought no return of joy. Day after day rolled on, but their state was immutable. Existence was to them a theatre of invariable melancholy; every moment was a moment of anguish, yet did they wish to prolong that moment, fearful that the coming period would bring a severer fate. They thought of the past with insupportable repentance, each man contented to give his right hand, to have again the choice of that peace and liberty, which he had unthinkingly bartered away. We talk of instruments of torture; Englishmen take credit to themselves for having banished the use of them from their happy shore! Alas, he that has observed the secrets of a prison, well knows that there is more torture in the lingering existence of a criminal, in the silent, intolerable minutes that he spends, than in the tangible misery of whips and racks!

Such were our days. At sun set our jailors appeared, and ordered each man to come away, and be locked into his dungeon. It was a bitter aggravation of our fate, to be under the arbitrary control of these fellows. They felt no man's sorrow; they were of all men least capable of any sort of feeling. They had a barbarous and sullen pleasure in issuing their detested mandates, and observing the mournful reluctance with which they were obeyed. Whatever they directed, it was in vain to expostulate; fetters, and bread and water, were the sure consequences of resistance. Their tyranny had no other limit than their own caprice; to whom shall the unfortunate felon appeal? To what purpose complain, when his complaints are sure to be received with incredulity? A tale of mutiny and necessary precaution is the unfailing refuge of the keeper, and this tale is an everlasting bar against redress.

Our dungeons were cells, 7½ feet by 6½, below the surface of the ground, damp, without window, light or air, except from a few holes worked for that purpose in the door. In some of these miserable receptacles three persons were put to sleep together. I was fortunate enough to have one to myself. It was now the approach of winter. We were not allowed to have candles; and, as I have already said, were thrust in here at sun set and not liberated till the returning day. This was our situation for fourteen or fifteen hours out of the four and twenty. I had never been accustomed to sleep more than six or seven hours, and my inclination to sleep was now less than ever. Thus was I reduced to spend half my day in this dreary abode and in complete darkness. This was no trifling aggravation of my lot.

Among my melancholy reflections I tasked my memory, and counted over the doors, the locks, the bolts, the chains, the massy walls and grated windows that were between me and liberty. 'These,' said I, 'are the engines that tyranny sits down in cold and serious meditation to invent. This is the empire that man exercises over man. Thus is a being, formed to expatiate, to act, to smile and enjoy, restricted and benumbed. How great must be his depravity or heedlessness who vindicates this scheme for changing health and gaiety and serenity, into the wanness of a dungeon and the deep furrows of agony and despair!'

'Thank God,' exclaims the Englishman, 'we have no Bastille! Thank God, with us no man can be punished with a crime!' Unthinking wretch! Is that a country of liberty where thousands languish in dungeons and fetters? Go, go, ignorant fool! and visit the scenes of our prisons! witness their unwholesomeness, their filth, the tyranny of their governors, the misery of their inmates! After that show me the man shameless enough to triumph, and say, 'England has no Bastille!' Is there any charge so frivolous upon which men are not consigned to those detested abodes? Is there any villainy that is not practised by justices and prosecutors? But against all this, perhaps you have been told, there is redress. Yes; a redress, that it is the consummation of insult so much as to name! Where shall the poor wretch, reduced to the last despair, and to whom acquittal perhaps comes just time enough to save him from perishing, – where shall this man find leisure, and much less money, to fee counsel and officers, and purchase the tedious dear-bought remedy of the law? No; he is too happy to leave his dungeon and the memory of his dungeon behind him; and the same tyranny and wanton oppression become the inheritance of his successor.

For myself I looked round upon my walls, and forward upon the premature death I had too much reason to expect; I consulted my own heart that whispered nothing but innocence; and I said, 'This is society. This is the object, the distribution of justice, which is the end of human reason. For this sages have toiled, and midnight oil has been wasted. This!'

The reader will forgive this digression from the immediate subject of my story. If it should be said, these are general remarks; let it be remembered that they are the dear bought result of experience. It is from the fulness of a bursting heart that invective thus flows to my pen. These are not the declamations of a man desirous to be eloquent. I have felt the iron of slavery grating upon my soul.

I believed that misery, more pure than that which I now endured, had never fallen to the lot of a human being. I recollected with astonishment my puerile eagerness to be brought to the test and have my innocence examined. I execrated it, as the vilest and most insufferable pedantry. I exclaimed in the bitterness of my heart, 'Of what value is a fair fame? It is the jewel of men formed to be amused with baubles. Without it I might have had serenity of heart and chearfulness of occupation, peace and liberty; why should I consign my happiness to other men's arbitration? But, if a fair fame were of the most inexpressible value, is this the method which common sense would prescribe to retrieve it? The language which these institutions hold out to the unfortunate is, 'Come, and be shut out from the light of day; be the associate of those whom society has marked out for her abhorrence, be the slave of jailers, be loaded with fetters; thus shall you be cleared from every unworthy aspersion, and restored to reputation and honour!' This is the consolation she affords to those whom malignity or folly, private pique or unfounded positiveness have without the smallest foundation loaded with calumny. For myself I felt my own innocence; and I soon found upon enquiry that three fourths of those who are regularly subjected to a similar treatment, are persons, whom even with all the superciliousness and precipitation of our courts of justice no evidence can be found sufficient to convict. How slender then must be that man's portion of information and discernment, who is willing to commit his character and welfare to such guardianship!

But my case was even worse than this. I intimately felt that a trial, such as [our] institution is able to make it, is only the worthy sequel of such a beginning. What chance had I, after the purgation I was now suffering, that I should come out acquitted at last? What probability was there that the trial I had endured in the house of Mr. Falkland was not just as fair as any that might be expected to follow? No; I already anticipated my own condemnation.

Thus was I cut off for ever from all that existence has to bestow, from all the high hopes I had so often conceived, from all the future excellence my soul so much delighted to imagine, to spend a few weeks in a miserable prison, and then to perish by the hand of the public executioner. No language can do justice to the indignant and soul-sickening loathing that these ideas excited. My resentment was not restricted to my prosecutor, but extended itself to the whole machine of human society. I could never believe that all this was the fair result of institutions inseparable from the general good. I regarded the whole human species as so many hangmen and torturers; I considered them as confederated to tear me to pieces; and this wide scene of inexorable persecution inflicted upon me inexpressible agony. I looked on this side and on that; I was innocent; I had a right to expect assistance; but every heart was steeled against me; every hand was ready to lend its force to make my ruin secure. No man that has not felt in his own most momentous concerns justice, eternal truth, unalterable equity engaged in his behalf, and on the other side brute force, impenetrable obstinacy and unfeeling insolence, can imagine the sensations that then passed through my mind. I saw treachery triumphant and enthroned; I saw the sinews of innocence crumbled into dust by the gripe of almighty guilt.

What relief had I from these sensations? Was it relief that I spent the day in the midst of profligacy and execrations, that I saw reflected from every coun-tenance agonies only inferior to my own? He that would form a lively idea of the regions of the damned, needed only to witness for six hours a scene to which I was confined for many months. Not for one hour could I withdraw myself from this complexity of horrors, or take refuge in the calmness of med-itation. Air, exercise, series, contrast, those grand enliveners of the human frame, I was for ever debarred, by the inexorable tyranny under which I was fallen. Nor did I find the solitude of my nightly dungeon less insupportable. Its only furniture was the straw that served me for my repose. It was narrow, damp and unwholesome. The slumbers of a mind, wearied like mine with the most detestable uniformity, to whom neither amusement nor occupation ever offered themselves to beguile the painful hours, were short, disturbed and unrefreshing. My sleeping, still more than my waking thoughts, were full of perplexity, deformity and disorder. To these slumbers succeeded the hours which by the regulations of our prison I was obliged though awake to spend in solitary and chearless darkness. Here I had neither books, nor pens, nor any thing upon which to engage my attention; all was a sightless blank. How was a mind, active and indefatigable like mine, to endure this misery? I could not sink it in lethargy; I could not forget my woes; they haunted me with un-intermitted and demoniac malice. Cruel, inexorable policy of human affairs, that condemns a man to torture like this; that sanctions it and knows not what is done under its sanction; that is too supine and unfeeling to enquire into these petty details; that calls this the ordeal of innocence and the protector of freedom! A thousand times I could have dashed my brains against the walls of my dungeon; a thousand times I longed for death, and wished with inex-pressible ardour for an end to what I suffered; a thousand times I meditated suicide, and ruminated in the bitterness of my soul upon the different means of escaping from the load of existence. What had I to do with life? I had seen enough to make me regard it with detestation. Why should I wait the lingering process of legal despotism, and not dare so much as to die but when and how its instruments decreed? Still some inexplicable suggestion withheld my hand. I clung with desperate fondness to this shadow of existence, its mysterious attractions and its hopeless prospects.

The Monk (1796)[*]

MATTHEW GREGORY LEWIS (1775–1818)

Lewis read a copy of Radcliffe's The Mysteries of Udolpho *in May 1794 as he crossed the Channel to take up his post as attaché at the British embassy at The Hague. He had been working desultorily on his own romance* The Monk *and was suddenly galvanized into completing it: 'I was induced to go on with it by reading "the Mysteries of Udolpho", which is in my opinion one of the most interesting Books that ever have been published' (letter to his mother, 18 May 1794). When* The Monk *appeared in March 1796 <u>it created an instant sensation due to its sexual violence and lurid descriptions</u>. Lewis foolishly bragged on the title page that he had just been elected a Member of Parliament, which made the novel's immorality even more threatening. (It is a curious irony that William Beckford's seat as MP for Hindon was taken by Monk Lewis.) In response to an attack by Mathias (see pp. 292ff.) urging that Lewis be prosecuted for blasphemy and obscenity, Lewis expurgated the offending passages from future editions. Coleridge agreed with Mathias in his criticism of the novel (see pp. 295ff.) and Byron, a flouter of convention himself, nevertheless noted in his journal that the offending parts of the novel 'ought to have been written by Tiberius at Caprea – they are forced – the philtered ideas of a jaded voluptuary'. Though Lewis's fame was established by this one novel – he was henceforth known as 'Monk Lewis' – he was also a very skilled poet (see pp. 240ff. and 245ff.) and a very popular dramatist (see pp. 188ff.).*

The novel reflects Lewis's homosexuality (he never married, and had a long relationship with William Kelly, son of Isabella Kelly, the author of half a dozen Gothic romances) as well as his subversive desire to shock his morally complacent elders (Lewis was 19 when he wrote the novel). Ambrosio falls in love with Matilda while she is disguised as a novice; his desire is not consummated until after she reveals herself as a woman, but a homoerotic ambience has been established, and is intensified when she later reveals herself as not really a woman either, but a male demon. However, Matilda exhibits passionate desires that are not congruent with the cold calculation of a demon. Lewis's analysis of repressed desire is compelling whether Matilda is male or female, human or demonic.

---

[*] M. G. Lewis, *The Monk*, 3 vols (Waterford: J. Saunders, 1796), vol. 2, pp. 174–9, 183–5, 192–6.

PLATE 5

TALES OF WONDER! James Gillray's caricature of ladies enthralled by Lewis's sensationalistic novel *The Monk*: 'This attempt to describe the effects of the Sublime & Wonderfull is dedicated to M. G. Lewis Esqr, MP.' From *The Caricatures of Gillray* (1818). By permission of the British Library 745.a.6.

The burst of transport was passed: Ambrosio's lust was satisfied. Pleasure fled, and Shame usurped her seat in his bosom. Confused and terrified at his weakness, he drew himself from Matilda's arms: his perjury presented itself before him: he reflected on the scene which had just been acted, and trembled at the consequences of a discovery: he looked forward with horror: his heart was despondent, and became the abode of satiety and disgust: he avoided the eyes of his partner in frailty. A melancholy silence prevailed, during which both seemed busied with disagreeable reflections.

Matilda was the first to break it. She took his hand gently, and pressed it to her burning lips.

'Ambrosio!' she murmured, in a soft and trembling voice.

The abbot started at the sound: he turned his eyes upon Matilda's; they were filled with tears; her cheeks were covered with blushes, and her supplicating looks seemed to solicit his compassion.

'Dangerous woman!' said he; 'into what an abyss of misery have you plunged me! Should your sex be discovered, my honour, nay, my life, must pay for the pleasure of a few moments. Fool that I was, to trust myself to your seductions! What can now be done? How can my offence be expiated? What atonement can purchase the pardon of my crime? Wretched Matilda, you have destroyed my quiet for ever!'

'To me these reproaches, Ambrosio? to me, who have sacrificed for you the world's pleasures, the luxury of wealth, the delicacy of sex, my friends, my fortune, and my fame! What have you lost which I preserved? Have *I* not shared in *your* guilt? Have *you* not shared in *my* pleasure? – Guilt, did I say? – In what consists ours, unless in the opinion of an ill-judging world? Let that world be ignorant of them, and our joys become divine and blameless! – Unnatural were your vows of celibacy; man was not created for such a state: and were love a crime, God never would have made it so sweet, so irresistible! Then banish those clouds from your brow, my Ambrosio. Indulge in those pleasures freely, without which life is a worthless gift. Cease to reproach me with having taught you what is bliss, and feel equal transports with the woman who adores you!'

As she spoke, her eyes were filled with a delicious languour: her bosom panted: she twined her arms voluptuously round him, drew him towards her, and glued her lips to his. Ambrosio again raged with desire: the die was thrown: his vows were already broken: he had already committed the crime, and why should he refrain from enjoying its reward? He clasped her to his breast with redoubled ardour. No longer repressed by the sense of shame, he gave a loose to his intemperate appetites; while the fair wanton put every invention of lust in practice, every refinement in the art of pleasure, which might heighten the bliss of her possession, and render her lover's transports still more exquisite. Ambrosio rioted in delights till then unknown to him. Swift fled the night, and the morning blushed to behold him still clasped in the embraces of Matilda.

Intoxicated with pleasure, the monk rose from the siren's luxurious couch: he no longer reflected with shame upon his incontinence, or dreaded the vengeance of offended heaven: his only fear was lest death should rob him of enjoyments, for which his long fast had only given a keener edge to his appetite. Matilda was still under the influence of poison; and the voluptuous monk trembled less for his preserver's life than his concubine's. Deprived of her, he would not easily find another mistress with whom he could indulge his passions so fully, and so safely; he therefore pressed her with earnestness to use the means of preservation which she had declared to be in her possession.

'Yes!' replied Matilda; 'since you have made me feel that life is valuable, I will rescue mine at any rate. No dangers shall appal me: I will look upon the consequences of my action boldly, nor shudder at the horrors which they present: I will think my sacrifice scarcely worthy to purchase your possession; and remember, that a moment passed in your arms in this world, o'erpays an age of punishment in the next. But before I take this step, Ambrosio, give me your solemn oath never to enquire by what means I shall preserve myself.'

He did so, in a manner the most binding.

'I thank you, my beloved. This precaution is necessary; for, though you know it not, you are under the command of vulgar prejudices. The business on which I must be employed this night might startle you from its singularity, and lower me in your opinion. Tell me, are you possessed of the key of the low door on the western side of the garden?'

'The door which opens into the burying-ground common to us and the sisterhood of St. Clare? I have not the key, but can easily procure it.'

'You have only this to do. Admit me into the burying-ground at midnight. Watch while I descend into the vaults of St. Clare, lest some prying eye should observe my actions. Leave me there alone for an hour, and that life is safe which I dedicate to your pleasures. To prevent creating suspicion, do not visit me during the day. Remember the key, and that I expect you before twelve. Hark! I hear steps approaching! Leave me; I will pretend to sleep.'

The friar obeyed, and left the cell. . . .

The night arrived. Ambrosio had taken care to procure from the porter the key of the low door opening into the cemetery. Furnished with this, when all was silent in the monastery, he quitted his cell, and hastened to Matilda's. She had left her bed, and was dressed before his arrival.

'I have been expecting you with impatience,' said she; 'my life depends upon these moments. Have you the key?'

'I have.'

'Away then to the garden. We have no time to lose. Follow me!'

She took a small covered basket from the table. Bearing this in one hand, and the lamp, which was flaming upon the hearth, in the other, she hastened from the cell. Ambrosio followed her. Both maintained a profound silence. She moved on with quick but cautious steps, passed through the cloisters, and reached the western side of the garden: her eyes flashed with a fire and wildness which impressed the monk at once with awe and horror. A determined desperate courage reigned upon her brow: she gave the lamp to Ambrosio; then taking from him the key, she unlocked the low door, and entered the cemetery. It was a vast and spacious square, planted with yew-trees; half of it belonged to the abbey, the other half was the property of the sisterhood of St. Clare, and was protected by a roof of stone: the division was marked by an iron railing, the wicket of which was generally left unlocked.

Thither Matilda bent her course: she opened the wicket, and sought for the door leading to the subterraneous vaults where reposed the mouldering bodies of the votaries of St. Clare. The night was perfectly dark; neither moon nor stars were visible. Luckily there was not a breath of wind, and the friar bore his lamp in full security: by the assistance of its beams, the door of the sepulchre was soon discovered. It was sunk within the hollow of a wall, and almost concealed by thick festoons of ivy hanging over it. . . .

Near an hour had elapsed since Matilda descended into the caverns; still she returned not. Ambrosio's curiosity was excited. He drew near the staircase – he listened – all was silent, except that at intervals he caught the sound of Matilda's voice, as it wound along the subterraneous passages, and was re-echoed by the sepulchre's vaulted roofs. She was at too great a distance for him to distinguish her words, and ere they reached him, they were deadened into a low murmur. He longed to penetrate into this mystery. He resolved to disobey her injunctions, and follow her into the cavern. He advanced to the staircase; he had already descended some steps, when his courage failed him. He remembered Matilda's menaces, if he infringed her orders; and his bosom was filled with a secret unaccountable awe. He returned up the stairs, resumed his former station, and waited impatiently for the conclusion of this adventure.

Suddenly he was sensible of a violent shock. An earthquake rocked the ground, the columns which supported the roof under which he stood were so strongly shaken, that every moment menaced him with its fall, and at the same moment he heard a loud and tremendous burst of thunder: it ceased, and his eyes being fixed upon the staircase, he saw a bright column of light flash along the caverns beneath. It was seen but for an instant. No sooner did it disappear, than all was once more quiet and obscure. Profound darkness again surrounded him, and the silence of night was only broken by the whirring bat, as she flitted slowly by him.

With every instant Ambrosio's amazement increased. Another hour elapsed, after which the same light again appeared, and was lost again as suddenly. It was accompanied by a strain of sweet but solemn music, which, as it stole through the vaults below, inspired the monk with mingled delight and terror. It had not long been hushed, when he heard Matilda's steps upon the staircase. She ascended from the cavern; the most lively joy animated her beautiful features.

'Did you see any thing?' she asked.

'Twice I saw a column of light flash up the staircase.'

'Nothing else?'

'Nothing.'

'The morning is on the point of breaking, let us retire to the abbey, lest day-light should betray us.'

With a light step she hastened from the burying-ground. She regained her cell, and the curious abbot still accompanied her. She closed the door, and disembarrassed herself of her lamp and basket.

'I have succeeded!' she cried, throwing herself upon his bosom; 'succeeded beyond my fondest hopes! I shall live, Ambrosio, shall live for you! The step which I shuddered at taking proves to me a source of joys inexpressible! Oh that I dared communicate those joys to you! Oh that I were permitted to share with you my power, and raise you as high above the level of your sex, as one bold deed has exalted me above mine!'

'And what prevents you, Matilda?' interrupted the friar. 'Why is your business in the cavern made a secret? Do you think me undeserving of your confidence? Matilda, I must doubt the truth of your affection, while you have joys in which I am forbidden to share.'

'You reproach me with injustice; I grieve sincerely that I am obliged to conceal from you my happiness: but I am not to blame; the fault lies not in me, but in yourself, my Ambrosio. You are still too much the monk, your mind is enslaved by the prejudices of education; and superstition might make you shudder at the idea of that which experience has taught me to prize and value. At present you are unfit to be trusted with a secret of such importance; but the strength of your judgment, and the curiosity which I rejoice to see sparkling in your eyes, makes me hope that you will one day deserve my confidence. Till that period arrives, restrain your impatience. Remember that you have given me your solemn oath, never to enquire into this night's adventures. I insist upon your keeping this oath; for though,' she added smiling, while she sealed his lips with a wanton kiss, 'though I forgive you breaking your vows to heaven, I expect you to keep your vows to me.'

Horrid Mysteries (1797)*

PETER WILL (trans.)

Rev. Peter Will was a minister of the German (i.e. Lutheran) Chapel in the Savoy who specialized in translating from the German. His books were published from 1795 through 1811, and include the Gothic novels The Victim of Magical Delusion *by Cajetan Tschink and* Horrid Mysteries, *his most popular work, translated from Karl Grosse's* Der Genius *(though some passages may be by Will himself). The former was published by G. Robinson, Mrs Radcliffe's publishers, and the latter by the Minerva Press.* Horrid Mysteries *is one of the 'horrid' novels mentioned in* Northanger Abbey, *and in Thomas Love Peacock's Gothic parody* Nightmare Abbey *a character modelled on Percy Bysshe Shelley sleeps with a copy of* Horrid Mysteries *under his pillow. Will also translated several works of German mysticism and works by the Illuminati, a secret society that professed a kind of Satanism. These 'magico-political' themes are explored in* Horrid Mysteries: *the extract describing a descent into the mystic forest may be a dramatized initiation ritual; the often-used word 'rosy' may be a coded reference to the Rosicrucians, the secret Society of the Rosy Cross.*

---

* *Horrid Mysteries. A Story from the German of the Marquis of Grose.* By P. Will, 2 vols (ed. Montague Summers) (London: Robert Holden, 1927), vol. 1, pp. 70–85.

We set out one morning, on horseback, and arrived at the cottage against noon, but it was empty. No vestige of human footsteps could be traced all around. What could that mean? Pedro, who already, on the road, had repented our rash undertaking, made this circumstance a pretext to abandon it entirely; and when I insisted upon the execution of my design, mounted his horse, and left me with visible satisfaction.

A dreadful wind arose with the setting in of night; the trees were violently shaken, and every new gust threatened to overturn the old, decayed cottage where I had taken shelter against the torrents of rain which poured down from the flood-gates of heaven. Having been near an hour in that uncomfortable situation, the intense darkness that involved me seemed to disperse gradually; but the faint glimmer, which now and then trembled through the window, was swallowed up again by black obscurity. My fear made me see every object double; and my imagination was, in these moments of anxiety, dreadfully assailed by the recollection of the adventurous rumours which I had heard related of that forest. My apprehensions were increased by the restlessness of my horse, whom I had tied to a post in the inner part of the cottage; and I may truly say that I never have seen a more dreadful night.

The awful silence which, for some time, had swayed around the cottage, began by degrees to be enlivened; my listening ear, in which the roaring of the storm, and the cracking of the trees, began to resound again, could plainly distinguish whispers, which seemed to proceed from different people. The whispers grew louder and louder; and I could, at length, plainly distinguish a word. I now began to tremble, instead of rejoicing, at being relieved from my horrid solitude by the society of men. The whisperers came, meantime, nearer and nearer; a pale glimmer flashed through the little window; somebody pushed against the unlocked door; it opened, and, to my greatest terror, I saw the old man enter. He had a lighted torch in his hand. As to the rest, he was still the same as when I saw him first; the same awful sternness prevailing in his looks.

'Is it you, Don Carlos?' he exclaimed, as soon as he observed me. 'I heard a horse kick and neigh!' 'My horse has not neighed.' 'Perhaps you did not regard it. Are you come to redeem your word?' 'Yes; I am come for that purpose,' I replied, rising from my seat. . . . 'Will you follow me now?' I consented. The horse was tied faster: he lighted a second torch, which he had under his arm, and gave it me in my hand. The door was then carefully bolted, and we began to push through the overgrown underwood. But no path being to be met with, every step we proceeded was attended with laborious difficulties. I ran against every protending branch that obstructed our passage, lost my hat, and could not get to an open spot that was before us without leaving part of my tattered garments behind. The old man seemed to be used to that difficult way; he improved every advantage, and followed me without receiving the least hurt. We rested a few minutes on that open spot. . . .

'Let us not tarry long here, Don Carlos,' he said; and this was the signal for breaking up. We began to proceed: the great extent of the open spot where we were began to grow narrower by degrees; and we were, at length, confined in a rocky passage, which led through wild shrubberies, almost horizontally, into the deep.

I could not help being chilled with a secret horror. The way seemed to lead us into a lonely abyss. All objects around us bore evident marks of a chaotic disorder and of violent devastation; yet we beheld everywhere the wrecks of former grandeur. The destructive hand of nature seemed to have exhausted here all her devastating powers. Enormous rocks, which were already half decayed, opposed a roaring cataract, which concealed its un-bridled fury beneath the gloomy darkness of bottomless abysses. Every thing bore the stamp of antiquity. A gray moss mournfully covered the mountains, and the slender shrubs trembled rustling in the flaring light of our torches; the rays of which, reflecting a pallid glimmer upon the darkness of the most distant bushes, along with the trembling shades, alter-nately raised the mind to the most elevated sentiments, and lulled it again into silent meditation. The change of the light, which sported between the leaves and the deep leafy darkness, every object around appeared to me to be a symbol of my life, in order to conduct me towards a happier futurity. I felt myself, as it were, new created, and dropped the cumbersome covering of time past with enthusiastic boldness.

'Whither do you lead me, Sennor?' I exclaimed, at length, involuntarily.

'Whither a man of boldness and feeling needs not be afraid to go. . . . A confederation of *men* awaits you. You wish, perhaps, to take a part in the great views which they prosecute; will you be able to submit to a voluntary yoke?' 'Yes, I shall; but what recompense may I expect?' 'You will be enabled to throw off an *involuntary* one.' 'Is that all?'

'Carlos, you ask this question too prematurely. You shall *one* time feel yourself happy. But how can you expect to receive your reward before you have earned it? Purified from our prejudices, united by indissoluble bonds with men of exalted virtue, and of an all-conquering spirit, you will learn to forget the little troubles of life, and be enabled, by the smiling light of truth, cheerfully to bear the burdens of your existence. But, are you un-biassed by opinion? is your mind unfettered by prejudice? do you think you are already deserving of such a union?' 'No, Sennor, and this is it what makes me uneasy. Can you say nothing that could dispel my uneasiness?' . . . 'Don't be afraid, Don Carlos; your merits will not be misconceived. They will expect rather too much than too little of you. Why should you then be afraid? If you should feel yourself undervalued, or deceived in your hopes, no one will force ties upon you which require the greatest liberty of will if you shall be useful to the society?'

'But how can freedom of will and ties of that nature be consistent with each other?'

'Nothing can be demonstrated easier than that. The connection of the whole body does not confine the different parts of which it is composed in the motions of which they *can* be capable. The freedom of will, which every member enjoys, suffers no abatement if impelled by its own voluntary choice. The charming garlands which bind a free, but purified, will, are kept together by a union which forms itself voluntarily, animated by a spirit of the highest cultivation. The more you prosecute it, the nicer and the more penetrating your looks grow in the examination of the nature of words; the more your perceptibility encreases, and the more sensible you are, that in the inane compass of a retired life the noblest springs of our spirit are lamed, the more powerfully you will be attracted by a point of union in which all the faculties revive as if roused from a lethargy.'

'What prospects! what hopes! Sennor!'

'Prospects! hopes!' he then resumed, with a gentle, but sarcastic, smile; 'what prospects and hopes have been held out to you? Don't speak of it. You are scarcely escaped from a miserable coast, and you presume already to see the shore of the opposite continent! You mistake clouds for the shore, Don Carlos: you see nothing but the coverings of rising tempests; a chaos big with terror. The rosy morn opens the gates of day with additional brightness after gloomy and boisterous nights.' . . .

We had, mean while, proceeded a great way through the rocky passage; and the mountains began, at length, to decrease gradually on the left and on the right. A valley opened to our view: the rising morn filled the apertures between the bushes with a sweet rosy dawn; and the objects we beheld assumed gradually a more romantic contour. As our torches began to become more useless and paler, we found ourselves and the whole valley involved in a thin vapour, out of which a uniform greenish-red back ground emerged. The objects around us began to lengthen, and every thing seemed to have dissolved itself to receive the rising day, and to be impregnated with its cheering light. Unutterable feelings crowded upon my senses; a rosy dream had lighted upon my inebriated soul, and all my ideas were floating in a dubious trance. I had frequently visited this forest on my hunting excursions, but never descried that spot, which seemed to be the production of my enraptured fancy. We entered, at length, a little wood of orange trees. . . . An antiquated fabric displayed itself at length to our view; a long avenue led towards it. Bending under the pressure of hoary time, its tottering ruins reclined against a hill, which protended over it in romantic beauty. Most of the windows were decayed; but those that had escaped the voracious tooth of all destroying time, I beheld, to my greatest astonishment, grated with new iron bars. An involuntary horror vibrated through my nerves at that ominous sight. I looked at my conductor, who walked by my side, absorpt in profound meditation. He seemed to have forgot that I was with him; his soul had unfolded herself on his countenance to a great expectation, and seemed to labour under the presension of an anticipated horror. I followed the old man through the gate, and we descended several steps. 'Don't fall, Don Carlos,' he said, lighting me with his torch. But this *don't fall* almost had thrown me headlong down the steps; I supported myself with difficulty by an iron bar, which was fixed into the wall; and it was high time that we reached the bottom, else I should certainly have dropt down fainting. But I now could support myself no longer. 'Give me leave to rest a little,' I said to my conductor, and seated myself on the undermost step: 'I am quite exhausted.'

The old man turned round with marks of surprise, and viewed me by the light of his torch. (Mine I had flung away at the entrance.) 'So soon, Don Carlos?' he exclaimed. 'Holy Virgin! how pale you are! Be a man.' . . . A long passage led us deeper into the fabric; steps which alternately led us up and down narrow ways; spacious caves variegated the scene every minute. We entered at length a regularly vaulted and very spacious apartment. 'Stay here, Don Carlos!' my conductor said, extinguishing his torch, and vanished suddenly. Not the least sound, not the most secret motion of air enabled me to find out whither he had turned. Whithersoever I extended my hands, I could find nothing but a dreary vacuity: I was in a spacious grave, the walls of which I could not discover. . . . The space around me began at length to grow visibly lighter, which probably was owing to the rising day, whose rays penetrated though a small aperture in the wall; and I could already discern myself again when a door was opened. Two masked men, with lighted torches, entered, and assisted me to get up. . . .

A numerous assembly of men, covered with white masks, offered themselves to my view on our entrance into a hall, which was splendidly illuminated by two large lustres, the light of which was reflected by a number of mirrors. They were seated on low arm chairs, which joined in the centre on an elevated spot, where, as it appeared, the chief of the society was sitting. He had a table before him, on which I beheld some books, a cross, a dagger, a goblet, and some unknown instruments. An empty chair, which seemed to be designed for me, was standing beneath the lustres. A profound solemn silence swayed for a few moments in that awful assembly, till my two conductors had taken their seats, when the chief, who sat opposite me, rose from his elevated seat. He stepped to the table, and uncovered his face. A noble and unspeakable enchanting countenance, where heavenly goodness, mixed with the vestiges of the bitterest experience, was enthroned, struck me with reverential awe. A clear look, which raised itself with peaceful serenity above the confines of this terrestrial life, and a brow, which braved the tempests of sorrow, captivated my soul. The silent plan of a new creation seemed to rest in the former, and the latter was a complete picture of the most perfect humanity. I could have prostrated myself before and adored that great man.

'Thou art come, Carlos, to get acquainted with us?' he now began, in a soft accent. I affirmed it silently. . . .

'What is your desire, Don Carlos?' he now resumed. 'To get acquainted with this society, reverend father.' 'And then to become a member of it?' 'I have duties incumbent on me as a man; duties which I have been taught to hold sacred: I am ready to become one of you, if you will not violate them.' 'And what duties are they?' 'To love mankind; to be charitable to every one that meets me; to forgive my enemy; to love every one who wishes me well.' 'Every one, Carlos?' 'Every one, my father.' 'Is this a duty which no circumstances will prompt thee to renounce, against which the arguments of reason, and the persuasion of your heart, never will prevail?' 'Neither my reason nor my heart will ever make me renounce it.' 'Then you are unfit for our society! – Lead him hence, my brethren.'

'Do not reject me too rashly, my father, (I replied:) do not condemn me without trial. Tell me what you desire, and what the bond of your brethren requires: I swear to be sincere in return, and to be entirely yours, if I can.' 'We require nothing of you, Carlos, except the very thing you have declared yourself not to be able to do. If you will become a deserving member of our community, you must dissolve all bonds whereby men bind themselves to men. Our property is only to be found in the world at large. Murder your father, poniard a beloved sister, and we shall receive you with open arms. When human society expels you, when the laws prosecute you, when the state execrates you, then you shall be welcome to us. However, our society rejects the tear of humanity. . . . Is it a miserable, cheating bargain, to exchange one sister for a thousand brothers? Would you not deem the preservation of millions worth one poor drop of blood from your own breast.'

'I understand your words, reverend father, but cannot comprehend their mystic sense. . . . Conduct me into the sanctuary of the principles by which your society is guided, and try me whether I am docile enough to be your pupil.' . . .

'You know the lamentable state of our country. The grievances of the whole nation cannot but affect you also. All ranks are confounded, or rather, are reduced to *one*, by despotism's galling scourge. The people are miserable slaves. Necessity has formed this society, and oppression has strengthened our mutual ties. Lurking dangers have forced us to be on our guard, and to court retirement and solitude. A century has made us wise. Experience taught us to proceed with moderation. The society chose their members from the ablest geniuses of the nation, who are intrusted with all our secrets, are wholly devoted to us, and feel themselves happy.'

'Have the views of the association always been entirely general?'

'They have never been otherwise. All countries of importance are ours through the members of our society. Here only is the centre of our united strength.' 'Do you aim at the dominion of the world?' 'To promote the happiness of the world is universal dominion.' 'And the means?' 'You see their symbols on this table. Faith, dagger and poison.' – I trembled with horror. . . . 'Well! then receive me into your society! I devote myself entirely to you. Tell me, what am I to do?' 'Nothing but to renounce every doubt; to confide in our decrees; to obey our orders, and to act your part well. Dagger and poison are the greatest friends of humankind. Thousands of new lives germinate from the urn of *one* man, whose doom is fixed, if the welfare of the human race requires it: his death is unavoidable in that case, though he be a monarch!' – . . .

Having suppressed my agitation, I exclaimed, with horror, 'Shocking! very shocking! The life of a *king*, did you say?' 'Yes, the life of a thousand kings. The liberty of man is an unalienable family property. Who steals it is a criminal; who artfully purchases it from the possessor for a false appearance of inane happiness is an impostor. Whoever feels himself strong enough to punish crimes, is his natural judge. Our forefathers gave us monarchs; we re-demand our rights, and summon them before a higher tribunal. . . . Believe me, dear Carlos,' he continued, taking me by the hand, and looking at me with an eye sparkling with a heavenly fire, '*you* also will, one time, confidently adopt our creed. The hallowed bosom of solitude inspires the soul with elevated, heavenly sentiments; the sublimest plans are generated in the profoundest darkness of night and obscurity: what an endless bliss to extend one's arms over the whole globe, to be entirely independent, to be no more exposed to the painful sensation of the wants of life, nor to the caprice of circumstances and the blasts of accidents?'

Being surprised and conquered, I sank into the arms of the venerable speaker. 'Approach, my brethren,' he resumed, 'and receive the oath of eternal love from his lips.'

I was in the twinkling of an eye encircled by every arm; and the horrid vow escaped my lips at the altar, amid the kisses of my new brethren. Being inebriated by a beverage out of the goblet, I dropped down at the foot of the altar, laying my hand upon the cross: my arm was uncovered, a vein opened with the point of a dagger, and the streaming blood circulated in a goblet among all my brethren. The old man embraced me once more. 'Go now, my son,' said he to me, 'go, and receive the reward which you deserve.'

The Midnight Bell (1798)*

FRANCIS LATHOM (1777–1832)

Francis Lathom wrote numerous satirical farces and comedies (e.g. All in a Bustle, *1795;* The Dash of the Day, *1800), some Oriental/Arabic Gothic tales and dramas (e.g.* The Castle of Ollada, *1794;* Orlando and Seraphina; or, The Funeral Pile, *1799), and about two dozen novels, mostly historical romances turning upon 'mysteries'. The editors of* Flowers of Literature *for 1803 observed that 'Mr. LATHOM has tried both the marvellous and the natural romance. In his marvellous romance, whose essence is much ado about nothing, he has adopted that kind of work which the German school first suggested, and the genius of Mrs. RADCLIFFE rendered popular. . . . In Mrs. RADCLIFFE's mysteries we find motives for most of the contrivances; but, in Mr. LATHOM's productions, there is mystery without any other motive than the love of mystery.' A spirit of satire and comedy pervades most of Lathom's work, though the use of comic characters, as in the following extract, may be intended to heighten the effect of terror in his readers. Jane Austen's father borrowed* The Midnight Bell *from the library in October 1798, and read it while her mother sat by the fire. The work is one of the 'horrid' novels listed in* Northanger Abbey.

Chapter XXII

How many things are there that the fancy makes terrible by night, which the day turns into ridicule!

SENECA'S MORALS

Fortunately for Alphonsus, who wished not to be known, the little inn had changed its inhabitants since he had last visited it; thus no suspicion of their being any other than common travellers was entertained by the landlord when they entered his dwelling.

Shortly after their arrival Alphonsus took occasion to lead to the subject on which his thoughts were unremittingly bent.

'That's a fine castle that stands about a league from hence,' said he, addressing his host.

'Yes, sir,' was the answer.

'Who inhabits it?'

'Nobody.'

'To whom does it belong?'

'To the Cohenburg family.'

---

* Francis Lathom, *The Midnight Bell, A German Story*, 3 vols (London: H. D. Symonds, 1798), vol. 3, pp. 114–40.

'And why do they not reside in it?'

'Ah, sir! they are all dead but one poor gentleman, the brother of him that used to live there, and he can no where find rest for his guilty mind: folks say he is gone into a monastery to repent of his sins, and make his peace with heaven.'

'Of what crime is he accused?'

'Why, sir, I have not lived here long, but as I have heard people say, count Frederic, the youngest brother, he that I now speak of, and who used to live in a handsome mansion about a league from hence to the left, and which is now inhabited by one count Radvelt, was so jealous of his brother's castle and riches, that he had him murdered by assassins in the Wolf's Wood, in his return home to his castle, from Vienna; and then killed his brother's wife and son with his own hand. The matter was pretty well hushed up at first; it was given out that the countess had died of grief for the loss of her husband, and that her son had killed himself in a fit of madness: nobody much believed it, but as nobody had any proofs to the contrary, nothing durst be said; but the villain soon betrayed himself, for he staid at the castle but two or three days, and then went no one knows whither.'

'And did he leave nobody in the castle?'

'No, sir, nobody; people do tell strange stories that it is haunted, and that he was frightened away by the ghost of the murdered count; and some say, that a bell is tolled by it every night at midnight.'

'I have a strange curiosity to visit this castle.'

'You had better not, sir.'

'Why so, friend?'

'Why, sir, people think that the reason of the ghost's ringing the bell is, that it is shut up by priestcraft within the walls of the castle, and prevented from coming out; and that it tolls the bell to call somebody in, that it may reveal the murder of its body to them, and frighten them into promising to revenge its death. Nobody goes near the castle on that account.'

Alphonsus pretended to smile at the tale related by his host, but it had an effect on his feelings which he could ill conceal: all his efforts to coerce the wish of immediately gratifying his curiosity he found to be in vain, and he declared to the count and Lauretta, that he felt an impulse he could not resist, to certify himself that night as to the tolling of the bell: in vain did they remonstrate, and endeavour to prevail with him not to leave the inn until the morning; but there was a resolute and anxious wildness in his countenance to follow the impulse he had described, which seemed to bid defiance to every objection.

The tears however of Lauretta, whose alarm was raised, she could hardly express on what account, to a pitch of agony, at the idea of Alphonsus that night approaching the castle, brought him to consent to defer his visit to the following day, on condition that if he could gain no light on the mystery which occupied his mind by traversing the castle, and examining his father's cabinet, she would not object to their there taking up their abode, which he declared would be an alleviation of his horrors and perplexities.

After a sleepless night, Alphonsus rose to an uneasy morn; every the most minute circumstance attendant on the mystery wherein his happiness was involved, had been turned over in his thoughts during the night; and as heretofore, instead of deriving any clue of elucidation from reflection, the mystery had only thickened upon increased conjecture.

Again he felt scruples arising in his mind against opposing the injunction laid on him by his mother: again his doubts were lulled by the secrecy he had vowed to maintain, relative to any discovery he might make in the castle, which, notwithstanding the strong impulse he felt to visit it, reason seemed to contradict he should do; and then again he felt a momentary fear, for which he shuddered to account, that a snare might be spread for taking his life if he returned to the castle.

Judging it however the most consistent with the faith he owed himself to go alone to the castle, he avowed his intention to his Lauretta, and resigning her after a fond embrace to the care of her father till his return, he departed, followed by the eyes of Lauretta till the intervening branches of the trees shut him from her sight.

Alphonsus rode swiftly forward, lost in a maze of fluctuating thought; at length taking a turn of the well-known road, Cohenburg castle burst full upon his sight; he beheld it with mingled sensations of melancholy pleasure, and awful apprehension. Crossing the moat, he proceeded to the stable from whence he had taken his steed on the morning on which he had last departed from the castle: fond remembrance was hasty to contrast the present gloom of desertion with former scenes of happier aspect; – recollection became too painful to be constrained, and burst its way from his eyes in burning drops of sorrow.

Having left his steed in the stable, he proceeded to the castle-gate; it was locked, and bade defiance to his repeated efforts to open it: he next attempted the postern-gate, it in like manner resisted his endeavours. He ran round the castle, gazing upon it in every part, and trying to recollect some window by which he might effect his entrance; he would not trust to recollection for believing them all too high, and too strongly barricaded to favour his attempts, but examined every one separately in the circuit of the castle.

Tortured by having his attempts thus baffled, he threw himself upon the ground in despair; in a few minutes, however, recollecting that inactivity could add little to forward his wishes, he rose from his situation, resolving to return to the inn, and ask advice of count Byroff how to proceed in his present dilemma. Once again he exerted his utmost endeavours to open the two gates, but they proved equally vain with his former efforts; he mounted his steed and returned to the inn.

Alphonsus immediately related his adventure, and opened a consultation with the count, on what steps were the best to be taken by him.

'Much deliberation,' the count said, 'seemed to be required on the subject of so delicate a nature: the gates of the castle being locked might be construed into an indication either of its being inhabited, or not being inhabited. If it was inhabited, the prevalent idea of its being deserted plainly proved it was the shelter of some person who wished to live in obscurity, and would, from this motive, perhaps, revenge the entrance of any one who dared to trespass on his retirement.'

'How can he wish to live unknown?' cried Alphonsus, 'who every night publicly announces his dwelling by tolling the castle bell?'

'Have you any proof of this?' said the count.

'The young miner, and now again our landlord, both assert that it is so.'

'But they never heard it; nor likely any one who trembles while he relates it, has any authority for it but the dream of some old woman, who having talked all day of the occurrences at the castle, had seen them in her sleep in aggravated colours.'

'I will certify myself in this point,' returned Alphonsus, 'before I proceed to any measures for entering the castle; I will watch the tolling of the bell this night.'

After promising Lauretta that he would use no means for entering the castle that night, she consented that he should watch on the outside, in order to learn the truth of the story which had been related of the midnight bell, provided her father accompanied him; but as Alphonsus declared that he could not leave her at the inn with satisfaction to himself, unless the count remained with her, it was at length agreed that Jacques Perlet should be the companion of Alphonsus on his nightly expedition.

As Alphonsus was well aware that his going out in the night could not fail being known by the host, and excite his curiosity, he determined to inform him, that he meant to go and listen for the tolling of the singular bell he had mentioned to be sounded every night at the castle; the host, unsuspicious that Alphonsus meant more than his words conveyed, endeavoured to dissuade him from his purpose by all the arguments of blind superstition, and vulgar fear; and finding him resolute in his purpose, besought him to wear a little cross on his expedition, which, he said, 'had belonged to his deceased wife, and which having been kissed by the pope, would secure him from the influence of the devil, and his fiends'.

To avoid the imputation of obstinacy and irreligion, Alphonsus accepted the offer of the sacred cross, and placed it within his waistcoat.

At a little after ten Alphonsus and Jacques set out for the castle on foot.

Where flesh and blood were to be contended with by day-light, Jacques was no coward, but a breath of wind, or a shadow in a dark night, were great settlers of his valour. Count Byroff knowing his disposition, had not made him acquainted with any of the particulars which constituted

Alphonsus's curiosity in regard to the bell which was sounded at the old castle; and as he fortunately had not heard of any dreadful appearance which had been seen in the vicinity of this building, he endeavoured all the way to keep up his courage by repeating to himself, 'that the sound of a bell in the night could be no more than the sound of a bell in the day'.

Alphonsus, wrapt in reflection, was not much disposed to converse, and they had proceeded nearly a third of the way without speaking, when Jacques suddenly exclaimed, 'Do you hear it, *monsieur?*'

'What?' asked Alphonsus.

'The bell, *monsieur?*'

'We are yet too distant from the castle to catch the sound,' returned Alphonsus.

'So I thought, *monsieur*: – that was the reason I asked.'

Had Jacques spoken the truth, he would have confessed that he found it very melancholy to proceed so far in silence, and that he despaired of drawing Alphonsus into conversation by any other subject, than the one on which his thoughts were then bent; his stratagem, however, answered but little to his wishes, for Alphonsus again sunk into silent reflection.

'The moon will be up presently, *monsieur*, it begins to grow a little light already.'

Alphonsus raised his eyes for a moment to the atmosphere, and again dropped them to their former situation.

'I wonder how many stars there are, *monsieur*: – did you ever count them?'

'No.'

'Nor I, *monsieur*; – I wonder whether any body ever did?'

No answer was returned.

'I dare say there are more than a thousand in all; I am sure I can see five hundred to-night, and there are often as many more on a clear night; a'n't there, *monsieur?*'

'Of what?'

'Stars, *monsieur.*'

Jacques now anxiously waited for a rejoinder, but his hopes were deceived. Alphonsus had spoken to the few words he had accidentally heard, without entering into the subject to which they belonged.

Now the silence had been once broken, its recommencement appeared more unpleasant to Jacques, than whilst it had remained totally un-interrupted; his tongue ached to relieve his eyes and ears, which were unremittingly looking out for shapeless monsters, and listening for uncouth sounds; singing and whistling by night he had heard ridiculed as betraying fear; and he could for some time think on no other expedient to divert the way; at last a lucky thought entered his head: 'I think I'll try and count the stars myself, *monsieur*,' he said, and immediately began counting, *une, deux, trois*, &c. passing them, as he pronounced the number, on his fingers: he chuckled at this happy expedient; it exercised both his eyes and tongue, and amused his hearing; thus passed on another third of the way; Jacques never the nearer in his knowledge of the numeration of the heavenly bodies, but quite as near in reality as he wished to be. At last wearied by his employment, and not at all satisfied with hearing only his own voice, he desisted from his calculation, and lowered his eyes to the spot where he supposed to find Alphonsus walking by his side; but he was not there; for a few moments he stood motionless, then looking round on all sides, as far as the slender light of the faintly shining stars would permit him to carry his sight, and not beholding his companion, he ran straight forward in the path along which he supposed Alphonsus to have proceeded, as fast as he could move his legs, and attended by all the noise his overstrained voice could make.

Alphonsus, inattentive to every object but what was passing in his own mind, had insensibly passed his companion, whose pace had been retarded by his pretended studies, and had gained some ground upon him ere Jacques perceived his advance; now, however, roused from his reflections by Jacques' exclamations, he stopped for him, and they were quickly again united, to the no small satisfaction of one party; when an explanation of their parting took place on both sides, and Jacques determining not to let the conversation he had now raised, flag, asked Alphonsus 'how many ghosts he had ever seen?'

'Not one,' replied Alphonsus.

'Then you have seen one less than me, *monsieur*; and that's what always makes me afraid of being alone in the dark.'

'Now I, on the contrary, should have supposed the dark to have been very agreeable to one of your credulous disposition.'

'Why so, *monsieur*?'

'Because I should conceive that in it you could see neither objects to please nor alarm you.'

'Oh dear, *monsieur*, how you talk! why ghosts always light themselves.'

Alphonsus had not spirits either to rally Jacques on his false ideas, or to endeavour to correct them by the arguments of reason, and he remained silent.

Jacques had now a clue for conversation, and he chattered on about spirits, ghosts, and witches, to his own joint amusement and terror, till a few minutes brought them within sight of Cohenburg castle, and all his faculties were then absorbed in the use of his eyes.

They advanced within a few yards of the building to a small elevation of the turf, where Alphonsus proposed they should sit down, and wait the expected sound of the bell. The moon was breaking from under a retiring cloud, and, shedding her partial influence on the building, while its shadow fell upon the place which Alphonsus had chosen for his watching post, gave a pleasing yet melancholy aspect to the scene. It produced sensations in the mind of Jacques which he felt at a loss to explain, and after repeated hesitations how to express himself, he exclaimed, 'Well, if ever I am to see another ghost, I am sure this is just the place I should expect to meet it in!'

'Folly!' cried Alphonsus: 'how should you expect to see what never existed?'

'*Mon Dieu, monsieur*, how you talk! why all the priests in the world should not make me believe, I did not see one that time I was going to mention to you.'

'Well, well, then you did,' said Alphonsus, softened by the scene into reflections too dear to be easily shaken off, and wishing to prevent their farther interruption by coalescing in opinion with his companion.

'I thought you would believe me at last, *monsieur*,' said Jacques, who flattered himself he had made a convert of Alphonsus: 'I'll tell you the whole story, – may I, *monsieur*?'

'Oh yes,' replied Alphonsus, thoroughly determined not to attend to it, and hoping, by this indulgence of his friend's garrulity, to free himself from the trouble of replying to his questions.

Having cast his eyes around, as a kind of security preparative to his dismal story, and moved a few inches nearer to Alphonsus, Jacques thus began: 'When I was about fifteen years old, *monsieur*, my father lived in a little village about a *lieue* from Desmartin, on the road to Paris; ours was a lonely little cottage, for it stood quite at the end of the village, and above a hundred paces distant from the next house; my grandmother was alive then, poor old soul, and she was as much afraid of a ghost as me; so one winter's evening, just before we went to bed, there comes a rap, or indeed it was more like a scratch at the door. "Come in," says my father; nobody answered, nor the door did not open; so my father bid me open it, and I did, but nobody was there to be seen; so as I thought it might be somebody that had a mind to frighten us, and had hid themselves behind the wood-stack at the corner of the house, I ran to look, for it was moon-light; and there I saw a man in black, kneeling down, without a head; and when I called out for help, he got up and ran away as fast as ever he could, and when he had got a little way off, his back looked as white as snow.

'Well, *monsieur*, frightened enough I was, as you may suppose, and so was my father, for he saw it too: and a little while after my grandmother died. "Now the murder's out," says my father: "that was a warning of *la bonne's* death: we shall see no more ghosts now." "I hope not, I am sure," said I; but he was wrong: for about a month after, one night when the wind was high, there was such a noise in the kitchen after we were gone to bed, that it waked us all, and in a minute or two the door between my father's chamber and mine burst open, as if *le diable lui même* had kicked it; then again we heard the noise in the kitchen, and in a few minutes came such a crack, as if the very roof had split over our heads; I covered myself with the bed cloaths; father said he would go down and see what it was, when, just as he was getting out of bed, there was such a rustling on the stairs; and then it seemed to come into the chamber under the door, and all on a sudden a long, deep, hoarse, frightful . . . . .' At this instant the bell in the south turret of the castle tolled several strokes, which sounded on the air hollow and dismal; Alphonsus started from his seat, and Jacques remained sitting on the turf in a state of fear scarcely a degree removed from petrifaction.

Koenigsmark the Robber
or, The Terror of Bohemia (c. 1802)*

Victor Jules Sarret

Koenigsmark the Robber, *an example of the chapbook 'robber romances', contains a series of loosely interlinked adventures having German sources. It was printed by Tegg and Castleman, 'at the Eccentric Book Warehouse', West Smith-field: their other chapbooks included* The Southern Tower; or, Conjugal Sacrifice, The Veiled Picture: or, The Mysteries of Gorgono, the Appennine Castle, A Tale of Mystery; or The Castle of Solitude, Father Innocent, Abbot of the Capuchins; or, The Crimes of Cloisters *(based upon Radcliffe's* The Italian*) and* Matilda; or The Adventures of an Orphan. *The following extract is just a small portion of the whole; though chapbooks were short, they were printed in a very tiny typeface and managed to squeeze a lot of excess into their few pages.*

'Bolfeld,' said Herman, addressing himself to the landlord, 'you will oblige my friend and myself by telling us the particulars of poor Rosenberg's death.' 'Herman,' answered Bolfeld, 'I will, since you desire it; but it is distressing to me; every one in the village knew Rosenberg, and every one revered him. Ah! we have all made a great loss!' He wiped his eyes and proceeded:

'Konigsal, you know, lies on the other side of this forest, at the distance of about twelve miles from this place. Rosenberg wished to cross the forest that night; his servant represented to him the danger of being in the forest at such an hour; he reminded him of the many murders and robberies which had been committed in that dreary place. Rosenberg would not listen to what his servant urged; he said, that duty and friendship impelled him to make every possible haste, and that a soldier could not know fear. The servant was silent, and they proceeded; as the distant clock struck twelve, they heard the cries of murder, seemingly issuing from a clump of trees at a short distance from them. "It is the cries of a female – some villains

---

* Victor Jules Sarrett, *Koenigsmark the Robber, or, The Terror of Bohemia* (London: Tegg and Castleman, n.d.), pp. 9–17.

are murdering her," exclaimed Rosenberg, seizing his pistols, and galloping towards the spot. His faithful servant followed; as they approached,
they saw a figure in white gliding through the trees with inconceivable
swiftness, and four men, apparently of a gigantick stature, following her
with the utmost speed; the forest resounded with her cries. Again the
servant remonstrated, but Rosenberg heeded him not – he still urged his
courser, and followed the white figure, convinced, that it was a female in
danger of being murdered! Alas, poor Rosenberg! he was flying to meet
death. Two assassins sprung from a thicket; one seized his horse's bridle,
and the other raised his arm, and held a dagger to his breast – Rosenberg's
pistols did not miss fire; both the ruffians fell in blood; but, at the same
moment, a dastardly villain buried his poniard in his back. Rosenberg fell
from his horse – in an instant he had ceased to live. The rest of the banditti
severely wounded the servant, and left him apparently lifeless; they then
stripped the wretched Rosenberg, carried away every thing which he had
about him, and left his corpse perfectly naked. The servant still breathed,
but was covered with wounds, and unable to move. At day-break, three
woodmen passed near the spot, and were greatly terrified at beholding two
men, stripped and bleeding: they humanely conveyed them to their
cottages, and endeavoured to restore animation by every means in their
power; with the servant they soon succeeded, but Adelaide's husband was
gone for ever! The servant gave an account of the event, similar to that
which I have just related, and told the woodmen the name and rank of his
beloved master. The fatal news were immediately sent to Colonel
Kæmpfer; he wisely resolved to conceal the dreadful intelligence from his
Adelaide, and, in the course of some time, to impart to her a forged letter,
giving an account of Rosenberg's illness. A few days after the receipt of it,
he intends to inform her, that her husband is much worse, and he hopes
that he will gradually prepare her to hear the dreadful tidings of his death;
but he is determined, that she shall never know that he was murdered in the
forest, within six miles of all that his soul held dear.

   'I saw the servant yesterday, he told me that Colonel Kæmpfer will not
long survive his dear Rosenberg; the shock has been fatal; he suffers still
more than he would do, if he could give way to his grief, but he endeavours
to appear cheerful, to prevent his unhappy child from guessing the truth.
He has written to Montecuculi, to communicate the melancholy event,
and to request him to send a letter to Adelaide, as if Rosenberg were indisposed: the servant added, that Adelaide would never survive the news of
her husband's death, and that it was but too probable that the villain who
had stabbed Rosenberg, had, at the same instant, mortally wounded his
father, wife, and child. That is all that I know of the event which you have
wished me to relate; I have obliged you, but it has cost me many pangs – I
dream of it every night. Poor Rosenberg! peace to his departed soul!'
Bolfeld concluded his narrative, and the tear of agony proclaimed that he

was a man. Theodore was greatly affected, and the friends were silent for some time. The company gradually recovered their spirits. Many strangers entered, and demanded whether they could sleep at the inn that night, for the weather was still very bad; the moon had risen about an hour, but though its pale orb was sometimes seen through the flying clouds, its silver light was too feeble to dispel the gloom which surrounded every object. The path through the forest was perceptible only when the transient light of Diana silvered the edge of a dark portending cloud. The wind howled with redoubled violence – every gust terrified the travellers who had intended to cross the forest that night; the story of Rosenberg's murder had appalled them; they almost fancied that they heard his groans on the blast – their dread increased. All those who had arrived that night, except *one*, resolved to sleep at the inn; even Theodore and Herman agreed to defer their return to their village until the next morning. Bolfeld having agreed to provide beds for his guests, they became more tranquil, and the conversation took a more lively turn: at last Bolfeld told the traveller who had not expressed a wish of sleeping at the inn, 'You, sir, seem determined to pursue your journey to night; you are alone; can you mean to cross the forest, on such a night particularly? Are you not afraid of – '

'Afraid!' answered the stranger, '*I* have never been afraid.'

The manner in which he answered – the look which he darted on Bolfeld – his piercing inquisitive eye, struck every one – every eye was immediately directed on him. He was a tall, strong, well-made man; his appearance excited terror and distrust. He perceived the effect which his answer had produced; he wrapped himself up in his mantle, and remained silent. It was some time before the company could resume their tranquillity. Bolfeld now and then cast a fearful glance on the terrible stranger; he looked expressively at Herman and his friend, but was afraid to speak. It began to grow late – some of his guests who were fatigued with their journey, retired to rest; Theodore, Herman, Bolfeld, and three or four more friends, remained. The dread unknown still remained in his place. A silence of a few minutes ensued; Theodore, less terrified at the sight of the stranger, and wishing to renew the conversation about Rosenberg, addressed himself to the landlord:

'Bolfeld,' said he, 'in giving us an account of the violent death of Rosenberg, you mentioned that he had heard appalling cries in the forest, and that when he approached the spot whence the cries appeared to issue, he beheld a tall figure in white, gliding through the trees, and endeavouring to escape from four gigantick men. Have you ever heard what became of that female, and what was the reason of –'

'In what does that concern you?' interrupted the stranger, starting from his chair.

'Concern me;' retorted Theodore, 'I wished to know what became of her; and I confess,' added he, looking at the stranger, and smiling contemptuously, 'that I did not think myself obliged to ask your leave before I put the question to the landlord.' The stranger hastily put his hand in his bosom, and Bolfeld thought that he saw the shining blade of a dagger. Theodore remained calm and undaunted. The stranger endeavoured to unknit his brow, but his dark scowling eye betrayed the workings of his soul; he at last composed himself, and said to Theodore, 'I meant not to offend you, but your question reminded me of a tradition which I have heard many times; the supernatural event which it records caused the death of one of my ancestors – it bears some resemblance to what Bolfeld has related, and the thought that one of my forefathers had perished by – affected me – made me furious. I did not intend – to offend you –'

The evident hesitating manner in which the terrifick stranger had concluded his speech, produced a violent effect on the mind of his hearers. Theodore alone remained firm, and, addressing himself to the unknown,

'Sir,' said he, 'I freely accept your apology, but I request, as a particular favour, that you would oblige me so far as to relate the tradition to which you alluded: it must record some dreadful deed. This night has been devoted to the awful: the account of Rosenberg's assassination has prepared our minds for every thing that is horrid and appalling – the fury of the elements seem to add to the horror of the narratives. We request you to oblige us with that tradition.'

'You will not like it,' said the stranger. 'On the twenty-seventh of November, 1401, one of my ancestors was crossing the northern part of this forest; it was nearly the same hour that it is now – it was almost midnight – he was very well armed, and like myself had never known fear.' The unknown assumed a hollow voice in pronouncing those last words: it was so exactly the same sepulchral voice in which he had uttered, 'Afraid!' when addressing himself to Bolfeld, that the landlord's blood ran cold in his veins. Theodore fixed his eye intently upon him; he did not seem to notice it: he resumed his stern, but tranquil voice, and continued: 'Passing under a lofty bower which was formed by the tall branches of elm-trees: his ears were assailed by the most appalling screams which he had ever heard. He galloped towards the spot, and perceived a beautiful female dishevelled, and in indescribable agony: she was imploring the mercy of heaven, and whenever she turned her eyes on the left side, she uttered the most terrifying yells. Romaldi (that was the name of the knight) asked her who had injured her, and what induced her to scream so violently, although no one was by her. "Oh! in the name of the Holy Virgin," she said, "destroy this terrible insect which is by me – make every possible haste, I conjure you by all that is dear to you." "Insect!" answered Romaldi, "and is it the sight of an insect which occasions all these cries? Where is this insect?" The unhappy woman, shuddering with horror, pointed to a large, black, horrid spider, which lay motionless by her. Romaldi, half inclined to laugh, good-naturedly alighted, and approached with the intention of trampling over this insect! but he started back with horror at perceiving the spider slowly increasing in size, and rolling two large yellow eyes, which glared frightfully. The wretched woman redoubled her cries: "By the host of saints," she exclaimed, "endeavour to destroy it, else we are both lost." During this time the insect was grown to a tremendous size. Romaldi was no coward – he drew his falchion, and struck a violent blow; it failed of effect – the sword rebounded as if it had struck a rock, and Romaldi disarmed, stood petrified with terror. The spider had disappeared; the wretched female, unable to speak, writhed in agony; unutterable horror seized Romaldi, when he beheld a hand grasping her by the throat – a loud peal of thunder shook the sky – all the winds seemed to be let loose – the hurricane was appalling – the trees were torn up by the roots – the storm lasted but a few minutes – the scene became calm. Romaldi fearfully looked around – his unhappy companion was gone – his knees shook under him; he lifted his hands to heaven, and recommended himself to the protection of every saint. A loud and reiterated laugh made him turn – at that instant something struck him on the face, and he fell with violence. A voice which seemed quite close to him, said in a whisper, "Thou shalt pay dearly for thy attempt." Romaldi, unable to support so many shocks, uttered a loud groan, and fainted away. He lay in a state of insensibility nearly an hour: when he opened his eyes, the dreadful adventure rushed upon his mind; his blood ran cold with horror. His horse was grazing near him; Romaldi crawled a few steps, and, with a great deal of trouble, mounted his courser, and endeavoured to reach an inn which was on the borders of the forest. It was day-light before he succeeded. When he arrived, the landlord came to receive him, but he stopped short, exclaiming, "My Lord, how pale you are! your lips are vivid, and your face has the pale ghastly hue of death. Have you been attacked? are you wounded?" "No," defiantly answered Romaldi, "I am unwell; give me some wine; I shall soon recover." The landlord complied; the wine was excellent, and Romaldi did not spare it, yet it was long ere he could recover his spirits. The dreadful screams; the supernatural insect; above all, the threatened punishment which still vibrated on his ear, recurred every moment on his agitated mind. He sometimes doubted his senses; he wished to persuade himself that he had been dreaming; but he had lost his sword; he had severely hurt himself when he fell in consequence of the invisible blow – all that convinced him but too plainly that he had really experienced a horrid adventure, and he considered what could be done to avert the appalling threat: he examined his conscience, and found it not quite still. "I will brave every thing," he said mentally; "it shall not be said that Romaldi is a coward." He called the landlord: "Muller," said he, "could you procure me a sword? I left mine at the place where I slept a few hours yesterday." "It is now two years, my lord," answered Muller, "since a noble knight breathed his last in my house; he was just returned from Palestine, and had no attendant with him;

his sword is hung in the apartment in which he died; I shall get it down."

'Romaldi was agreeably surprised at finding that it was a most excellent sword; the blade was well tempered, and the mounting was magnificent. Romaldi generously paid the landlord for it, and gradually recovered his tranquillity. He resolved to stop at that inn two or three days, and then proceed to Vienna. The next day in the evening, Count Clodomir arrived with his attendants and a great many dogs, intending to hunt in the forest early on the succeeding morning. Romaldi, who had met Clodomir at several tournaments, was overjoyed at his arrival, and Clodomir was delighted to find a companion. "Romaldi," said he, "thou shalt hunt with me to-morrow; the number of bears and wolves is incredible: they are fierce, I am told – we shall signalize ourselves. I mean to rise before day; what sayst thou? Wilt thou accompany me?" Romaldi promised he would. At five the next morning, Clodomir and his friend were equipped and well armed; their attendants joined them, and they plunged into the thickest part of the forest. The dogs soon seized an immense bear, which Clodomir put to death with his spear: Romaldi was soon equally successful, and after a space of two hours, their horses were so fatigued, that Clodomir proposed returning to the inn; his friend assented to the proposal. At the same instant, a prodigiously large wolf passed by them – Romaldi pursued him: Clodomir called out, "My horse is so fatigued that I shall wait here for thee." One of his servants, who was very well mounted, called two of his fiercest dogs, and galloped after Romaldi. The wolf fled with inconceivable rapidity, and had considerably the start of his pursuers: at last the dogs seemed to gain on him; Romaldi and the servant encouraged them. The wolf entered a long avenue, and, without seeming to be any longer afraid, he rested at the foot of a large tree. Romaldi, who was at some distance, perceived it, and again spurred his courses; when he came up, the wolf had disappeared, and, instead of him, he beheld a man dressed in a peasant's habit, and sitting in the very place where the wolf had rested. Romaldi was thunderstruck. The servant crossed himself, and waited in awful expectation the end of that diabolical transformation. The dogs barked violently, but seemed afraid of attacking the man.

'Romaldi became furious; he sprang from his horse, and, rushing on the unknown, wounded him severely in the breast: "Thou diest," he exclaimed, holding his sword over him: "thou diest, unless thou tell me by what power thou canst transform thyself into a wolf at pleasure." "Mercy, noble knight," answered the man, "mercy! save my life and I will tell you all: it is a secret which I received from my father. But help! oh, help; I expire!" He sunk to the ground. Romaldi ordered his servant to support him on horseback, and if he were too weak, to endeavour to carry him as far as the place where they had left Clodomir. The servant, who was very athletick, took up the wounded man on his shoulders, and they proceeded towards the place where they had parted from their friends. As they approached, Clodomir said to his friend, "So, thou hast been pursuing a wolf, and thou returnest with a wounded man!" "Forbear thy jokes," answered Romaldi, very gravely. "When thou knowest our adventure, thou shalt not smile; but this is no time to relate it to thee. Let us hasten to the inn, and get the wound of this wretch properly dressed, though he is very undeserving of any care; I will then relate every thing to thee. Great God!" continued Romaldi; "I believe that I am doomed to experience the most horrible adventures." In a short time they reached the inn: the unknown was carried by two servants, and, to all appearance, was lifeless. Clodomir and Romaldi entered the yard – at that instant a frightful scream was heard – Clodomir turned suddenly round – he beheld his two servants motionless on the ground, and the wounded man had disappeared. Clodomir, struck with horror, called Romaldi, but no Romaldi answered. Clodomir grew pale with terror, and his heart scarcely palpitated. He at last ventured to look towards the spot where Romaldi was when he heard the scream – no trace of the knight was to be seen: the situation of Clodomir is indescribable. While he stared in vacant manner on the spot where his friend stood but a minute before, something brushed by him, and the words, "Romaldi receives the punishment due to his crimes," were whispered near his ear.

'Clodomir, dreadfully terrified, prostrated himself, and prayed with fervour. His courage gradually returned – he entered, and desired the landlord to take care of his servants, who had been stunned at the moment that the wounded unknown had disappeared. They had not been much hurt; they were unable to describe the manner in which that man had been torn from them; all that they recollected was, that a strong sulphurous smell had suddenly issued – their sight had grown dim, and they had lost the powers of perception. From that moment,' continued the stranger, raising his voice, 'from that moment, Romaldi was seen no more. Clodomir, greatly affected at the awful event, departed for Spain, intended to seek for adventures, that he might dispel the gloom which enveloped his mind: he was present at a tournament at Seville, and lost his life fighting bravely against a Spanish knight. That is the tradition which you demanded;' said the unknown, addressing himself to Theodore, and fixing him fiercely, 'You see that there is a great similarity between the adventure which befell Romaldi and, that, which Bolfeld says, happened to Rosenberg.' 'I thank you for your narrative,' replied Theodore calmly, 'but must confess that I do not see a great resemblance between the adventures: it is true that Romaldi heard the screams of a female in the forest, but when he approached, he beheld only a woman, who was probably beset by a fiend, perhaps for some crime which she had committed: the whole of the adventure which you have related is supernatural; quite different is that which Rosenberg met with in the forest – there is nothing of the marvellous in that . . .'

Zofloya; or, The Moor (1806)*

CHARLOTTE DACRE (*c.* 1782–*c.* 1841)

Charlotte Dacre was one of two daughters of the Jewish radical writer and blackmailer John King. She was twice married, but little is known of her life. Several passages in her best novel Zofloya *are borrowed from Radcliffe's* The Italian, *but all her works were strongly influenced by Matthew Gregory Lewis, to whom she dedicated her novel* The Confessions of the Nun of St. Omer *(1805). She wrote under the pseudonym 'Rosa Matilda' (other novels were* The Libertines, *1807, and* The Passions, *1811). Her works were very well known in the early nineteenth century (much loved by Shelley and Thackeray), and at least* Zofloya *should be classed among the first rank of Gothic novels. In this novel, subtitled 'A Romance of the Fifteenth Century', Laurina is seduced by Count Ardolph, who kills her husband, a disgrace condemned by her wild and imperious daughter Victoria. By the end of the novel Victoria becomes a heroine-villain who slowly poisons her husband to death (after first experimenting on an elderly female relative). These and other horrid acts are facilitated by Zofloya the Moor, servant to her husband's brother (with whom Victoria has fallen in love, and whose wife she imprisons and torments). The Moor haunts Victoria's disturbing dreams, in which he turns into a skeleton before she awakes in terror, and sinisterly appears and disappears, a 'mysterious being' whom we perceive to be the Devil (as dark within as without). To escape punishment for the horrors she has perpetrated, Victoria swears to Zofloya her soul, whereupon he reveals himself as Satan, and without further ado hurls her into the dreadful abyss (as Satan did Ambrosio in Lewis's* The Monk). *The novel would be called misogynistic if the author were a man, and most of its obsessions and conventions are unarguably Lewisian (and Sadean). But it has much to say about mother–daughter relations, female desire, power, race and 'the other', and challenges our assumptions about what differentiates 'the female Gothic' from 'the male Gothic'.*

It may naturally be supposed that the character of Victoria, by nature more prone to evil than to good, and requiring at once the strong curb of wisdom and example to regulate it, had not, since the death of her father, obtained much opportunity of improvement. She saw exemplified, in the conduct of her mother, the flagrant violation of a most sacred oath – she saw every principle of delicacy and of virtue apparently contemned – and, although the improper bias of her mind led her infinitely to prefer the gay though horrible state of degradation in which she lived, to the retirement and seclusion so strongly insisted on by the dying Marchese, yet had she reflection and discrimination enough, fully to perceive and condemn the

* Charlotte Dacre, *Zofloya; or, The Moor*, 3 vols (London: Longman, Hurst, Rees, and Orme, 1806), vol. 1, pp. 75–90.

flagitious disregard those dying commands had received. But Victoria was a girl of no common feelings – her ideas wildly wandered, and to every circumstance and situation she gave rather the vivid colouring of her own heated imagination, than that of truth.

Berenza had awakened in her breast feelings and passions which had till now remained dormant, mighty and strong, like the slumbering lion, even in their inactivity. Slight, indeed, was the spur which they required to rouse them. She had even contemplated the seductive, and, in appearance, delightful union of her mother with Ardolph, with such sentiments as were at the time inexplicable to herself; but when Berenza singled her out, when he addressed her in the language of love, she then discovered that her sentiments were those of envy, and of an ardent consuming desire to be situated *like* that unhappy mother – like her, to receive the attentions, listen to the tenderness, and sink beneath the ardent glances of a lover. Such, such were the baleful effects of parental vice upon the mind of a daughter – a mind that required the strongest power of precept and virtuous conduct to correct it.

'At length, then,' with secret exultation, she exclaimed – 'at length, I too have found a lover – I shall now be as happy as my mother, at least, if Berenza should love *me* as Count Ardolph loves *her*.'

But it happened that the heart of Berenza had acquired a *real* passion, while that of Victoria was susceptible only of novel and seducing sensations – of anticipations of future pleasure. Berenza *loved* – Victoria was only roused and *flattered*. Upon consideration, but not certainly impartial consideration, the enamoured philosopher concluded that it would not be an act of baseness or guilt to withdraw Victoria from her present dangerous and ineligible situation – to acknowledge his passion to her, and induce her, if possible, to abandon the contaminated roof under which she resided. The pride of the Venetian, however, must have been stronger than his love, for it rejected the idea of making her his wife; while he determined to leave no means untried to cause her to become his mistress.

Pursuant to this idea he sought the earliest opportunity of obtaining a private interview with Victoria. An opportunity early presented itself; and having declared to his delighted auditress the ardent love with which she had inspired him, he delicately but frankly proposed to her the plan upon which he had for some time past suffered himself to dwell enraptured.

The boldly organised mind, the wild and unrestrained sentiments of Victoria, prevented her from being offended at the proposition of Berenza: had she for an instant conceived, that his strict ideas deemed her incapable of being legally his, she must, with all her desire for a lover, have spurned him indignantly from her; but pride here acted as the preservative of pride, and her vanity easily led her to believe that Berenza thought marriage a degrading and unnecessary tie to love like his.

Under this impression she gave him her hand: Berenza seized it with ardour, as the earnest of consent; and, seating himself at the feet of his mistress, who smiled with high and unusual joy, he entered more fully into his arrangements, and the means by which he proposed she should quit Monte Bello unsuspected. Victoria listened with lively emotions; pleasure flushed triumphant her animated cheek, and shone in her wild eyes with an almost painful brilliance: her heart glowed with the love of enterprize; she felt capable of deeds which, though in their *conception* they dilated and seduced her soul, she could neither *comprehend* nor *identify*; but she felt inspired for action, and the enthusiasm which burnt in her bosom, lighted up every feature with lambent and etherial fire. Suddenly, in the very midst of her felicitations, while Berenza, still at her feet, was pouring in her intoxicated ears his various plans for their future happiness, in rushed, rage and horror depicted in her countenance, the half frantic Laurina!

'Wretch!' she exclaimed, seizing violently the arm of Victoria – 'wretch! is it thus you recompence my indulgence towards you – the fond, the foolish confidence, which your mother has ever placed in you? – And *you*, Signor Berenza, monster of depravity! is it thus *you* recompence the hospitality of Count Ardolph, in seeking to seduce our only happiness, the innocent Victoria?'

'Signora,' replied Berenza, with a disdainful smile, '*you* are indeed well qualified to arraign those who *trample on the rights of hospitality!*'

The eyes of the conscience-struck Laurina sought for an instant the ground – her countenance became suffused with a guilty blush – her heart beat with violence, and scarcely could she support her trembling frame! Berenza, with dignified calmness, took the hand of Victoria – 'I do not,' he continued, in a firm deliberate voice, 'I do not plead guilty to the charge of attempting to *seduce* your daughter. – I wish,' he added, in a severe accent, 'to *save* her from seduction. Pardon me, if I say, that under *this* roof, I conceive it inevitably awaits her.'

'Victoria,' cried Laurina, recovering from her agitation, but awed by the manner of Berenza from replying to *him* – 'Victoria, I command you to leave the room – yes, for the first time in my life, I *command* you never more to hold converse with Il Conte Berenza!'

Berenza fixed his proud and enquiring eyes upon the countenance of Victoria. Whether she caught a spark of the fire which emanated from them, or thus for the first time asserted the bold and independent sentiments of her bosom, is immaterial; but, withdrawing proudly her hand from Berenza, as though she needed not his aid, and advancing a few steps towards her mother, she thus replied –

'That you never, Signora, *commanded* me till now, is true; that you command me now, when it is too late, is equally so. I *determine* to quit this roof, which is no protection to me, for that of Il Conte Berenza, which I trust will be.'

'Oh, Victoria! – Victoria! – are thou *mad!*' exclaimed Laurina, clasping her hands, and now beginning to feel the terrible commencement of those retributive pangs so justly ordained as the punishment of those parents who corrupt their children – 'Art thou mad, my child? or wouldst thou voluntarily plunge me in eternal disgrace?'

'Plunge *you* in disgrace!' contemptuously returned Victoria.

'Oh, my child! my child!' cried the distracted mother, sinking under the overpowering excess of remorseful anguish, 'wouldst thou indeed *abandon* me?'

'*You* abandoned *me* – my *brother* – and my *father!*' sternly replied the torturing Victoria.

'Oh, daughter! – oh, Victoria!' groaned Laurina, – 'this from thee!'

'Mother – *eternally* has *thou* disgraced us!' she replied. 'For me, no one has ever thought me worthy of love but Il Conte Berenza. Let me, then, *accept* his love, and be happy. Why, I ask you, should considerations of *your* happiness sway me in opposition to my *own?* When *you* loved Count Ardolph, you know, mother, that you fled with him, regardless of the misery you gave my father. Do you not remember too – '

'Cease, scorpion! – cease, for *God's* sake!' shrieked Laurina, in agony.

'Let me, then, depart with Il Conte Berenza. Remember, it is your fault,' pursued the pitiless girl, 'that ever I saw him. Had *you* but kept the oath – the *oath*, mother, that – that you swore at the death-bed of my father –'

The images conjured up by the forked tongue of a reproaching child, were too much even for the guilty Laurina to endure; and, in a convulsion of irrepressible anguish, she sunk upon the floor.

Berenza, who had at first listened with delight and surprize to the independence of spirit, as he considered it, evinced by the undaunted Victoria, now became visibly shocked at her persevering and remorseless cruelty to a mother, whose personal tenderness for her had at least merited some little gratitude. Scarcely willing to analyse if his love for her had not already somewhat diminished by the display of a trait so offensive to a delicate and feeling mind as filial ingratitude and unkindness, he approached, and raised Laurina from the floor. When she became in a degree recovered, he assisted her, with respectful forbearance, to her chamber; and whispering to Victoria, in rather a serious voice, to be tender towards her mother, retired, and left them together.

But the slight shade of reserve which marked the countenance of Berenza, as he waved his hand to Victoria in parting, had not failed to make even more than its due impression on her: her vivid imagination easily led her to trace the occasion of his altered air. She saw that her cruel recriminations on her mother had excited his disgust: alarmed at the remotest idea of becoming indifferent to him, she instantly determined on regaining his esteem. Approaching her weeping mother, therefore, with a conciliating air, she endeavoured to soothe her into composure; but having awakened the remorse of the conscious Laurina, she no sooner beheld in the artful Victoria a disposition to softness, than she resolved to take immediate advantage of it to withdraw her, if possible, from the vortex of guilt and libertinism into which she saw her plunging. A keener pang assailed the heart of the mother, as she acknowledged, in dreadful conviction, the fatal effects of her own example: to alleviate, therefore, the tortures of her mind, to save her loaded conscience from such an addition of guilt, she sought with energy to preserve her daughter. To every persuasion, however, even to every supplication to give up her distracting resolution without reserve, the wild impassioned Victoria was wholly deaf. The utmost that Laurina could obtain, was a reluctant promise to see Il Conte Berenza no more for that day. Even this would not have been granted, had not the deeply-meaning Victoria imagined, that, by debarring her lover from seeing her for a few hours, he would begin so far to feel the loss of her society, as wholly to forget, in his uneasiness, the cause he had had for displeasure against her.

Laurina, after some hours of more poignant wretchedness than she had almost ever experienced, separated at length, for the night, from her daughter. She flew instantly to Ardolph, and imparted to him this new and unexpected cause, to her, of unhappiness. So keen, indeed, were her compunctious feelings, that, with bitter tears, she vowed she would quit him on the morrow, and retire at once, with Victoria, to some seclusion, where, experience now convinced her, she ought long since to have been.

The Midnight Groan (1808)*

The excerpt reproduces one-third of a chapbook, which, like many examples of the form, was marketed on the basis of its title – The Midnight Groan; or The Spectre of the Chapel: involving An Exposure of the Horrible Secrets of the Nocturnal Assembly. A Gothic Romance – and its illustration, a frontispiece showing a knight facing a skeleton spectre.

'Farewell, my young friend! when next we meet it will, I hope, be in happier circumstances: time will wipe away that sorrow which now overspreads your brow, and restore tranquillity to your breast.' Such were the last words of the Lord Manfredoni to the young Horatio, as the latter mounted his horse, to depart from that castle, in which his earliest infancy had been passed, and which was rendered dear to him, by a thousand tender considerations; but in particular, by its being the residence of the

---

* *The Midnight Groan; or The Spectre of the Chapel: involving An Exposure of the Horrible Secrets of the Nocturnal Assembly. A Gothic Romance* (London: T. and R. Hughes, 1808), pp. 1–8.

PLATE 6

'And as Horatio gazed, the beautious features vanish'd and presented to view a perfect skeleton.' Frontispiece to the chapbook *The Midnight Groan; or The Spectre of the Chapel: involving An Exposure of the Horrible Secrets of the Nocturnal Assembly. A Gothic Romance* (1808). By permission of the British Library 12330.aaa.b.2.

young and beautiful Miranda. Some singular events now called the youthful lover away from the place where his soul's affections were deposited, which will, in due time, be unfolded to the reader. As Horatio turned from the castle, his eye involuntarily sought for the figure of Miranda. She appeared at the window of her apartment; for a few moments their eyes were immoveably fixed on each other: no words were uttered, but their looks transfused into each other's heart, the substance of a thousand volumes. Every moment that Horatio gazed, increased his reluctance to depart; but go he must, and at length, after a severe internal struggle, he desperately applied the spurs to his horse, and was, in a few moments, beyond the utmost stretch of vision. 'He is gone!' cried Miranda, bursting into an involuntary flood of tears, 'he is gone, perhaps for ever!' She threw herself on a sofa, and gave full scope to the sorrow which weighed on her heart. Nearly eighteen summers had shed their ripening bloom over Miranda's countenance; she had, from her infancy, been the companion of Horatio; she had never formed a wish to roam beyond the precincts of the castle, nor did she ever indulge an idea, from which Horatio was detached. Her mind was the seat of innocence and feminine rectitude; attractive grace: her figure was tall, and slight; her face admirably proportioned; her eyes, black as jet, were replete with fire and intelligence, her disposition singularly amiable, little heightened by a redundancy of bright chesnut [*sic*] hair, which meandered down her shoulders, and wantoned in amorous curls round the clear convexity of her forehead. As was observed before, Miranda and Horatio had been companions of each other from their earliest years, and as they both grew up, their juvenile intimacy had been consolidated, by a similarity of tastes and sentiments, into a mutual, and deep-rooted passion. Lord Manfredoni had long suspected their attachment, and at length received ocular demonstration that his suspicions were not unfounded: he discovered the lovers one evening exchanging their mutual vows, in one of the romantic retreats surrounding the castle. That same night, he summoned Horatio to a private conference in one of the most retired chambers of the ancient edifice; he chose this remote place, that the subject of their discourse should not possibly be overheard. The place where Horatio was conducted by Lord Manfredoni, surprised him not a little, such a gloomy desolation reigned round the awful spot: the lamp they carried with them faintly illuminated the apartment, and afforded partial glimpses of half-decayed furniture; but the chief part of the room was involved in shadow. 'I have for some time,' began Manfredoni, 'suspected that there existed a partiality between you and Miranda, but before I proceed any further, I require you to give me your solemn oath you will not divulge the substance of our discourse to her.' This introduction astonished Horatio; he however gave the required security, and crossing his sword with that of his patron, he swore everlasting secrecy. 'Now then I will unfold the whole business,' said my lord, 'the *whole* of the business!' repeated a voice, the hollow sepulchral tone of which struck a transient horror into the hearts of its hearers: starting suddenly, they both fixed their eyes on each other in awful astonishment: 'The circular form of this spacious chamber, returns the sound,' said my lord; but his pale countenance showed that the reason he had assigned did not satisfy himself. 'I will now briefly,' said he, 'tell you what I wished to communicate: I totally disapprove of the nature of your attachment to Miranda; I will go farther, it shocks my soul to think of it; for – (mark me, and remember your oath) she is your sister!' Astonishment and horror were painted on the countenance of Horatio on hearing these fatal words; they included a mystery, which his soul trembled to have unravelled! he staggered back at the shocking sound, and faintly echoed the word 'Sister!' 'I see this information has struck you with an horrible surprise; but nothing is more true, though I shall not enter into a developement [*sic*] of the mysteries connected with your and her birth: I once more repeat that Miranda is your sister: to tell you how to act on this occasion would be an insult to your own integrity.' It was some moments before Horatio could overcome the astonishment and emotion which these disagreeable tidings inspired. At length, 'Alas!' cried he, 'my lord, you have rendered me completely miserable.' That night, the pillow of Horatio was planted with the sharpest thorns: if his eyes caught a moment's slumber, the most horrible visions haunted his fancy; and when the shackles of Morpheus were completely dissolved, he only awoke to the more fatal realities of existing events. The sight of Miranda now tormented him; for as he could not behold her with eyes of indifference, he severely reproached himself for indulging an affection little short of incestuous. What increased his anguish, was the necessary silence which his oath imposed on him, which would occasion Miranda to view his altered behaviour, as the effect of fickleness and inconstancy. This was in some measure actually the case. Miranda soon became sensible of an alteration in his conduct, the cause of which she, in vain, endeavoured to investigate: that delicate affection, which he had formerly showed her, was now exchanged for the most frigid politeness: he always appeared embarrassed in her company, and took the earliest opportunity to quit it; yet in spite of these symptoms of alienated affection, she still observed an expression of amorous sorrow lingering in his eye; which at length induced her to think that some mysterious secret was lodged at his heart. Lord Manfredoni observing the struggle of love and virtue in the breast of Horatio, and that the daily sight of Miranda added fuel to his passion, advised him to depart from the castle, for a time, and endeavour to forget his unhappy attachment on the various scenes he should meet with in his travels. This was the state of affairs when we opened this history, and such was the cause of Miranda's sorrow. Horatio soon got out of sight of the castle, and entered upon a gloomy forest, which seemed of immeasurable extent. The dull uniformity of the scene was ill calculated to divert his mind from dwelling on its own miseries: for hours he travelled without discerning a human habitation, and the shades of night deepened upon the earth, while yet he seemed in the very bosom of the forest; the wind arose, sweeping in hollow gusts through the trees; a large, heavy mass of clouds began to gather in the air, sweating with their liquid load; the vivid lightning, in expansive sheets, seemed to set the heavens in a transient blaze, while the bursting thunder was rendered more horrid by the responsive echoes of the shaggy monsters of the shades. Horatio, during this ethereal war, was obliged to call into practice a great part of his skill in horsemanship; for the steed on which he rode, waked by the noise of the thunder, as by the trumpet's sound, exhibited all the fiery energies peculiar to his breed: he pranced, champed the bit, erected his main [*sic*], dilated his nostrils, and emitted flashes of martial fire from his terrific eye. As Horatio proceeded cautiously through the perilous obscurities of the place, a dreadful flash of lightning shot from the angry gloom, and discovered the battlements of a castle, rising over the heads of the trees. This was a welcome sight to our harassed traveller; he soon came up to the building: but the indistinct view which the night afforded of it, rendered it, to appearance, an heterogeneous mass of confused materials: the draw bridge was up, and the moat almost chocked [*sic*] up with rubbish, composed partly of the materials of the fallen battlements, so that all approach to the interior of the castle, seemed impossible without encountering danger. However the violence of the storm obliged him to make an effort to get within the castle, and therefore, hazardous as the attempt was, he began to explore his way over the moat, and at length arrived unhurt, on the other side. He now found himself within an enormous archway, which issuing in an open area, he discerned right before him, by the lightning's glare, a ponderous marble stair-case; this he began to ascend with caution; its vast height and spiral form, rendered it a considerable time before he could reach the top, and when he did, so thoroughly fatigued was he, that he laid down on the landing-place, and resigned himself to sleep; but it is truly said by Young, that the downy god 'flies from woe, and lights on lids unsullied with a tear.' Horatio, weary as he was courted in vain the influence of the somnific deity: his thoughts flew to Miranda and fancy gave him all her charms; then would he start in distraction on reflecting on the fatal information which Manfredoni gave him concerning her. In the midst of his reverie, he imagined he heard a deep groan and turning his head, he saw, to his inexpressible astonishment, a figure clothed in white, round which was diffused a fiery radiance, rendering it awfully conspicuous even in the depth of midnight gloom; a transparent veil, through which appeared features of the most exquisite beauty, fell from her forehead to waist. The phantom approached Horatio. 'Gracious heaven!' exclaimed he, 'what do I see?' at the same time a torpor spread over all his powers, and he lay, for some moments, quite insensible. From this state he was roused by a sensation so peculiar and uncommon, that all his nerves were instantly awakened: it was occasioned by the cold icy touch of the spectre. It beckoned Horatio with the hand; and mustering all his resolution, he drew his sword, and followed it along the dark and gloomy gallery; when the phantom arrived at the end of the gallery, it halted a moment, and by this means, Horatio discovered that it stood on the brink of a flight of steps. It suddenly disappeared from there, and became visible about half-way down the dark descent. Horatio hesitated, the figure beckoned, and he began cautiously to descend, still pointing his sword before him; quick as lightning, the appearance vanished from its station, and stood conspicuous at the bottom of the steps. Horatio still followed, and had nearly reached the bottom, when the ghost again moved onward. The adventurous youth hesitated again, he appeared to be in a dungeon, and the gloomy horror of the spot roused the energies of human fear; on the other hand a dreadful curiosity impelled him to see the issue of this extraordinary affair; the spectre still retreated farther into the dungeon, till it came to an obscure recess; here again it became stationary. Horatio gazed in dreadful expectation on its beauteous face; a deep groan burst from its bosom, and in a hollow, sepulchral voice, it uttered these words: 'Remember the desolate chamber!' Instantly the veil dropped from its face, and as Horatio gazed, the beauteous features vanished, and a ghastly death's head appeared in its stead! the clothing in like manner suddenly flew off, and presented to view a perfect human skeleton!! The horrible transition was too much for mortal sight to encounter, and the youth, overcome with terror and astonishment, fell prostrate on the earth, and remained there for some time, destitute of sense or reflection. . . .

Tales of the Dead (1812)*

Sarah Brown Utterson (trans.) (*c.* 1782–1851)

Mary Shelley has described how, during a rainy spell during the summer of 1816, she, Percy Shelley, Lord Byron, his physician John Polidori and his mistress Claire Clairmont gathered around the fire of Villa Diodati on Lake Leman outside Geneva and amused themselves in the evening with reading – and writing – ghost stories. The book that they read was Fantasmagoriana, ou Recueil d'Histoires d'Apparitions de Spectres, Revenans, Fantômes, etc. *(1812), which was a French translation (by Jean Baptiste Benoit Eyries) of macabre German fairytales by Friedrich Schulze (under the pseudonym of Friedrich Laun) and which Johann Apel published in the five-volume* Gespensterbuch *(1811–15). Five of these ghost stories (some from the German original and some from the French translation) were*

---

* *Tales of the Dead.* Principally translated from the French (London: Chite, Cochrane, and Co., 1813), pp. 15–25.

translated into English by Sarah Elizabeth Brown Utterson, together with one native English folktale, and published in 1812 as Tales of the Dead. *Mrs Utterson's husband was an antiquarian whose book on chivalric legends was published by the same publisher as* Tales of the Dead. *Mary Shelley particularly remembered one story in which a group of friends share with each other their stories about ghostly apparitions, much in the manner of those assembled in the Villa Diodati, from which the following extract is reproduced. Matthew Gregory Lewis was also struck by the same story, which he probably read in the German original, and which he recounted to Shelley in August 1816. The authorship of the various stories, and their reappearance in different versions in a large number of chapbooks, German, French and English, lead into one of the more intricate labyrinths of Gothic bibliography.*

The Family Portraits

Ferdinand began in these words: – 'One day, when I was arguing with the friend of whom I am about to make mention, on apparitions and omens, he told me the following story: –'

'I had been invited,' said he, 'by one of my college companions, to pass my vacations with him at an estate of his father's. The spring was that year unusually late, owing to a long and severe winter, and appeared in consequence more gay and agreeable, which gave additional charms to our projected pleasures. We arrived at his father's in the pleasant month of April, animated by all the gaiety the season inspired.

'As my companion and I were accustomed to live together at the university, he had recommended to his family, in his letters, so to arrange matters that we might live together at his father's also: we in consequence occupied two adjoining rooms, from whence we enjoyed a view of the garden and a fine country, bounded in the distance by forests and vineyards. In a few days I found myself so completely at home in the house, and so familiarised with its inhabitants, that nobody, whether of the family or among the domesticks, made any difference between my friend and myself. His younger brothers, who were absent from me in the day, often passed the night in my room, or in that of their elder brother. Their sister, a charming girl about twelve years of age, lovely and blooming as a newly blown rose, gave me the appellation of brother, and fancied that under this title she was privileged to shew me all her favourite haunts in the garden, to gratify my wishes at table, and to furnish my apartment with all that was requisite. Her cares and attention will never be effaced from my recollection; they will long outlive the scenes of horror that *château* never ceases to recall to my recollection. From the first of my arrival, I had remarked a huge portrait affixed to the wall of an antechamber through which I was obliged to pass to go to my room; but, too much occupied by the new objects which on all sides attracted my attention, I had not particularly examined it. Meanwhile I could not avoid observing that, though the two younger brothers of my friend were so much attached to me, that they would never permit me to go at night into my room without them, yet they always evinced an unaccountable dread in crossing the hall where this picture hung. They clung to me, and embraced me that I might take them in my arms; and whichever I was compelled to take by the hand, invariably covered his face, in order that he might not see the least trace of the portrait.

'Being aware that the generality of children are afraid of colossal figures, or even of those of a natural height, I endeavoured to give my two young friends courage. However, on more attentively considering the portrait which caused them so much dread, I could not avoid feeling a degree of fear myself. The picture represented a knight in the costume of a very remote period; a full grey mantle descended from his shoulders to his knees; one of his feet placed in the foreground, appeared as if it was starting from the canvass; his countenance had an expression which petrified me with fear. I had never before seen any thing at all like it in nature. It was a frightful mixture of the stillness of death, with the remains of a violent and baneful passion, which not even death itself was able to overcome. One would have thought the artist had copied the terrible features of one risen from the grave, in order to paint this terrific portrait. I was seized with a terror little less than the children, whenever I wished to contemplate this picture. Its aspect was disagreeable to my friend, but did not cause him any terror: his sister was the only one who could look at this hideous figure with a smiling countenance; and said to me with a compassionate air, when I discovered my aversion to it, "That man is not wicked, but he is certainly very unhappy." My friend told me that the picture represented the founder of his race, and that his father attached uncommon value to it; it had, in all probability, hung there from time immemorial, and it would not be possible to remove it from this chamber without destroying the regularity of its appearance.

'Meanwhile, the term of our vacation was speedily drawing to its close, and time insensibly wore away in the pleasures of the country. The old count, who remarked our reluctance to quit him, his amiable family, his *château*, and the fine country that surrounded it, applied himself with kind and unremitting care, to make the day preceding our departure a continual succession of rustic diversions: each succeeded the other without the slightest appearance of art; they seemed of necessity to follow each other. The delight that illumined the eyes of my friend's sister when she perceived her father's satisfaction; the joy that was painted in Emily's countenance (which was the name of the charming girl) when she surprised even her father by her arrangements, which outstripped his projects, led me to discover the entire confidence that existed between the father and daughter, and the active part Emily had taken in directing the order which reigned in that day's festivities.

'Night arrived; the company in the gardens dispersed; but my amiable companions never quitted my side. The two young boys skipped gaily before us, chasing the may-bug, and shaking the shrubs to make them come out. The dew arose, and aided by the light of the moon formed silver spangles on the flowers and grass. Emily hung on my arm; and an affectionate sister conducted me, as if to take leave, to all the groves and places I had been accustomed to visit with her, or with the family. On arriving at the door of the *château*, I was obliged to repeat the promise I had made to her father, of passing some weeks in the autumn with him. "That season," said she, "is equally beautiful with the spring!" With what pleasure did I promise to decline all other engagements for this. Emily retired to her apartment, and, according to custom, I went up to mine, accompanied by my two little boys: they ran gaily up the stairs; and in crossing the range of apartments but faintly lighted, to my no small surprise their boisterous mirth was not interrupted by the terrible portrait.

'For my own part, my head and heart were full of the intended journey, and of the agreeable manner in which my time had passed at the count's *château*. The images of those happy days crowded on my recollection; my imagination, at that time possessing all the vivacity of youth, was so much agitated, that I could not enjoy the sleep which already overpowered my friend. Emily's image, so interesting by her sprightly grace, by her pure affection for me, was present to my mind like an amiable phantom shining in beauty. I placed myself at the window, to take another look at the country I had so frequently ranged with her, and traced our steps again probably for the last time. I remembered each spot illumined by the pale light the moon afforded. The nightingale was singing in the groves where we had delighted to repose; the little river on which while gaily singing we often sailed, rolled murmuringly her silver waves.

'Absorbed in a profound reverie, I mentally exclaimed: With the flowers of spring, this soft pure peaceful affection will probably fade; and as frequently the after seasons blight the blossoms and destroy the promised fruit, so possibly may the approaching autumn envelop in cold reserve that heart which, at the present moment, appears only to expand with mine!

'Saddened by these reflections, I withdrew from the window, and overcome by a painful agitation I traversed the adjoining rooms; and on a sudden found myself before the portrait of my friend's ancestor. The moon's beams darted on it in the most singular manner possible, insomuch as to give the appearance of a horrible moving spectre; and the reflection of the light gave to it the appearance of a real substance about to quit the darkness by which it was surrounded. The inanimation of its features appeared to give place to the most profound melancholy; the sad and glazed look of the eyes appeared the only hinderance to its uttering its grief.

'My knees tremblingly knocked against each other, and with an unsteady step I regained my chamber: the window still remained open; I reseated myself at it, in order that the freshness of the night air, and the aspect of the beautiful surrounding country, might dissipate the terror I had experienced. My wandering eyes fixed on a long vista of ancient linden trees, which extended from my window to the ruins of an old tower, which had often been the scene of our pleasures and rural *fêtes*. The remembrance of the hideous portrait had vanished; when on a sudden there appeared to me a thick fog issuing from the ruined tower, which advancing through the vista of lindens came towards me.

'I regarded this cloud with an anxious curiosity: it approached; but again it was concealed by the thickly spreading branches of the trees.

On a sudden I perceived, in a spot of the avenue less dark than the rest, the same figure represented in the formidable picture, enveloped in the grey mantle I so well knew. It advanced towards the *château*, as if hesitating: no noise was heard of its footsteps on the pavement; it passed before my window without looking up, and gained a back door which led to the apartments in the colonnade of the *château*.

'Seized with trembling apprehension, I darted towards my bed, and saw with pleasure that the two children were fast asleep on either side. The noise I made awoke them; they started, but in an instant were asleep again. The agitation I had endured took from me the power of sleep, and I turned to awake one of the children to talk with me: but no powers can depict the horrors I endured when I saw the frightful figure at the side of the child's bed.

'I was petrified with horror, and dared neither move nor shut my eyes. I beheld the spectre stoop towards the child and softly kiss his forehead: he then went round the bed, and kissed the forehead of the other boy.

'I lost all recollection at that moment; and the following morning, when the children awoke me with their caresses, I was willing to consider the whole as a dream.

'Meanwhile, the moment for our departure was at hand. We once again breakfasted all together in a grove of lilacs and flowers. "I advise you to take a little more care of yourself," said the old count in the midst of other conversation; "for I last night saw you walking rather late in the garden, in a dress ill suited to the damp air; and I was fearful such imprudence would expose you to cold and fever. Young people are apt to fancy they are invulnerable; but I repeat to you, Take advice from a friend."

'"In truth," I answered, "I believe readily that I have been attacked by a violent fever, for never before was I so harassed by terrifying visions: I can now conceive how dreams afford to a heated imagination subjects for the most extraordinary stories of apparitions."

'"What would you tell me?" demanded the count in a manner not wholly devoid of agitation. I related to him all that I had seen the preceding night; and to my great surprise he appeared to me in no way astonished, but extremely affected.

'"You say," added he in a trembling voice, "that the phantom kissed the two children's foreheads?" I answered him, that it was even so. He then exclaimed, in accents of the deepest despair, "Oh heavens! they must then both die!"'–

Till now the company had listened without the slightest noise or interruption to Ferdinand: but as he pronounced the last words, the greater part of his audience trembled; and the young lady who had previously occupied the chair on which he sat, uttered a piercing shriek.

'Imagine,' continued Ferdinand, 'how astonished my friend must have been at this unexpected exclamation. The vision of the night had caused him excess of agitation; but the melancholy voice of the count pierced his heart, and seemed to annihilate his being, by the terrifying conviction of the existence of the spiritual world, and the secret horrors with which this idea was accompanied. It was not then a dream, a chimera, the fruit of an over-heated imagination! but a mysterious and infallible messenger, which, dispatched from the world of spirits, had passed close to him, had placed itself by his couch, and by its fatal kiss had dropt the germ of death in the bosom of the two children. . . . Three days afterwards the young count received news of the death of his two younger brothers. They were both taken off in the same night.'

Frankenstein; or, The Modern Prometheus (1818)*

MARY SHELLEY (1797–1851)

Mary Shelley's Frankenstein *is part of the tradition of the radical 'philosophical romance' developed by the circle around her father William Godwin. As an active member of that circle, she was intrigued by the new sciences emerging at the turn of the century – electricity, magnetism, galvanism – and the image of the 'mad scientist', as in Godwin's novel about alchemy,* St. Leon, *and in Rosicrucian novels about the search for hidden knowledge.* Frankenstein *is the finest tale to have emerged from the sharing of ghost stories at the Villa Diodati in 1816 (see pp. 152ff. and 161ff.), and many critics consider it to have laid the cornerstone for the new genre of science fiction. The metaphysical theme of the novel, as indicated by its subtitle, focuses upon the Romantic image of the over-reacher, as in* Prometheus Unbound, *which her husband Percy Bysshe Shelley was working on at the same time, and whose themes they debated together. Despite all these factors that place Mary Shelley firmly within the tradition of*

---

* Mary Shelley, *Frankenstein; or, The Modern Prometheus*, 3 vols (London: Lackington, Hughes, Harding, Mavor, & Jones, 1818), vol. 1, pp. 97–109.

the 'male Gothic', her work has been placed at the heart of the 'female Gothic'. This is due primarily to the interpretation of the novel as a birth myth, and the presence of dreams and images suggesting that Mary Shelley may have felt herself to be 'monstrous' for having caused the death in childbirth of her mother Mary Wollstonecraft Godwin. The nineteenth-century view of Mary Shelley as an appendage to her more famous father and husband has been superseded by the feminist–psychoanalytical view of Mary Shelley as mother and daughter, both views being reductive in their different ways.

It was on a dreary night of November that I beheld the accomplishment of my toils [writes Victor Frankenstein]. With an anxiety that almost amounted to agony, I collected the instruments of life around me, that I might infuse a spark of being into the lifeless thing that lay at my feet. It was already one in the morning; the rain pattered dismally against the panes, and my candle was nearly burnt out, when, by the glimmer of the half-extinguished light, I saw the dull yellow eye of the creature open; it breathed hard, and a convulsive motion agitated its limbs.

How can I describe my emotions at this catastrophe, or how delineate the wretch whom with such infinite pains and care I had endeavoured to form? His limbs were in proportion, and I had selected his features as beautiful. Beautiful! – Great God! His yellow skin scarcely covered the work of muscles and arteries beneath; his hair was of a lustrous black, and flowing; his teeth of a pearly whiteness; but these luxuriances only formed a more horrid contrast with his watery eyes, that seemed almost of the same colour as the dun-white sockets in which they were set, his shrivelled complexion and straight black lips.

The different accidents of life are not so changeable as the feelings of human nature. I had worked hard for nearly two years, for the sole purpose of infusing life into an inanimate body. For this I had deprived myself of rest and health. I had desired it with an ardour that far exceeded moderation; but now that I had finished, the beauty of the dream vanished, and breathless horror and disgust filled my heart. Unable to endure the aspect of the being I had created, I rushed out of the room and continued a long time traversing my bed-chamber, unable to compose my mind to sleep. At length lassitude succeeded to the tumult I had before endured; and I threw myself on the bed in my clothes, endeavouring to seek a few moments of forgetfulness. But it was in vain: I slept indeed, but I was disturbed by the wildest dreams. I thought I saw Elizabeth, in the bloom of health, walking in the streets of Ingolstadt. Delighted and surprised, I embraced her; but as I imprinted the first kiss on her lips, they became livid with the hue of death; her features appeared to change, and I thought that I held the corpse of my dead mother in my arms; a shroud enveloped her form, and I saw the grave-worms crawling in the folds of the flannel. I started from my sleep with horror; a cold dew covered my forehead, my teeth chattered, and every limb became convulsed; when, by the dim and yellow light of the moon, as it forced its way through the window-shutters, I beheld the wretch – the miserable monster whom I had created. He held up the curtain of the bed; and his eyes, if eyes they may be called, were fixed on me. His jaws opened, and he muttered some inarticulate sounds, while a grin wrinkled his cheeks. He might have spoken, but I did not hear; one hand was stretched out, seemingly to detain me, but I escaped and rushed downstairs. I took refuge in the court-yard belonging to the house which I inhabited, where I remained during the rest of the night, walking up and down in the greatest agitation, listening attentively, catching and fearing each sound as if it were to announce the approach of the demoniacal corpse to which I had so miserably given life.

Oh! no mortal could support the horror of that countenance. A mummy again endued with animation could not be so hideous as that wretch. I had gazed on him while unfinished; he was ugly then, but when those muscles and joints were rendered capable of motion, it became a thing such as even Dante could not have conceived.

I passed the night wretchedly. Sometimes my pulse beat so quickly and hardly, that I felt the palpitation of every artery; at others, I nearly sank to the ground through languor and extreme weakness. Mingled with this horror, I felt the bitterness of disappointment: dreams that had been my food and pleasant rest for so long a space, were now become a hell to me; and the change was so rapid, the overthrow so complete!

Morning, dismal and wet, at length dawned and discovered to my sleep-less and aching eyes the church of Ingolstadt, its white steeple and clock, which indicated the sixth hour. The porter opened the gates of the court, which had that night been my asylum, and I issued into the streets, pacing them with quick steps, as if I sought to avoid the wretch whom I feared every turning of the street would present to my view. I did not dare return to the apartment which I inhabited, but felt impelled to hurry on, although drenched by the rain which poured from a black and comfortless sky.

I continued walking in this manner for some time, endeavouring, by bodily exercise, to ease the load that weighed upon my mind. I traversed the streets, without any clear conception of where I was, or what I was doing. My heart palpitated in the sickness of fear; and I hurried on with irregular steps, not daring to look about me:

> Like one who, on a lonely road,
>   Doth walk in fear and dread,
> And, having once turn'd round, walks on,
>   And turns no more his head;
> Because he knows a frightful fiend
>   Doth close behind him tread.
> (Coleridge's 'Ancient Mariner.')

Continuing thus, I came at length opposite to the inn at which the various diligences and carriages usually stopped. Here I paused, I knew not why; but I remained some minutes with my eyes fixed on a coach that was coming towards me from the other end of the street. As it drew nearer I observed that it was the Swiss diligence: it stopped just where I was standing; and on the door being opened, I perceived Henry Clerval, who, on seeing me, instantly sprung out. 'My dear Frankenstein,' exclaimed he, 'how glad I am to see you! How fortunate that you should be here at the very moment of my alighting!'

Nothing could equal my delight on seeing Clerval; his presence brought back to my thoughts my father, Elizabeth, and all those scenes of home so dear to my recollection. I grasped his hand, and in a moment forgot my horror and misfortune; I felt suddenly, and for the first time during many months, calm and serene joy. I welcomed my friend, there- fore, in the most cordial manner, and we walked towards my college. Clerval continued talking for some time about our mutual friends, and his own good fortune in being permitted to come to Ingolstadt. 'You may easily believe,' said he, 'how great was the difficulty to persuade my father that all necessary knowledge was not comprised in the noble art of book- keeping; and, indeed, I believe I left him incredulous to the last, for his constant answer to my unwearied entreaties was the same as that of the Dutch schoolmaster in *The Vicar of Wakefield*: "I have ten thousand florins a year without Greek, I eat heartily without Greek." But his affection for me at length overcame his dislike of learning, and he has permitted me to undertake a voyage of discovery to the land of knowledge.'

'It gives me the greatest delight to see you; but tell me how you left my father, brothers, and Elizabeth.'

'Very well, and very happy, only a little uneasy that they hear from you so seldom. By the bye, I mean to lecture you a little upon their account myself. – But, my dear Frankenstein,' continued he, stopping short, and gazing full in my face, 'I did not before remark how very ill you appear; so thin and pale; you look as if you had been watching for several nights.'

'You have guessed right; I have lately been so deeply engaged in one occupation, that I have not allowed myself sufficient rest, as you see: but I hope, I sincerely hope, that all these employments are now at an end, and that I am at length free.'

I trembled excessively; I could not endure to think of, and far less to allude to the occurrences of the preceding night. I walked with a quick pace, and we soon arrived at my college. I then reflected, and the thought made me shiver, that the creature whom I had left in my apartment might still be there, alive, and walking about. I dreaded to behold this monster: but I feared still more that Henry should see him. Entreating him therefore to remain a few minutes at the bottom of the stairs, I darted up towards my own room. My hand was already on the lock of the door before I recollected myself. I then paused; and a cold shivering came over me. I threw the door forcibly open, as children are accustomed to do when they expect a spectre to stand in waiting for them on the other side; but nothing appeared. I stepped fearfully in: the apartment was empty; and my bedroom was also freed from its hideous guest. I could hardly believe that so great a good-fortune could have befallen me; but when I became assured that my enemy had indeed fled, I clapped my hands for joy and ran down to Clerval.

We ascended into my room, and the servant presently brought breakfast; but I was unable to contain myself. It was not joy only that possessed me; I felt my flesh tingle with excess of sensitiveness, and my pulse beat rapidly. I was unable to remain for a single instant in the same place; I jumped over the chairs, clapped my hands, and laughed aloud. Clerval at first attributed my unusual spirits to joy on his arrival; but when he observed me more attentively, he saw a wildness in my eyes for which he could not account; and my loud, unrestrained, heartless laughter frightened and astonished him.

'My dear Victor,' cried he, 'what, for God's sake, is the matter? Do not laugh in that manner. How ill you are! What is the cause of all this?'

'Do not ask me,' cried I, putting my hands before my eyes, for I thought I saw the dreaded spectre glide into the room; '*he* can tell. – Oh, save me! save me!' I imagined that the monster seized me; I struggled furiously and fell down in a fit.

Poor Clerval! what must have been his feelings? A meeting, which he anticipated with such joy, so strangely turned to bitterness. But I was not the witness of his grief; for I was lifeless and did not recover my senses for a long, long time.

The Vampyre (1819)⋆

JOHN POLIDORI (1795–1821)

Dr John Polidori served as the physician and companion to George Gordon, Lord Byron, during the latter's travels on the Continent in 1816–17. His short novella The Vampyre *is one of the stories that resulted from the telling of ghost stories at the Villa Diodati in 1816 (see pp. 152–3); Byron himself composed a brief fragment of a vampire tale, but never developed it. Partly because it was mistakenly attributed to Byron,* The Vampyre *was very successful and gave rise to many imitations, and dramatic and operatic adaptations. Polidori named his vampire Lord Ruthven, the same name that Byron's rejected lover Lady Caroline Lamb gave to the Byron figure*

⋆ 'The Vampyre: a Tale by Lord Byron', *New Monthly Magazine*, **11** (April 1819), pp. 194–5.

in her novel Glenarvon. *The central relationship in Polidori's novel is the narrator Aubrey's fascination with Lord Ruthven, a possible reflection of the troubled homosexual relationship between Byron and Polidori, who was dismissed by Byron for being vain and ill-tempered. Polidori's brief attempt at a literary career failed, and he killed himself at the age of 26. Vampire literature was popular in Germany (e.g. Bürger's* Lenore, *1774, and Goethe's* Die Braut von Korinth, *1797), and some British vampires pre-dated Polidori's (e.g. Southey's* Thalaba the Destroyer, *1801; John Stagg's 'The Vampyre', 1810; Coleridge's 'Christabel', 1816). In much vampire literature, the folklore of vampirism can be as fascinating as the fictional (or poetic) narratives themselves, and historical accounts of vampires, werewolves and other* revenants *who fed on the living were popular in Northern Europe in the mid-1700s. In the excerpt, Polidori reviews the origins of his tale.*

Extract of a Letter to the Editor

There is a society three or four miles from Geneva, the centre of which is the Countess of Breuss, a Russian lady, well acquainted with the *agrémens de la Société*, and who has collected them round herself at her mansion. It was chiefly here, I find, that the gentleman who travelled with Lord Byron, as physician, sought for society. He used almost every day to cross the lake by himself, in one of their flat-bottomed boats, and return after passing the evening with his friends about eleven or twelve at night, often whilst the storms were raging in the circling summits of the mountains around. As he became intimate, from long acquaintance, with several of the families in this neighbourhood, I have gathered from their accounts some excellent traits of his lordship's character, which I will relate to you at some future opportunity. I must, however, free him from one imputation attached to him – of having in his house two sisters as the partakers of his revels. This is, like many other charges which have been brought against his lordship, entirely destitute of truth. His only companion was the physician I have already mentioned. The report originated from the following circumstance: Mr. Percy Bysshe Shelly [*sic*], a gentleman well known for extravagance of doctrine, and for his daring in their profession, even to sign himself with the title of Αθεος [atheist] in the Album at Chamouny, having taken a house below, in which he resided with Miss M. W. Godwin [i.e. the future Mrs Mary Shelley] and Miss Clermont, (the daughters of the celebrated Mr. Godwin) they were frequently visitors at Diodati, and were often seen upon the lake with his Lordship, which gave rise to the report, the truth of which is here positively denied.

Among other things which the lady, from whom I procured these anecdotes, related to me, she mentioned the outline of a ghost story by Lord Byron. It appears that one evening Lord B., Mr. P. B. Shelly, two ladies and the gentleman before alluded to, after having perused a German work, entitled *Phantasmagoriana*, began relating ghost stories; when his lordship having recited the beginning of *Christabel*, then unpublished, the whole took so strong a hold of Mr. Shelly's mind, that he suddenly started up and ran out of the room. The physician and Lord Byron followed, and discovered him leaning against a mantle-piece, with cold drops of perspiration trickling down his face. After having given him something to refresh him, upon enquiring into the cause of his alarm, they found that his wild imagination having pictured to him the bosom of one of the ladies with eyes (which was reported of a lady in the neighbourhood where he lived) he was obliged to leave the room in order to destroy the impression. It was afterwards proposed, in the course of conversation, that each of the company present should write a tale depending upon some supernatural agency, which was undertaken by Lord B., the physician, and Miss M. W. Godwin. My friend, the lady above referred to, had in her possession the outline of each of these stories, I obtained them as a great favour, and herewith forward them to you, as I was assured you would feel as much curiosity as myself, to peruse the *ebauches* of so great a genius, and those immediately under his influence.

Introduction

The superstition upon which this tale is founded is very general in the East. Among the Arabians it appears to be common: it did not, however, extend itself to the Greeks until after the establishment of Christianity; and it has only assumed its present form since the division of the Latin and Greek churches; at which time, the idea becoming prevalent, that a Latin body could not corrupt if buried in their territory, it gradually increased, and formed the subject of many wonderful stories, still extant, of the dead rising from their graves, and feeding upon the blood of the young and beautiful. In the West it spread, with some slight variation, all over Hungary, Poland, Austria, and Lorraine, where the belief existed, that vampyres nightly imbibed a certain portion of the blood of their victims, who became emaciated, lost their strength, and speedily died of consumptions; whilst these human blood-suckers fattened – and their veins became distended to such a state of repletion, as to cause the blood to flow from all the passages of their bodies, and even from the very pores of their skins.

In the *London Journal* of March, 1732, is a curious, and of course *credible* account of a particular case of vampyrism, which is stated to have occurred at Madreyga, in Hungary. It appears, that upon an examination of the commander-in-chief and magistrates of the place, they positively and unanimously affirmed, that, about five years before, a certain Heyduke, named Arnold Paul, had been heard to say, that, at Cassovia, on the frontiers of the Turkish Servia, he had been tormented by a vampyre, but had found a way to rid himself of the evil, by eating some of the earth out of the vampyre's grave, and rubbing himself with his blood. This precaution, however, did not prevent him from becoming a vampyre himself (The universal belief is, that a person sucked by a vampyre becomes a vampyre himself, and sucks in his turn.); for, about twenty or thirty days after his death and burial, many persons complained of having been tormented by him, and a deposition was made, that four persons had been deprived of life by his attacks. To prevent further mischief, the inhabitants having con-sulted their Hadagni, (Chief bailiff) took up the body, and found it (as is supposed to be usual in cases of vampyrism) fresh, and entirely free from corruption, and emitting at the mouth, nose, and ears, pure and florid blood. Proof having been thus obtained, they resorted to the accustomed remedy. A stake was driven entirely through the heart and body of Arnold Paul, at which he is reported to have cried out as dreadfully as if he had been alive. This done, they cut off his head, burned his body, and threw the ashes into his grave. The same measures were adopted with the corses of those persons who had previously died from vampyrism, lest they should, in their turn, become agents upon others who survived them.

We have related this monstrous rodomontade, because it seems better adapted to illustrate the subject of the present observations than any other instance which could be adduced. In many parts of Greece it is considered as a sort of punishment after death, for some heinous crime committed whilst in existence, that the deceased is [not only] doomed to vampyrise, but be compelled to confine his infernal visitations solely to those beings he loved most while upon earth – those to whom he was bound by ties of kindred and affection. This supposition is, we imagine, alluded to in the following fearfully sublime and prophetic curse from the *Giaour* [by Byron].

> But first on earth, as Vampyre sent,
> Thy corse shall from its tomb be rent;
> Then ghastly haunt the native place,
> And suck the blood of all thy race;
> There from thy *daughter, sister, wife*,
> At midnight drain the stream of life;
> *Yet loathe the banquet which perforce*
> Must feed thy livid living corse,
> Thy victims, ere they yet expire,
> Shall know the demon for their sire;
> As cursing thee, thou cursing them,
> Thy flowers are withered on the stem.
> But one that for *thy crime* must fall,
> The youngest, best beloved of all,
> Shall bless thee with a *father*'s name –
> That word shall wrap thy heart in flame!

Yet thou must end thy task and mark
Her cheek's last tinge – her eye's last spark,
And the last glassy glance must view
Which freezes o'er its lifeless blue;
Then with unhallowed hand shall tear
The tresses of her yellow hair,
Of which, in life a lock when shorn
Affection's fondest pledge was worn –
But now is borne away by thee
Memorial of thine agony!
Yet with thine own best blood shall drip
Thy gnashing tooth, and haggard lip;
Then stalking to thy sullen grave,
Go – and with Gouls and Afrits rave,
Till these in horror shrink away
From spectre more accursed than they.

Mr. Southey has also introduced in his wild but beautiful poem of *Thalaba*, the vampyre corse of the Arabian maid Oneiza, who is represented as having returned from the grave for the purposes of tormenting him she best loved whilst in existence. But this cannot be supposed to have resulted from the sinfulness of her life, she being pourtrayed throughout the whole of the tale as a complete type of purity and innocence. The veracious Tournefort gives a long account in his travels [*Relation d'un Voyage du Levant*, 1717] of several astonishing cases of vampyrism, to which he pretends to have been an eye-witness; and Calmet, in his great work upon this subject [*Traité sur les Apparitions des Esprits, et sur les Vampires*, 1751], besides a variety of anecdotes, and traditionary narratives illustrative of its effects, has put forth some learned dissertations, tending to prove it to be a classical, as well as barbarian error.

We could add many curious and interesting notices on this singularly horrible superstition, and we may, perhaps, resume our observations upon it at some future opportunity; for the present, we feel that we have very far exceeded the limits of a note, necessarily devoted to the explanation of the strange production to which we now invite the attention of our readers; and we shall therefore conclude by merely remarking, that though the term Vampyre is the one in most general acceptation, there are several others synonymous with it, made use of in various parts of the world, namely, Vroucolocha, Vardoulacha, Goul, Broucoloka, &c.

Melmoth the Wanderer (1820)*

CHARLES ROBERT MATURIN (1782–1824)

Charles Robert Maturin supplemented his inadequate income as curate at Saint Peter's, Dublin, by writing novels and plays, though only Bertram, *performed at Drury Lane in 1816 (see pp. 205ff.) was a financial success. His last years were poverty-stricken, and he contemplated suicide. Contemporary critics accused Maturin of sadomasochism in* Melmoth; *this term had not yet been coined, but the* Edinburgh Review *pointed out his obsession with scenes such as cannibalism and burning alive, and the* New Monthly Review *noted that 'He is a passionate connoisseur in agony.' Maturin himself acknowledged, in his preface to the* Milesian Chief, *that his talent lay in 'painting life in extremes, and representing those struggles of passion when the soul trembles on the verge of the unlawful and unhallowed.' He does not seem to have been wholly in control of what he called 'the criminals of the imagination' as he worked long into the night on* Melmoth. *Modern critics feel that this work is best illuminated by using the tools of 'morbid' psychology, though we should also bear in mind that many scenes in the novel bear witness to his Calvinist hatred of Roman Catholicism. (See a review of* Melmoth, *pp. 332ff.; and Scott's criticism of* The Fatal Revenge, *pp. 318ff.)*

Preface

The hint of this Romance (or Tale) was taken from a passage in one of my Sermons, which (as it is to be presumed very few have read) I shall here take the liberty to quote. The passage is this.

> At this moment is there one of us present, however we may have departed from the Lord, disobeyed his will, and disregarded his word – is there one of us who would, at this moment, accept all that man could bestow, or earth afford, to resign the hope of his salvation? – No, there is not one – not such a fool on earth, were the enemy of mankind to traverse it with the offer!

This passage suggested the idea of *Melmoth the Wanderer*. The Reader will find that idea developed in the following pages, with what power or success *he* is to decide.

The 'Spaniard's Tale' has been censured by a friend to whom I read it, as containing too much attempt at the revivification of the horrors of Radcliffe-Romance, of the persecutions of convents, and the terrors of the Inquisition.

---

* Charles Robert Maturin, *Melmoth the Wanderer*, 4 vols (Edinburgh: Archibald Constable and Company, 1820), vol. 1, pp. ix–xii, 272–82.

I defended myself, by trying to point out to my friend, that I had made the misery of conventual life depend less on the startling adventures one meets with in romances, than on that irritating series of petty torments which constitutes the misery of life in general, and which, amid the tideless stagnation of monastic existence, solitude gives its inmates leisure to invent, and power combined with malignity, the full disposition to practise. I trust this defence will operate more on the conviction of the Reader, than it did on that of my friend.

For the rest of the Romance, there are some parts of it which I have borrowed from real life.

The story of John Sandal and Elinor Mortimer is founded in fact.

The original from which the Wife of Walberg is imperfectly sketched is a living woman [i.e. Maturin's wife], and *long may she live*.

I cannot again appear before the public in so unseemly a character as that of a writer of romances, without regretting the necessity that compels me to it. Did my profession furnish me with the means of subsistence, I should hold myself culpable indeed in having recourse to any other, but – am I allowed the choice?

DUBLIN,
31st August 1820

The Spaniard's Tale

The oscillations of a convent vibrate within a very short interval. One day all is relaxation, another all is inexorable discipline. Some following days I received a striking proof of that foundation on which, in despite of a miracle, my repugnance to a monastic life rested. Some one, it was said, had committed a slight breach of monastic duty. The *slight breach* was *fortunately* committed by a distant relation of the Archibishop of Toledo, and con-sisted *merely in his entering the church intoxicated*, (a rare vice in Spaniards), attempting to drag the matin preacher from the pulpit, and failing in that, getting astride as well as he could on the altar, dashing down the tapers, overturning the vases and the pyx, and trying to scratch out, as with the talons of a demon, the painting that hung over the table, uttering all the while the most horrible blasphemies, and even *soliciting the portrait of the Virgin* in language not to be repeated. A consultation was held. The com-munity, as may be guessed, was in an uproar while it lasted. Every one but myself was anxious and agitated. There was much talk of the Inquisition, – the scandal was so atrocious, – the outrage so unpardonable, – and atone-ment so impracticable. Three days afterwards the archbishop's mandate came to stop all proceedings; and the following day the youth who had committed this sacrilegious outrage appeared in the hall of the Jesuits, where the Superior and a few monks were assembled, read a short exercise which one of them had written for him on the pithy word 'Ebrietas,' [drunkenness] and departed to take possession of a large benefice in the diocese of the archbishop his relative. The very next day after this scandalous scene of compromise, imposture, and profanation, a monk was detected in the act of going, after the permitted hour, to an adjacent cell to return a book he had borrowed. As a punishment for this offence, he was compelled to sit for three days at refection, while we were dining, barefooted and his tunic reversed, on the stone floor of the hall. He was compelled to accuse himself aloud of every crime, and of many not at all fit to be mentioned to our ears, and exclaim at every interval, 'My God, my punishment is just.' On the second day, it was found that a mat had been placed under him by some merciful hand. There was an immediate commotion in the hall. The poor wretch was labouring under a complaint that made it worse than death to him to be compelled to sit or rather lie on a stone floor; some merciful being had surreptitiously conveyed to him this mat. An investigation was immediately commenced. A youth whom I had not noticed before, started from the table, and kneeling to the Superior, confessed *his guilt*. The Superior assumed a stern look, retired with some old monks to consult on this new crime of humanity, and in a few moments the bell was rung, to give every one notice to retire to their cells. We all retired trembling, and while we prostrated ourselves respectively before the crucifix in our cells, wondered who would be the next victim, or what might be his punishment. I saw that youth but once again. He was the son of a wealthy and powerful family, but even his wealth was no balance against his contumacy, in the opinion of the convent, that is, of four monks of rigid principles, whom the Superior consulted that very evening. The Jesuits are fond of courting power, but they are still fonder of keeping it, if they can, to themselves. The result of their debate was, that the offender should undergo a severe humiliation and penance in their presence. His sentence was announced to him, and he submitted to it. He repeated every word of contrition they dictated to him. He then bared his shoulders, and applied the scourge till the blood flowed, repeating between every stroke, 'My God, I ask pardon of thee for having given the slightest comfort or relief to Fra Paolo, during his merited penance.' He performed all this, cherishing in the bottom of his soul an intention still to comfort and relieve Fra Paolo, whenever he could find opportunity. He then thought all was over. He was desired to retire to his cell. He did so, but the monks were not satisfied with this examination. They had long suspected Fra Paolo of irregularity, and imagined they might extort the confession of it from this youth, whose humanity increased their suspicion. The virtues of nature are always deemed vices in a convent. Accordingly, he had hardly been in bed when they surrounded him. They told him they came by command of the Superior to enjoin him a further penance, unless he disclosed the secret of the interest he felt for Fra Paolo. It was in vain he exclaimed, 'I have no interest but that of humanity and compassion.' Those were words they did not understand. It was in vain he urged, 'I will inflict whatever penance the

Superior is pleased to order, but my shoulders are bleeding still,' – and he shewed them. The executioners were pitiless. They compelled him to quit his bed, and applied the scourge with such outrageous severity, that at last, mad with shame, rage and pain, he burst from them, and ran through the corridor calling for assistance or for mercy. The monks were in their cells, none dared to stir, – they shuddered, and turned on their straw pallets. It was the vigil of Saint John the Lesser, and I had been commanded what is called in convents an hour of recollection, which was to be passed in the church. I had obeyed the order, and remained with my face and body prostrate on the marble steps of the altar, till I was almost unconscious, when I heard the clock strike twelve. I reflected the hour had elapsed without a single recollection on my part. 'And thus it is to be always,' I exclaimed, rising from my knees; 'they deprive of the power of thinking, and then they bid me recollect.' As I returned through the corridor, I heard frightful cries – I shuddered. Suddenly a phantom approached me – I dropt on my knees – I cried, 'Satana vade retro – apage Satana.' ['Satan get thee behind me, Satan begone.'] A naked human being, covered with blood, and uttering screams of rage and torture, flashed by me; four monks pursued him – they had lights. I had shut the door at the end of the gallery – I felt they must return and pass me – I was still on my knees, and trembling from head to foot. The victim reached the door, found it shut, and rallied. I turned, and saw a groupe worthy of Murillo. A more perfect human form never existed than that of this unfortunate youth. He stood in an attitude of despair – he was streaming with blood. The monks, with their lights, their scourges, and their dark habits, seemed like a groupe of demons who had made prey of a wandering angel, – the groupe resembled the infernal furies pursuing a mad Orestes. And, indeed, no ancient sculptor ever designed a figure more exquisite and perfect than that they had so barbarously mangled. Debilitated as my mind was by the long slumber of all its powers, this spectacle of horror and cruelty woke them in a moment. I rushed forward in his defence – I struggled with the monks – I uttered some expressions which, though I hardly was conscious of, they remembered and exaggerated with all the accuracy of malice.

I have no recollection of what followed; but the issue of the business was, that I was confined to my cell for the following week, for my daring interference in the discipline of the convent. And the additional penance of the unfortunate novice, for resisting that discipline, was inflicted with such severity, that he became delirious with shame and agony. He refused food, he got no rest, and died the eighth night after the scene I had witnessed. He was of a temper unusually mild and amiable – he had a taste for literature, and even the disguise of a convent could not conceal the distinguished graces of his person and manners. Had he lived in the world, how these qualities would have embellished it! Perhaps the world would have abused and perverted them – true; but would the abuses of the world ever have brought them to so frightful and disastrous a conclusion? – would he have been first lashed into madness, and then lashed out of existence? He was interred in the church of the convent, and the Superior himself pronounced his eulogium – the Superior! by whose order, or else permission, or at least connivance, he had been driven mad, in order to obtain a trivial and imaginary secret.

During this exhibition, my disgust arose to a degree incalculable. I had loathed the conventual life – I now despised it; and every judge of human nature knows, that it is harder to eradicate the latter sentiment than the former. . . .

'The Adventure of the German Student' (1824)*

WASHINGTON IRVING (1783–1859)

A Gothic atmosphere pervades the fiction of the American Romantics Charles Brockden Brown, Nathaniel Hawthorne, Herman Melville, Edgar Allan Poe, James Fennimore Cooper, Washington Irving, and many less well known writers influenced by Brown and Irving, such as James Kirke Paulding and William Gilmore Simms. In very many of his stories, Washington Irving combines the German Gothic tradition (folklore, ballads, stories of the Illuminati) with the American humorist tradition, as in his 'legendary' and 'ghostly' tales 'The Legend of Sleepy Hollow' and 'Rip Van Winkle'. Tales of a Traveller (1824), from which the following story comes, begins with a series of 'Strange Stories by a Nervous Gentleman', mostly told in the Radcliffean style of Sentimental Gothic: ghost stories set in ancient French châteaux, tales of pictures that possess a strange fascination, a long 'Story of the Young Italian' of extreme sensibility shut up in a convent, and humorous tales drawing upon New York Dutch traditions such as 'The Bold Dragoon' which tells of furniture that comes to life and gambols about the room – or was it just a dream? Further series were added, some employing Irving's popular 'Diedrich Knickerbocker' persona, with tales about banditti and pacts with the Devil. We can see the urbane professional writer smiling bemusedly behind most of the tales, and his gentle satire prevents any truly frightening effects – except perhaps in the following.

On a stormy night, in the tempestuous times of the French revolution, a young German was returning to his lodgings, at a late hour, across the old part of Paris. The lightning gleamed, and the loud claps of thunder rattled through the lofty, narrow streets – but I should first tell you something about this young German.

---

* Washington Irving, *Tales of a Traveller* (London: John Murray, (1824), vol. I, pp. 71–83).

Gottfried Wolfgang was a young man of good family. He had studied for some time at Göttingen, but being of a visionary and enthusiastic character, he had wandered into those wild and speculative doctrines which have so often bewildered German students. His secluded life, his intense application, and the singular nature of his studies, had an effect on both mind and body. His health was impaired; his imagination diseased. He had been indulging in fanciful speculations on spiritual essences until, like Swedenborg, he had an ideal world of his own around him. He took up a notion, I do not know from what cause, that there was an evil influence hanging over him; an evil genius or spirit seeking to ensnare him and ensure his perdition. Such an idea working on his melancholy temperament produced the most gloomy effects. He became haggard and desponding. His friends discovered the mental malady that was preying upon him, and determined that the best cure was a change of scene; he was sent, therefore, to finish his studies amidst the splendours and gaieties of Paris.

Wolfgang arrived at Paris at the breaking out of the revolution. The popular delirium at first caught his enthusiastic mind, and he was captivated by the political and philosophical theories of the day: but the scenes of blood which followed shocked his sensitive nature; disgusted him with society and the world, and made him more than ever a recluse. He shut himself up in a solitary apartment in the *Pays Latin*, the quarter of students. There in a gloomy street not far from the monastic walls of the Sorbonne, he pursued his favourite speculations. Sometimes he spent hours together in the great libraries of Paris, those catacombs of departed authors, rummaging among their hoards of dusty and obsolete works in quest of food for his unhealthy appetite. He was, in a manner, a literary ghoul, feeding in the charnel-house of decayed literature.

Wolfgang, though solitary and recluse, was of an ardent temperament, but for a time it operated merely upon his imagination. He was too shy and ignorant of the world to make any advances to the fair, but he was a passionate admirer of female beauty, and in his lonely chamber would often lose himself in reveries on forms and faces which he had seen, and his fancy would deck out images of loveliness far surpassing the reality.

While his mind was in this excited and sublimated state, he had a dream which produced an extraordinary effect upon him. It was of a female face of transcendent beauty. So strong was the impression it made, that he dreamt of it again and again. It haunted his thoughts by day, his slumbers by night; in fine he became passionately enamoured of this shadow of a dream. This lasted so long, that it became one of those fixed ideas which haunt the minds of melancholy men, and are at times mistaken for madness.

Such was Gottfried Wolfgang, and such his situation at the time I mentioned. He was returning home late one stormy night, through some of the old and gloomy streets of the *Marais*, the ancient part of Paris. The loud claps of thunder rattled among the high houses of the narrow streets. He came to the Place de Grève, the square where public executions are performed. The lightning quivered about the pinnacles of the ancient Hôtel de Ville, and shed flickering gleams over the open space in front. As Wolfgang was crossing the square, he shrunk back with horror at finding himself close by the guillotine. It was the height of the reign of terror, when this dreadful instrument of death stood ever ready, and its scaffold was continually running with blood of the virtuous and the brave. It had that very day been actively employed in the work of carnage, and there it stood in grim array amidst a silent and sleeping city, waiting for fresh victims.

Wolfgang's heart sickened within him, and he was turning shuddering from the horrible engine, when he beheld a shadowy form cowering as it were at the foot of the steps which led up to the scaffold. A succession of vivid flashes of lightning revealed it more distinctly. It was a female figure, dressed in black. She was seated on one of the lower steps of the scaffold, leaning forward, her face hid in her lap, and her long dishevelled tresses hanging to the ground, streaming with the rain which fell in torrents. Wolfgang paused. There was something awful in this solitary monument of wo[e]. The female had the appearance of being above the common order. He knew the times to be full of vicissitude, and that many a fair head, which had once been pillowed on down, now wandered houseless. Perhaps this was some poor mourner whom the dreadful axe had rendered desolate, and who sat here heartbroken on the strand of existence, from which all that was dear to her had been launched into eternity.

He approached, and addressed her in the accents of sympathy. She raised her head and gazed wildly at him. What was his astonishment at beholding, by the bright glare of the lightning, the very face which had haunted him in his dreams. It was pale and disconsolate, but ravishingly beautiful.

Trembling with violent and conflicting emotions, Wolfgang again accosted her. He spoke something of her being exposed at such an hour of the night, and to the fury of such a storm, and offered to conduct her to her friends. She pointed to the guillotine with a gesture of dreadful signification.

'I have no friend on earth!' said she.

'But you have a home,' said Wolfgang.

'Yes – in the grave!'

The heart of the student melted at the words.

'If a stranger dare make an offer,' said he, 'without danger of being misunderstood, I would offer my humble dwelling as a shelter; myself as a devoted friend. I am friendless myself in Paris, and a stranger in the land; but if my life could be of service, it is at your disposal, and should be sacrificed before harm or indignity should come to you.'

There was an honest earnestness in the young man's manner that had its effect. His foreign accent, too, was in his favour; it showed him not to be a hackneyed inhabitant of Paris. Indeed there is an eloquence in true enthusiasm that is not to be doubted. The homeless stranger confided herself implicitly to the protection of the student.

He supported her faltering steps across the Pont Neuf, and by the place where the statue of Henry the Fourth had been overthrown by the populace. The storm had abated, and the thunder rumbled at a distance. All Paris was quiet; that great volcano of human passion slumbered for a while, to gather fresh strength for the next day's eruption. The student conducted his charge through the ancient streets of the *Pays Latin*, and by the dusky walls of the Sorbonne to the great, dingy hotel which he inhabited. The old portress who admitted them stared with surprise at the unusual sight of the melancholy Wolfgang with a female companion.

On entering his apartment, the student, for the first time, blushed at the scantiness and indifference of his dwelling. He had but one chamber – an old fashioned saloon – heavily carved and fantastically furnished with the remains of former magnificence, for it was one of those hotels in the quarter of Luxembourg palace which had once belonged to nobility. It was lumbered with books and papers, and all the usual apparatus of a student, and his bed stood in a recess at one end.

When lights were brought, and Wolfgang had a better opportunity of contemplating the stranger, he was more than ever intoxicated by her beauty. Her face was pale, but of a dazzling fairness, set off by a profusion of raven hair that hung clustering about it. Her eyes were large and brilliant, with a singular expression that approached almost to wildness. As far as her black dress permitted her shape to be seen, it was of perfect symmetry. Her whole appearance was highly striking, though she was dressed in the simplest style. The only thing approaching to an ornament which she wore was a broad, black band round her neck, clasped by diamonds.

The perplexity now commenced with the student how to dispose of the helpless being thus thrown upon his protection. He thought of abandoning his chamber to her, and seeking shelter for himself elsewhere. Still he was so fascinated by her charms, there seemed to be such a spell upon his thoughts and senses, that he could not tear himself from her presence. Her manner, too, was singular and unaccountable. She spoke no more of the guillotine. Her grief had abated. The attentions of the student had first won her confidence, and then, apparently, her heart. She was evidently an enthusiast like himself, and enthusiasts soon understand each other.

In the infatuation of the moment Wolfgang avowed his passion for her. He told her the story of his mysterious dream, and how she had possessed his heart before he had even seen her. She was strangely affected by his recital, and acknowledged to have felt an impulse toward him equally unaccountable. It was the time for wild theory and wild actions. Old prejudices and superstitions were done away; everything was under the sway of the 'Goddess of reason.' Among other rubbish of the old times, the forms and ceremonies of marriage began to be considered superfluous bonds for honourable minds. Social compacts were the vogue. Wolfgang was too much of a theorist not to be tainted by the liberal doctrines of the day.

'Why should we separate?' said he: 'our hearts are united; in the eye of reason and honour we are as one. What need is there of sordid forms to bind high souls together?'

The stranger listened with emotion: she had evidently received illumination at the same school.

'You have no home nor family,' continued he; 'let me be everything to you, or rather let us be everything to one another. If form is necessary, form shall be observed – there is my hand. I pledge myself to you for ever.'

'For ever?' said the stranger, solemnly.

'For ever!' repeated Wolfgang.

The stranger clasped the hand extended to her: 'Then I am yours,' murmured she, and sunk upon his bosom.

The next morning the student left his bride sleeping, and sallied forth at an early hour to seek more spacious apartments, suitable to the change in his situation. When he returned, he found the stranger lying with her head hanging over the bed, and one arm thrown over it. He spoke to her, but received no reply. He advanced to awaken her from her uneasy posture. On taking her hand, it was cold – there was no pulsation – her face was pallid and ghastly. – In a word – she was a corpse.

Horrified and frantic, he alarmed the house. A scene of confusion ensued. The police were summoned. As the officer of police entered the room, he started back on beholding the corpse.

'Great heaven!' cried he, 'how did this woman come here?'

'Do you know anything about her?' said Wolfgang, eagerly.

'Do I?' exclaimed the police officer: 'she was guillotined yesterday!'

He stepped forward; undid the black collar round the neck of the corpse, and the head rolled on the floor!

The student burst into a frenzy. 'The fiend! the fiend has gained possession of me!' shrieked he: 'I am lost for ever!'

They tried to soothe him, but in vain. He was possessed with the frightful belief that an evil spirit had reanimated the dead body to ensnare him. He went distracted, and died in a madhouse.

Here the old gentleman with the haunted head finished his narrative.

'And is this really a fact?' said the inquisitive gentleman.

'A fact not to be doubted,' replied the other. 'I had it from the best authority. The student told it me himself. I saw him in a madhouse at Paris.'

— 4 —

𝔇rama

ALL THE MAJOR GOTHIC NOVELS were dramatized, often in more than one version. The first Gothic drama was Robert Jephson's *The Count of Narbonne* (1781), a dramatization of Walpole's *The Castle of Otranto*; James Boaden adapted several Gothic novels; and Mary Shelley's *Frankenstein* gave rise to several different productions. George Colman dramatized Godwin's *Caleb Williams*, titled *Falkland*, in 1796, with an excellent Gothic library for the stage set; he also satirized the genre. Sometimes the route by which the novels went on stage is curious: Planché's *The Vampire*, for example, is based on a French translation of Polidori's *The Vampyre* rather than directly on Polidori's novel. Lewis and Maturin wrote original, and very successful, productions for the stage, and Lewis adapted German Gothic novels for the English stage.

According to Montague Summers, Thomas Holcroft's Gothic play *Tales of Mystery* (1802) was the first time that the word 'melodrama' was used on the title page of an English play. Modern critics debate whether to call these productions melodramas or dramas or tragedies. The action in most of them is very stilted, and in any modern performances an audience might be tempted to call them farces. But Walpole's *The Mysterious Mother*, Lewis's *The Castle Spectre*, Maturin's *Bertram* and Baillie's *De Monfort* all carry poetic conviction, and these titles still give pleasure, at least as 'closet plays' if not on the stage. I have not included Romantic dramatic poems such as Byron's *Manfred* (1817) or Shelley's *The Cenci* (1819), though they derive much inspiration from Gothic productions at Covent Garden and Drury Lane. The most interesting characters of Gothic dramas were invariably the villains, including some women as well as men. Much of the critical attack on 'hobgobliana' was specifically an attack upon Gothic melodrama, which had the highest profile in attracting a popular audience.

A literary anthology is at a disadvantage in demonstrating the pleasures of drama, which of course depend heavily on action and spectacle, and even music. Gothic drama was especially 'spectacular', and achieved some notable successes. The setting of Act V, Scene VI in Robert Jephson's *The Count of Narbonne* (first performed at Covent Garden on 17 November 1781) was not untypical: 'The inside of a Convent, with ailes [*sic*] and Gothic arches, part of an altar appearing on one side; the statue of Alphonso in armour in the centre. Other statues and monuments also appearing.

Adelaide veiled, rising from her knees before the statue of Alphonso.'
Walpole himself supervised the production, instructing the actors, adjust-
ing their costumes, even loaning medieval garb from his own collection.
Walpole's arguments with Jephson over the set – Walpole felt it was more
authentic for the statue of Alphonso to be recumbent on his tomb, whereas
Jephson thought it should stand erect – led to their estrangement.

It is difficult to adequately represent dramas in anthologies, for they take
up so much space; even selection of an entire act will not show how the
dramatic action develops over the whole course of the play, which has
dramatic reversals, surprises, comic interludes and so on. In any case, the
action that took place on stage is not necessarily accurately reflected by the
printed play: Lewis's *The Castle Spectre*, for example, was cut to half the
length of the printed text before it was performed on the stage. I have placed
the Gothic drama in context by including contemporary reviews of dramas,
and contemporary discussions of 'behind the scenes' activities, such as how
to most effectively portray a spectre on the stage, or how the audience
reacted to the acting of Mrs Siddons, Britain's greatest tragic actress.

The Mysterious Mother (1768)*

HORACE WALPOLE (1717–97)

Scene III

BENEDICT, MARTIN [two friars]

BENEDICT. Ay! sift her, sift her –
    As if I had not prob'd her very soul,
    And wound me round her heart – I tell thee, brother,
    This woman was not cast in human mould:
    Ten such would soil a council, would unbuild
    Our Roman church – In her, devotion's real:
    Our beads, our hymns, our saints, amuse her not:
    Nay, not confession, not repeating o'er
    Her darling sins, has any charms for her.
    I have mark'd her praying: not one wand'ring thought
    Seems to steal meaning from her words. – She prays
    Because she feels, and feels, because a sinner.
MARTIN. What is this secret sin; this untold tale,
    That art cannot extract, nor penance cleanse?
    Loss of a husband, sixteen years enjoy'd,

---

* Horace Walpole, *The Mysterious Mother. A Tragedy* (Printed at Strawberry Hill, 1768), pp.
10–13; Postscript, pp. 1–6.

And dead as many, could not stamp such sorrow.
Nor could she be his death's artificer,
And now affect to weep it. – I have heard,
That chasing as he homeward rode, a stag,
Chas'd by the hounds, with sudden onset slew
Th' adventurous Count.

BENEDICT.   'Twas so; and yet, my brother,
My mind has more than once imputed blood
To this incessant mourner Beatrice,
The damsel for whose sake she holds in exile
Her only son, has never, since the night
Of his incontinence, been seen or heard of.

MARTIN. 'Tis clear, 'tis clear; nor will her prudent tongue
Accuse its owner.

BENEDICT.   Judge not rashly, brother.
I oft have shifted my discourse to murder:
She notes it not. Her muscles hold their place,
Nor discompos'd, nor firm'd to steadiness.
No sudden flushing, and no falt'ring lip:
Nor, tho' she pities, lifts she to her eyes
Her handkerchief, to palliate her disorder.
There the wound rankles not. – I fix'd on love,
The failure of her sex, and aptest cause
Of each attendant crime –

MARTIN.   Ay, brother, there
We master all their craft. Touch but that string –

BENEDICT. Still, brother, do you err. She own'd to me,
That, tho' of nature warm, the passion love
Did ne'er anticipate her choice. The Count,
Her husband, so ador'd and so lamented,
Won not her fancy, till the nuptial rites
Had with the sting of pleasure taught her passion.
This, with such modest truth, and that truth heighten'd
By conscious sense, that holds deceit a weakness,
She utter'd, I would pawn my order's credit
On her veracity.

MARTIN.   Then whither turn
To worm her secret out?

BENEDICT.   I know not that.
She will be silent, but she scorns a falshood [*sic*].
And thus while frank on all things, but her secret,
I know, I know it not.

MARTIN.   Till she disclose it,
Deny her absolution.

BENEDICT.   She will take none:
    Offer'd, she scoffs it; and withheld, demands not.
    Nay, vows she will not load her sinking soul
    With incantations.
MARTIN.   This is heresy;
    Rank heresy; and holy church should note it.
BENEDICT. Be patient, brother – Tho' of adamant
    Her reason, charity dissolves that rock,
    – And surely we have tasted of the stream.
    Nay, one unguarded moment may disclose
    This mystic tale – then, brother, what a harvest,
    When masters of her bosom-guilt! – Age too
    May numb her faculties. – Or soon, or late,
    A praying woman must become our spoil. . . .

Postscript

From the time that I first undertook the foregoing scenes, I never flattered myself that they would be proper to appear on the stage. The subject is so horrid, that I thought it would shock, rather than give satisfaction to an audience. Still I found it so truly tragic in the two essential springs of terror and pity, that I could not resist the impulse of adapting it to the scene, though it should never be practicable to produce it there. I saw too that it would admit of great situations, of lofty characters, and of those sudden and unforeseen strokes, which have singular effect in operating a revolution in the passions, and in interesting the spectator. It was capable of furnishing, not only a contrast of characters, but a contrast of vice and virtue in the same character: and by laying the scene in what age and country I pleased, pictures of ancient manners might be drawn, and many allusions to historic events introduced to bring the action nearer to the imagination of the spectator. The moral resulting from the calamities attendant on unbounded passion, even to the destruction of the criminal person's race, was obviously suited to the purpose and object of tragedy.

    The subject is more truly horrid than even that of Œdipus; and yet I do not doubt but a Grecian poet would have made no scruple of exhibiting it on the theatre. Revolting as it is, a son assassinating his mother, as Orestes does, exceeds the guilt that appears in the foregoing scenes. As murder is the highest crime that man can commit against his fellow beings, parricide is the deepest degree of murder. No age but has suffered such guilt to be represented on the stage. And yet I feel the disgust that must arise at the catastrophe of this piece; so much is our delicacy more apt to be shocked than our good-nature. Nor will it be an excuse that I thought the story founded on an event in real life.

    I had heard, when very young, that a gentlewoman, under uncommon agonies of mind, had waited on archbishop Tillotson, and besought his counsel. A damsel that served her had, many years before, acquainted her that she was importuned by the gentlewoman's son to grant him a private meeting. The mother ordered the maiden to make the assignation, when, she said, she would discover herself, and reprimand him for his criminal passion: but being hurried away by a much more criminal passion herself, she kept the assignation without discovering herself. The fruit of this horrid artifice was a daughter, whom the gentlewoman caused to be educated very privately in the country: but proving very lovely, and being acciden-tally met by her father-brother, who had never had the slightest suspicion of the truth, he had fallen in love with and actually married her. The wretched guilty mother, learning what had happened, and distracted with the consequence of her crime, had now resorted to the archbishop to know in what manner she should act. The prelate charged her never to let her son and daughter know what had passed, as they were innocent of any criminal intention. For herself, he bade her almost despair.

Some time after I had finished the play on this ground-work, a gentle-man to whom I had communicated it, accidentally discovered the origine [*sic*] of the tradition in the novels of the queen of Navarre, vol. I. nov. 30. and to my great surprise I found a strange concurrence of circumstances between the story as there related, and as I had adapted it to my piece: for though I believed it to have happened in the reign of king William, I had, for a purpose mentioned below, thrown it back to the even of the reforma-tion; and the queen, it appears, dates the event in the reign of Louis XII. I had chosen Narbonne for the scene; the queen places it in Languedoc. These rencounters are of little importance; and perhaps curious to nobody but the author.

In order to make use of a canvas so shocking, it was necessary as much as possible to palliate the crime, and raise the character of the criminal. To attain the former end, I imagined the moment in which she had lost a beloved husband, when grief, disappointment and a conflict of passions might be supposed to have thrown her reason off its guard, and exposed her to the danger under which she fell. Strange as the moment may seem for vice to have seized her, still it makes her less hatefull, than if she had cooly meditated so foul a crime. I have endeavoured to make her very fondness for her husband in some measure the cause of her guilt.

But as that guilt could not be lessened without destroying the subject itself, I thought that her immediate horror and consequential repentance were essential towards effectuating her being suffered on the stage. Still more was necessary: the audience must be prejudiced in her favour; or an uniform sentiment of disgust would have been raised against the whole piece. For this reason I suppressed the story till the last scene; and bestowed every ornament of sense, unbigotted piety, and interesting contrition, on the character that was at last to raise universal indignation; in hopes that some degree of pity would linger in the breasts of the audience; and that a whole life of virtue and penance might in some measure atone for a moment, though a most odious moment, of a depraved imagination.

Some of my friends have thought that I have pushed the sublimity of sense and reason, in the character of the Countess, to too great a height, considering the dark and superstitious age in which she lived. They are of opinion that the excess of her repentance would have been more likely to have thrown her into the arms of enthusiasm. Perhaps it might – but I was willing to insinuate that virtue could and ought to leave more lasting stings in a mind conscious of having fallen; and that weak minds alone believe or feel that conscience is to be lulled asleep by the incantations of bigotry. However, to reconcile even the seeming inconsistence objected to, I have placed my fable at the dawn of the reformation: consequently the strength of mind in the Countess may be supposed to have borrowed aid from other sources, besides those she found in her own understanding.

Her character is certainly new, and the cast of the whole play unlike any other that I am acquainted with. The incidents seem to me to flow naturally from the situation; and with all the defects in the writing, of many of which I am conscious, and many more no doubt will be discovered, still I think, as a tragedy, its greatest fault is the horror which it must occasion in the audience; particularly in the fairer, more tender, and less criminal part of it. . . .

Memoirs of Mrs. Siddons (1783)*

JAMES BOADEN (1762–1839)

Mr. Cumberland has a name in the drama, which demands attention to every effort not very much below himself. The *Mysterious Husband*, acted at Covent Garden, on the 28th of January [1783], is in many respects one of his best productions. Before the play went into rehearsal, he brought it to Henderson's house to read to him. Mrs. Henderson, with a very natural feeling, exclaimed to him, 'Well, Mr. Cumberland, I hope at last you will find Mr. Henderson to be *good for something* on the stage.' 'Madam,' replied the poet, '*I can't afford it* – a VILLAIN he *must be.*' And, to be sure, of all the *causeless* depravity, in the great moral massacre of the English tragedy, the character of Lord Davenant, in the present play, affords the completest specimen. It seems to have been suggested by [Horace Walpole] Lord Orford's mysterious *Mother*, which had been printed in 1768 at Strawberry Hill, and presented to his friends, with the express stipulation, that neither Garrick, nor Dr. Johnson, should be permitted to read it. The Doctor

---

* James Boaden, *Memoirs of Mrs. Siddons*, 2 vols (London: Henry Colburn, 1827), vol. 2, pp. 3–6, 129–30, 133–5.

would call this a 'very *angry*, but *unnecessary* prohibition.' It would severely mortify Mr. Garrick, who, however idly, hoped for universal esteem.

I do not wonder that Walpole, when, in 1781, he consented to a publication of this play from his own copy, pronounced a subject so horrid unsuited to the stage; and it should be remembered, that, in horrors, the *Mysterious Mother* greatly transcends either Phædra or Jocasta. But the nervous dignity of its composition will for ever delight in the closet. Yet, when we have in the mind's eye, such an actress as Mrs. Siddons, it is impossible to read some of its passages without attempting to conceive the astonishing effect they must receive from her *look* and *utterance*. The fifth scene of the first act, where an artful friar is endeavouring to worm out the cause of her remorse, that he may be master of her wealth, offers a few points that are irresistible, among many that are fine.

> *Bened.* The church could seal
>   Your pardon, but you scorn it. In your pride
>   Consists your danger. Yours are pagan virtues.
> *Countess.* Father, my *crimes* are pagan: my belief
>   Too orthodox to trust to erring man.

When the reader, who has known this magician in her strength, has a little considered the effect of *one word* in this reply, he may be disposed to go on with her in a speech so calculated for her powers.

> What! shall I, foul with guilt, and self-condemn'd,
> Presume to kneel, where angels kneel appal'd,
> And plead a *priest's certificate* for pardon?
> While HE, perchance, before my blasted eyes
> Shall sink to woes endless unutterable,
> For having *fool'd* me into that presumption.
> *Bened.* Is HE to blame, *trusting* to what he grants?
> *Countess.* Am I to blame, NOT trusting to what he grants?

Nor is the power of the poet at all weakened to the very end of the first act; where, with some of the *forms*, and more of the *spirit*, he adopts the interrogative style of Cato to Labienus in the ninth book of Lucan. Of its *forms* in the outset:

> *Countess.* Good father, wherefore? what should I inquire?
>   Must I be taught of him, that guilt is woe?
>   That innocence alone is happiness?

Of its *spirit* about the middle of her speech:

We want no preacher to distinguish vice
From virtue. At our birth the god reveal'd
All conscience needs to know.

As Mr. Cumberland chose a slighter degree of *incest* for the subject of his play, I wish he had not written it in prose, and that with the dexterity of Walpole, he had thrown the occurrence back a few centuries. In hearing or reading the vices of another and distant age, we have a twofold consolation: an involuntary suspicion that the facts may never have been true; and a voluntary belief, that our own times exhibit nothing like them. . . .

To use the language of the late Dr. Parr, when speaking of Warburton, on the 2nd of February, 1785, – 'from her towering and distant heights she rushed down upon her prey, and disdaining the ostentatious prodigalities of cruelty, destroyed it at a blow.' She [Mrs. Siddons] acted Lady Macbeth on that night, and criticism, and envy, and rivalry sunk at once before her. The subject was as fortunate to her as to the GREAT POET himself, and from that hour her dominion over the passions was undisputed, her genius pronounced to be at least equal to her art, and Sir Joshua's happy thought of identifying her person with the muse of tragedy confirmed by the immutable decree of the public. . . .

When Mrs. Siddons came on with the letter from Macbeth (the first time we saw her,) such was the impression from her form, her face, her deportment – the distinction of sex was only external – 'her spirits' informed their tenement with the apathy of a demon. The commencement of this letter is left to the reader's imagination. 'They met me in the day of success,' shews that he had previously mentioned the witches. Her first novelty was a little suspension of the voice, 'they made themselves – *air:*' that is, less astonished at it as a miracle of nature, than attentive to it as a manifestation of the reliance to be built upon their assurances. She read the whole letter with the greatest skill, and, after an instant of reflection, exclaimed –

Glamis thou art, and Cawdor – and SHALT BE
What thou art *promised.*

The amazing burst of energy upon the words *shalt be*, perfectly electrified the house. The determination seemed as uncontrollable as *fate* itself. The searching analysis of Macbeth, which she makes, was full of meaning – the eye and the hand confirmed the logic. Ambition is the soul of her very phrase: –

Thou'dst have, *great* Glamis.

Great Glamis! this of her *husband!* metaphysical speculation, calculated estimate – as if it had regarded Cæsar or Pompey. He is among the means before me – how is such a nature to be worked up to such *unholy* objects? . . .

The murmured mysteriousness of the address to the spirits 'that tend on mortal thoughts,' became stronger as she proceeded: –

> Come to my WOMAN'S BREASTS,
> And take my *milk* for GALL, you murd'ring ministers.

A beautiful thought, be it observed; as if these sources of infant nourishment could not even *consent* to mature destruction, without some loathsome change in the very stream itself which flowed from them.

When the actress, invoking the destroying ministers, came to the passage –

> Wherever in your sightless substances
> You wait on nature's mischief,

the elevant of her *brows*, the full *orbs* of sight, the raised shoulders, and the hollowed hands, seemed all to endeavour to explore what yet were pronounced no possible objects of vision. Till then, I am quite sure, a figure so terrible had never bent over the pit of a theatre; that night crowded with intelligence and beauty, in its seven front rows. . . .

'A Ghostly Performance' (1794)*

JAMES BOADEN (1762–1839)

The dramatist and theatre manager James Boaden exploited the popularity of Gothic novels by adapting some of them for the stage, including Lewis's The Monk *as* Aurelio and Miranda *(1799) and Radcliffe's* The Italian *as* The Italian Monk *(1797) (see pp. 186ff.). Boaden's earliest adaptation was of Radcliffe's* The Romance of the Forest, *which he read with great pleasure when it came out. He admired 'the singular address by which Mrs Radcliffe contrived to impress the mind with all the terrors of the ideal world; and the sportive resolution of all that had excited terror into very common natural appearances'. It struck him that the novel would provide 'the ground-work of a drama of more than usual effect'. During the winter of 1793 he began work on* Fontainville Forest, *which grew to a full five acts and was produced at Covent Garden (of which he was the manager) on 25 March 1794. It was designed specifically to compete with a production of Handel's*

---

* James Boaden, *Memoirs of the Life of John Philip Kemble*, 2 vols (London: Longman, Hurst, Rees, Orme, Brown, and Green, 1825), vol. 2, pp. 115–19.

Oratorios with which John Philip Kemble was opening his New Drury Lane Theatre that season. The pièce de résistance of Boaden's medieval set was the appearance of a spectre inspired by Fuseli's painting of Hamlet, exhibited in the Shakespeare Gallery on Pall Mall. Not to be outdone, New Drury Lane followed with Macbeth *on 21 April that year, with Kemble and Mrs Siddons in the title roles. But Covent Garden drew the crowds back with Henry Siddons's dramatization of* A Sicilian Romance; or, The Apparition of the Cliffs, *an Opera – based upon Radcliffe's earlier novel.*

.⌒⌒.

On the 12th of March (1794) the town was at once astonished and delighted by the opening of the new Theatre Royal, Drury Lane. Its spaciousness was entirely sunk in its lightness and proportion. Had I the construction of twenty theatres, this should be their model. It seemed to grow out of the pointed architecture, from its effect; though its parts did not imitate that mysterious order, or perhaps disorder, of composition. Why, *since*, theatres have affected so solid an inside front, it were perhaps fruitless to enquire. As to their exterior, convenience is the only principle that is imperative in such piles; and that, consequently, has been put out of sight altogether. The carriages have hardly any space to move in, and the audience are exposed to the wet, as speedily as possible, on their leaving the lobbies. The exit doors are still too few.

The oratorios were naturally well attended; and the coup d'oeil of the orchestra, piled up in Capon's actual building of a Gothic chapel, magnificent and even sublime. The house was at once ascertained to be a fine musical structure; and when applied to its positive purposes, with a company upon its stage seldom equalled and never surpassed – with all the leading beauties of England at the head of the polite, the liberal, the intelligent public – again, I say, our dear Kemble's heart might swell with pride at being manager of such a theatre.

I am brought back to the rival theatre, by being myself selected to supply part of the means by which Drury Lane was to be opposed. I have already ventured, some pages back, to interest the reader in the discussion, how the supernatural may best be exhibited upon the stage: and I, at the same time, showed that the author [i.e. Boaden himself] of *Fontainville Forest* meditated some improvements which were suggested to him by the sister art of painting. How far the stage execution might correspond with his notion was matter of experiment. A ludicrous misconception of his instructions might have ruined his whole design. Perhaps the reader may find some amusement in the *miseries* of an author. The great contrivance was, that the spectre should appear through a blueish-grey gauze, so as to remove the too corporeal effect of a 'live actor,' and convert the moving substance into a gliding essence.

As, to speak the absolute truth, any great effect in this play depended on the management of the ghost scene, Mr. Harris ordered a night rehearsal of it, that the author might judge how happily the stage had seconded his conceptions. Mrs. Pope had charmed us with the pathos of her recitation – the entrance of the spectre approached. On came good, honest, jolly Thompson, 'in his habit as he liv'd,' with the leathern pilch, 'time out of mind the player's armour' – as thick nearly as he was long, –

> And over all, that he might be
> Equipt from top to toe,
> His *grey gause* VEIL, as buckram stiff,
> Right manfully did throw.

No; never, except a river god in some procession, with all his *sedge* about him; never did I behold such a figure! I was rivetted to my seat with astonishment. Mr. Harris, who sat in the front by my side, said he thought the effect very good. But not staying to dispute this opinion, I made no secret of my distress and alarm; and clearly explained to him what my own idea really was. He laughed heartily at the mistake, and we soon found, across a portal of the scene, a proper place for the gauze worn by old Thompson. The clumsy effect of the traditional stage armour he did not so soon admit, and asked at last, rather briskly, how it could be made better? I told him that, in the first place, the present ghost must be *laid*, and a much higher spirit be invoked; and at length we found the tall, sweeping figure, that was to freeze the spectator with horror, in the person of Follet, the clown so royally celebrated for the eating of *carrots* in the pantomimes. Follet readily agreed to lend his person on this momentous occasion – his stride might have delighted Mr. Fuseli himself – his figure was of the heroic height – his action whatever you chose to order. But notwithstanding all these requisites for the part, there occurred one formidable difficulty. The ghost had but two words to utter, 'PERISH'D HERE:' – now 'that will be exactly the case with the author,' said Follet, 'if *I* speak them.' The fable had taught every body, that though the animal might be concealed, the *voice* would betray him. We therefore settled it, that, in imitation of the ancients, he should be only the MIME, to make the action on the stage, and that poor Thompson, disencumbered from the pilch [coarse garment] of the Majesty of Denmark, should yet at the wing, with hollow voice, pronounce the two important words; to which the extended arm of Follet might give the consentaneous action.

All that remained now was to dress the spirit; for which purpose I recommended a dark blue grey stuff, made in the shape of armour, and sitting close to the person; and when Follet (of course unknown) was thus drest, and faintly visible behind the gauze or crape spread before the scene, the whisper of the house, as he was about to enter, – the breathless silence, while he floated along like a shadow, – proved to me, that I had achieved the great desideratum; and the often-renewed plaudits, when the curtain fell, told me that the audience had enjoyed

> That sacred terror, that severe delight,

for which alone it is excusable to overpass the ordinary limits of nature.

For a whimsical dilemma that occurred, I may be excused in speaking of myself. I can only add that the public was extremely indulgent to my effort, and that I found the author's receipts very considerable indeed.

Review of Boaden's *The Italian Monk* (1797)⋆

Boaden's The Italian Monk *opened at the Haymarket on 15 August 1797 and was performed twelve times during the season. Boaden absurdly reclaimed Schedoni and restored him to domestic happiness, and the piece was diversified with music and songs by Colman. The actor Mr Palmer, when he took leave of the acting profession a year or two later, took Boaden aside and said that 'he could not quit London without in a particular manner thanking me for the part of Schedoni'. The following review is interesting for showing how, first, a novel may be rendered less subversive by the conventions of the theatre, and second, how subversive meanings in the novel can be reinserted by the actors despite the text of the adaptation.*

This play is founded upon a late romance of Mrs. Radcliffe's, entitled *The Italian; or, The Confessional of the Black Penitents.*

The privilege of borrowing the plot of a play from a novel has never been denied to the dramatic writer. Shakspere drew nearly all his materials from the same source. But we are apt to question the prudence of adhering too strictly to the original author. To compress an entire story into the narrow limits of a drama, is a work of extreme difficulty, and, after all, the interest must suffer by the transposition.

Mr. Boaden, however, seems to possess the enviable talent of conveying the leading points of a novel into a play, without any material injury to the whole; he knows, at once, what can be appropriated to dramatic use; and, by judiciously abstracting the less interesting parts of the narrative, he contrives to communicate, in a very short compass, the spirit of many hundred pages.

It was thus he treated a former production of Mrs. Radcliffe, in his play of *Fontainville Forest*, *Herman of Unna* a German novel, in his *Secret Tribunal*,

---

⋆ *Monthly Mirror*, **4** (July 1797), pp. 100–2.

and, in the same manner, though with evident improvement, he has now employed his skill upon the ITALIAN MONK.

The only point in which the author has essentially differed from the romance, is in blending the two characters of *Ansaldo*, and *The Monk of Paluzzi*. The plot is consequently much simplified, and a probable way prepared for the reform and eventual preservation of Schedoni; for, instead of being an *Agent of Mischief*, assuming an air of mystery to reveal the guilt, and occasion the destruction of Schedoni, and thereby to gratify his own revenge, he appears here as a *Guardian Minister*, watching the conduct, and frustrating the schemes, of the *Monk*, and is, at last, the means of securing the happiness of all parties. The motives, too, for this mysterious intervention, are accounted for with more probability than in the book. Schedoni's confession made to Ansaldo, on the eve of San Marco, is supposed to awaken his pity; and being himself implicated, as the suitor of Schedoni's wife when she received the poniard of her husband, he manages to gain his confidence, and is thus enabled to prevent the accomplishment of his dark intentions.

With the *Plot* Mr. Boaden has occasionally adopted the *sentiments* of the novel; but these he has cloathed in the language of blank-verse; and his style bears no resemblance to the feeble dialogue of modern tragedy, but is bold, nervous, and, in several passages, sublime. The interview between *Schedoni and the Marchioness*, and that between *Ansaldo and Vivaldi* in the prison of the inquisition, are very forcibly sustained in this respect. Nor have we often witnessed finer declamation than that put into the mouth of Ellena when she replies to the arguments of the *Abbess*. The author has evidently studied in the school of Shakspere, and fortunately discovers more of the strength than quaintness of his master's muse; that is, he has not been content with a mere imitation of his *phraseology*.

Though the fable is conducted with great art, it is yet not perfect; – for instance, a languor is sometimes induced by the repetition of circumstances which have previously past in action – this is the case with the *old woman's* account of Paulo's bravery, and Vivaldi's relation of Ansaldo's visit. The argument also between the *assassins* in the second act breaks in upon the interest; but the ingenuity with which the catastrophe is concealed is admirable.

The *comic* characters are by no means so well supported as the serious, though, indeed, it is obvious that the author thrust in the *humour* against his own inclination, to avert the fate which now attends all exhibitions purely tragic. Paulo, however, is just the merry, faithful domestic Mrs. Radcliffe has drawn him, and he serves very well to relieve the gloomy passages of the play. We beg leave here to correct a mistake of one of the daily critics, who taxed the author with inconsistency, in making Paulo a *Coward* in one scene, and a *desperado* in another. The censor forgot that Paulo's fear was entirely *superstitious*; and this sort of timidity is by no means incompatible with natural courage.

THE CHARACTERS. —

Schedoni . . . . Mr. Palmer
Ansaldo. . . . . Mr. Aickin
Vivaldi . . . . Mr. C. Kemble
Spalatro . . . . Mr. R. Palmer
Paulo . . . . Mr. Suett
The Marchioness . . . . Mrs. Harlowe
Olivia . . . . Miss Heard
Ellena. . . . . Miss De Camp.

THE ACTING. — We often hear of a dramatic production being supported and kept alive by the performers. The success of the *Italian Monk*, however, can never be attributed to the excellence of the *acting*: not that we mean to impute negligence to any individual concerned in the cast, for we believe they exerted themselves to the utmost; but the female part of the company is positively so inadequate, in point of ability as well as number, to the purposes even of the most subordinate provincial theatre in the kingdom, that a serious drama is sacrificed and ruined in such miserable hands. Where all is so very indifferent, we will not create any jealousy by determining which is the *worst*. We will venture, however, to intimate to Miss De Camp, who is really a very clever young actress, that she is by far *too boisterous* in the scene before alluded to with the *Abbess*. It is only intended that Ellena should be firm in her replies, dignified in her deportment, animated in her action, and resolute in her determination; as one who is maintaining the rights of truth and justice against the sophistry of the cloister, and the wrongs of oppression; Whereas the excessive violence of Miss De Camp almost alarmed us for the personal safety of poor Mrs. Hale, another fine tragic actress of the Haymarket theatre, who seemed to sit very uneasy in her *elbow chair*.

Palmer looked *Schedoni* admirably well, nor did he play it amiss; only he has a sad habit of relying on the extremes of his voice, and leaving the middle tone unexercised, so that we are either condemned to *hear nothing*, or, like Sir Richard Steele, when his workmen reminded him of their unpaid labours, *to hear too well*. . . .

The Castle Spectre (1797)*

MATTHEW GREGORY LEWIS (1775–1818)

M. G. Lewis was more prolific as a dramatist than as a novelist; his plays performed at Drury Lane or Covent Garden include Adelmorn, the Outlaw *(1801),*

---

* M.G. Lewis, *The Castle Spectre* (London: John Cumberland, n.d.), pp. 11, 13–14, 46–51.

Alfonso *(1802),* The Harper's Daughter *(1803) (adapted from Schiller's* Kabale und Liebe*),* Rugantino; or The Bravo of Venice *(1805) (adapted from J. H. D. Zschökke's novel* Abällino, der grosse Bandit*),* The Wood Daemon; or The Clock Has Struck *(1807), and* Venoni; or The Novice of St. Mark's *(1808). The section on Raymond and Agnes (and the Bleeding Nun) from his novel* The Monk *was adapted for the stage by himself and by others, and even became the basis for a ballet pantomime. Several of his plays became the basis of toy theatres designed by James Skelton – 'penny plain and tuppence coloured'. His most popular play* The Castle Spectre, *a 'Dramatic Romance, in Five Acts', was first performed at the Theatre Royal, Drury Lane, on 14 December 1797. Boaden, the manager of rival Covent Garden, noted that the play 'filled the treasury nightly'. It is estimated that Lewis earned some £18,000 for the first three months of its performance. Coleridge told Wordsworth that 'The merit of the Castle Spectre consists wholly in its situations. These are all borrowed and absolutely pantomimical' (letter, 23 January 1798).*

Costume

EARL OSMOND. – Yellow tunic, trimmed with silver spangles and buttons; purple velvet belt, white pantaloons spangled, short blue velvet robe trimmed with fur only, open sleeves. Second dress. – Handsome satin morning-gown.

PERCY. – Slate-coloured shirt tunic, trimmed with black galloon, flesh pantaloons. Second dress. – Green old English suit, with puffs trimmed, steel breastplate, long scarlet satin sash, leather belts; black velvet hat, white feathers, gauntlets, russet boots, ruff.

KENRIC. – Brown velvet shape, puffed with blue, cloak of the same, brown stockings.

HASSAN. – White body with sleeves looped up, trowsers of same, black leggings and arms, black velvet flys, silver buttons, sandals.

SAIB. }
MULEY. } Ditto.

ALARIC. – Not quite so good.

MOTLEY. – Touchstone's dress.

FATHER PHILIP. – Friar's grey gown, with Falstaff's belly, a cord round the waist, flesh stockings and sandals.

ALLAN. – An old English dress, drab trimmed with black.

HAROLD. – Blue tunic with yellow binding, blue stockings, short breeches.

EDRIC. – Blue Flushing great coat, blue trowsers, striped Guernsey shirt, blue cap, fishing stockings and boots.

REGINALD. – Brown tunic and pantaloons, with a loose torn cloak or drapery, flesh legs and arms, old sandals, the whole dress much torn.

SOLDIERS. – Green tunics with scarlet bindings, and stockings, boots, and breastplates.

Sold by J. REDINGTON, 208, Hoxton Old Town.

and Wholesale by Moss HYAMS, 15, Mint St, Borough.

GREEN'S
CHARACTERS AND SCENES
IN THE
CASTLE OF OTRANTO
OR
HARLEQUIN & THE
GIANT HELMET
3 Pl Tricks
8 Plates Characters.
10 Scenes. 4 Wings.
Nº 2. 5. 6. 17

Book Price 4ᵈ

Prince Manfred.

Pantaloon.

Theodore afterwards Harlequin.　　Lady Isabella afterwards Columbine.　　Princess Hippolyta afterwards Clown.
London Pub Dec 25 1841 by J K GREEN 34 Lambeth Square New Cut.　　　Price Halfpenny.

PLATE 7

A scene from J. K. Green's toy theatre version of *The Castle of Otranto; or Harlequin & the Giant Helmet* (1841). Author's collection.

ANGELA. – Handsome embroidered white satin dress.

ALICE. – Black open gown trimmed with point lace, red stuff petticoat, black hood, high heel'd shoes, with buckles.

SPECTRE. – Plain white muslin dress, white head dress, or binding under chin, light loose gauze drapery.

Prologue

FAR from the haunts of men, of vice the foe,
The moon-struck child of genius and of woe,
Versed in each magic spell and dear to fame,
A fair enchantress dwells, Romance her name.
She loathes the sun, or blazing taper's light.
The moon-beam'd landscape and tempestuous night,
Alone she loves; and oft, with glimmering lamp,

Near graves new open'd, or 'midst dungeons damp,
Drear forests, ruin'd aisles, and haunted towers,
Forlorn she roves, and raves away the hours!
Anon, when storms howl loud, and lash the deep,
Desperate she climbs the sea-rock's beetling steep;
There wildly strikes her harp's fantastic strings,
Tells to the moon how grief her bosom wrings;
And while her strange song chants fictitious ills,
In wounded hearts Oblivion's balm distils.

    A youth, who yet has liv'd enough to know
That life has thorns, and taste the cup of woe,
As late near Conway's time-bowed towers he stray'd,
Invok'd this bright enthusiast's magic aid.
His prayer was heard. With arms and bosom bare,
Eyes flashing fire, loose robes, and streaming hair,
Her heart all anguish, and her soul all flame,
Swift as her thoughts, the lovely maniac came!
High heav'd her breasts, with struggling passions rent,
As prest to give some fear-fraught mystery vent:
And oft, with anxious glance and altered face,
Trembling with terror, she relaxed her pace,
And stopt! and listened! – then with hurried tread
Onwards again she rushed, yet backwards bent her head,
As if from murderous swords or following fiend she fled.

    Soon as near Conway's walls her footsteps drew,
She bade the youth their ancient state renew.
Eager he sped, the fallen towers to rear:
'Twas done, and Fancy bore the fabric here.
Next, choosing from great Shakspeare's comic school;
The gossip crone, gross friar, and gibing fool –
These, with a virgin fair and lover brave,
To our young author's care the enchantress gave;
But charged him, 'ere he bless'd the brave and fair,
To lay the exulting villain's bosom bare;
And, by the torments of his conscience, shew,
That prosperous vice is but triumphant woe!

    The pleasing task, congenial to his soul,
Oft from his own sad thoughts our author stole:
Blest be his labours, if with like success
They soothe their sorrows whom I now address.
Beneath this dome, should some afflicted breast
Mourn slighted talents, or desert opprest,
False friendship, hopeless love, or faith betray'd,
Our author will esteem each toil o'er-paid,

If, while his muse exerts her livelier vein,
Or tells imagin'd woes in plaintive strain,
Her flight and fancies make one smile appear
On the pale cheek, where trickled late a tear;
Or if *her* fabled sorrows steal one groan,
Which else her hearers would have given their own.

ACT IV.

SCENE I. – *The Castle-Hall. The lamps are lighted.*

Enter FATHER PHILIP, R.

F. Phil. 'Tis near midnight, and the earl is already retired to rest. What if I ventured now to the lady's chamber? Hark! I hear the sound of footsteps!

Enter ALICE, L.

F. Phil. (R.) How, Alice, is it you?

Alice. (L.) So, so! have I found you at last, father? I have been in search of you these four hours! – Oh! I've been so frightened since I saw you, that I wonder I keep my senses!

F. Phil. So do I; for I'm sure they're not worth the trouble. And, pray, what has alarmed you thus? I warrant you've taken an old cloak pinned against the wall for a spectre, or discovered the devil in the shape of a tabby-cat.

Alice. [*Looking round in terror.*] For the love of heaven, father, don't name the devil! or, if you must speak of him, pray mention the good gentleman with proper politeness. I'm sure, for my own part, I had always a great respect for him, and he hears me, I dare say he'll own as much, for he certainly haunts this castle in the form of my late lady.

F. Phil. Form of a fiddle-stick! – Don't tell me of your –

Alice. Father, on the word of a virgin, I saw him this very evening in Lady Angela's bed!

F. Phil. In Lady Angela's? On my conscience, the devil has an excellent taste! But, Alice! Alice! how dare you trot about the house at this time of night, propagating such abominable falsehoods? One comfort is, that nobody will believe you. Lady Angela's virtue is too well known and I'm persuaded she wouldn't suffer the devil to put a single claw into her bed for the universe.

Alice. How you run on! Lord bless me, she wasn't in bed herself.

F. Phil. Oh! was she not?

Alice. No to be sure: but you shall hear how it happened. We were in the cedar-room together; and while we were talking of this and that, Lady Angela suddenly gave a great scream. I looked round, and what should I see but a tall figure, all in white, extended upon the bed! At the same time I heard a voice, which I knew to be the Countess Evelina's, pronounce in a hollow tone – 'Alice! Alice! Alice!' three times. You may be certain that I was frightened enough. I instantly took to my heels; and just as I got with outside of the door, I heard a loud clap of thunder.

F. Phil. Well done, Alice! A very good story, upon my word. It has but one fault – 'tis not true.

Alice. Odds my life, father, how can you tell any thing about it? Sure I should know best; for I was there, and you were not. I repeat it – I heard the voice as plain as I hear yours: do you think I've no ears!

F. Phil. Oh! far from it: I think you've uncommonly good ones; for you not only hear what has been said, but what has not. As to this wonderful story of yours, Alice, I don't believe one word of it; I'll be sworn that the voice was no more like your lady's than like mine; and that the devil was no more in the bed than I was. Therefore, take my advice, set your heart at rest, and go quietly to your chamber, as I am now going to mine. Good night.   [*Exit*, L.

Alice. There, he's gone! – Dear heart! dear heart! what shall I do now? 'Tis past twelve o'clock, and stay by myself I dare not. I'll e'en wake the laundry-maid, make her sit up in my room all night; and 'tis hard if two women a'n't a match for the best devil in christendom.   [*Exit*, R.

Enter SAIB *and* HASSAN, L.

Saib. The earl then has forgiven me! A moment longer and his pardon would have come too late. Had not Kenric held his hand, by this time I should be at supper with St. Peter.

Has. Your folly well deserved such a reward. Knowing the earl's hasty nature, you should have shunned him till the first storm of passion was past, and circumstances had again made your ministry needful. Anger then would have armed his hand in vain; for interest, the white man's God, would have blunted the point of his dagger.

Saib. I trusted that his gratitude for my past services –

Has. European gratitude? Seek constancy in the winds, fire in ice, darkness in the blaze of sunshine! But seek not gratitude in the breast of an European!

Saib. Then why so attached to Osmond? For what do you value him?

Has. Not for his virtues, but for his vices, Saib; can there for me be a greater cause to love him? Am I not branded with scorn? Am I not marked out for dishonour? Was I not free, and am I not a slave? Was I not once beloved, and am I not now despised? What man, did I tender my service, would accept the negro's friendship? What woman, did I talk of affection, would not turn from the negro with disgust? Yet, in my own dear land, my friendship was courted, my love was returned. I had parents, children, wife! Bitter thought, in one moment all were lost to me! Can I remember this, and not hate these white men? Can I think how cruelly they have wronged me, and not rejoice when I see them suffer? Attached to Osmond, say you? – Said, I hate him! Yet viewing him as an avenging fiend sent hither to torment his fellows, it glads me that he fills his office so well! Oh! 'tis a thought which I would not barter for empires, to know that in this world he makes others suffer, and will suffer himself for their tortures in the next!   [*Crosses*, R.

Saib. (L.) Hassan, I will sleep no more in the lion's den. My resolve is taken: I will away from the castle, and seek, in some other service, that security –

Osm. [*Within*, M. D.] What, hoa! help! lights there! lights!

Has. Hark! Surely 'twas the earl!

OSMOND *rushes in wildly at* M. D.

Osm. (C.) Save me! Save me! They are at hand! Oh! let them not enter!
[*Sinks into the arms of Saib.*

Saib. (L.) What can this mean? How violently he trembles!

Has. (R.) Speak, my lord! Do you not know us?

Osm. [*Recovering himself.*] Ha! whose voice? Hassan's? And Saib too here? Oh! was it then but a dream? Did I not hear those dreadful, those damning words? Still, still they ring in my ears. Hassan! Hassan! Death must be bliss, in flames or on the rack, compared to what I have this night suffered!

Has. Compose yourself, my lord. Can a mere dream unman you thus?

Osm. A mere dream, say'st thou? Hassan, 'twas a dream of such horror! Did such dreams haunt my bitterest foe, I should wish him no severer punishment. Mark you not how the ague of fear still makes my limbs tremble? Roll not my eyes as if still gazing on the spectre? Are not my lips convulsed, as were they yet pressed by the kiss of corruption? Oh! 'twas a sight that might have bleached joy's rose cheek for ever, and strewed the snows of age upon youth's auburn ringlets! Hark, fellows! Instruments of my guilt, listen to my punishment! Methought I wandered through the low-browed caverns, where repose the reliques of my ancestors! Suddenly a female form glided along the vault; it was Angela! She smiled upon me, and beckoned me to advance. I flew towards her; my arms were already unclosed to clasp her; when, suddenly, her figure changed, her face grew pale, a stream of blood gushed from her bosom! Hassan, 'twas Evelina!

Saib and Has. Evelina!

Osm. Such as when she sank at my feet expiring, while my hand grasped the dagger still crimsoned with her blood! 'We meet again this night!' murmured her hollow voice! 'Now rush to my arms – but first see what you have made me! Embrace me, my bridegroom! We must never part again!' While speaking, her form withered away: the flesh fell from her bones; her eyes burst from their sockets; a skeleton, loathsome and meagre, clasped me in her mouldering arms!

Saib. Most horrible!

Osm. And now blue dismal flames gleamed along the walls; and tombs were rent asunder, bands of fierce spectres rushed around me in frantic dance; furiously they gnashed their teeth, while they gazed upon me, and shrieked in loud yell 'Welcome, thou fratricide! Welcome, thou lost for ever!' Horror burst the bands of sleep; distracted I flew hither: But my feelings – words are too weak, too powerless to express them.

[*Crosses*, L.

Saib. (C.) My lord! my lord! this was no idle dream! it was a celestial warning; 'twas your better angel that whispered, 'Osmond, repent your former crimes! Commit not new ones!' Remember, that this night should Kenric –

Osm. Kenric? Oh, speak! Drank he the poison?

Saib. Obedient to your orders, I presented it at supper; but ere the cup reached his lips, his favourite dog sprang upon his arm, and the liquor fell to the ground untasted.

Osm. Praised be heaven! Then my soul is lighter by a crime! Kenric shall live, good Saib. What though he quit me, and betray my secrets? Proofs he cannot bring against me, and bare assertions will not be believed. At worst, should his tale be credited, long ere Percy can wrest her from me, shall Angela be mine. [*Crosses,* C.] Hassan, to your vigilance I leave the care of my beloved. Fly to me that instant, should any unbidden footstep approach yon chamber-door. I'll to my couch again. Follow me, Saib, and watch me while I sleep. Then, if you see my limbs convulsed, my teeth clenched, my hair bristling, and cold dews trembling on my brow, seize me – rouse me – snatch me from my bed! I must not dream again. Oh! how I hate thee, sleep! Friend of virtue, oh! how I hate thy coming!   [*Exit with Saib, through* M. D.

Has. Yes, thou art sweet, vengeance! Oh! how it joys me when the white man suffers! Yet weak are his pangs, compared to those I felt when torn from thy shores, oh, native Africa! from thy bosom, my faithful Samba! – Oh! when I forget my wrongs, may I forget myself! When I forbear to hate these Christians, God of my fathers, may'st thou hate me! – Ha! Whence that light? A man moves this way with a lamp! How cautiously he steals along! He must be watched. This friendly column will shield me from his regards. Silence! He comes.   [*Retires,* L. S. E.

Enter KENRIC, *softly, with a lamp,* R.

Ken. All is hushed! the castle seems buried in sleep. Now then to Angela!

[*Exit*, L.

Has. [*Advancing*.] – It was Kenric! – Still he moves onwards – Now he stops – 'Tis at the door of Angela's chamber! – He unlocks it! – He enters! – Away then to the earl: Christian, soon shall we meet again!

[*Exit*, M. D.

'Reminiscences of M. G. Lewis' (1797)*

Michael Kelly (1762?–1826)

On the 14th December [1797], the celebrated romance, called *The Castle Spectre*, was produced at Drury Lane, written by M. G. Lewis, Esq. It had a prodigious run; John Kemble performed in it, as did Mrs. Jordan, and Mrs. Powell, who made a splendid spectre. The first night of its representation, the sinking of the Ghost in a flame of fire, and the beauty of the whole scene, had a most sublime effect. I composed the music for the piece; but for the situation in which the Ghost first appears in the oratory to her daughter, and in which the acting both of Mrs. Powell and Mrs. Jordan, without speaking, rivetted the audience, I selected the chacoone of Jomelli, as an accompaniment to the action. This chacoone had been danced at Stutgard, by Vestris, and was thought an odd choice of mine for so solemn a scene; but the effect which it produced, warranted the experiment.

Mr. M. Lewis, the author of this drama, though eccentric, had a great deal of genius. I knew him well, and have passed many pleasant hours in his society. I composed his Operas of *Adelmorn the Outlaw*; *The Wood Dæmon*; *Venoni*; *Adelgitha*; all for Drury Lane; and a romantic drama, which he never brought forward, called *Zoroaster*. The last I composed was, *One o'Clock*, produced at the Lyceum. Of all his dramas the *Castle Spectre* was his favourite, perhaps from its having been the most attractive and popular; and yet it has been said, it was the indirect cause of his death.

After his father's decease he went to Jamaica, to visit his large estate. When there, for the amusement of his slaves, he caused his favourite drama, *The Castle Spectre*, to be performed; they were delighted, but of all parts which struck them, that which delighted them most was the character of Hassan, the black. He [i.e. Lewis] used indiscreetly to mix with these people in the hours of recreation, and seemed, from his mistaken urbanity and ill-judged condescension, to be their very idol. Presuming on indulgence, which they were not prepared to feel or appreciate, they petitioned him to emancipate them. He told them, that during his lifetime it could not be done; but gave them a solemn promise, that at his *death*, they should

---

* *Reminiscences of Michael Kelly*, 2 vols (London: Henry Colburn, 1826), vol. 2, pp. 140–3.

have their freedom. Alas! it was a fatal promise for him, for on the passage homeward he died; it has been said, by poison, administered by three of his favourite black brethren, whom he was bringing to England to make free British subjects of, and who, thinking that by killing their master they should gain their promised liberty; in return for all his liberal treatment, put an end to his existence at the first favourable opportunity.

This anecdote I received from a gentleman, who was at Jamaica when Mr. Lewis sailed for England, and I relate it as I heard it, without pledging myself to its entire authenticity.

De Monfort: A Tragedy (1798)*

JOANNA BAILLIE (1762–1851)

The Scottish poet and dramatist Joanna Baillie spent most of her life in Hampstead, London, and moved in Bluestocking circles from an early age. Her major work was A Series of Plays . . . on the Passions, *each 'passion' being the subject of a tragedy and then of a comedy, beginning in 1798 and enlarged to a total of 26 plays over the following years. The finest was the early tragedy on 'hate',* De Monfort, *which was produced at Drury Lane in 1800, with Mr Kemble as De Monfort and his sister Mrs Siddons as Jane Monfort, sister of De Monfort. The senior designer of Drury Lane, William Capon, was an enthusiast for Gothic architecture, and his design for the convent chapel in* De Monfort *employed all available levels of side-wing grooves in its 52-foot vista of nave, aisles, and choir, with a storm beating against a pointed-arch window, through which a grave was visible in the distance. The setting was acclaimed more universally than the play, and was adapted for later Gothic plays. The collection as a whole was an instant success when it first appeared anonymously in 1798: many people called the author — presumed to be a man — a second Shakespeare, and there was much speculation about the author's identity (see pp. 344ff., 353ff.) until Baillie finally made herself known in the 1800 edition. Baillie continued to be praised among literary women, but, according to Mrs Piozzi, 'No sooner, however, did an unknown girl own the work, than the value so fell, her booksellers complained they could not get themselves paid for what they did, nor did their merits ever again swell the throat of public applause' (letter, March 1819). Baillie became a great friend of Sir Walter Scott from 1808, and wrote increasingly on Scottish themes and in Scottish ballad metres. Her Scottish Gothic melodrama* The Family Legend, *performed in Edinburgh in 1810 with Mrs Siddons again in the leading role, was a great success. Her late play on the passion of 'horror',* Orra (1812), *was very popular, but Byron was not successful in his efforts to revive* De Monfort *for Drury Lane in 1815.*

---

* Joanna Baillie, *A Series of Plays: in which it is attempted to delineate* The Stronger Passions of the Mind, 4th edn, 3 vols (London: T. Cadell, Jun. and W. Davies, 1802), vol. 1, pp. 302, 335–44.

Persons of the Drama.

MEN

DE MONFORT.
REZENVELT.
COUNT FREBERG, *Friend to* De Monfort *and* REZENVELT.
MANUEL, *Servant to* De Monfort.
JEROME, De Monfort's *old Landlord.*
CONRAD, *an artful knave.*
BERNARD, *a Monk.*

Monks, Gentlemen, Officers, Page, *&c. &c.*

WOMEN

JANE DE MONFORT, *Sister to* De Monfort.
COUNTESS FREBERG, *Wife to* Freberg.
THERESA, *Servant to the* Countess.

Abbess, Nuns, *and a* Lay Sister, Ladies, *&c.*

Scene, a Town in Germany.

ACT II. SCENE II.

De Monfort's *apartments. Enter* DE MONFORT, *with a disordered air, and his hand pressed upon his forehead, followed by* JANE.

De Mon. No more, my sister, urge me not again:
    My secret troubles cannot be reveal'd.
    From all participation of its thoughts
    My heart recoils: I pray thee be contented.
Jane. What, must I, like a distant humble friend,
    Observe thy restless eye, and gait disturb'd,
    In timid silence, whilst with yearning heart
    I turn aside to weep? O no! De Monfort!
    A nobler task thy nobler mind will give;
    Thy true entrusted friend I still shall be.
De Mon. Ah, Jane, forbear! I cannot e'en to thee.
Jane. Then fy upon it! fy upon it, Monfort!
    There was a time when e'en with murder stain'd,
    Had it been possible that such dire deed
    Could e'er have been the crime of one so piteous,
    Thou would'st have told it me.

De Mon. So would I now – but ask of this no more.
    All other trouble but the one I feel
    I had disclosed to thee. I pray thee spare me.
    It is the secret weakness of my nature.
Jane. Then secret let it be; I urge no farther.
    The eldest of our valiant father's hopes,
    So sadly orphan'd, side by side we stood,
    Like two young trees, whose boughs in early strength,
    Screen the weak saplings of the rising grove,
    And brave the storm together –
    I have so long, as if by nature's right,
    Thy bosom's inmate and adviser been,
    I thought thro' life I should have so remain'd,
    Nor ever known a change. Forgive me, Monfort,
    A humbler station will I take by thee:
    The close attendant of thy wand'ring steps;
    The cheerer of this home, with strangers sought;
    The soother of those griefs I must not know,
    This is mine office now: I ask no more.
De Mon. Oh Jane! thou doest constrain me with thy love!
    Would I could tell it thee!
Jane. Thou shalt not tell me. Nay I'll stop mine ears,
    Nor from the yearnings of affection wring
    What shrinks from utt'rance. Let it pass, my brother.
    I'll stay by thee; I'll cheer thee, comfort thee:
    Pursue with thee the study of some art,
    Or nobler science, that compels the mind
    To steady thought progressive, driving forth
    All floating, wild, unhappy fantasies;
    Till thou, with brow unclouded, smilest again;
    Like one who, from dark visions of the night,
    When th' active soul within its lifeless cell
    Holds its own world, with dreadful fancy press'd
    Of some dire, terrible, or murd'rous deed,
    Wakes to the dawning morn, and blesses heaven.
De Mon. It will not pass away: 'twill haunt me still;
Jane. Ah! say not so, for I will haunt thee too;
    And be to it so close an adversary,
    That, though I wrestle darkling with the fiend,
    I shall o'ercome it.
De Mon.   Thou most gen'rous woman!
    Why do I treat thee thus? It should not be –
    And yet I cannot – O that cursed villain!
    He will not let me be the man I would.

Jane. What say'st thou, Monfort? Oh! what words are these?
    They have awaked my soul to dreadful thoughts.
    I do beseech thee speak!
    (*He shakes his head and turns from her; she following him.*)
    By the affection thou didst ever bear me;
    By the dear mem'ry of our infant days;
    By kindred living ties, ay, and by those
    Who sleep i' the tomb, and cannot call to thee,
    I do conjure thee speak!
    (*He waves her off with his hand, and covers his face with the other, still turning
    from her.*)
                                Ha! wilt thou not?
    (*Assuming dignity.*) Then, if affection, most unwearied love,
    Tried early, long, and never wanting found,
    O'er gen'rous man hath more authority,
    More rightful power than crown and sceptre give,
    I do command thee.
    (*He throws himself into a chair greatly agitated.*)
    De Monfort, do not thus resist my love.
    Here I entreat thee on my bended knees. (*Kneeling.*)
    Alas! my brother!
    (DE MONFORT *starts up, and catching her in his arms, raises her up, then
    placing her in the chair, kneels at her feet.*)
De Mon.   Thus let him kneel who should the abased be,
    And at thine honour'd feet confession make.
    I'll tell thee all – but oh! thou wilt despise me.
    For in my breast a raging passion burns,
    To which thy soul no sympathy will own.
    A passion which hath made my nightly couch
    A place of torment; and the light of day,
    With the gay intercourse of social man,
    Feel like th' oppressive airless pestilence.
    O Jane! thou wilt despise me.
Jane.   Say not so:
    I never can despise thee, gentle brother.
    A lover's jealousy and hopeless pangs
    No kindly heart contemns.
De Mon.   A lover, say'st thou?
    No, it is hate! black, lasting, deadly hate!
    Which thus hath driven me forth from kindred peace,
    From social pleasure, from my native home,
    To be a sullen wand'rer on the earth,
    Avoiding all men, cursing and accursed.
Jane. De Monfort, this is fiend–like, frightful, terrible!

What being, by th' Almighty Father form'd,
Of flesh and blood, created even as thou,
Could in thy breast such horrid tempest [m]ake,
Who art thyself his fellow?
Unknit thy brows, and spread those wrath-clench'd hands?
Some sprite accurst within thy bosom mates
To work thy ruin. Strive with it, my brother!
Strive bravely with it; drive it from thy breast:
'Tis the degrader of a noble heart:
Curse it, and bid it part.

De Mon. It will not part. (*His hand on his breast.*) I've lodged it here too long:
With my first cares I felt its rankling touch;
I loathed him when a boy.

Jane. Who did'st thou say?

De Mon.   Oh! that detested Rezenvelt;
E'en in our early sports, like two young whelps
Of hostile breed, instinctively reverse,
Each 'gainst the other pitch'd his ready pledge,
And frown'd defiance. As we onward pass'd
From youth to man's estate, his narrow art,
And envious gibing malice, poorly veil'd
In the affected carelessness of mirth,
Still more detestable and odious grew.
There is no living being on this earth
Who can conceive the malice of his soul,
With all his gay and damned merriment,
To those, by fortune or by merit placed
Above his paltry self. When, low in fortune,
He look'd upon the state of prosp'rous men,
As nightly birds, roused from their murky holes,
Do scowl and chatter at the light of day,
I could endure it; even as we bear
Th' impotent bite of some half-trodden worm,
I could endure it. But when honours came,
And wealth and new-got titles fed his pride;
Whilst flatt'ring knaves did trumpet forth his praise,
And grov'ling idiots grinn'd applauses on him;
Oh! then I could no longer suffer it!
It drove me frantick. – What! what would I give!
What would I give to crush the bloated toad,
So rankly do I loathe him!

Jane. And would thy hatred crush the very man
Who gave to thee that life he might have ta'en?
That life which thou so rashly did'st expose

To aim at his! Oh! this is horrible!

De Mon. Ha! thou hast heard it, then? From all the world,
But most of all from thee, I thought it hid.

Jane. I heard a secret whisper, and resolved
Upon the instant to return to thee.
Did'st thou receive my letter?

De Mon. I did! I did! 'twas that which drove me hither.
I could not bear to meet thine eye again.

Jane. Alas! that, tempted by a sister's tears,
I ever left thy house! these few past months,
These absent months, have brought us all this woe.
Had I remain'd with thee it had not been.
And yet, methinks, it should not move you thus.
You dared him to the field; both bravely fought;
He more adroit disarm'd you; courteously
Return'd the forfeit sword, which, so return'd,
You did refuse to use against him more;
And then, as says report, you parted friends.

De Mon. When he disarm'd this cursed, this worthless hand
Of its most worthless weapon, he but spared
From dev'lish pride, which now derived a bliss
In seeing me thus fettr'd, shamed, subjected
With the vile favour of his poor forbearance;
Whilst he securely sits with gibing brow,
And basely bates me like a muzzled cur
Who cannot turn again. –
Until that day, till that accursed day,
I knew not half the torment of this hell,
Which burns within my breast. Heaven's lightnings blast him!

Jane. O this is horrible! Forbear, forbear!
Lest heaven's vengeance light upon thy head,
For this most impious wish.

De Mon.   Then let it light.
Torments more fell than I have felt already
It cannot send. To be annihilated,
What all men shrink from; to be dust, be nothing,
Were bliss to me, compared to what I am!

Jane. Oh! would'st thou kill me with these dreadful words?

De Mon. (*raising his arms to heaven.*) Let me but once upon his ruin look,
Then close mine eyes for ever!
(JANE *in great distress, staggers back, and supports herself upon the side scene.*
DE MON. *alarm'd, runs up to her with a soften'd voice.*)
Ha! how is this? thou'rt ill; thou'rt very pale.
What have I done to thee? Alas, alas!

I meant not to distress thee. – O my sister!

Jane. (shaking her head.) I cannot speak to thee.

De Mon.   I have kill'd thee.

Turn, turn thee not away! look on me still!

Oh! droop not thus, my life, my pride, my sister;

Look on me yet again.

Jane.   Thou too, De Monfort,

In better days, were wont to be my pride.

De Mon. I am a wretch, most wretched in myself,

And still more wretched in the pain I give.

O curse that villain! that detested villain!

He hath spread mis'ry o'er my fated life:

He will undo us all.

Jane. I've held my warfare through a troubled world,

And borne with steady mind my share of ill,

For then the helpmate of my toil wert thou.

But now the wain of life comes darkly on,

And hideous passion tears me from my heart,

Blasting thy worth. – I cannot strive with this.

De Mon. (affectionately.) What shall I do?

Jane.   Call up thy noble spirit;

Rouse all the gen'rous energy of virtue;

And with the strength of heaven-endued man,

Repel the hideous foe. Be great; be valiant.

O, if thou could'st! E'en shrouded as thou art

In all the sad infirmities of nature,

What a most noble creature would'st thou be!

De Mon. Ay, if I could: alas! alas! I cannot.

Jane. Thou can'st, thou may'st, thou wilt.

We shall not part till I have turn'd thy soul.

Enter MANUEL.

De Mon. Ha! some one enters. Wherefore com'st thou here?

Man. Count Freberg waits your leisure.

De Mon. (angrily.) Be gone, be gone! – I cannot see him now.

[EXIT MANUEL.

Jane. Come to my closet; free from all intrusion,

I'll school thee there; and thou again shall be

My willing pupil, and my gen'rous friend,

The noble Monfort I have loved so long,

And must not, will not lose.

De Mon. Do as thou wilt; I will not grieve thee more.

[EXEUNT.

'On the Absurdities of the Modern Stage' (1800)*

'ACADEMICUS'

MR. EDITOR,

The subject of the following, needs no preface. It will be sufficient to observe, that its object is, like Prospero's wand, to cause the ghostly spirits of dramatic poesy, the terrific, wild, and numerous apparitions that haunt Old Drury and Covent Garden, 'to vanish into thin air, and, like the baseless fabric of a vision, leave not a wreck behind.' Happy shall I be, and I shall have gained the object I had in view, if I can but dissolve the spell, and convince my readers, that the fairy tales; the Cock Lane Ghost; *Mother Bunch's* romances; or even the mighty magician of *Udolpho*, *Aladin* [*sic*] and the *Wonderful Lamp*, or the *Castle Spectre*, are very well in the nursery, will please children, when the *coral* will not, but are not to be endured by men of sense and judgment, or who have ceased to think or act *like* children. Cannot these inspired writers, 'these fickle pensioners of Morpheus' train,' cannot they let the dead be at peace? Must they be ever raking their ashes to conjure up 'shadowy forms' and ideal mockeries, and horrible spectres? And cannot they indulge fancy's fire, without diving into mysteries more sacred than the Eleusinian, or pretending to search beyond the grave? They are the offspring, the undoubted progeny of Cerberus and Midnight; nay more, instead of shooting folly as it flies, they are the warmest patrons and guardians of it; they are either fools, or think every one of their country-men so.

— Are we to have prodigies and monstrous omens, horrid shapes, and the fruits of brooding darkness forced on us at a place to which we resort to be instructed and amused? Are we to expect to meet fiction instead of reality, on the stage? Cannot sober melancholy be pourtrayed without the aid of turrets and gloomy Gothic corridors haunted by ghosts? Better, should honest John Bull, from the one shilling gallery, call out for Rule Britannia, in the heart of the representation – Atque ursum et pugiles media inter carmina noscat ['like calling for a bear and boxers in the middle of the song'; Horace, *Epistles 2*]. I would rather the gods, noisy and vociferous as they are in their mirth, would put to flight the souls of the departed, than that they should make their appearance to the disgrace of the good sense of a British audience. . . .

---

* Academicus, 'On the Absurdities of the Modern Stage', *Monthly Mirror*, **10** (September 1800), pp. 180–2.

'A Performance of *Julia and Agnes*' (1800)*

MARY RUSSELL MITFORD (1787–1855)

It has just occurred to me that when a young girl, some eleven years old or less, I went with my father to the pit of one of the theatres – Drury Lane, I believe; yes, Drury Lane – to see a tragedy from *The Monk* (Sotheby's *Julia and Agnes*, 1800). Kemble played the hero, and Mrs. Siddons the heroine. *She* had to go into a dungeon where a frail nun had produced an infant, or rather she had to come out of a small door on to the stage, with the supposed baby in her arms. The door was what is technically called 'practicable,' that is to say, a *real* door, frame and all, made to open in the scene, and to sustain the illusion of a dungeon, as well as in that huge stage such an illusion can be sustained – for, paradoxical as it sounds, so many are the discrepancies in the present ambitious state of scenery, that I am quite convinced that in the days of Shakespeare, when all was trusted to the imagination of the spectator, the fitting state of willing illusion was much more frequently obtained than now – however, to make the scene as dungeon-like as possible, the door was deeply arched, hollow and low; and Mrs. Siddons, miscalculating the width, knocked the head of the huge wax doll she carried so violently against the wooden framework that the unlucky figure broke its neck with the force of the blow, and the waxen head came rolling along the front of the stage. Lear could not have survived such a *contretemps*. The theatre echoed and re-echoed with shouts of laughter, and the tragedy being comfortably full of bombast, not only that act, but the whole piece, finished amidst peals of merriment unrivalled since the production of *Tom Thumb*. I remember it as if it were yesterday.

Bertram; or, The Castle of St. Aldobrand (1816)†

CHARLES ROBERT MATURIN (1782–1824)

Maturin's five-act tragedy Bertram, *starring Edmund Kean in the title role, was performed at Drury Lane on 9 May 1816 and ran for 22 nights. Maturin received £1000 for the play, which had seven editions in 1816. On the basis of its great popularity, Maturin hoped to become a successful playwright, but his dramas never*

---

* *The Life of Mary Russell Mitford, Related in a Selection from Her Letters to Her Friends*, 3 vols, ed. A. G. L'Estrange (London: Richard Bentley, 1870), letter to Miss Barrett, 2 March 1842, vol. 3, pp. 139–40.
† C. R. Maturin, *Bertram; or, The Castle of St. Aldobrand*, 2nd edn (London: John Murray, 1816), pp. 1–7, 46–57.

again achieved the same public approval. In this very Shakespearean work, Imogine,
wife of St Aldobrand, many years past had once loved Count Bertram, but married
Aldobrand to raise the sinking fortunes of her house and father. Bertram's unexpected
reappearance after a shipwreck revives her desire for him. At the end of the final Act,
Bertram stabs Aldobrand, who dies at the feet of Imogine; Imogine goes mad and
when the monks discover her dead son lying on the tomb of Aldobrand she says
'(with a frantic laugh) The forest fiend hath snatched him – He rides the night-
mare through the wizard woods'. Bertram is captured, and Imogine dies at his feet
just before he is killed by his captors.

ACT IV.
Scene II.

Imogine in her apartment – a lamp burning on the Table – She walks some time in
great agitation and then pushes the light away.

Imo. Away, thou glarest on me, thy light is hateful;
    Whom doth the dark wind chide so hollowly?
    The very stones shrink from my steps of guilt,
    All lifeless things have come to life to curse me:
    Oh! that a mountain's weight were cast on me;
    Oh! that the wide, wild ocean heaved o'er me;
    Oh! that I could into the earthy centre
    Sink and be nothing.
    Sense, memory, feeling, life extinct and swallowed,
    With things that are not, or have never been,
    Lie down and sleep the everlasting sleep –

                           (She sinks on the ground.)

    If I run mad, some wild word will betray me,
    Nay – let me think – what am I? – no, what was I?

                              (A long pause.)

    I was the honoured wife of Aldobrand;
    I am the scorned minion of a ruffian.

                                Enter Clotilda.

Imo. Who art thou that thus comest on me in darkness?
Clot. The taper's blaze doth make it bright as noon.
Imo. I saw thee not, till thou wert close to me.
    So steal the steps of those who watch the guilty;
    How darest thou gaze thus earnestly upon me;
    What seest thou in my face?
Clot.   A mortal horror.

    If aught but godless souls at parting bear
    The lineaments of despair, such face is thine.
Imo. See'st thou despair alone?
    Nay, mock me not, for thou hast read more deeply,
    Else why that piercing look.
Clot.   I meant it not –
    But since thy lonely walk upon the rampart –
    Strange hath been thy demeanour, all thy maidens
    Do speak in busy whispers of its wildness –
Imo. Oh hang me shuddering on the baseless crag –
    The vampire's wing, the wild-worm's sting be on me,
    But hide me, mountains, from the man I've injured –
Clot. Whom hast thou injured?
Imo.   Whom doth woman injure?
    Another daughter dries a father's tears;
    Another sister claims a brother's love;
    An injured husband hath no other wife,
    Save her who wrought him shame.
Clot. I will not hear thee.
Imo. We met in madness, and in guilt we parted –
    Oh! I see horror rushing to thy face –
    Do not betray me, I am penitent –
    Do not betray me, it will kill my Lord –
    Do not betray me, it will kill my boy,
    My little one that loves me.
Clot.   Wretched woman –
    Whom guilt hath flung at a poor menial's feet –
    Rise, rise, how canst thou keep thy fatal secret?
    Those fixt and bloodshot eyes, those wringing hands –
Imo. And were I featureless, inert, and marble –
    Th' accuser *here* would speak –
Clot. Wilt thou seek comfort from the holy prior?
Imo. When I was innocent, I sought it of him –
    For if his lip of wrath refused my pardon,
    My heart would have absolved me –
    Now when that heart condemns me, what avails
    The pardon of my earthly erring judge?
Clot. Yet, hie from hence, upon their lady's bower
    No menial dares intrude.
Imo.   That seat of honour –
    My guilty steps shall never violate –
    What fearful sound is that?
Clot. Alas, a feller trial doth abide thee;
    I hear thy lord's approach.

  Madness is in thy looks, he'll know it all –
Imo. Why, I am mad with horror and remorse –
  He comes, he comes in all that murderous kindness;
  Oh Bertram's curse is on me.

             Enter Aldobrand.

Ald. How fares my dame? give me thy white hand, love.
  Oh it is pleasant for a war-worn man
  To couch him on the downy lap of comfort –
  And on his rush-strewn floors of household peace
  Hear his doffed harness ring – Take thou my helmet;
           (To page who goes out.)
  Well may man toil for such an hour as this.
Imo. (standing timidly near him)
  Yea, happier they, who on the bloody field
  Stretch when their toil is done –
Ald. – What means my love?
Imo. Is there not rest among the quiet dead;
  But is there surely rest in mortal dwellings?
Ald. Deep loneliness hath wrought this mood in thee,
  For like a cloistered votaress, thou hast kept,
  Thy damsels tell me, this lone turret's bound –
  A musing walk upon the moonlight ramparts,
  Or thy lute's mournful vespers all thy cheering –
  Not thine to parley at the latticed casement
  With wandering wooer, or –
Imo. (wildly)   For mercy's sake forbear –
Ald. How farest thou?
Imo. (recovering) Well – well – a sudden pain o' th' heart.
Ald. Knowest thou the cause detained me hence so long,
  And which again must call me soon away?
Imo. (trying to recollect herself) – Was it not war?
Ald. – Aye, and the worst war, love –
  When our fell foes are our own countrymen.
  Thou knowest the banished Bertram – why, his name
  Doth blanch thy altered cheek, as if his band
  With their fierce leader, were within these towers –
Imo. Mention that name no more – on with thy tale –
Ald. I need not tell thee, how his mad ambition
  Strove with the crown itself for sovereignty –
  The craven monarch was his subject's slave –
  In that dread hour my country's guard I stood,
  From the state's vitals tore the coiled serpent,

    First hung him writhing up to public scorn,
    Then flung him forth to ruin.
Imo. Thou need'st not tell it –
Ald. Th'apostate would be great even in his fall –
    On Manfredonia's wild and wooded shore
    His desperate followers awed the regions round –
    Late from Taranto's gulf his bark was traced
    Right to these shores, perchance the recent storm
    Hath spared me further search, but if on earth
    His living form be found –
Imo.   Think'st thou he harbours here –
    Go, crush thy foe – for he is mine and thine –
    But tell me not when thou hast done the deed.
Ald. Why are thou thus, my Imogine, my love?
    In former happier hours thy form and converse
    Had, like thy lute, that gracious melancholy
    Whose most sad sweetness is in tune with joy –
    Perhaps I've been to thee a rugged mate –
    My soldier's mood is all too lightly chafed –
    But when the gust hath spent its short-liv'd fury,
    I bowed before thee with a child's submission,
    And wooed thee with a weeping tenderness.
Imo. (after much agitation) Be generous, and stab me –
Ald. Why is this?
    I have no skill in woman's changeful moods,
    Tears without grief and smiles without a joy –
    My days have passed away 'mid war and toil –
    The grinding casque hath worn my locks of youth;
    Beshrew its weight, it hath ploughed furrows there,
    Where time ne'er drove its share – mine heart's sole wish
    Is to sit down in peace among its inmates –
    To see mine home for ever bright with smiles,
    'Mid thoughts of past, and blessed hopes of future,
    Glide through the vacant hours of waning life –
    Then die the blessed death of aged honour,
    Grasping thy hand of faith, and fixing on thee
    Eyes that, though dim in death, are bright with love.
Imo. Thou never wilt – thou never wilt on me –
    Ne'er erred the prophet heart that grief inspired
    Thou joy's illusions mock their votarist –
    I'm dying, Aldobrand, a malady
    Preys on my heart, that medicine cannot reach,
    Invisible and cureless – look not on me
    With looks of love, for then it stings me deepest –

When I am cold, when my pale sheeted corse
Sleeps the dark sleep no venomed tongue can wake
List not to evil thoughts of her whose lips
Have then no voice to plead –
Take to thine arms some honourable dame,
(Blessed will she be within thine arms of honour)
And – if he dies not on his mother's grave –
Still love my boy as if that mother lived.

Ald. Banish such gloomy dreams –
'Tis solitude that makes thee speak thus sadly –
No longer shalt thou pine in lonely halls.
Come to thy couch, my love –

Imo. Stand off – unhand me. –
                              Forgive me, oh my husband;
I have a vow – a solemn vow is on me –
And black perdition gulf my perjured soul
If I ascend the bed of peace and honour
'Till that –

Ald. 'Till what?

Imo. My penance is accomplished.

Ald. Nay, Heav'n forefend I should disturb thy orisons –
The reverend prior were fittest counsellor –
Farewell! – but in the painful hour of penance
Think upon me, and spare thy tender frame.

Imo. And doest thou leave me with such stabbing kindness?

Ald. *(to Clotilda who goes out)* Call to my page
To bring the torch and light me to my chamber –

Imo. *(with a sudden impulse falling on her knees)*
  Yet, ere thou goest, forgive me, oh my husband –

Ald. Forgive thee! – What? –

Imo. Oh, we do all offend –
There's not a day of wedded life, if we
Count at its close the little, bitter sum
Of thoughts, and words, and looks unkind and froward,
Silence that chides and woundings of the eye –
But prostrate at each others' feet, we should
Each night forgiveness ask – then what should I? –

Ald. *(not hearing the last words)* Why take it freely;
I well may pardon, what I ne'er have felt.

Imo. *(following him on her knees, and kissing his hand)*
Dost thou forgive me from thine inmost soul –
God bless thee, oh, God bless thee –

Ald. Farewell – mine eyes grow heavy, thy sad talk
Hath stolen a heaviness upon my spirits –

I will unto my solitary couch – Farewell.

[*Exit Aldobrand.*

Imo. There is no human heart can bide this conflict –
    All dark and horrible, – Bertram must die –
    But oh, within these walls, before mine eyes,
    Who would have died for him, while life had value; –
    He shall not die, – Clotilda, ho, come forth –
    He yet may be redeemed, though I am lost –
    Let him depart, and pray for her he ruin'd.
    Hah! was it fancy's work – I hear a step –
    It hath the speech-like thrilling of *his* tread:
    It is himself.

Enter Bertram.

    It is a crime in me to look on thee –
    But in whate'er I do there now is crime –
    Yet wretched thought still struggles for thy safety –
    Fly, while my lips without a crime may warn thee –
    Would thou hadst never come, or sooner parted.
    Oh God – he heeds me not;
    Why comest thou thus, what is thy fearful business?
    I know thou comest for evil, but its purport
    I ask my heart in vain.
Ber. Guess it, and spare me. *(A long pause, during which she gazes at him)*
    Canst thou not read it in my face?
Imo. I dare not;
    Mixt shades of evil thought are darkening there;
    But what my fears do indistinctly guess
    Would blast me to behold – *(turns away, a pause.)*
Ber. Dost thou not hear it in my very silence?
    That which no voice can tell, doth tell itself.
Imo. My harassed thought hath not one point of fear,
    Save that it must not think.
Ber. *(throwing his dagger on the ground.)*
    Speak thou for me, –
    Shew me the chamber where thy husband lies,
    The morning must not see us both alive.
Imo. *(screaming and struggling with him.)*
    Ah! horror! horror! off – withstand me not,
    I will arouse the castle, rouse the dead,
    To save my husband; villain, murderer, monster,
    Dare the bayed lioness, but fly from me.
Ber. Go, wake the castle with thy frantic cries;

Those cries that tell my secret, blazon thine.
Yea, pour it on thine husband's blasted ear.
Imo. Perchance his wrath may kill me in its mercy.
Ber. No, hope not such a fate of mercy from him;
    He'll curse thee *with his pardon.*
    And would his death-fixed eye be terrible
    As its ray bent in love on her that wronged him?
    And would his dying groan affright thine ear
    Like words of peace spoke to thy guilt – in vain?
Imo. I care not, I am reckless, let me perish.
Ber. No, thou must live amid a hissing world,
    A thing that mothers warn their daughters from,
    A thing the menials that do tend thee scorn,
    Whom when the good do name, they tell their beads,
    And when the wicked think of, they do triumph;
    Canst thou encounter this?
Imo. I must encounter it – I have deserved it;
    Begone, or my next cry shall wake the dead.
Ber. Hear me.
Imo. No parley, tempter, fiend, avaunt.
Ber. Thy son – *(she stands stupified.)*
    Go, take him trembling in thy hand of shame,
    A victim of the shrine of public scorn –
    Poor boy! his sire's worst foe might pity him,
    Albeit his mother will not –
    Banished from noble halls, and knightly converse,
    Devouring his young heart in loneliness
    With bitter thought – my mother was – a wretch.
Imo. *(falling at his feet.)*
    I am a wretch – but – who hath made me so?
    I'm writhing like a worm, beneath thy spurn.
    Have pity on me, I have had much wrong.
Ber. My heart is as the steel within my grasp.
Imo. *(still kneeling.)* Thou hast cast me down from light,
    From my high sphere of purity and peace,
    Where once I walked in mine uprightness, blessed –
    Do not thou cast me into utter darkness.
Ber. *(looking on her with pity for a moment.)* Thou fairest flower –
    Why didst thou fling thyself across my path,
    My tiger spring must crush thee in its way,
    But cannot pause to pity thee.
Imo. Thou must,
    For I am strong in woes – I ne'er reproached thee –
    I plead but with my agonies and tears –

Kind, gentle Bertram, my beloved Bertram,
For thou were gentle once, and once beloved,
Have mercy on me – Oh thou couldst not think it –
(Looking up, and seeing no relenting in his face, she starts up wildly.)
By heaven and all its host, he shall not perish.

Ber. By hell and all its host, he shall not live.
This is no transient flash of fugitive passion –
His death hath been my life for years of misery –
Which else I had not lived –
Upon that thought, and not on food, I fed,
Upon that thought, and not on sleep, I rested –
I come to do the deed that must be done –
Nor thou, nor sheltring angels, could prevent me.

Imo. But man shall – miscreant – help.

Ber. Thou callest in vain –
The unarmed vassals all are far from succour –
Following St. Anselm's votarists to the convent –
My band of blood are darkening in their halls –
Wouldst have him butchered by their ruffian hands
That wait my bidding?

Imo. (falling on the ground.) – Fell and horrible
I'm sealed, shut down in ransomless perdition.

Ber. Fear not, my vengeance will not yield its prey,
He shall fall noble, by my hand shall fall –
But still and dark the summons of its fate,
So winds the coiled serpent round his victim.

'On "German" Drama' (1816)*

SAMUEL TAYLOR COLERIDGE (1772–1834)

*Coleridge's critique of current dramatic fashion was prompted by the popularity of
Maturin's play* Bertram, *which opened in May 1816 (see preceding selection).
Coleridge was perhaps resentful that his own play* Zapolya *was rejected by Drury
Lane that July. His criticism of* Bertram *appeared anonymously, as 'Letters to the
Editor' in the* Courier *on 29 August, 7, 9, 10 and 11 September 1816 (and was
later included in his collection* Biographia Literaria, *from which the extract comes).
He argues that so-called 'German' drama is in fact a native English product,*

---

* Samuel Taylor Coleridge, *Biographia Literaria*, 2 vols (London: Rest Fenner, 1817) vol. 2,
pp. 256–60.

influenced by such works as Edward Young's The Complaint; or Night
Thoughts on Life, Death, and Immortality *(1742–5); James Hervey's* Meditations among the Tombs *(1748); Samuel Richardson's* Clarissa *(1748); as
well as by the German dramatist Kotzebue (1761–1819).*

But before I enter on the examination of *Bertram, or the Castle of St. Alde-
brand*, I shall interpose a few words, on the phrase *German Drama*, which I
hold to be altogether a misnomer. At the time of Lessing, the German
stage, such as it was, appears to have been a flat and servile copy of the
French. It was Lessing who first introduced the name and the works of
Shakespeare to the admiration of the Germans; and I should not perhaps go
too far, if I add, that it was Lessing who first proved to all thinking men,
even to Shakespeare's own countrymen, the true nature of his apparent
irregularities. These, he demonstrated, were deviations only from the *Accidents* of the Greek Tragedy; and from such accidents as hung a heavy
weight on the wings of the Greek Poets, and narrowed their flight within
the limits of what we may call the *Heroic Opera*. He proved, that in all the
essentials of art, no less than in the truth of nature, the Plays of Shakespeare
were incomparably more coincident with the principles of Aristotle, than
the productions of Corneille and Racine, notwithstanding the boasted regularity of the latter. Under these convictions, were Lessing's own dramatic
works composed. Their deficiency is in depth and in imagination: their
excellence is in the construction of the plot; the good sense of the sentiments; the sobriety of the morals; and the high polish of the diction and
dialogue. In short, his dramas are the very antipodes of all those which it has
been the fashion of late years at once to abuse and to enjoy, under the name
of the German Drama. Of this latter, Schiller's *Robbers* was the earliest
specimen; the first fruits of his youth (I had almost said of his boyhood) and
as such, the pledge, and promise of no ordinary genius. Only as *such*, did the
maturer judgement of the author tolerate the Play. During his whole life he
expressed himself concerning this production with more than needful
asperity, as a monster not less offensive to good taste, than to sound morals;
and in his latter years his indignation at the unwonted popularity of the
Robbers seduced him into the *contrary* extremes, viz. a studied feebleness of
interest (as far as the interest was to be derived from incidents and the
excitement of curiosity); a diction elaborately metrical; the affectation of
rhymes; and the pedantry of the chorus.

But to understand the true character of the *Robbers*, and of the countless
imitations which were its spawn, I must inform you, or at least call to your
recollection, that about that time, and for some years before it, three of
the most popular books in the German language were, the translations
of *Young's Night Thoughts*, *Harvey's Meditations*, and *Richardson's Clarissa
Harlow*. Now we have only to combine the bloated style and peculiar

rhythm of Harvey, which is poetic only on account of its utter unfitness for prose, and might as appropriately be called prosaic, from its utter unfitness for poetry; we have only, I repeat, to combine these Harveyisms with the strained thoughts, the figurative metaphysics and solemn epigrams of Young on the one hand; and with the loaded sensibility, the minute detail, the morbid consciousness of every thought and feeling in the whole flux and reflux of the mind, in short the self-involution and dreamlike continuity of Richardson on the other hand; and then to add the horrific incidents, and mysterious villains, (geniuses of supernatural intellect, if you will take the author's words for it, but on a level with the meanest ruffians of the condemned cells, if we are to judge by their actions and contrivances) – to add the ruined castles, the dungeons, the trap-doors, the skeletons, the flesh-and-blood ghosts, and the perpetual moonshine of a modern author, (themselves the literary brood of the *Castle of Otranto*, the translations of which, with the imitations and improvements aforesaid, were about that time beginning to make as much noise in Germany as their originals were making in England), – and as the compound of these ingredients duly mixed, you will recognize the so called *German* Drama. The *Olla Podrida* [Spanish stew] thus cooked up, was denounced, by the best critics in Germany, as the mere cramps of weakness, and orgasms [immoderate excitements] of a sickly imagination on the part of the author, and the lowest provocation of torpid feeling on that of the readers. The old blunder however, concerning the irregularity and wildness of Shakespeare, in which the German did but echo the French, who again were but the echoes of our own critics, was still in vogue, and Shakespeare was quoted as authority for the most anti-Shakspearean Drama. We have indeed two poets who wrote as one, near the age of Shakespeare, to whom (as the worst characteristic of their writings), the Coryphæus [leader of the chorus in Greek drama] of the present Drama may challenge the honour of being a poor relation, or impoverished descendant. For if we would charitably consent to forget the comic humour, the wit, the felicities of style, in other words, *all* the poetry, and nine-tenths of all the genius of Beaumont and Fletcher, that which would remain becomes a Kotzebue.

The so-called *German* Drama, therefore, is *English* in its *origin*, *English* in its *materials*, and *English* by re-adoption; and till we can prove that Kotzebue, or any of the whole breed of Kotzebues, whether dramatists or romantic writers, or writers of romantic dramas, were ever admitted to any other shelf in the libraries of well-educated Germans than were occupied by their originals, and apes' apes in their mother country, we should submit to carry our own brat on our own shoulders; or rather consider it as a lack-grace returned from transportation with such improvements only in growth and manners as young transported convicts usually come home with.

The Vampire; or, The Bride of the Isles (1820)[*]

James Robinson Planché (1796–1880)

J. R. Planché wrote more than 150 plays and operas, of which The Vampire *was the most popular. This two-act 'Romantic Melo-Drama' was performed at the Theatre Royal, English Opera House, on 9 August 1820. Planché acknowledged it as 'a free translation' of a French drama, which he transposed to Scotland. The ultimate source is Polidori's* The Vampyre *(see pp. 161ff.), which was translated into French and German. The extracts illustrate two characteristic features of Gothic melodrama: spectacle and comic characters, which are necessary to both sustain and contrast with the sublimity of the work. I have included a description of the costumes from a later performance, as Planché was famous for his designs.*

Dramatis Personæ

IN THE VISION.

Unda, *Spirit of the Flood*
Ariel, *Spirit of the Air*
A Vampire
Lady Margaret

IN THE MELO-DRAME.

Ruthven, *Earl of Marsden*
Ronald, *Baron of the Isles*
Robert, *an English Attendant on the Baron*
M'Swill, *the Baron's Henchman*
Andrew, *Steward to Ruthven*
Father Francis
Lady Margaret, *Daughter to Ronald*
Effie, *Daughter to Andrew*
Bridget, *Lord Ronald's Housekeeper*
Retainers, Peasants, Bargemen, &c. &c.

[Unda is costumed in 'White satin dress, trimmed with shells, &c., blue satin robe, hair in long ringlets, tiara, wand'; Ariel in 'White muslin dress, with spangles, sky-blue robe, wings, tiara, silver wand'; the Vampire (Ruthven) in 'Silver breast-plate, studded with steel buttons, plaid kelt, cloak, flesh arms and leggings, sandals, gray cloak, to form the attitude as he ascends from the tomb'; Lady Margaret in 'White satin dress, trimmed with

[*] J. R. Planché, *The Vampire; or, The Bride of the Isles* (London: John Lowndes, 1820), pp. 4–12.

plaid and silver, plaid silk sash, Scotch hat and feather'; Bridget in 'Black velvet body and tabs, plaid petticoat, trimmed with black, blue ribbon in the hair, plaid sash'; Robert in 'Gray shirt, trimmed with yellow binding, drab pantaloons, gray hat, with black feathers, sword and belt, russet boots and collar'; and M'Swill in 'Red plaid jacket, waistcoat, and kelt, philibeg, flesh leggings, plaid stockings, black shoes and buckles, Scotch cap'.]

Introductory Vision

The Curtain rises to slow Music, and discovers the Interior of the Basaltic Caverns of Staffa; at the extremity of which is a Chasm opening to the Air. The Moonlight streams through it, and partially reveals a number of rude Sepulchres. On one of these, LADY MARGARET *is seen, stretched in a heavy Slumber. The Spirit of the Flood rises to the Symphony of the following*

INCANTATION.

SOLO. – UNDA.

SPIRIT! Spirit of the Air!
Hear and heed my spell of power;
On the night breeze swift repair
Hither from thy starry bower.

CHORUS.

Appear! Appear!

UNDA.

By the sun that hath set,
In the waves I love;
By the spheres that have met
In the heavens above.
By the latest dews
That fall to earth;
On the Eve that renews
The fair moon's birth.

CHORUS.

Appear! Appear!

QUARTETTO.

By the charm of might and the word of fear,
Which must never be breath'd to mortal ear.
Spirit! Spirit of the air,
Hither at my call repair!

(Music. – The Spirit of the Air descends through the Chasm, on a Silvery Cloud, which she leaves and advances.)

Ariel. Why, how now, sister! wherefore am I summoned?
    What in the deep and fearful caves of Staffa
    Demands our presence or protection? – Speak!
Unda. Spirit of the Air! thy sister Unda claims
    Thy powerful aid; – not idly from thy blue
    And star-illumin'd mansion art thou call'd
    To Fingal's rocky sepulchre – Look here.

                                   [*Pointing to Lady Margaret.*

Ariel. A maiden, and asleep!
Unda. Attend thee, Ariel.
    Her name is Margaret, the only daughter
    Of Ronald, the brave Baron of the Isles.
    A richer, lovelier, more virtuous lady
    This land of Flood and Mountains never boasted.
    To-morrow Marsden's Earl will claim her hand,
    Renown'd through Europe for his large possessions,
    His clerkly knowledge, and his deeds of arms.
Ariel. How came she in this den of death and horror?
Unda. Chasing the red-deer with her father Ronald,
    A storm arose, and parted from her train,
    She sought a shelter here – calmly she sleeps,
    Nor dreams to-morrow's hymeneal rites,
    Will give her beauties to a Vampire's arms.
Ariel. A Vampire, say'st thou! – Is then Marsden's Earl –
Unda. Thou knowest, Ariel, that wicked souls
    Are, for wise purposes, permitted oft
    To enter the dead forms of other men;
    Assume their speech, their habits, and their knowledge,
    And thus roam o'er the earth. But subject still,
    At stated periods, to a dreadful tribute.
Ariel. Aye, they must wed some fair and virtuous maiden,
    Whom they do after kill, and from her veins
    Drain eagerly the purple stream of life;
    Which horrid draught alone hath pow'r to save them
    From swift extermination.
Unda. Yes; that state
    Of nothingness – total annihilation!
    The most tremendous punishment of heaven.
    Their torture then being without resource,
    They do enjoy all power in the present.
    Death binds them not – from form to form they fleet,

And though the cheek be pale, and glaz'd the eye,
Such is their wond'rous art, the hapless victim
Blindly adores, and drops into their grasp,
Like birds when gaz'd on by the basilisk.
Ariel. Say on. –
Unda. Beneath this stone the relics lie
Of Cromal, called the bloody. Staffa still
The reign of fear remembered. For his crimes,
His spirit roams, a Vampire, in the form
Of Marsden's Earl; – to count his victims o'er,
Would be an endless task – suffice to say
His race of terror will to-morrow end,
Unless he wins some virgin for his prey,
Ere sets the full-orb'd moon.
Ariel. And with this view
He weds the Lady Margaret.
Unda. Aye, Ariel;
Unless our blended art can save the maid.
Ariel. What can be done? – our power is limited.
What can be done, my sister?
Unda. We must warn
The maiden of her fate. Lend me thine aid,
To raise a vision of her sleeping sight.
Ariel. Let us about it.

(They perform Magical Ceremonies to the Symphony of the following Charm.)

CHARM. – ARIEL and UNDA.

Phantom, from thy tomb so drear,
    At our bidding swift arise;
Let thy Vampire-corpse appear,
    To this sleeping maiden's eyes.
Come away! come away!
        That the form she may know
        That would work her woe;
And shun thee, till the setting ray
Of the morn shall bid thy pow'r decay;
        Phantom, from thy tomb so drear,
        At our bidding rise! – appear!

[*Thunder.*

CHORUS – ARIEL and UNDA.

Appear! Appear! Appear!

(A Vampire succeeds from the Tomb of Cromal, and springs towards Margaret.)
Vam. Margaret!
Ariel. Foul spirit, retire!
Vam. She is mine!
Ariel. The hour is not yet come.
Unda. Down, thou foul spirit; – extermination waits thee:
    Down, I say.

(Music. – The Vampire sinks again, shuddering, and the Scene closes.)

Act the First.
Scene I.

A Hall in the Castle of Lord Ronald. M'Swill, and a group of Retainers are seen seated round a Table in hunting dresses, drinking. The Sun is seen just rising behind the hills through the large Gothic window at the back of the scene.

CHORUS.

Tune – '*Johnny Cope.*'

Come fill, let the parting glass go round
With a stirrup cup, be our revelry crown'd,
See the sun that set to our bugles sound
    Is changing the night into morning.

As darkness shrinks from his rising ray,
So sorrow and care will we keep at bay,
By the bowl at night and the 'Hark away,'
    That awakes us, brave boys, in the morning.

Enter BRIDGET *and* ROBERT. – *M'Swill gets under the Table.*

Brid. Very pretty doings upon my word! Here's our poor mistress, the Lady
    Margaret, been lost for nearly the whole night in the forest; and no
    sooner is she by good fortune found again and trying to get a little rest in
    her own apartments, but you make all this noise, as if on purpose to
    disturb her.
Rob. Nay, Mrs. Bridget, don't be angry with them. They've been celebrat-
    ing my lady's return.
Brid. Return! Don't tell me. – They never want an excuse to get drunk –
    out of the castle directly – don't stand ducking and scraping there – go
    along directly, when I tell you. [*Exeunt Retainers.*] Where is that rascal,
    M'Swill? he's at the bottom of all this; – but if I – [*M'Swill attempts to steal
    off.*] Oh! oh! there you are, sir – come here, sir. [*Seizes him by the ear, and
    brings him forward.*] Down on your knees directly, and ask my pardon.

M'Swill. I do, Mrs. Bridget.

Brid. How came you under the table?

M'Swill. What a question, when a man has been drinking all night.

Brid. Will you never leave off taking your drops?

M'Swill. I don't take *drops*, Mrs. Bridget.

Brid. Here has poor Robert been running through the forest all night, seeking my lady, and peeking in all the holes of the grotto, whilst you –

M'Swill. The grotto, Mrs. Bridget! Good guide us! Why, you didn't go into the grotto, did you?

Brid. And why not, booby?

M'Swill. O, dear! O, dear! the ignorance of some people – but you're an Englishman, and that accounts for it. Why, didn't you know that the grotto was haunted.

Rob. Ha! ha! ha!

M'Swill. Aye! aye! laugh away, do – but I can tell you it's full of kelpies and evil spirits of all sorts; only ask Mrs. Bridget.

Brid. It's very true, Robert, and you shou'dn't laugh, for they always owe a grudge to any body that jests about them.

M'Swill. Did you never hear the story of Lady Blanch?

Brid. Hush! don't talk so loud.

M'Swill. You know it, Mrs. Bridget.

Brid. No! but Lord Ronald is very angry with every body who circulates stories of that description – so speak lower, if you are going to tell it.

M'Swill. Well, then – once upon a time –

Rob. Ha! ha! ha! – Mother Bunch's fairy tales.

M'Swill. Well, isn't that the proper way to begin a story?

Brid. Go on.

M'Swill. Once upon a time –

Rob. You've said that once twice.

M'Swill. Will you be quiet with your fun. I won't tell it at all.

Rob. Well, well, then – Once upon a time – what happened?

M'Swill. Once on a time, there lived a lady named Blanch, in this very castle, and she was betrothed to a rich Scotch nobleman; all the preparations for the wedding were finished, when, on the evening before it was to take place, the lovers strolled into the forest –

Brid. Alone?

M'Swill. No; together to be sure.

Brid. Well, sot, I mean that; and I think it was highly improper.

M'Swill. Well, they were seen to enter the grotto, and –

Rob. And what?

M'Swill. They never came out again.

Rob. Bravo! – an excellent story.

M'Swill. But that isn't all. – The next morning the body of the lady was found covered with blood, and the marks of human teeth on her throat, but no trace of the nobleman could be discovered, and from that time to this he has never been heard of; and they do say, (I hope nobody hears us) they do say that the nobleman was a *Vampire*, for a friar afterwards confessed on his death bed, that he had privately married them in the morning by the nobleman's request, and that he fully believed it some fiend incarnate, for he could not say the responses without stuttering.

Rob. Better and better! and how came you by this precious legend?

M'Swill. The great uncle of my grandfather had it from the great grand-father of the steward's cousin, by the mother's side, who lived with a branch of the family when the accident happened; and moreover, I've heard my great uncle say, that these horrible spirits, call'd Vampires, kill and suck the blood of beautiful young maidens, whom they are obliged to marry before they can destroy. – And they do say that such is the condition of their existence, that if, at stated periods, they should fail to obtain a virgin bride, whose life blood may sustain them, they would instantly perish. Oh, the beautiful young maidens! –

Brid. Oh beautiful young maidens – merciful powers! what an escape I've had. – I was in the cavern myself one day.

M'Swill. Lord, Mrs. Bridget, I'm sure there's no occasion for you to be frightened.

Brid. Why, you saucy sot, I've a great mind to –

A BELL RINGS.

I declare there's my lady's bell – no occasion, indeed – an impudent fellow; but men, now-a-days, have no more manners than hogs. (*Bell rings.*)

[*Exit Mrs. Bridget.*

M'Swill. There's a she devil for you. I don't think there's such another vixen in all Scotland. She's little and hot, like a pepper-corn. What a lug she gave me by the ear.

Rob. Nay, nay, you musn't mind that; all old ladies have their odd ways.

M'Swill. Curse such odd ways as that, tho'; I shall feel the pinch for a month. – Pray, Mr. Robert, as you've been in London with Lord Ronald, do you know who this Earl is that the Lady Margaret is to be married to?

Rob. I only know that he is the Earl of Marsden, and master of the castle on the coast facing this island.

M'Swill. What? where the pretty Effie, your intended lives?

Rob. Exactly.

M'Swill. He'll arrive just in time, then, to be present at the wedding.

Rob. I hope so.

M'Swill. That will be glorious! two weddings in one day – such dancing, such eating, such drinking –

Brid. M'Swill!

M'Swill. Ugh, choak you, you old warlock! what's in the wind now, I wonder?

Brid. M'Swill, I say!

M'Swill. Coming, Mrs. Bridget.   [*Exit M'Swill*.

Rob. Yes, as soon as the Earl arrives, I shall certainly take an opportunity to request him to honour the wedding with his presence – how pleas'd my dear Effie would be. Charming girl, I shall never forget the hour when first we met. . . .

— 5 —

𝕻oetry

WILLIAM WORDSWORTH in his Preface to *Lyrical Ballads* (1800), which was a kind of manifesto for Romantic poetry, complained that

> The invaluable works of our elder writers, I had almost said the works of Shakespeare and Milton, are driven into neglect by frantic novels, sickly and stupid German Tragedies, and deluges of idle and extravagant stories in verse. – When I think upon this degrading thirst after outrageous stimulation, I am almost ashamed to have spoken of the feeble endeavour made in these volumes to counteract it.

Wordsworth's desire for plain language and his contempt for the Gothic, however, were contradicted by his colleague Coleridge's focus upon the supernatural in poems such as 'Rime of the Ancient Mariner', 'Christabel' and 'Kubla Khan; or, A Vision in a Dream'. The major Romantic poets (even Wordsworth, in *The Borderers*) owed something to Ann Radcliffe, without whom we probably would not have Keats's 'Eve of St Agnes' and 'Isabella' or Byron's *Manfred* and other poems in which he creates the brooding 'Byronic hero' – or indeed Edgar Allan Poe's 'The Raven'.

Such works are important specimens of the Gothic poetic tradition, but are too well known to need inclusion here. I have selected two almost unknown early works by the major poets: Coleridge's 'The Mad Monk', which, when it was first published was described (presumably by an editor) as being written 'in Mrs. Ratcliffe's manner'; and Shelley's 'Ballad', which was written a year or two before his Gothic novel *St Irvyne* (1808–9). According to his boyhood friend Medwin,

> Such was the sort of poetry Shelley wrote at this period – and it is valuable, inasmuch as it served to shew the disposition and bent of his mind in 1808 and 1809, which ran on bandits, castles, ruined towers, wild mountains, storms and apparitions – the Terrific, which according to Burke is the great machinery of the Sublime.

Two lines from Charlotte Smith's *The Emigrants* (a political poem about the persecution following the French Revolution that forced the French clergy to flee to England) – 'by the blunted light/That the dim moon thro' painted casements lends' – were quoted by Ann Radcliffe in *The Mysteries of Udolpho*, and are believed to have suggested to Keats the 'Charm'd magic casements, opening on the foam/Of perilous seas, in faery lands forlorn' which are used to symbolize the romantic imagination in his 'Ode to a Nightingale'. Keats pretended that any similarity of his work to Gothic literature was superficial: 'In my next Packet as this is one by the way, I shall send you the Pot of Basil, St Agnes eve, and if I should have finished it a little thing call'd the "eve of St Mark" you see what fine mother Radcliff names I have' (letter, 14 February 1819). But Coleridge, Byron and Shelley literally plagiarized passages from Radcliffe's *Mysteries of Udolpho*.

What we today refer to as the Romantics were known in their own time as the Lake School (referring to England's Lake District where Wordsworth lived), though we have forgotten their minor members such as Lloyd, Lovell, and Allan Cunningham, and teachers tend to downplay how very many of their poems are concerned with ghosts, witches and fairies. For David Macbeth Moir, delivering lectures at the Edinburgh Philosophical Association in 1850/51, there were two main streams of poetry: the 'Darwinian School' of artificial verse by Erasmus Darwin, Anna Seward, Hayley and the insipid Della Cruscans – versus the 'Lewis School', i.e. the Romantics, 'of which Matthew Gregory Lewis ought to be set down as the leader, and John Leyden, Walter Scott, Coleridge, Southey, James Hogg, Mrs Radcliffe, Anna Maria Porter, and Anne Bannerman, as the chief disciples'. Perhaps it is just as well that today we have largely forgotten once-popular works such as James Montgomery's 'The Vigil of St. Mark' (1806) and Anne Bannerman's 'The Perjured Nun' (1802), but the poetry in this section, however 'Gothic' and 'minor', would have been seen as characteristic of the Romantic School by its contemporary readers.

The Minstrel; or, The Progress of Genius (1771)*

JAMES BEATTIE (1735–1803)

XIX.

Lo! where the stripling, wrapt in wonder, roves
Beneath the precipice o'erhung with pine;
And sees, on high, amidst th' encircling groves,
From cliff to cliff the foaming torrents shine:
While waters, woods, and winds, in concert join,

---

* James Beattie, *The Minstrel; or, The Progress of Genius,* 5th edn (London: Edward and Charles Dilly; Edinburgh: William Creech, 1775), pp. 10–12, 16–17.

And Echo swells the chorus to the skies.
Would Edwin this majestic scene resign
For aught the huntsman's puny craft supplies?
Ah! no: he better knows great Nature's charms to prize.

XX.

And oft he traced the uplands, to survey,
When o'er the sky advanced the kindling dawn,
The crimson cloud, blue main, and mountain grey,
And lake, dim-gleaming on the smoky lawn;
Far to the west the long long vale withdrawn,
Where twilight loves to linger for a while;
And now he faintly kens the bounding fawn,
And villager abroad at early toil. –
But, lo! the sun appears! and heaven, earth, ocean, smile.

XXI.

And oft the craggy cliff he loved to climb,
When all in mist the world below was lost.
What dreadful pleasure! there to stand sublime,
Like shipwreck'd mariner on desert coast,
And view th' enormous waste of vapour, tost
In billows, lengthening to th' horizon round,
Now scoop'd in gulfs, with mountains now emboss'd!
And hear the voice of mirth and song rebound,
Flocks, herds, and waterfalls, along the hoar profound!

XXII.

In truth he was a strange and wayward wight,
Fond of each gentle, and each dreadful scene.
In darkness, and in storm, he found delight:
Nor less, than when on ocean-wave serene
The southern sun diffused his dazzling shene.
E'en sad vicissitude amused his soul:
And if a sigh would sometimes intervene,
And down his cheek a tear of pity roll,
A sign, a tear, so sweet, he wish'd not to control.

. . .

XXX.

See, in the rear of the warm sunny shower,
The visionary boy from shelter fly!
For now the storm of summer-rain is o'er,

And cool, and fresh, and fragrant, is the sky.
And, lo! in the dark east, expanded high,
The rainbow brightens to the setting sun!
Fond fool, that deem'st the streaming glory nigh,
How vain the chace thine ardour has begun!
'Tis fled afar, ere half thy purposed race be run.

XXXI.

Yet couldst thou learn, that thus it fares with age,
When pleasure, wealth, or power, the bosom warm,
This baffled hope might tame thy manhood's rage,
And Disappointment of her sting disarm. –
But why should foresight thy fond heart alarm?
Perish the lore that deadens young desire!
Pursue, poor imp, th' imaginary charm,
Indulge gay Hope, and Fancy's pleasing fire:
Fancy and Hope too soon shall of themselves expire.

XXXII.

When the long-sounding curfew from afar
Loaded with loud lament the lonely gale,
Young Edwin, lighted by the evening star,
Lingering and listening, wander'd down the vale.
There would he dream of graves, and corses pale;
And ghosts, that to the charnel-dungeon throng,
And drag a length of clanking chain, and wail,
Till silenced by the owl's terrific song,
Or blast that shrieks by fits the shuddering isles along.

XXXIII.

Or, when the setting moon, in crimson dyed,
Hung o'er the dark and melancholy deep,
To haunted stream, remote from man, he hied,
Where Fays of yore their revels wont to keep;
And there let Fancy roam at large, till sleep
A vision brought to his intranced sight.
And first, a wildly-murmuring wind 'gan creep
Shrill to his ringing ear; then tapers bright,
With instantaneous gleam, illumed the vault of Night.

'Written on the Sea Shore' (1784)*

CHARLOTTE SMITH (1749–1806)

Sonnet xii. Written on the Sea Shore. – October, 1784

On some rude fragment of the rocky shore
    Where on the fractur'd cliff, the billows break,
    Musing, my solitary seat I take,
And listen to the deep and solemn roar.

O'er the dark waves the winds tempestuous howl;
    The screaming sea-bird quits the troubled sea:
    But the wild gloomy scene has charms for me,
And suits the mournful temper of my soul.

Already shipwreck'd by the storms of Fate,
    Like the poor mariner methinks I stand,
    Cast on a rock; who sees the distant land
From whence no succour comes – or comes too late.
Faint and more faint are heard his feeble cries,
'Till in the rising tide, the exhausted sufferer dies.

The Emigrants (1793)†

CHARLOTTE SMITH (1749–1806)

    Oft have I heard the melancholy tale,
Which, all their native gaiety forgot,
These Exiles tell – How Hope impell'd them on,
Reckless of tempest, hunger, or the sword,
Till order'd to retreat, they knew not why,
From all their flattering prospects, they became
The prey of dark suspicion and regret:
Then, in despondence, sunk the unnerv'd arm
Of gallant Loyalty – At every turn
Shame and disgrace appear'd, and seem'd to mock
Their scatter'd squadrons; which the warlike youth,

* Charlotte Smith, *Elegiac Sonnets*, 6th edn (London: T. Cadell, 1792).
† Charlotte Smith, *The Emigrants, a Poem* (London: T. Cadell, 1793), pp. 54–9.

Unable to endure, often implor'd,
As the last act of friendship, from the hand
Of some brave comrade, to receive the blow
That freed the indignant spirit from its pain.
To a wild mountain, whose bare summit hides
Its broken eminence in clouds; whose steeps
Are dark with woods; where the receding rocks
Are worn by torrents of dissolving snow,
A wretched Woman, pale and breathless, flies!
And, gazing round her, listens to the sound
Of hostile footsteps – No! it dies away:
No noise remains, but of the cataract,
Or surly breeze of night, that mutters low
Among the thickets, where she trembling seeks
A temporary shelter – clasping close
To her hard-heaving heart her sleeping child,
All she could rescue of the innocent groupe [*sic*]
That yesterday surrounded her – Escap'd
Almost by miracle! Fear, frantic Fear,
Wing'd her weak feet: yet, half repentant now
Her headlong haste, she wishes she had staid
To die with those affrighted Fancy paints
The lawless soldier's victims – Hark! again
The driving tempest bears the cry of Death,
And, with deep sudden thunder, the dread sound
Of cannon vibrates on the tremulous earth;
While, bursting in the air, the murderous bomb
Glares o'er her mansion. Where the splinters fall,
Like scatter'd comets, its destructive path
Is mark'd by wreaths of flame! – Then, overwhelm'd
Beneath accumulated horror, sinks
The desolate mourner; yet, in Death itself,
True to maternal tenderness, she tries
To save the unconscious infant from the storm
In which she perishes; and to protect
This last dear object of her ruin'd hopes
From prowling monsters, that from other hills,
More inaccessible, and wilder wastes,
Lur'd by the scent of slaughter, follow fierce
Contending hosts, and to polluted fields
Add dire increase of horrors – But alas!
The Mother and the Infant perish both! –
      The feudal Chief, whose Gothic battlements
Frown on the plain beneath, returning home

From distant lands, alone and in disguise,
Gains at the fall of night his Castle walls,
But, at the vacant gate, no Porter sits
To wait his Lord's admittance! – In the courts
All is drear silence! – Guessing but too well
The fatal truth, he shudders as he goes
Thro' the mute hall; where, by the blunted light
That the dim moon thro' painted casements lends,
He sees that devastation has been there:
Then, while each hideous image to his mind
Rises terrific, o'er a bleeding corse
Stumbling he falls; another interrupts
His staggering feet – all, all who us'd to rush
With joy to meet him – all his family
Lie murder'd in his way! – And the day dawns
On a wild raving Maniac, whom a fate
So sudden and calamitous has robb'd
Of reason; and who round his vacant walls
Screams unregarded, and reproaches Heaven! –
Such are thy dreadful trophies, savage War!
And evils such as these, or yet more dire,
Which the pain'd mind recoils from, all are thine –
The purple Pestilence, that to the grave
Sends whom the sword has spar'd, is thine; and thine
The Widow's anguish and the Orphan's tears! –
Woes such as these does Man inflict on Man;
And by the closet murderers, whom we style
Wise Politicians, are the schemes prepar'd,
Which, to keep Europe's wavering balance even,
Depopulate her kingdoms, and consign
To tears and anguish half a bleeding world! –

'Invocation to Horror' (1787)⋆

HANNAH COWLEY ('ANNA MATILDA') (1743–1809)

FAR be remov'd each painted scene!
What is to *me* the sapphire sky?
What is to *me* the earth's soft dye?
    Or fragrant vales which sink between
Those velvet hills? yes, there I see –

⋆ *The British Album*, 4th edn, 2 vols (London: John Bell, 1792), vol. 1, pp. 39–42.

(Why do those beauties burst on me?)
Pearl-dropping groves bow to the sun;
Seizing his beams, bright rivers run
    That dart redoubled day:
Hope ye vain scenes, to catch the mind
To torpid sorrow all resign'd,
    Or bid my heart be gay?
False are those hopes! – I turn – I fly,
Where no enchantment meets the eye,
    Or soft ideas stray.

HORROR! I call thee from the *mould'ring tower*,
The *murky church-yard*, and *forsaken bower*,
    Where 'midst unwholesome damps
    The vap'ry gleamy lamps
Of *ignes fatui*, shew the thick-wove night,
    Where morbid MELANCHOLY sits,
    And weeps, and sings, and raves by fits,
And to her bosom strains the fancied sprite.

    Or, if amidst the arctic gloom
    Thou toilest at thy sable loom,
Forming the hideous phantoms of Despair –
    Instant thy grisly labours leave,
    With raven wing the concave cleave,
Where floats, self-borne, the dense nocturnal air.

    Oh! bear me to th'impending cliff,
    Under whose brow the dashing skiff
Behold *Thee* seated on thy rocky throne;
    There, 'midst the shrieking wild wind's roar,
    Thy influence, HORROR, I'll adore,
And at thy magic touch congeal to stone.

    Oh! hide the Moon's obtrusive orb,
    The gleams of ev'ry star absorb,
And let CREATION be a moment thine!
    Bid billows dash; let whirlwinds roar,
    And the stern, rocky-pointed shore,
The stranded bark, back to the waves resign!
    Then, whilst from yonder turbid cloud,
    Thou roll'st thy thunders long, and loud,
And light'nings flash upon the deep below,
    Let the *expiring Seaman's* cry,

The *Pilot*'s agonizing sigh
Mingle, and in the dreadful chorus flow!

HORROR! far back thou dat'st thy reign;
Ere KINGS th' *historic page* could stain
With records black, or deeds of lawless power:
Ere empires *Alexanders* curst,
Or Faction, madd'ning *Cæsars* nurst,
The frighted World receiv'd thy awful dower!

Whose pen JEHOVAH's self inspir'd;
He, who in eloquence attir'd,
Led *Israel's squadrons* o'er the earth,
Grandly terrific, paints thy birth.
Th' ALMIGHTY, 'midst his fulgent seat on high,
Where glowing *Seraphs* round his footstool fly,
Beheld the wanton cities of the plain,
With acts of deadly name his laws disdain;
He gave th' irrevocable sign,
Which mark'd to man the hate divine;
And sudden from the starting sky
The Angels of his wrath bid fly!
Then, HORROR! thou presided'st o'er the whole,
And fill'd, and rapt, each self-accusing soul!
Thou did'st ascend to guide the burning shower –
On THEE th' Omnipotent bestow'd the hour!

'Twas thine to scourge the sinful land,
'Twas thine to toss the fiery brand;
Beneath thy glance the temples fell,
And mountains crumbled at thy yell.
ONCE MORE thou'lt triumph in fiery storm;
ONCE MORE the Earth behold thy direful form;
Then shalt thou seek, as holy prophets tell,
Thy *native throne*, amidst th' *eternal shades of* HELL!

'Superstition. An Ode' (1790)*

ANN RADCLIFFE (1764–1823)

High mid Alverna's awful steeps,
　　Eternal shades, and glooms, and silence dwell,
Save, when the lonely gale resounding sweeps,
　　Sad, solemn strains are faintly heard to swell:

Enthron'd amid the wild impending rocks,
　　Involv'd in clouds, and brooding future woe,
The demon Superstition Nature shocks,
　　And waves her Sceptre o'er the world below.

Around her throne, amid the mingling glooms,
　　Wild – hideous forms are slowly seen to glide;
She bids them fly to shade earth's brightest blooms,
　　And spread the blast of Desolation wide.

See! in the darkened air their fiery course!
　　The sweeping ruin settles o'er the land,
Terror leads on their steps with madd'ning force,
　　And Death and Vengeance close the ghastly band!

　　　　Mark the purple streams that flow!
　　　　Mark the deep empassioned woe!
　　　　Frantic Fury's dying groan!
　　　　Virtue's sigh, and Sorrow's moan!

Wide – wide the phantoms swell the loaded air
With shrieks of anguish – madness and despair!
　　Cease your ruin! spectres dire!
　　　Cease your wild terrific sway!
　　Turn your steps – and check your ire,
　　　Yield to peace and mourning day!

★ Ann Radcliffe, *A Sicilian Romance*, 2 vols (London: T. Hookham, 1790), vol. 2, pp. 30–1.

'To the Visions of Fancy' (1791)*

ANN RADCLIFFE (1764–1823)

Dear, wild illusions of creative mind!
    Whose varying hues arise to Fancy's art,
And by her magic force are swift combin'd
    In forms that please, and scenes that touch the heart:
Oh! whether at her voice ye soft assume
    The pensive grace of sorrow drooping low;
Or rise sublime on terror's lofty plume,
    And shake the soul with wildly thrilling woe;
Or, sweetly bright, your gayer tints ye spread,
    Bid scenes of pleasure steal upon my view,
Love wave his purple pinions o'er my head,
    And wake the tender thought to passion true;
O! still – ye shadowy forms! attend my lonely hours,
Still chase my real cares with your illusive powers!

'Night' (1791)†

ANN RADCLIFFE (1764–1823)

Now Ev'ning fades! her pensive step retires,
    And Night leads on the dews, and shadowy hours:
Her awful pomp of planetary fires,
    And all her train of visionary pow'rs.

These paint with fleeting shapes the dream of sleep,
    These swell the waking soul with pleasing dread;
These through the glooms in forms terrific sweep,
    And rouse the thrilling horrors of the dead!

Queen of the solemn thought – mysterious Night!
    Whose step is darkness, and whose voice is fear!
Thy shades I welcome with severe delight,
    And hail thy hollow gales, that sigh so drear!

---

* Ann Radcliffe, *The Romance of the Forest*, 3 vols (London: T. Hookham and J. Carpenter, 1791), vol. 1, pp. 86–7.
† *Ibid.*, vol. 1, pp. 207–9.

When, wrapt in clouds, and riding in the blast,
    Thou roll'st the storm along the sounding shore,
I love to watch the whelming billows, cast
    On rocks below, and listen to the roar.

Thy milder terrors, Night, I frequent woo,
    Thy silent lightnings, and thy meteor's glare,
Thy northern fires, bright with ensanguine hue,
    That light in heaven's high vault the fervid air.

But chief I love thee, when thy lucid car
    Sheds through the fleecy clouds a trembling gleam,
And shews the misty mountain from afar,
    The nearer forest, and the valley's stream:

And nameless objects in the vale below,
    That floating dimly to the musing eye,
Assume, at Fancy's touch, fantastic shew,
    And raise her sweet romantic visions high.

Then let me stand amidst thy glooms profound
    On some wild woody steep, and hear the breeze
That swells in mournful melody around,
    And faintly dies upon the distant trees.

What melancholy charm steals o'er the mind!
    What hallow'd tears the rising rapture greet!
While many a viewless spirit in the wind
    Sighs to the lonely hour in accents sweet!

Ah! who the dear illusions pleas'd would yield,
    Which Fancy wakes from silence and from shades,
For all the sober forms of Truth reveal'd,
    For all the scenes that Day's bright eye pervades!

'To the River Dove' (*c.* 1798/1800)★

ANN RADCLIFFE (1764–1823)

Oh! stream beloved by those,
With Fancy who repose,
And court her dreams 'mid scenes sublimely wild,
Lulled by the summer-breeze,
Among the drowsy trees
Of thy high steeps, and by thy murmurs mild,

My lonely footsteps guide,
Where thy blue waters glide,
Fringed with the Alpine shrub and willow light;
'Mid rocks and mountains rude,
Here hung with shaggy wood,
And there upreared in points of frantic height.

Beneath their awful gloom,
Oh! blue-eyed Nymph, resume
The mystic spell, that wakes the poet's soul!
While all thy caves around
In lonely murmur sound,
And feeble thunders o'er these summits roll.

O shift the wizard scene
To banks of pastoral green
When mellow sun-set lights up all thy vales;
And shows each turf-born flower,
That, sparkling from the shower,
Its recent fragrance on the air exhales.

When Evening's distant hues
Their silent grace diffuse
In sleepy azure o'er the mountain's head;
Or dawn in purple faint,
As nearer cliffs they paint,
Then lead me 'mid thy slopes and woodland shade.

★ Ann Radcliffe, *Posthumous Works*, in *Gaston de Blondeville* (London: Henry Colburn, 1826), vol. 4, pp. 236–8.

Nor would I wander far,
When Twilight lends her star,
And o'er thy scenes her doubtful shades repose;
Nor when the Moon's first light
Steals on each bowery height,
Like the winged music o'er the folded rose.

Then, on thy winding shore,
The fays and elves, once more,
Trip in gay ringlets to the reed's light note;
Some launch the acorn's *ring*,
Their sail – Papilio's wing,
Thus shipped, in chace of moon-beams, gay they float.

But, at the midnight hour,
I woo thy thrilling power,
While silent moves the glow-worm's light along,
And o'er the dim hill-tops
The gloomy red moon drops,
And in the grave of darkness leaves thee long.

Even then thy waves I hear,
And own a nameless fear,
As, 'mid the stillness, the hight winds do swell,
Or (faint from distance) hark
To the lone watch-dog's bark!
Answering a melancholy far sheep bell.

O! Nymph fain would I trace
Thy sweet awakening grace,
When summer dawn first breaks upon thy stream;
And see thee braid thy hair;
And keep thee ever there,
Like thought recovered from an antique dream!

'Ode to Superstition' (1793)*

NATHAN DRAKE (1766–1836)

The prolific essayist and critic Nathan Drake called Ann Radcliffe 'the Shakespeare of Romance Writers', for he felt that she ably carried on the native British 'Celtic/Gothic' tradition since the time of 'Ossian' and Shakespeare. Her novels inspired him to write several 'Gothic tales', such as 'The Abbey of Clunedale', 'Montmorenci', 'Henry FitzOwen', 'Sir Egbert' and 'The Spectre'. His 'Ode to Superstition', first published in July 1793 and subsequently revised, was designed to contain examples of 'the two species of Gothic superstition, the terrible and the sportive'. His collected literary essays contain detailed criticism of the Gothic writings by Walpole, John Aikin and Mrs Barbauld, Reeve, Charlotte Smith, Radcliffe, Lewis, Beckford, and others now forgotten.

Saw ye that dreadful shape? heard ye the scream
    That shook my trembling soul?
E'en now, e'en now, where yon red lightnings gleam
    Wan forms of terror scowl –
I know thee, Superstition! fiend, whose breath
    Poisons the passing hours,
Pales the young cheek, and o'er the bed of death
    The gloom of horror pours!
Of ghastly Fear, and darkest Midnight born,
    Far in a blasted dale,
Mid Lapland's woods, and noisome wastes forlorn,
    Where lurid hags the moon's pale orbit hail:
There, in some vast, some wild and cavern'd cell,
    Where flits the dim blue flame,
They drink warm blood, and act the deed of hell,
    The 'deed without a name.'
    With hollow shriek and boding cry,
    Round the wither'd witches hie,
    On their uncouth features dire,
    Gleams the pale and livid fire;
    The charm begins, and now arise
    Shadows foul, and piercing cries,
    Storm and tempest loud assail,
    Beating wind and rattling hail;

---

* Nathan Drake, *Literary Hours: or Sketches Critical, Narrative, and Poetical*, 3 vols, 3rd edn (London: T. Cadell and W. Davies, 1804), vol. 1, pp. 150–4 (originally published in the *British Critic*, 1793).

Thus, within th' infernal wood,
Dance they round the bubbling blood,
Till sudden from the wond'ring eye,
Upborne on harpy wing they fly,
Where, on the rude inhospitable wild,
   Fir'd by the lightning's arrowy stroke,
Oft at the balmy close of evening mild,
   They're seen to hurry round the blasted oak:
Then rise strange spectres to the pilgrim's view,
     With horrid lifeless stare,
And gliding float upon the noxious dew,
     And howling rend the air.
Oft near yon leaf-clad solitary fane,
     While morn yet clasps the night,
Some ghost is heard to sound his clanking chain,
Beheld mid moon-beam pale and dead to sight;
Nor less unfrequent the lone trav'ller hears
     The sullen-sounding bell,
And the dim-lighted tow'r awakes to fears
Of haunted mansion, brake, or darkling dell,
     Haste thee, Superstition! fly,
     Perish this thy sorcery!
Why in these gorgon terrors clad,
But to affright, afflict the bad,
'Tis thee, O Goddess! thee I hail,
Of Hesper born, and Cynthia pale,
That wont the same rude name to bear,
Yet gentle all, and void of fear;
O, come, in Fancy's garb array'd,
In all her lovely forms display'd,
And o'er the poet's melting soul,
Bid the warm tide of rapture roll,
To dying music, warbling gales,
'Mid moon-light scenes, and woody vales,
Where Elves, and Fays, and Sprites disport,
And nightly keep their festive court;
There, 'mid the pearly flood of light,
In tincts cerulean richly dight,
Light-sporting o'er the trembling green,
Glance they quick thro' the magic scene,
And from the sparkling moss receive,
Shed by the fragrant hand of Eve,
The silver dew, of matchless pow'r,
To guard from harm, at midnight hour,

The lonely wight, who lost, from far,
Views not one friendly guiding star,
Or one kind lowly cottage door,
To point his track across the moor;
Whilst the storm howling, prompts his mind
Dark Demons ride the northern wind,
And, plaining, mourn their cruel doom,
On tempest hurl'd, and wint'ry gloom:
Oft too, along the vales at eve,
Shall Sprites the songs of gladness weave,
With many a sweet and varied flight,
Soft warbling hymn the setting light,
Heard far th' echoing hills among,
Whilst chanting wild their heav'nly song,
Till lost in ether dies away,
The last, long, faint and murm'ring lay;
These on the lonely Bard attend,
With him the mountain's side ascend,
Or in the valley's lowly plain,
To Rapture breathe the melting strain;
These lift his soul beyond her clime,
To daring flights of thought sublime,
Where, warm'd by Fancy's brightest fire,
He boldly sweeps the sounding lyre:
Come then, with wild flow'rs, come array'd,
O Superstition, magic maid!
And welcome then, suggesting pow'r!
At evening close, or midnight hour.

'Alonzo the Brave and Fair Imogine' (1796)⋆

Matthew Gregory Lewis (1775–1818)

A warrior so bold, and a virgin so bright
    Conversed, as they sat on the green;
They gazed on each other with tender delight;
Alonzo the Brave was the name of the knight,
    The maid's was the Fair Imogine.

⋆ M. G. Lewis, *The Monk*, 3 vols (London: J. Bell, 1796), vol. 3, pp. 63–6.

'And, oh!' said the youth, 'since to-morrow I go
    To fight in a far distant land,
Your tears for my absence soon leaving to flow,
Some other will court you, and you will bestow
    On a wealthier suitor your hand.'

'Oh! hush these suspicions,' Fair Imogine said,
    'Offensive to love and to me!
For, if you be living, or if you be dead,
I swear by the Virgin, that none in your stead
    Shall husband of Imogine be.

'If e'er I, by lust or by wealth led aside,
    Forget my Alonzo the Brave,
God grant, that to punish my falsehood and pride
Your ghost at the marriage may sit by my side,
May tax me with perjury, claim me as bride,
    And bear me away to the grave!'

To Palestine hastened the hero so bold;
    His love, she lamented him sore:
But scarce had a twelvemonth elapsed, when behold,
A Baron all covered with jewels and gold
    Arrived at Fair Imogine's door.

His treasure, his presents, his spacious domain
    Soon made her untrue to her vows:
He dazzled her eyes; he bewildered her brain;
He caught her affections so light and so vain,
    And carried her home as his spouse.

And now had the marriage been blest by the priest;
    The revelry now was begun:
The tables they groaned with the weight of the feast;
Nor yet had the laughter and merriment ceased,
    When the bell at the castle told – 'one!'

Then first with amazement Fair Imogine found
    That a stranger was placed by her side:
His air was terrific; he uttered no sound;
He spoke not, he moved not, he looked not around,
    But earnestly gazed on the bride.

His vizor was closed, and gigantic his height;
 His armour was sable to view:
All pleasure and laughter were hushed at his sight;
The dogs as they eyed him drew back in affright;
 The lights in the chamber burned blue!

His presence all bosoms appeared to dismay;
 The guests sat in silence and fear.
At length spoke the bride, while she trembled; 'I pray,
Sir Knight, that your helmet aside you would lay,
 And deign to partake of our chear.'

The lady is silent: the stranger complies.
 His vizor he slowly unclosed:
Oh! God! what a sight met Fair Imogine's eyes!
What words can express her dismay and surprise,
 When a skeleton's head was exposed!

All present then uttered a terrified shout;
 All turned with disgust from the scene.
The worms they crept in, and the worms they crept out,
And sported his eyes and his temples about,
 While the spectre addressed Imogine.

'Behold me, thou false one! behold me!' he cried;
 'Remember Alonzo the Brave!
God grants, that to punish thy falsehood and pride
My ghost at thy marriage should sit by thy side,
Should tax thee with perjury, claim thee as bride,
 And bear thee away to the grave!'

Thus saying, his arms round the lady he wound,
 While loudly she shrieked in dismay;
Then sank with his prey through the wide-yawning ground:
Nor ever again was Fair Imogine found,
 Or the spectre who bore her away.

Not long lived the Baron; and none since that time
 To inhabit the castle presume;
For chronicles tell that, by order sublime,
There Imogine suffers the pain of her crime,
 And mourns her deplorable doom.

At midnight four times in each year does her spright,
　　When mortals in slumber are bound,
Arrayed in her bridal apparel of white,
Appear in the hall with the Skeleton-Knight,
　　And shriek as he whirls her around.

While they drink out of skulls newly torn from the grave,
　　Dancing round them the spectres are seen:
Their liquor is blood, and this horrible stave
They howl: – 'To the health of Alonzo the Brave,
　　And his consort, the False Imogine!'

'The Voice from the Side of Etna or, The Mad Monk' (1800)*

SAMUEL TAYLOR COLERIDGE (1772–1834)

AN ODE, in Mrs. RATCLIFF's manner.

I heard a voice from Etna's side,
　　Where o'er a Cavern's mouth,
　　That fronted to the South,
A chesnut spread its umbrage wide.
A Hermit, or a Monk, the man might be,
But him I could not see:
And thus the music flow'd along,
In melody most like an old Sicilian song.

There was a time when earth, and sea, and skies,
　　The bright green vale and forest's dark recess,
When all things lay before my eyes
　　In steady loveliness.
But now I feel on earth's uneasy scene
　　Such motions as will never cease!
　　I only ask for peace –
Then wherefore must I know, that such a time has been?

　　A silence then ensu'd.
　　　Till from the cavern came
　　　A voice. It was the same:

★ *Morning Post and Gazetteer*, 13 October 1800, p. 3.

And thus that mournful voice its dreary plaint renew'd.
Last night, as o'er the sloping turf I trod,
    The smooth green turf to me a vision gave:
        Beneath my eyes I saw the sod,
        The roof of ROSA's grave.

My heart has need with dreams like these to strive,
For when I wak'd, beneath my eyes I found
        That plot of mossy ground,
On which so oft we sate when ROSA was alive.
Why must the rock, and margin of the flood,
    Why must the hills so many flow'rets bear,
Whose colours to a wounded woman's blood
        Such sad resemblance wear?

I struck the wound – this hand of mine!
    For, oh! thou Maid divine,
        I loved to agony!
    The youth, whom thou call'dst thine,
        Did never love like me.

    It is the stormy clouds above,
        That flash so red a gleam
        On yonder downward trickling stream;
    'Tis not the blood of her I love.
The sun torments me from his western bed!
    O let him cease for ever to diffuse
    Those crimson spectre hues!
O let me lie in peace, and be for ever dead!

Here ceas'd the voice! In deep dismay,
Down thro' the forest I pursu'd my way.
The twilight fays came forth in dewy shoon,
    Ere I within the cabin had withdrawn,
    The goat-herd's tent upon the open lawn.
That night there was no moon!!

CASSIANI, jun.

Tales of Terror (1801)*

MATTHEW GREGORY LEWIS (attrib.) (1775–1818)

A major feature of both Gothic and Romantic poetry was the use of 'German' and 'Old English' folk tales and the recreation of the ancient ballad tradition. Tales of Terror and Tales of Wonder, to which Sir Walter Scott as well as Lewis contributed, were extremely popular. Tales of Terror consists mostly of Spanish, Scottish, Swedish and Welsh ballads, many imitating and dedicated to M. G. Lewis, some attributed to him. It is worth listing the titles to illustrate the taste of the times: The Stranger; Hrim Thor, or the Winter-King; The Wolf-King, or Little Red-riding-hood; The Wanderer of the Wold; Gonzalvo; Albert of Werdendorff, or the Midnight Embrace; The Maid of Donalblayne; The Pilgrim of Valencia; The Grey Friar of Winton, or the Death of King Rufus; Grim, King of the Ghosts, or the Dance of Death; Osric and Ella; Martel, or the Conqueror's Return; Ellen of Eglantine; The Black Canon of Elmham, or Saint Edmond's Eve; The Scullion-Sprite, or the Garret-Goblin; The Troubadour, or Lady Alice's Bower; The Sprite of the Glen; The House upon the Heath; The Mud-King, or Smedley's Ghost; The Abbot of Leiston. Rather than include them here – like all folk songs, they are interminable – I have selected the prefatory remarks, in which Lewis defends the genre.

Introductory Dialogue

FRIEND
WHAT, scribble tales? Oh! cease to play the fool!
Christmas is past, and children gone to school;
E'en active Harlequin abash'd retired,
Neglected witches quench the cauldron's fires,
Whilst fairy phantoms vanish swift away,
And sense and nature reassume their sway.

What gain, what pleasure, can your labours crown?
A nurs'ry's praise shall be your best renown;
Each feeble tale ingloriously expire,
A gossip's story at a winter's fire!

AUTHOR
Oh! cease this rage, this misapplied abuse,
Satire gives weapons for a nobler use;
Why draw your sword against my harmless quill,
And strive in vain a *ghostly muse* to kill?

* *Tales of Terror with An Introductory Dialogue*, 2nd edn (London: Printed for L. Bell by Bulmer & Co., 1808), pp. 1–7.

That task is *ours*: if I can augur well,
Each day grows weaker her unheeded spell,
Her eager votaries shall fix her doom,
And lay her spirit in Oblivion's tomb.

FRIEND
Yes! thus I oft my drooping hopes revive,
Prepost'rous births are seldom known to thrive;
These scribblers soon shall mourn their useless pains,
And weep the short-lived product of their brains,
These active panders to perverted taste
Shall mar their purpose by too anxious haste.

As earthquakes nature's harmony restore,
And air grows purer in the tempest's roar,
So the strange workings of a monstrous mind
Will quickly fade, and leave no trace behind;
Like brilliant bubbles, glitter for a day,
Till, swoll'n too big, they burst, and pass away.
We need not call ethereal spirits down
To rouse the torpid feelings of the town;
Or bid the dead their ghastly forms uprear,
To freeze some silly female breast with fear;
No – I have hopes you'll find this *rage* decreas'd,
And send a dish too much to Terror's feast;
The vicious taste, with such a rich supply
Quite surfeited, 'will sicken, and so die.'

AUTHOR
My friend, believe me, with indifferent view
I mark opinion's ever-varying hue,
Let tasteless fashion guide the public heart,
And, without feeling, scan the poet's art.
Fashion! dread name in criticism's field,
Before whose sway both sense and judgement yield,
Whether she loves to hear, 'midst deserts bleak,
The untaught savage moral axioms speak;
O'er modern, six weeks, epic strains to dose,
To sigh in sonnets, or give wings to prose;
Or bids the bard, by leaden rules confined,
To freeze the bosom, and confuse the mind,
While feeling stagnates in the drawler's veins,
And Fancy's fetter'd in didactic chains; –
Or rouses the dull German's gloomy soul,

And Pity leaves for Horror's wild controul,
Pouring warm tears for *visionary* crimes,
And softening sins to mend these *moral* times;
It boots not *me* – *my* taste is still my own,
Nor heeds the gale by wavering fashion blown.
My mind unalter'd views, with fix'd delight,
The wreck of learning snatch'd from Gothic night;
Chang'd by no time, unsettled by no place,
It feels the Grecian fire, the Roman grace;
Exulting marks the flame of ancient days,
In Britain with triumphant brightness blaze!

Yet still the soul for *various* pleasure form'd,
By Pity melted, and by Terror storm'd,
Loves to roam largely through each distant clime,
And 'leap the flaming bounds of space and time!'
The mental eye, by constant lustre tires,
Forsakes, fatigued, the object it admires,
And, as it scans each various nation's doom,
From classic brightness turns to Gothic gloom.

Oh! it breathes awe and rapture o'er the soul
To mark the surge in wild confusion roll,
And when the forest groans, and tempest lours,
To wake Imagination's darkest powers!
How throbs the breast with terror and delight,
Fill'd with rude scenes of Europe's barbarous night!
When restless war with papal craft combined,
To shut each softening ray from lost mankind;
When nought by Error's fatal light was shown,
And taste and science were alike unknown;
To mark the soul, benumb'd its active powers,
Chain'd at the foot of superstition's towers;
To view the pale-eyed maid in penance pine,
To watch the votary at the sainted shrine;
And, while o'er blasted heaths the night-storm raves,
To hear the wizzard wake the slumb'ring graves;
To view war's glitt'ring front, the trophied field,
The hallow'd banner, and the red-cross shield;
The tourney's knights, the tyrant baron's crimes,
'Pomp, pride, and circumstance,' of feudal times!

Th' enraptured mind with fancy loves to toil
O'er rugged Scandinavia's martial soil;

With eager joy the 'venturous spirit goes
O'er Morven's mountains, and through Lapland's snows;
Sees barbarous chiefs in fierce contention fall,
And views the blood-stain'd feasts of Odin's hall;
Hears Ossian's harp resound the deeds of war,
While each grey soldier glories in his scar;
Now marks the wand'ring ghost, at night's dull noon,
Howl out its woes beneath the silent moon;
Sees Danish pirates plough th' insulted main,
Whilst Rapin's outcry shakes the sacred fane;
Observes the Saxon baron's sullen state,
Where rival pride enkindles savage hate;
Each sound, each sight, the spell-bound sense appalls
Amid some lonely abbey's ivied walls!
The night-shriek loud, wan ghost, and dungeon damp,
The midnight cloister, and the glimm'ring lamp,
The pale procession fading on the sight,
The flaming tapers, and the chaunted rite,
Rouse, in the trembling breast, delightful dreams,
And steep each feeling in romance's streams!
Streams which afar in restless grandeur roll,
And burst tremendous on the wond'ring soul!
Now gliding smooth, now lash'd by magic storms,
Lifting to light a thousand shapeless forms;
A vapourous glory floats each wave around,
The dashing waters breathe a mournful sound,
Pale Terror trembling guards the fountain's head,
And rouses Fancy on her wakeful bed;
'From realms of viewless spirits tears the veil,
'And half reveals the unutterable tale!'
                                    March 1, 1801.

Review of Lewis's *Tales of Wonder* (1801)[*]

Tales of Wonder: Written and collected by M. G. Lewis, Esq. M.P. Author of the Monk, Castle Spectre, Love of Gain, &c. 2 Vols. large 8vo. Pp. 480. 2l. 2s.

Far from being inclined to join in the censure which has been directed against Mr. Lewis for compiling the present volumes, we think he is much

---

[*] *Anti-Jacobin Review and Magazine*, **8** (March 1801), pp. 322–3.

better employed than in most of his former productions, at least, with reference to his well-known romance, entitled *The Monk*, a work that has tended more to vitiate juvenile minds, and poison the fountains of morality than any thing of the kind that has fallen within our notice for a long period. Indeed we hardly know of any work of so licentious a complexion, and of so mischievous a tendency, except the political crudities of the detestable Citizen PAINE. From all that we have read or heard of Mr. Lewis and his works, he seems to us to possess a singular turn of mind. His fancy appears to be chiefly attracted by, and absorbed in, *the terrible, the horrible, the hideous*, and *the impossible*; nor can we conceive what has been his bent of education that has led him into so uncommon a track of study. He certainly does not want abilities, or knowledge, but his talents are strangely perverted, and he sometimes seems even to be employed in throwing a ridicule upon himself. But to the present work. It consists of as many tales as the author could collect in order to scare the minds of children, and impress a terror upon the imagination through life. Some indeed of the compositions, to be found in these volumes, are of a pathetic, interesting, and moral cast; but they bear a small proportion to the works of the other tendency. Several pieces were written by Mr. Lewis himself, and others are well known. We shall extract an imitation from the German, by WALTER SCOTT, as a specimen of the works which these volumes contain, as he seems to be the best of the new species of *horror-breeding* Bards. [omitted]

PLATE 8

Frontispiece to *Tales of Terror* (1801), a collection of supernatural ballads written by or imitating Matthew Gregory Lewis. By permission of the British Library 11660.e.39.

'Ballad' (*c.* 1807)[★]

Percy Bysshe Shelley (1792–1822)

The death-bell beats,
The mountain repeats
The echoing sound of the knell;
And the dark monk now
Wraps the cowl round his brow,
As he sits in his lonely cell.

And the cold hand of death
Chills his shuddering breath,
As he lists to the fearful lay,
Which the ghosts of the sky,
As they sweep wildly by,
Sing to departed day.
And they sing of the hour
When the stern Fates had power
To resolve Rosa's form to its clay.

But that hour is past,
And that hour was the last,
Of peace to the dark monk's brain;
Bitter tears from his eyes gush'd silent and fast,
And he strove to suppress them in vain.
Then his fair cross of gold he dashed on the floor,
When the death-knell struck on his ear –
'Delight is in store for her evermore,
But for me is fate, horror, and fear.'

Then his eyes wildly rolled,
When the death-bell tolled,
And he raged in terrific woe;
And he stamped on the ground,
But when ceased the sound,
Tears again begun to flow.

And the ice of despair
Chilled the wild throb of care,

★ Thomas Medwin, *The Life of Percy Bysshe Shelley*, 2 vols (London: Thomas Cautley Newby, 1847), vol. 1, pp. 79–83.

And he sate in mute agony still:
Till the night-stars shone thro' the cloudless air,
And the pale moonbeam slept on the [hill.]

Then he knelt in his cell,
And the horrors of hell
Were delights to his agonised pain,
And he prayed to God to dissolve the spell,
Which else must ever remain.

And in fervent prayer he knelt to the ground,
Till the abbey bell struck one;
His feverish blood ran chill at the sound,
And a voice hollow, horrible, murmured around,
'The term of thy penance is done.'

Grew dark the night;
The moonbeam bright
Waxed faint on the mountain high;
And from the black hill
Went a voice cold and shrill –
'Monk! thou art free to die.'

Then he rose on his feet,
And his heart loud did beat,
And his limbs they were palsied with dread;
Whilst the grave's clammy dew
O'er his pale forehead grew;
And he shuddered to sleep with the dead.

And the wild midnight storm
Raved around his tall form,
As he sought the chapel's gloom;
And the sunk grass did sigh
To the wind, bleak and high,
As he search'd for the new-made tomb.

And forms dark and high
Seem'd around him to fly,
And mingle their yells with the blast;
And on the dark wall
Half-seen shadows did fall,
And enhorror'd he onward pass'd.

And the storm fiends wild rave
O'er the new made grave,
And dread shadows linger around,
The monk call'd on God his soul to save,
And in horror sank on the ground.

Then despair nerved his arm,
To dispel the charm,
And he burst Rosa's coffin asunder.
And the fierce storm did swell
More terrific and fell,
And louder peal'd the thunder.

And laugh'd in joy the fiendish throng,
Mix'd with ghosts of the mouldering dead;
And their grisly wings, as they floated along,
Whistled in murmurs dread.

And her skeleton form the dead nun rear'd,
Which dripp'd with the chill dew of hell.
In her half-eaten eye-balls two pale flames appear'd,
But triumphant their gleam on the dark monk glar'd,
As he stood within the cell.

And her long hand lay on his shuddering brain,
But each power was nerv'd by fear. –
'I never, henceforth, may breathe again;
Death now ends mine anguish'd pain;
The grave yawns – we meet there.'

And her skeleton lungs did utter the sound,
So deadly, so lone, and so fell,
That in long vibrations shudder'd the ground,
And as the stern notes floated around,
A deep groan was answer'd from Hell!

'The Vampyre' (1810)*

John Stagg (1770–1823)

In his Prefatory Apology, Stagg observes that 'the present perversion of taste, and the romance mania so prevalent now-a-days, almost demonstrates to me, that Essays of a more serious and regular nature would not be universally received with such a degree of encouragement. The avidity with which the works of Lewis, Wordsworth, Southey, and Scott, are at present perused, determined me to attempt this species of composition; and as there are a great many historical and romantic legends existing in Cumberland; with a number of other Gothic stories prevalent in the North, the scenes and subjects of which were unfixed and unconnected with any particular spot, I felt myself convinced, that a versification of these stories, which in some manner were topographical, and to localize others, would not prove ungratifying to a great number of readers, especially the admirers of Gothic and romantic literature. How far I have been successful, the world will soon inform me; and on its candour and clemency are founded all my expectations.'

'Why looks my lord so deadly pale?
 Why fades the crimson from his cheek?
What can my dearest husband ail?
 Thy heartfelt cares, O Herman, speak!

'Why, at the silent hour of rest,
 Dost thou in sleep so sadly mourn?
Hast tho' with heaviest grief oppress'd,
 Griefs too distressful to be borne.

'Why heaves thy breast? – why throbs thy heart?
 O speak! and if there be relief,
Thy Gertrude solace shall impart,
 If not, at least shall share thy grief.

'Wan is that cheek, which once the bloom
 Of manly beauty sparkling shew'd;
Dim are those eyes, in pensive gloom,
 That late with keenest lustre glow'd.

★ John Stagg, *The Minstrel of the North; or, Cumbrian Legends*. Being a Poetical Miscellany of Legendary, Gothic, and Romantic, Tales (London: Printed by Hamblin and Seyfang, for the Author, 1810), pp. 262–8.

'Say why, too, at the midnight hour,
    You sadly pant and tug for breath,
As if some supernat'ral pow'r
    Were pulling you away to death?

'Restless, tho' sleeping, still you groan,
    And with convulsive horror start;
O Herman! to thy wife make known
    That grief which preys upon thy heart.'

'O Gertrude! how shall I relate
    Th' uncommon anguish that I feel;
Strange as severe is this my fate, –
    A fate I cannot long conceal.

'In spite of all my wonted strength,
    Stern destiny has seal'd my doom;
The dreadful malady at length
    Will drag me to the silent tomb!'

'But say, my Herman, what's the cause
    Of this distress, and all thy care,
That, vulture-like, thy vitals gnaws,
    And galls thy bosom with despair?

'Sure this can be no common grief,
    Sure this can be no common pain?
Speak, if this world contain relief,
    That soon thy Gertrude shall obtain.'

'O Gertrude, 'tis a horrid cause,
    O Gertrude, 'tis unusual care,
That, vulture-like, my vitals gnaws,
    And galls my bosom with despair.

'Young Sigismund, my once dear friend,
    But lately he resign'd his breath;
With others I did him attend
    Unto the silent house of death.

'For him I wept, for him I mourn'd,
    Paid all to friendship that was due;
But sadly friendship is return'd,
    Thy Herman he must follow too!

'Must follow to the gloomy grave,
 In spite of human art or skill;
No pow'r on earth my life can save,
 'Tis fate's unalterable will!

'Young Sigismund, my once dear friend,
 But now my persecutor foul,
Doth his malevolence extend
 E'en to the torture of my soul.

'By night, when, wrapt in soundest sleep,
 All mortals share a soft repose,
My soul doth dreadful vigils keep,
 More keen than which hell scarcely knows.

'From the drear mansion of the tomb,
 From the low regions of the dead,
The ghost of Sigismund doth roam,
 And dreadful haunts me in my bed!

'There, vested in infernal guise,
 (By means to me not understood,)
Close to my side the goblin lies,
 And drinks away my vital blood!

'Sucks from my veins the streaming life,
 And drains the fountain of my heart!
O Gertrude, Gertrude! dearest wife!
 Unutterable is my smart.

'When surfeited, the goblin dire,
 With banqueting by suckled gore,
Will to his sepulchre retire,
 Till night invites him forth once more.

'Then will he dreadfully return,
 And from my veins life's juices drain;
Whilst, slumb'ring, I with anguish mourn,
 And toss with agonizing pain!

'Already I'm exhausted, spent;
 His carnival is nearly o'er,
My soul with agony is rent,
 To-morrow I shall be no more!

'But, O my Gertrude! dearest wife!
    The keenest pangs hath last remain'd –
When dead, I too shall seek thy life,
    Thy blood by Herman shall be drain'd!

'But to avoid this horrid fate,
    Soon as I'm dead and laid in earth,
Drive thro' my corpse a jav'lin straight; –
    This shall prevent my coming forth.

'O watch with me, this last sad night,
    Watch in your chamber here alone,
But carefully conceal the light
    Until you hear my parting groan.

'Then at what time the vesper-bell
    Of yonder convent shall be toll'd,
That peal shall ring my passing knell,
    And Herman's body shall be cold!

'Then, and just then, thy lamp make bare,
    The starting ray, the bursting light,
Shall from my side the goblin scare,
    And shew him visible to sight!'

The live-long night poor Gertrude sate,
    Watch'd by her sleeping, dying lord;
The live-long night she mourn'd his fate,
    The object whom her soul ador'd.

Then at what time the vesper-bell
    Of yonder convent sadly toll'd,
Then, then was peal'd his passing knell,
    The hapless Herman he was cold!

Just at that moment Gertrude drew
    From 'neath her cloak the hidden light;
When, dreadful! she beheld in view
    The shade of Sigismund! – sad sight!

Indignant roll'd his ireful eyes,
    That gleam'd with wild horrific stare;
And fix'd a moment with surprise,
    Beheld aghast th' enlight'ning glare.

His jaws cadaverous were besmear'd
    With clott'd carnage o'er and o'er,
And all his horrid whole appear'd
    Distent, and fill'd with human gore!

With hideous scowl the spectre fled;
    She shriek'd aloud; – then swoon'd away!
The hapless Herman in his bed,
    All pale, a lifeless body lay!

Next day in council 'twas decreed,
    (Urg'd at the instance of the state,)
That shudd'ring nature should be freed
    From pests like these ere 'twas too late.

The choir then burst the fun'ral dome
    Where Sigismund was lately laid,
And found him, tho' within the tomb,
    Still warm as life, and undecay'd.

With blood his visage was distain'd,
    Ensanguin'd were his frightful eyes,
Each sign of former life remain'd,
    Save that all motionless he lies.

The corpse of Herman they contrive
    To the same sepulchre to take,
And thro' both carcases they drive,
    Deep in the earth, a sharpen'd stake!

By this was finish'd their career,
    Thro' this no longer they can roam;
From them their friends have nought to fear,
    Both quiet keep the slumb'ring tomb.

'Annabel Lee' (1849)★

EDGAR ALLAN POE (1809–49)

It was many and many a year ago,
    In a kingdom by the sea,

★ E. A. Poe, *The Poetical Works of Edgar Allan Poe* (London: Addey, 1853), pp. 43–4.

That a maiden there lived whom you may know
    By the name of ANNABEL LEE;
And this maiden she lived with no other thought
    Than to love and be loved by me.
I was a child and *she* was a child,
    In this kingdom by the sea:
But we loved with a love that was more than love –
    I and my Annabel Lee;
With a love that the winged seraphs of heaven
    Coveted her and me.

And this was the reason that, long ago,
    In this kingdom by the sea,
A wind blew out of a cloud, chilling
    My beautiful Annabel Lee;
So that her highborn kinsmen came
    And bore her away from me,
To shut her up in a sepulchre
    In this kingdom by the sea.

The angels, not half so happy in heaven,
    Went envying her and me –
Yes! – that was the reason (as all men know,
    In this kingdom by the sea)
That the wind came out of the cloud by night,
    Chilling and killing my Annabel Lee.

But our love it was stronger by far than the love
    Of those who were older than we –
    Of many far wiser than we;
And neither the angels in heaven above,
    Nor the demons down under the sea,
Can ever dissever my soul from the soul
    Of the beautiful Annabel Lee.

For the moon never beams, without bringing me dreams
    Of the beautiful Annabel Lee;
And the stars never rise, but I feel the bright eyes
    Of the beautiful Annabel Lee;
And so, all the night-tide, I lie down by the side
Of my darling – my darling – my life and my bride,
    In the sepulchre there by the sea,
    In her tomb by the sounding sea.

6

𝕻𝖆𝖗𝖔𝖉𝖞

GOTHIC LITERATURE WAS FREQUENTLY SATIRIZED and parodied from 1796 through the 1820s. For example, William Godwin's novel *St. Leon* (1799) was parodied by 'Count Reginald de St Leon' as *St. Godwin: A Tale of the xvi, xvii and xviii Century* (1800); Lewis's *The Monk* was satirized in Thomas Dermody's *The Harp of Erin* (1807); and *The New Monk* (1798) by 'R.S.' was a rewriting of Lewis's *The Monk* with the action transferred from the Inquisition to a boarding school and Methodist chapel. Lewis's verse was satirized in Charles Few's *A Parody upon the poem of Alonzo the Brave and the Fair Imogine* (1799). Full-scale burlesques upon Radcliffe's works include Mrs F. C. Patrick's *More Ghosts!* (1798), Mary Charlton's *Rosella, or Modern Occurrences* (1799), Sarah Green's *Romance Readers and Romance Writers* (1810), and Eaton Stannard Barrett's *The Heroine, Or Adventures of Cherubina* (1813). Barrett's novel 'very much amused' Jane Austen, whose own satire, *Northanger Abbey*, was begun in 1797. In *Love and Horror: an Imitation of the Present and a Model for all future Romances* (1815), by 'Ircastrensis', the dull normal young man falls in love with Ethelinda Tit, dead these 200 years, and contrives adventures that allow him to transform himself into a Gothic hero – a standard pattern for Gothic parodies.

It was perceived that some Gothic novelists just followed the fashion rather than wrote from their hearts, and satirists focused upon their formulaic techniques and conventions. The ubiquitous veil of mystery cast over all the stories from the Radcliffe School was derided. T. Ferguson in *Gothalbert of the Tyne, or The Gothic Minstrel's Progress from Parnassus to the Press* (1823) develops his tale at a leisurely pace because it is best to keep

> Some portion of our *Gothic* hist'ry,
> Envelop'd in a sort of myst'ry –
> A mode, which, if I don't mistake,
> Keeps Curiosity awake; . . .
> So Novel writers throw a veil
> Of myst'ry, o'er each magic tale,
> In order to allure us on,
> Till each successive *Tome* is done.

The most effective weapon employed in political attacks on the Gothic novel was satirical mockery. For example, Thomas James Mathias in his barbed satire *The Pursuits of Literature, or What You Will* (1794 onwards), attacked popular literature such as Charlotte Smith's *Celestina* in these terms:

> Is it for me to creep, or soar, or doze,
> In Modish song, or fashionable prose:
> To pen with garreteers obscure and shabby
> Inscriptive nonsense in a fancied *Abbey*.

But Mathias's underlying censure was that works by the women novelists 'now and then are tainted with democracy'. There is a good political satire of Mat Lewis MP as 'The Old Hag in a Red Cloak. A Romance' in *The Spirit of Anti-Jacobinism for 1802*. Satirical pastiches on the Gothic were popular in the 1810s, and David Macbeth Moir in 1851 (see pp. 335ff.) suggested that Gothic melodrama and the school of Lewis were abandoned in the face of ridicule and burlesque. However, my impression is that many inferior critics and poets were simply leaping to the attack upon an already dying horse.

It should also be noted that many Gothic novels contain an element of self-satire. This may be an authorial acknowledgement that the events they record are not wholly believable. Eliza Parsons' cynical exploitation of a fashion in her novel *Lucy,* published by the Minerva Press in 1794 (in the same month as *The Mysteries of Udolpho*), is revealed when she says that Lucy in her wanderings through the castle 'was so exceedingly fatigued, and out of humour, that she went quietly into her own room to boil her potatoes, and reserved the vaulted passages for her afternoon's walk'.

Some modern critics feel that the Gothic novelists didn't trust their form, and lapsed into satire by accident. My feeling is that the Gothic novelists were very aware of the artificiality of their form, and simply enjoyed poking fun at it. By having profane comic characters as well as sacred serious characters, the Gothic novelist could puncture the balloon of the supernatural while at the same time affirming the power of the imagination. Even Ann Radcliffe – who was certainly serious about her work – employed humorous characters to satirize her own bag of Gothic tricks. For example, the maid Annette – the mischievous *alter ego* of another Ann, the author – explains to Ludovico that she has little reason to fear running about a castle full of drunken men on the loose:

> 'I only want to go to my young lady's chamber, and I have only to go, you know, along the vaulted passage and across the great hall and up the marble stair-case and along the north gallery and through the west wing of the castle, and I am in the corridor in a minute.'

It is hard to fling such mockery against the Gothic novelists, since they have already employed it themselves, whether cynically or sincerely.

Azemia (1797)*

WILLIAM BECKFORD (1760–1844)

Beckford wrote two parodies of the Gothic romance, Modern Novel Writing, or, The Elegant Enthusiast *(1796) by 'Lady Harriet Marlow', and* Azemia *(1797), subtitled 'A Novel: Containing Imitations of the Manner, Both in Prose and Verse, of Many of the Authors of the Present Day'.* Azemia *was published under the pseudonym J. A. M. Jenks, the editor of the* Biographical Dictionary of Living Authors *in 1816, perhaps colluding in the joke, identified her as Miss Jacquetta Agneta Mariana Jenks, of Bellegrove Priory, Wales. Some contemporary critics, and Hester Lynch Piozzi, believed the author to be Robert Merry, the famous 'Della Cruscan' poet. The novel has a clever appendix containing anticipatory reviews, written in the style of each of the leading literary journals. The heroine Azemia is a native of Constantinople (giving Beckford an opportunity to indulge his Arabic interests), in search of romantic adventure in Britain. The following incident takes place in the grounds of an English country house.*

Wrapt in this sad but soothing contemplation, as in a pelisse, she advanced till it grew late, and a wheelbarrow, left there by the carelessness of the under gardener, obstructed an opening path apparently designed to lead to some place (as most paths do, except in novels); its winding turns serpentined imperceptibly up an easy ascent: she was roused from her reverie by finding herself at the top of the hill, where, contrary to all expectation, she beheld a mausoleum of *black* marble, which put her extremely in mind of a mosque or a minaret in her own country. (The ideas of these two things were not very distinct in her own mind.) She did not greatly enjoy the discovery, for it was now almost dark; and though the moon could not choose but rise on one side, the sun had entirely sunk on the other.

Azemia, however, entered the gloomy building – she knew not why – (We know not neither, unless, because she was guided by some *invisible impulse*; and because it is now necessary in novels for all the heroines to go into black marble mausoleums and grey-stone ruins whenever they meet with them) – However, Azemia approached; – the door stood a-jar: the gloom of the surrounding evergreens, particularly the cypresses, cast a solemn shade upon the occasion; and an owl from a neighbouring ivy bush hooted audibly, and cried, 'Tee-whit!' which Azemia had heard from Mrs. Blandford's old housekeeper was always a bad sign. She stopped – she shuddered – she was inspired with a secret terror! – she felt herself irresistibly impelled as by an invisible hand to penetrate this drear abode.

---

* J. A. M. Jenks [i.e. William Beckford], *Azemia, A Novel*, 2nd edn, 2 vols (London: Sampson Low, 1798), vol. 2, pp. 89–93, 236–40.

The noise she made in entering alarmed her: the door grated on its rusty hinges; the owl again cried, 'Tee-whit!' – and the wind howl'd – All served to increase these sepulchral horrors of this lugubrious residence of mouldering-mortality.

Azemia trembled, as fearfully, she beheld the dome; for the moon now opportunely coming from behind a cloud, threw a feeble light through the long casements of painted glass. Azemia fancied herself Juliet in the vault of the Capulets – (for, unlike other foreigners, she understood Shakespeare to a miracle) – and again shuddered: a door was half open on the right hand; she pushed it gently, and found it led from the mausoleum into the chapel. She entered the aisle – something white appeared at the farther end; the rays of the moon fell directly upon it, and it seemed to move. – suddenly the great bell in the turret tolled, and Azemia was overcome with horrible dread, and unable to retreat. The tolling ceased, but she heard the tread of feet: she became immovable; she uttered a faint scream – a *form* appeared. *It* perceived her fears – *it* flew to support her in *its* arms – it sunk with her on the black marble pavement (on which her *white* drapery gracefully floated); and nobody can tell how this terrific scene might have ended, if Mrs. Blandford, alarmed at the absense of Azemia, had not most fortunately arrived at that moment in search of her, attended by a footman with a candle and lantern, who found Lord Scudabout supporting Azemia, yet laughing excessively at the fear he had put her into. Mrs. Blandford severely reproving him, he ran to the stables, mounted his horse, and galloped back to his companions at Lord Oddberry's, from which he had suddenly escaped to execute this frolic, as if he had foreseen Azemia's evening excursion.

Mrs. Blandford soon soothed to peace the agitated bosom of her fair ward; and Lady Dorothy Dawdle, who presided as mistress of this hospitable mansion, declared that Lord Scudabout should never enter it again, and that she would the next day go with her ponies to the Marchioness, his mother, who lived about ten miles off, and complain of the indecorous behaviour he had been guilty of.

. . .

To the Reviewers of all the Reviews

To attain the masculine force and strong colouring of the great dramatist and Novelist of the present day, Mr. [Richard] Cumberland, was quite beyond my slender attainment; but I have paid a due tribute to his taste, sagacity, and knowledge of *womankind*. Thrown at a great distance from the most engaging models among my own sex, I yet look up with more confidence to attain, at some future day, a seat on that point of Parnassus where they hold such eminent rank. In this hope I have sometimes assumed the stately step with which the pupils of the Burney school follow in *solemn,* yet *inadequate* march, *their inimitable leader.* This, however, I have attempted in *style* only. I have not seen enough of the world to sketch even in the way of a scholar, such admirable characters. With less dissidence, though still with greater humility, I have ventured with shuddering feet into the World of Spirits, in modest emulation of the soul-petrifying Ratcliffe [Ann Radcliffe] – but, alas!

Within that circle none dare walk but she.

Even if I *had* ever had the fortune to see a *real natural ghost*, I could never describe it with half the terrific apparatus that fair Magician can conjure up in some dozen or two of pages, interspersed with convents, arches, pillars, cypresses, and banditti-bearing cliffs, beetling over yawning and sepulchral caverns. Her pictures,

Dark as Poussin, and as Salvator wild,

can only be faintly copied; – to rival them is impossible. – I own I do *not* feel quite so disheartened, when I try at making something like the luminous page of Mrs. Mary Robinson: I even flatter myself that I have, in more than one instance, caught the *air of probability* so remarkable in her delectable histories, as well as her glowing description and applicable metaphors.

To Mrs. [Susannah] Gunning's Novels, and those of her amiable daughter [Elizabeth Gunning], I owe all in these little volumes that pretends to draw the characters and manners of high life. With due humility and trepidation I have seized the mimic pencil: I feel that I cannot wield it with their happy freedom and felicity – *faut d'usage*. . . .

From the parterres of Miss [Harriet or Sophia] Lee, Mrs. [Elizabeth] Inchbald, and Mrs. [Charlotte] Smith, I have culled here and there a flower; and I should have enlarged my bouquet with buds and blossoms of other very agreeable writers, of whom I could make (like Mr. Pratt) a very respectable list, if I could have induced my publisher to have allowed my work to be enlarged to what I intended it, viz. six *very* large volumes. . . .

Northanger Abbey (1798–9/1818)★

JANE AUSTEN (1775–1817)

Jane Austen began writing Northanger Abbey *in 1798, then revised and completed it by 1803, when it was sold to Crosby, the publisher of Godwin's* Caleb Williams, *for £10. But it was left unpublished until one of Jane Austen's brothers*

★ Jane Austen, *Northanger Abbey: and Persuasion*, 4 vols (London: John Murray, 1818), vol. 1, pp. 60–5, 66–70; vol. 2, pp. 185–94.

bought the manuscript back in 1816, and had it published in 1818, the year after Jane Austen's death. This satire on the Gothic novel has been wrongly credited with killing off the Gothic novel, but by the time of its posthumous publication in 1818 the Gothic tradition was already in serious decline. The most sensational events and nightmarish images from Radcliffe's A Sicilian Romance *and* The Romance of the Forest *(for it is these which form the base texts of* Northanger Abbey, *rather than* The Mysteries of Udolpho*) are deflated by being placed in prosaic settings, but Catherine's apprehension that General Tilney is an oppressive domestic tyrant is absolutely correct, and the Radcliffean prototypes of cruel father and oppressed mother support rather than conflict with the social realism of Austen's novel. Austen was engaged in an affectionate rather than a cruel satire, and we should note that Radcliffe's influence upon her went beyond* Northanger Abbey; *for example, Fanny Price's room in* Mansfield Park *is modelled upon Emily's room in the castle of Udolpho. The authors of all of the 'horrid' novels whose titles are read out by Isabella Tilney are represented in the present anthology.*

The progress of the friendship between Catherine and Isabella was quick as its beginning had been warm, and they passed so rapidly through every gradation of increasing tenderness, that there was shortly no fresh proof of it to be given to their friends or themselves. They called each other by their Christian name, were always arm in arm when they walked, pinned up each other's train for the dance, and were not to be divided in the set; and if a rainy morning deprived them of other enjoyments, they were still resolute in meeting in defiance of wet and dirt, and shut themselves up, to read novels together. Yes, novels; – for I will not adopt that ungenerous and impolitic custom so common with novel writers, of degrading by their contemptuous censure the very performances, to the number of which they are themselves adding – joining with their greatest enemies in bestowing the harshest epithets on such works, and scarcely ever permitting them to be read by their own heroine, who, if she accidentally take up a novel, is sure to turn over its insipid pages with disgust. Alas! if the heroine of one novel be not patronized by the heroine of another, from whom can she expect protection and regard? I cannot approve of it. Let us leave it to the Reviewers to abuse such effusions of fancy at their leisure, and over every new novel to talk in threadbare strains of the trash with which the press now groans. Let us not desert one another; we are an injured body. Although our productions have afforded more extensive and unaffected pleasure than those of any other literary corporation in the world, no species of composition has been so much decried. From pride, ignorance, or fashion, our foes are almost as many as our readers. And while the abilities of the nine-hundredth abridger of the History of England, or of the man who collects and publishes in a volume some dozen lines of Milton, Pope, and Prior, with a paper from the Spectator, and a chapter from Sterne, are eulogized by a thousand pens, – there seems almost a general wish of decrying the capacity and undervaluing the labour of the novelist, and of slighting the performances which have only genius, wit, and taste to recommend them. 'I am no novel reader – I seldom look into novels – Do not imagine that *I* often read novels – It is really very well for a novel.' – Such is the common cant. – 'And what are you reading, Miss ——?' 'Oh! it is only a novel!' replies the young lady; while she lays down her book with affected indifference, or momentary shame. – 'It is only Cecilia, or Camilla, or Belinda;' or, in short, only some work in which the greatest powers of the mind are displayed, in which the most thorough knowledge of human nature, the happiest delineation of its varieties, the liveliest effusions of wit and humour are conveyed to the world in the best chosen language. Now, had the same young lady been engaged with a volume of the Spectator, instead of such a work, how proudly would she have produced the book, and told its name; though the chances must be against her being occupied by any part of that voluminous publication, of which either the matter or manner would not disgust a young person of taste: the substance of its papers so often consisting in the statement of improbable circumstances, unnatural characters, and topics of conversation, which no longer concern any one living; and their language, too, frequently so coarse as to give no very favourable idea of the age that could endure it.

The following conversation, which took place between the two friends in the Pump-room one morning, after an acquaintance of eight or nine days, is given as a specimen of their very warm attachment, and of the delicacy, discretion, originality of thought, and literary taste which marked the reasonableness of that attachment.

They met by appointment; and as Isabella had arrived nearly five minutes before her friend, her first address naturally was – 'My dearest creature, what can have made you so late? I have been waiting for you at least this age!'

'Have you, indeed! – I am very sorry for it; but really I thought I was in very good time. It is but just one. I hope you have not been here long?'

'Oh! these ten ages at least. I am sure I have been here this half hour. But now, let us go and sit down at the other end of the room, and enjoy ourselves. I have an hundred things to say to you. In the first place, I was so afraid it would rain this morning, just as I wanted to set off; it looked very showery, and that would have thrown me into agonies! Do you know, I saw the prettiest hat you can imagine, in a shop window in Milsom-street just now – very like yours, only with coquelicot ribbons instead of green; I quite longed for it. But, my dearest Catherine, what have you been doing with yourself all this morning? – Have you gone on with Udolpho?'

'Yes, I have been reading it ever since I woke; and I am got to the black veil.'

'Are you, indeed? How delightful! Oh! I would not tell you what is behind the black veil for the world! Are not you wild to know?'

'Oh! yes, quite; what can it be? – But do not tell me – I would not be told upon any account. I know it must be a skeleton, I am sure it is Laurentina's skeleton. Oh! I am delighted with the book! I should like to spend my whole life in reading it. I assure you, if it had not been to meet you, I would not have come away from it for all the world.'

'Dear creature! how much I am obliged to you; and when you have finished Udolpho, we will read the Italian together; and I have made out a list of ten or twelve more of the same kind for you.'

'Have you, indeed! How glad I am! – What are they all?'

'I will read you their names directly; here they are, in my pocket-book. Castle of Wolfenbach, Clermont, Mysterious Warnings, Necromancer of the Black Forest, Midnight Bell, Orphan of the Rhine, and Horrid Mysteries. Those will last us some time.'

'Yes, pretty well; but are they all horrid, are you sure they are all horrid?'

'Yes, quite sure; for a particular friend of mine, a Miss Andrews, a sweet girl, one of the sweetest creatures in the world, has read every one of them.'

. . .

[Henry Tilney realizes that Catherine has suspected that his father has murdered his mother:] 'If I understand you rightly, you had formed a surmise of such horror as I have hardly words to – Dear Miss Morland, consider the dreadful nature of the suspicions you have entertained. What have you been judging from? Remember the country and the age in which we live. Remember that we are English, that we are Christians. Consult your own understanding, your own sense of the probable, your own observation of what is passing around you – Does our education prepare us for such atrocities? Do our laws connive at them? Could they be perpetrated without being known, in a country like this, where social and literary intercourse is on such a footing; where every man is surrounded by a neighbourhood of voluntary spies, and where roads and newspapers lay every thing open? Dearest Miss Morland, what ideas have you been admitting?'

They had reached the end of the gallery; and with tears of shame she ran off to her own room.

The visions of romance were over. Catherine was completely awakened. Henry's address, short as it had been, had more thoroughly opened her eyes to the extravagance of her late fancies than all their several disappointments had done. Most grievously was she humbled. Most bitterly did she cry. It was not only with herself that she was sunk – but with Henry. Her folly, which now seemed even criminal, was all exposed to him, and he must despise her for ever. The liberty which her imagination had dared to take with the character of his father, could he ever forgive it? The absurdity of her curiosity and her fears, could they ever be forgotten? She hated herself more than she could express. . . .

Her thoughts being still chiefly fixed on what she had with such causeless terror felt and done, nothing could shortly be clearer, than that it had been all a voluntary, self-created delusion, each trifling circumstance receiving importance from an imagination resolved on alarm, and every thing forced to bend to one purpose by a mind which, before she entered the Abbey, had been craving to be frightened. She remembered with what feelings she had prepared for knowledge of Northanger. She saw that the infatuation had been created, the mischief settled long before her quitting Bath, and it seemed as if the whole might be traced to the influence of that sort of reading which she had there indulged.

Charming as were all Mrs. Radcliffe's works, and charming even as were the works of all her imitators, it was not in them perhaps that human nature, at least in the midland counties of England, was to be looked for. Of the Alps and Pyrenees, with their pine forests and their vices, they might give a faithful delineation; and Italy, Switzerland, and the South of France, might be as fruitful in horrors as they were there represented. Catherine dared not doubt beyond her own country, and even of that, if hard pressed, would have yielded the northern and western extremities. But in the central part of England there was surely some security for the existence even of a wife not beloved, in the laws of the land, and the manners of the age. Murder was not tolerated, servants were not slaves, and neither poison nor sleeping potions to be procured, like rhubarb, from every druggist. Among the Alps and Pyrenees, perhaps, there were no mixed characters. There, such as were not as spotless as an angel, might have the dispositions of a fiend. But in England it was not so; among the English, she believed, in their hearts and habits, there was a general though unequal mixture of good and bad. Upon this conviction, she would not be surprized if even in Henry and Eleanor Tilney, some slight imperfection might hereafter appear; and upon this conviction she need not fear to acknowledge some actual specks in the character of their father, who, though cleared from the grossly injurious suspicions which she must even blush to have entertained, she did believe, upon serious consideration, to be not perfectly amiable.

Her mind made up on these several points, and her resolution formed, of always judging and acting in future with the greatest good sense, she had nothing to do but to forgive herself and be happier than ever; and the lenient hand of time did much for her by insensible gradations in the course of another day. . . . The anxieties of common life began soon to succeed to the alarms of romance.

'The Scribbler' (1799)*

MARY ALCOCK (*c.* 1742–98)

Another Novel! Pray, have you read it, Sir? or you? Who the deuce would? cried an elderly gentleman (laying down the news-paper, and taking off his spectacles). I have already, Sir, waded through such an inundation of hobgoblin nonsense, of haunted castles, mysterious caverns, yawning graves, bleeding ghosts, &c. that, had they not a ready passage out of my head, I should expect to find my night-cap rise perpendicular from it, and every hair turned white with horror; yes, yes, Sir, such would be the effect every bloody-minded novel-writer wishes to inflict upon you; but I no sooner see the drift and cruelty of his intention, than I grow enraged at my author, arm myself with a coat of mail, not like Don Quixote, to fight my opponents as giants, but prepared to dispute the pass with them, to strip off their *white sheets*, to pluck out their *goggle eyes*, and shew them as nature designed them. There are another species of novel writers, rejoined a pale-faced and emaciated lady, far more difficult to combat, I mean your *professed* sentimental authors, who most ingeniously rack every corner of their brain to invent new tortures for your nerves; who deliberately probe every fibre in your heart, where, if any recent sorrow is lulled or suppressed, it is again torn open. Against these writers there is no appeal, for whilst there are readers found who not only *chuse* to waste their time, but *like* to be made unhappy into the bargain, there will ever be plenty of authors to assist them to the utmost of their wishes in the accomplishment of both. At the conclusion of this harrangue, I observed the gentleman who had unintentionally brought on this volley of abuse (by simply asking, have you read the new novel) slily slip two volumes into the chaos of trash upon the counter, and take two others from the shelf, saying, as he hobbled out, there, Mr. Librarian, I have taken Joe Miller's Jests and the Pilgrim's Progress, as I begin to think it is better after all to be merry and wise than sad and silly. And a good exchange he has made indeed, replied a lady; for the two books he had before singled out, I perceive, were the Sorrows of Werter, and the Self-Tormentor. As I had gotten possession of an arm-chair by the fire-side, to observe the important business of a circulating library, I found myself too comfortable, and too well entertained, to quit my seat hastily, particularly as at that instant three beautiful young ladies pressed in, and with animated and inquiring countenances requested the catalogue to chuse their studies from, when all crowding over it, the tallest of the three called out, Oh, my dearest Lydia, I have now met with the book I have been mad after, and absolutely dying for. I am told by Mrs. Dozer (who reads every thing) it is a most enchanting novel, and so affecting, it is enough to break your heart. She assured me she was blind with crying, and that poor Counsel-

* Mary Alcock, *Poems* (London: C. Dilly, 1799), pp. 173–6.

lor Winifred declared it had destroyed his appetite, and broke his night's rest for some time, for there are seven volumes. Seven volumes! repeated my elderly gentleman; seven plagues and seven furies! No sooner had this exclamation escaped his lips, than the three young ladies burst into a loud laugh, and cried, 'What a gig he is, I quizzed him the instant I came in.'

A young lady in a loose morning dress now tripped in, and whispered [to] a young man behind the counter, but not so low but I could hear her enquiry was for the *Monk*; and on the man assuring her all his sets were from home, she cried, 'that is deplorable indeed; to be kept just at the most critical and interesting part waiting for the last volume; I wish your master would buy more sets of a novel on which so much is said and written.' I was sorry to hear my friend in the corner had not overheard the whisper of the fair enquirer, being well assured he would not have suffered a book of such an alarming tendency (particularly in the hands of so young a student) to have been named without his admonition to the reader, and his anathema against the writer. I felt pained (on contemplating the innocent countenance of the young lady) to think that blasphemy and obscenity should ever meet her eye? I wished to speak and stop the contagion of the evil, as it seemed as yet not to have diffused its baneful influence; but to accost her, and to counsel her, would be uncommon, and be deemed impertinent. How superior, thought I, are those characters, who, regardless of the punctilios of breeding, will dare to do good to their fellow creatures, by obtruding their advice unasked. With this reflection I arose dissatisfied with myself, and having lost all the comfort, quitted the amusements, of my arm-chair. In my way home I tried to divert my mind by a walk through the park; it was in vain; the young lady and her companion the Monk occupied my mind too much to admit of it. I now accused myself of a breach of christianity in not warning her of the dangerous tendency of such studies to young and unformed minds; I lamented the fashions of the world, which lead us to comply with the follies and vices of it, instead of guarding ourselves and others from them.

'A Village Circulating Library' (1804)*

CHARLES DIBDIN (1745–1814)

Scenery. – A house neatly fitted up in the modern cottage style; a door in the centre of the scene and one on each side: over the centre, the words 'Circulating Library,' in large letters; on one side, 'The Reading Room,' on the opposite 'Academy.'

---

* Francis William Blagdon (ed.), *Flowers of Literature; for 1804* (London: B. Crosby, 1805), pp. 384–5; from Dibdin's five-act comedy *Guilty or Not Guilty*, performed at Covent Garden in 1804.

Trian. – . . . So, so – in times like these it requires every man of business to be as watchful as Cerberus, in order to obtain a decent livelihood – and, egad, if I hadn't, like Cerberus, a triple head, I should never have managed to become, at once, the superintendant of three literary departments, [*looking round*] 'Academy,' 'Library,' and 'Reading Room,' – by which means I draw the whole village to my interest; the women read my novels, the men my newspapers, and the children come to school. To be sure, the news-room is a little too close to the academy, for my customers can't read for the chattering of the boys, and the scholars can't study for the quarrels of the newspaper politicians, who, while they damn the *Times*, and upset the *Globe*, are all ready to fight for the honour of the *British Press*.

Enter DICKY.

Well, Dicky, you have carried out the books?

Dicky. – Yes, Sir; here is the list of what's delivered and what is wanting.

Trian. – Oh, let's see [*reads*] 'Counselor Crab wants *Liberal Opinions*' – I'm sorry for that, for it's not at home. 'The taylor's wife has had *Mysterious Warnings*, and the apothecary's journeyman, *Pills to purge Melancholy*.' Now you must take *Tales of Terror* to the widow Tremor – *More Ghosts* to the sexton's daughter, the *Curse of Sentiment* to the butcher, *Melting Moments* to the tallow chandler, and *Old Nick* to the attorney.

Dicky. – Yes, Sir; he! he! he! I'll take the attorney to Old Nick.

Trian. – No, no, there'll be no necessity for that. Get along, and do as I bid you. [*Exit* Dicky.]

'To Make a Novel' (1810)*

A novel may be made out of a romance, or a romance out of a novel, with the greatest ease, by scratching out a few terms, and inserting others. . . . From any romance to make a novel. Where you find –

A castle,	put An house.
A cavern,	A bower.
A groan,	A sigh.
A giant,	A father.
A blood-stained dagger,	A fan.
Howling blasts,	Zephyrs.
A knight,	A gentleman without whiskers.
A lady who is the heroine,	Need not be changed, being versatile.

* *The Age; A Poem* (London: Vernor, Hood, and Sharpe, 1810), pp. 209–10.

Assassins, ...	Killing glances.
A monk, ...	An old steward.
Skeletons, skulls, &c	Compliments, sentiments, &c.
A lamp, ...	A candle.
A magic book sprinkled with blood, .	A letter bedewed with tears.
Mysterious voices, ...	Abstruse words, (easily found in a dictionary).
A secret oath, ...	A tender hint accompanied with naiveté.
A gliding ghost, ...	A usurer, or an attorney.
A witch, ...	An old housekeeper.
A wound, ...	A kiss.
A midnight murder, ...	A marriage.

The same table of course answers for transmuting a novel into a romance.

The Age; A Poem (1810)*

Say who is this mysterious creature
So bitterly accusing nature,
With loose attire, and mien so wild?
She looks like madness or her child.
Pursue her steps! yet still beware
Of some bewitchment or a snare.
She goes with look enthusiastic
To yonder edifice fantastic,
Where fancy speaking from its trances
Gives inspiration of romances.
Here vot'ries crowd of all conditions
To view the fleeting exhibitions;
And, well as crazy brain permits
Sketch down each vision as it flits:
While deeper mysteries are brewing
They see at first a gothic ruin.
(This seems to be a rule of late
From which none dare to deviate)
'Tis castle large with turrets high
Intruding always on the sky;
And as they're old in place of clothes
Around them ivy kindly grows;

---

* *The Age; A Poem* (London: Vernor, Hood, and Sharpe, 1810), pp. 201–9.

Somewhat like Adam's coat or Eve's,
Except for fig, they're ivy leaves.
On ev'ry tow'r, to please the sight,
The moon bestows a speck of light
Like patches stuck on ladies' skin,
To shew how fair, or p'rhaps how thin.
The stairs and passages so wind,
The way's impossible to find;
And who to venture in them durst
Must always lose himself at first.
The windows close, thro' which, about
Each hour, some curious Ghost peeps out;
As if he had a slight suspicion
Folks might walk in without permission:
For all such castles, with their rights
Are ever property of sprites;
And Lords who think they own them still
Are merely tenantry at will.
Woods all around are thickly set
Which 'stead of green, are black as jet.
Beyond these rise a ridge of rocks
At which imagination shocks;
While each his horrid face out pushes
Like robbers peeping over bushes.
Then comes a true and valiant Knight
Who only seems to live to fight;
One moment never free from toils
If possible, and cruel broils;
To whom, cuts, gashes, wounds, and bruises
Are toys, with which he self amuses.
Whene'er good humour'd, nought but grace
Should dare intrude upon his face;
But, when his looks to anger waken
From Cerberus they should be taken.
That which he rides, a milk-white steed
Most usually's of fairy breed,
What road to take, if slow or faster,
Seems to know better than his master.
Next comes a monk with disposition
Endeav'ring solely for perdition;
Without design or end in view
For which the devil's work he'll do.
Attend! for lo, a virgin form
Swells on 'the zephyr's bosom warm;'

From her blue eye a magic glance
Must lay the valiant Knight in trance;
For special purpose, that which much
Ado, she may his hand just touch:
He seldom the occasion misses
Upon her hand to perch some kisses,
Which should thereon be seen to linger
More plain than rings upon her finger.
Whene'er she moves 'tis done by notes
Nor e'er walks vulgarly, 'She floats:'
. . .

    On her misfortunes swiftly press
To plunge her into deep distress,
Borne off by night by wizard rogue or
A giant, griffon, or an ogre;
Which accident the Knight must hear
By furies screech'd within his ear;
With some small share rejoicing too
As giving him somewhat to do;
Then on his steed exactly flies
To where his virgin captive lies:
The dreadful castle where no breath
Can stir, but thro' the jaws of Death;
Thro' darkness ever he must grope,
Locks burst, doors fly, and windows ope;
Bells toll, and while his ears are dinning
A dozen ghosts at eyes are grinning.
'Till starting up a sulph'rous flame
Without intending, shews the dame.
Then strange to tell! when tale is done
The reader learns 'twas all in fun.
And easy the enchantment's broke
By saying it was but a joke.

    This species seems to rank most high
Of all amid romantic fry;
When, in innumerable hosts
Rise up mock wizards, gorgons, ghosts.
'Twas one like these that Quixote made
To turn upon knight-errant trade;
As most unluckily his head
Had never the conclusion read.
And in these days, the Gothic sect
Can scribble with a good effect,

Whene'er these tales like lighted match
Can fire imagination's thatch:
Yet strange! by those who're undeceiv'd
Such frauds are o'er again believ'd,
And for their sake, from meals they fast
But to be cheated at the last.
Some breeds there are whose sullen brain
Can scarce such lofty flights attain;
Not fully gifted in their fancy
With artificial necromancy:
But all must conjure castles, knights,
And virgins, noises, mystic lights,
With plot of an infernal hue,
Impervious to the keenest view:
For myst'ries puzzles in relation
Essential are to their formation,
As much as is to bullets, lead,
Or flour and water are to bread.

. . .

   Hail! Germany most favored, who
Seems a romantic rendezvous;
Thro'out whose large and tumid veins
The unmixt Gothic current reigns!
Much thou hast giv'n of precious hosts
Of monsters, wizards, giants, ghosts:
Yet, give our babes of fancy more
Impart to novelists thy store!
'Till classic science dull monastic
Dissolves in flood enthusiastic.

. . .

The Heroine; or Adventures of Cherubina (1813)*

EATON STANNARD BARRETT (1786–1820)

Eaton Stannard Barrett was a political writer, prolific satirical poet and occasional writer of farces. His best novel, The Heroine, *is a series of letters written by 15-year-old Cherry to her former governess, recording her attempts to find a romantic alternative to her middle-class respectability. Her father burns all the novels in the house, so she runs away from home. After a series of adventures, she mistakes*

---

* Eaton Stannard Barrett, *The Heroine, or Adventures of Cherubina*, 2nd edn, 3 vols (London: Henry Colburn, 1814), vol. 1, pp. 33–5, 44–6, 153–6; vol. 2, pp. 151–2, 156–60, 163–4.

Covent Garden Theatre for a castle, and falls in love with the mad actor Abraham Grundy, who claims his real name is Lord Altamont Mortimer Montmorenci. The novel has large set-piece parodies of scenes from Radcliffe's The Mysteries of Udolpho *(and some plagiarism), and some amusing one-liners: Lady Bontein has 'one shoulder of the Gothic order', and Jerry O'Sullivan, a woollen-draper whom Cherry takes on as her servant, is renamed Jeronymo, for 'Nothing can equal Italian names ending in O.' By the end of the third volume Cherry inherits a genuine Gothic castle, but lacking the money for feudal splendour manages to decorate only one room, dubbed 'THE BLACK CHAMBER'. Unable to endure the cold and damp of her dilapidated Castello, she returns to a comfortable life of 'balls, operas, and familiar parties' and gives up reading novels. Jane Austen wrote to her sister Cassandra on 2/3 March 1814: 'I finished the Heroine last night & was very much amused by it. I wonder James did not like it better. It diverted me exceedingly. – We went to bed at 10. . . . It is Even* [3 March]*. We have drank tea & I have torn through the 3^d vol. of the Heroine, & do not think it falls off. – It is a delightful burlesque, particularly on the Radcliffe style.'*

But you must naturally wish to learn what has happened here since your departure. I was in my boudoir, reading the Delicate Distress, when I heard a sudden bustle below and 'Out of the house, this moment,' vociferated my father. The next minute he was in my room with a face like fire.

'There!' cried he, 'I knew what your famous romances would do for us at last.'

'Fie!' said I, playfully spreading my fingers over his face. 'Don't frown so, but tell me what these famous romances have done?'

'Only a kissing match between the Governess and the Butler,' answered he. 'I caught them at the sport in the pantry.'

I was petrified. 'Dear Sir,' said I, 'you must surely mistake.'

'No such thing,' cried he. 'The kiss was too much of a smacker for that. – Egad, it rang through the pantry like the smash of twenty plates. But she shall never darken my doors again, never. I have just packed the pair of wrinkled sweethearts off together; and what is better, I have ordered all the novels in the house to be burnt, by way of purification. They talk so much of flames, that I suppose they will like to feel them.' He spoke, and ran raging out of the room.

Adieu, then, ye dear romances, adieu for ever. No more shall I sympathize with your heroines, while they faint and blush, and weep, through four half-bound octavos. Adieu, ye Edwins, Edgars, and Edmunds; ye Selinas, Evelinas, Malvinas: ye inas all adieu! The flames will consume all. The melody of Emily, the prattle of Annette, and the hoarseness of Ugo, will be confounded in one indiscriminate crackle. The Casa and Castello will blaze with equal fury; nor will the virtue of Pamela aught avail to save;

nor Wolmar delighting to see his wife in a swoon; nor Werter shelling peas and reading Homer, nor Charlotte cutting bread and butter for the children. . . .

Soon after my last letter, I was summoned to dinner. What heroine in distress but starves? so I sent a message that I was unwell, and then solaced myself with a volume of the Mysteries of Udolpho, which had escaped the conflagration. Afterwards I flung myself on my bed, in hopes to have dreams portentous of my future fate; for heroines are remarkably subject to a certain prophetic sort of night-mare. You remember the story which Ludovico read, of a spectre that beckons a Baron from his castle in the dead of night, and leading him into a forest, points to his own corpse, and bids him bury it. Well, owing, I suppose, to my having just read this episode, and to my having fasted so long, I had the following dreams.

Methought a delicious odour of viands attracted me to the kitchen, where I found an iron pot upon the fire simmering in unison with my sighs. As I looked at it with a longing eye, the lid began to rise, and I beheld a half-boiled turkey stalk majestically forth. It beckoned me with its claw. I followed. It led me into the yard, and pointed to its own head and feathers, which were lying in a corner.

What a vulgar, what a disgusting vision, when I ought to have dreamt of nothing but coffins and ladies in black! . . .

[Abraham Grundy begins to tell his tale to Cherry:]
'All was dark. The hurricane howled, the wet rain fell, and the thunder rolled in an awful and Ossianly manner.

'On a beetling rock, lashed by the Gulph of Salerno, stood Il Castello di Grimgothico.

'"My lads, are your carbines charged, and your sabres sharpened?" cried Stiletto.

'"If they an't, we might load our carbines with this hail, and sharpen our sabres against this north wind," cried Poignardi.

'"The wind is east-south-east," cried Daggeroni.

'At that moment the bell of Grimgothico tolled one. The sound vibrated through the long corridors, the spiral staircases, the suites of tapestried apartments, and the ears of the personage who has the honour to address you. Much alarmed, I started from my couch; but conceive my horror when I beheld my chamber filled with banditti! They were sent by Napoleon (that awful oddity) to dispatch me, because of my glorious struggle against him in Italy.

'Snatching my faulchion, I flew to the armoury for my coat of mail. The bravos rushed after me; but I fought and dressed, and dressed and fought, till I had perfectly completed my unpleasing toilette. . . .

'At length I murdered my way down to my little skiff, embarked in it, and arrived at this island. As I first touched foot on its chalky beach, "Hail, happy land," cried I, "hail, thrice hail!"

"'There is no hail here, Sir," said a child running by; "but come with me, and I will shew you a wedding."

"'And who are to be married," asked I, lifting the little innocent in my arms.

"'The Marquis de Furioso, and the Lady Sympathina, daughter to Baron Hildebrand," answered little Billy. . . .'

[Cherry discovers her supposed mother in the subterranean dungeon:]
 When I retired to rest, I found this note on my toilette.

To the Lady Cherubina.

Your mother lives! and is confined in a subterranean vault of the villa. At midnight two men will tap at your door, and conduct you to her. Be silent, courageous, and circumspect.

What a flood of new feelings gushed upon my soul, as I laid down the billet, and lifted my filial eyes to heaven! Mother – endearing name! I pictured that unfortunate lady, stretched on a mattrass [*sic*] of straw, her eyes sunken in their sockets, yet retaining a portion of their youthful fire; her frame emaciated, her voice feeble, her hand damp and chill. Fondly did I depict our meeting – our embrace; she gently pushing me from her, and baring my forehead to gaze on the lineaments of my countenance. . . .

[My conductor] stopped, and unlocked a door.

'Enter,' said he, 'and behold your mother!'

He led me forward, tore the bandage from my eyes, and retiring, locked the door after him.

Agitated already by the terrors of my dangerous expedition, I felt additional horror in finding myself within a dismal cell, lighted with a lantern; where, at a small table, sat a woman suffering under a corpulency unparalleled in the memoirs of human monsters. Her dress was a patchwork of blankets and satins, and her grey tresses were like horse's tails. Hundreds of frogs leaped about the floor; a piece of mouldy bread, and a mug of water, lay on the table; some straw, strewn with dead snakes and sculls, occupied one corner, and the distant end of the cell was concealed behind a black curtain.

I stood at the door, doubtful, and afraid to advance; while the prodigious prisoner sat examining me all over.

At last I summoned courage to say, 'I fear, Madam, I am an intruder here. I have certainly been shewn into the wrong room.'

'It is, it is my own, my only daughter, my Cherubina!' cried she, with a tremendous voice. 'Come to my maternal arms, thou living picture of the departed Theodore!'

'Why, Ma'am,' said I, 'I would with great pleasure, but I am afraid – Oh, Madam, indeed, indeed, I am quite sure you cannot be my mother!'

'Why not, thou unnatural girl?' cried she.

'Because, Madam,' answered I, 'my mother was of thin habit; as her portrait proves.'

'And so was I once,' said she. 'This deplorable plumpness is owing to want of exercise. But I thank the Gods I am as pale as ever!'

'Heavens! no,' cried I. 'Your face, pardon me, is a rich scarlet.'

'And is this our tender meeting?' cried she. 'To disown me, to throw my fat in my teeth, to violet the lilies of my skin, with a dash of scarlet? Hey diddle diddle, the cat and the fiddle! Tell me, girl, will you embrace me, or will you not?'

'Indeed, Madam,' answered I, 'I will presently.'

'Presently!'

'Yes, depend upon it I will. Only let me get over the first shock.'

'Shock!'

Dreading her violence, and feeling myself bound to do the duties of a daughter, I kneeled at her feet, and said:

'Ever respected, ever venerable author of my being, I beg thy maternal blessing!'

My mother raised me from the ground, and hugged me to her heart, with such cruel vigour, that, almost crushed, I cried out stoutly, and struggled for release.

'And now,' said she, relaxing her grasp, 'let me tell you of my sufferings. Ten long years, I have eaten nothing but bread. Oh, ye favourite pullets, oh, ye inimitable tit-bits, shall I never, never taste you more? It was but last night, that maddened by hunger, methought I beheld the Genius of dinner in my dreams. His mantle was laced with silver eels, and his locks were dropping with soups. He had a crown of golden fishes upon his head, and pheasants' wings at his shoulders. A flight of little tartlets fluttered about him, and the sky rained down comfits. As I gazed on him, he vanished in a sigh, that was impregnated with the fumes of brandy. Hey diddle diddle, the cat and the fiddle.'

I stood shuddering, and hating her more and more every moment. . . .

Such was the detestable adventure of to-night. Oh, Biddy, that I should live to meet this mother of mine! How different from the mothers that other heroines rummage out in northern turrets and ruined chapels! I am out of all patience. Liberate her I must, of course, and make a suitable provision for her too, when I get my property; but positively, never will I sleep under the same roof with – (ye powers of filial love forgive me!) such a living mountain of human horror.

7

Theory and Criticism

THE CONTEMPORARY CRITICAL DEBATE about the Gothic novel centred on three interrelated issues: the power of fear and the supernatural to stimulate the creative imagination (for both writer and reader); the tendency of the genre to deprave and corrupt its readers; and the subversive or revolutionary political nature of the genre. These three aesthetic, moral and ideological critiques are linked by the repeated charge that such literature appeals to and is created by 'the distempered imagination'.

The aesthetic discussion at its highest level concerned the nature of terror and 'the sublime', and, at its lowest, 'hobgobliana'. Whether the creator of such literature was considered to be a romantic genius or a terrifier of children in the nursery and a panderer to vulgar taste depended partly on the political stance of the critic and the perceived politics of the novelist. At the height of the rage for the Gothic, the categories of the Beautiful, the Sublime, the Picturesque and the Pathetic (or Melancholic) were all formally analysed into their constituent subdivisions. Sublime sounds, for example, were analysed by Rev. Archibald Allison, famous organist and music theorist: 'The noise of an engagement heard from a distance, is dreadfully Sublime' whereas 'The firing of a Review is scarcely more than magnificent.' The artificiality of this kind of 'associationism' was sometimes criticized, for example Gilpin was reproached for his insensitivity in appreciating the 'picturesqueness' of impoverished peasants in the foreground of landscapes.

The argument over the moral tendency of the genre centred on the obscenity and blasphemy in M. G. Lewis's *The Monk* (1796). Lewis's advertisement of the fact that he was a Member of Parliament created a public scandal. Thomas James Mathias, Treasurer to the Queen and Librarian at Buckingham Palace, and highly respected editor of Thomas Gray's works, argued that Lewis should be prosecuted at law, with the effect that Lewis quickly suppressed the offending passages in the second edition of his novel. The blasphemy and obscenity may be mild by modern standards, but they undoubtedly exist, and even today Lewis succeeds in his apparent intention to shock and to subvert conventional morality.

The political dimension of the debate may be better appreciated today, with our postmodern sensitivity to ideological issues. Much criticism of Gothic literature is class-based: subscribers to circulating libraries are often characterized as possessing the vulgar taste of the lower classes. By the end of 'the first wave' the predominant critique was that Gothic novels were suitable only for kitchen maids. But the underlying fear was that Gothic novels were a threat both to the bourgeois middle class and to the established upper class. Novelists were perceived as advocates of the principles of the French Revolution – which in many cases they were. Writers such as Anna Laetitia Barbauld, Ann Radcliffe and Charlotte Smith came from Dissenting backgrounds that opposed the rigid hierarchy of Anglicanism and were 'democratically inclined'. The Marquis de Sade observed in 1800 that Gothic novels were 'the inevitable fruit of the revolutionary shocks felt by the whole of Europe' (*Idée sur les Romans*). William Hazlitt said that Radcliffe's mouldering castles 'derived part of their interest, no doubt, from the supposed tottering state of all old structures at the time'. Free thinking was practised and defended by the circle of political radicals around William Godwin and Mary Wollstonecraft. Their friend Mary Hays, in her feminist novel *Memoirs of Emma Courtney* (1796), linked the names of Godwin, Wollstonecraft, Rousseau, Radcliffe, Lewis and Holcroft, and the critic Allan Cunningham in 1834 remarked that 'William Godwin is the Anne Radcliffe of moral order and social law'. Reactionary journals such as the *Anti-Jacobin Review* attacked sensibility and the Gothic as being sickly, effeminate, revolutionary and French: in a word, un-English. And most of the conservative attacks on the Terrorist School were blatantly sexist attacks upon women, characterized as viragos:

> Ye female scribes! who write without a blot,
> 'Mysterious Warnings' of – the Lord knows what;
> O quit this trade, exert your proper skill,
> Resume the needle, and lay down the quill.
> (*Aberdeen Magazine*, 1798)

In addition to covering the main issues in such debates, I have included reviews of the major novelists, often by major critics (though Coleridge is mistakenly taken as the reviewer of Radcliffe's *Mysteries of Udolpho*), and critical commentary on their respective merits. The chronological arrangement of the selections charts the steady increase in the popularity of Gothic fiction, and the last few selections record its steep decline. There is general agreement that although the Gothic tradition had some outstanding writers, their imitators lacked their skill and could not maintain it, and were no match for the new fashion for picturesque realism, as in the novels of Sir Walter Scott. This section concludes with one of six lectures that D. M. Moir gave to the Edinburgh Philosophical Institution in 1850/51, which constitutes an admirable summing up of the first wave of the Gothic, and indicates the extent to which Lewis and the 'German' School of Horror rather than Radcliffe and the sentimental School of Terror would come to dominate the second wave.

'On the Pleasure Derived from Objects of Terror' (1773)*

Anna Laetitia Aikin (1743–1825)

Anna Laetitia Aikin was the daughter of Dr John Aikin, a teacher at the famous Warrington Academy in the North West Midlands, the Dissenting alternative to the Anglican universities of Cambridge and Oxford. She married Rochemont Barbauld, a former student at Warrington Academy (who went insane and killed himself in 1808). She moved in Unitarian circles, advocating the abolition of the slave trade, freedom of speech, and freedom of religion. In 1810 she edited a 50-volume collection of the British Novelists (which contained the major Gothic novels), with critical introductions and a comprehensive essay 'On the Origin and Progress of Novel-Writing', in which she pointed out that 'it may safely be affirmed that we have more good writers in this walk living at the present time, than at any period since the days of Richardson and Fielding. A very great proportion of these are ladies: and surely it will not be said that either taste or morals have been losers by their taking the pen in hand.' She was a defender of the Goddess of Liberty long before, and after, the French Revolution. She was so severely attacked for her political poem on freedom, Eighteen Hundred and Eleven (1812), that she ceased writing and even stopped preparations for the publication of her collected works. The following essay preceded her brother's fragmentary tale Sir Bertrand *(see pp. 7ff.), which was meant to illustrate the two sorts of terrifying pleasure she discusses.*

That the exercise of our benevolent feelings, as called forth by the view of human afflictions, should be a source of pleasure, cannot appear wonderful to one who considers that relation between the moral and natural system of man, which has connected a degree of satisfaction with every action or emotion productive of the general welfare. The painful sensation immediately arising from a scene of misery, is so much softened and alleviated by the reflex sense of self-approbation on attending virtuous sympathy, that we find, on the whole, a very exquisite and refined pleasure remaining, which makes us desirous of again being witnesses to such scenes, instead of flying from them with disgust and horror. It is obvious how greatly such a provision must conduce to the ends of mutual support and assistance. But the apparent delight with which we dwell upon objects of pure terror, where our moral feelings are not in the least concerned, and no passion seems to be excited by the depressing one of fear, is a paradox of the heart, much more difficult of solution.

The reality of this source of pleasure seems evident from daily observation. The greediness with which the tales of ghosts and goblins, or murders, earthquakes, fires, shipwrecks, and all the most terrible disasters attending

★ J. and A. L. Aikin, *Miscellaneous Pieces, in Prose* (London: J. Johnson, 1773), pp. 119–27.

human life, are devoured by every ear, must have been generally remarked. Tragedy, the most favourite work of fiction, has taken a full share of those scenes; 'it has supt full with horrors' – and has, perhaps, been more indebted to them for public admiration than to its tender and pathetic parts. The ghost of Hamlet, Macbeth descending into the witches' cave, and the tent scene in Richard, command as forcibly the attention of our souls as the parting of Jaffeir and Belvidera, the fall of Wolsey, or the death of Shore. The inspiration of *terror* was by the antient critics assigned as the peculiar province of tragedy; and the Greek and Roman tragedians have introduce[d] some extraordinary personages for this purpose: not only the shades of the dead, but the furies, and other fabulous inhabitants of the infernal regions. Collins, in his most poetical ode to Fear, has finely enforced this idea.

> Tho' gentle Pity claim her mingled part,
> Yet all the thunders of the scene are thine.

The old Gothic romance and the Eastern tale, with their genii, giants, enchantments, and transformations, however a refined critic may censure them as absurd and extravagant, will ever retain a most powerful influence on the mind, and interest the reader independently of all peculiarity of taste. Thus the great Milton, who had a strong bias [*sic*] to these wildnesses of the imagination, has with striking effect made the stories 'of forests and enchantments drear,' a favourite subject with his *Penseroso*; and had undoubtedly their awakening images strong upon his mind when he breaks out,

> Call up him that left half-told
> The story of Cambuscan bold; &c.

How are we then to account for the pleasure derived from such objects? I have often been led to imagine that there is a deception in these cases; and that the avidity with which we attend is not a proof of our receiving real pleasure. The pain of suspense, and the irresistible desire of satisfying curiosity, when once raised, will account for our eagerness to go quite through an adventure, though we suffer actual pain during the whole course of it. We rather chuse to suffer the smart pang of a violent emotion than the uneasy craving of an unsatisfied desire. That this principle, in many instances, may involuntarily carry us through what we dislike, I am convinced from experience. This is the impulse which renders the poorest and most insipid narrative interesting when once we get fairly into it; and I have frequently felt it with regard to our modern novels, which, if lying on my table, and taken up in an idle hour, have led me through the most tedious and disgusting pages, while, like Pistol eating his leek, I have swallowed and execrated to the end. And it will not only force us through dullness, but through actual torture – through the relation of a Damien's execution, or an inquisitor's act of faith. When children, therefore, listen with pale and mute attention to the frightful stories of apparitions, we are not, perhaps, to imagine that they are in a state of enjoyment, any more than the poor bird which is dropping into the mouth of the rattlesnake – they are chained by the ears, and fascinated by curiosity. This solution, however, does not satisfy me with respect to the well-wrought scenes of artificial terror which are formed by a sublime and vigorous imagination. Here, though we know beforehand what to expect, we enter into them with eagerness, in quest of a pleasure already experienced. This is the pleasure constantly attached to the excitement of surprise from new and wonderful objects. A strange and unexpected event awakens the mind, and keeps it on the stretch; and where the agency of invisible beings is introduced, of 'forms unseen, and mightier far than we,' our imagination, darting forth, explores with rapture the new world which is laid open to its view, and rejoices in the expansion of its powers. Passion and fancy co-operating elevate the soul to its highest pitch; and the pain of terror is lost in amazement.

Hence, the more wild, fanciful, and extraordinary are the circumstances of a scene of horror, the more pleasure we receive from it; and where they are too near common nature, though violently borne by curiosity through the adventure, we cannot repeat it or reflect on it, without an over-balance of pain. In the *Arabian nights* [sic] are many most striking examples of the terrible joined with the marvellous: the story of Aladdin and the travels of Sinbad are particularly excellent. The *Castle of Otranto* is a very spirited modern attempt upon the same plan of mixed terror, adapted to the model of Gothic romance. The best conceived, and most strongly worked-up scene of mere natural horror that I recollect, is in Smollett's *Ferdinand count Fathom* [sic]; where the hero, entertained in a lone house in a forest, finds a corpse just slaughtered in the room where he is sent to sleep, and the door of which is locked upon him. It may be amusing for the reader to compare his feelings upon these, and from thence form his opinion of the justness of my theory.

'Illustrations on Sublimity' (1783)*

JAMES BEATTIE (1735–1803)

The Scottish poet and philosopher James Beattie occupied the chair of moral philosophy and logic at Marischal College, Aberdeen (and later taught in Edinburgh). He was a friend of many Scottish worthies, and in the 1770s became a good friend of

---

* James Beattie, *Dissertations Moral and Critical* (London: S. Strahan; T. Cadell; Edinburgh: W. Creech, 1783), pp. 615–16.

John Gray, Dr Johnson, Garrick, Mrs Montagu and her circle of Bluestockings. He
wrote a famous Essay on Truth *(1770) attacking the rational scepticism of Hume*
and Voltaire, and later added essays on Poetry and Music, Laughter and Ludicrous
Composition, and related subjects. Beattie would sit up all night under the open sky
admiring the romantic scenery. His poem The Minstrel *(see pp. 225ff.) uses the*
Spenserian stanza and develops the theme of the romantic enthusiast.

. . . the Sublime, in order to give pleasing astonishment, must be either
imaginary, or not immediately pernicious.

There is a kind of horror, which may be infused into the mind both by
natural appearances, and by verbal description; and which, though it make
the blood seem to run cold, and produce a momentary fear, is not unpleasing, but may be even agreeable: and therefore, the objects that produce it
are justly denominated sublime. Of natural appearances that affect the mind
in this manner, are vast caverns, deep and dark woods, overhanging
precipices, and agitation of the sea in a storm: and some of the sounds
above-mentioned have the same effect, as those of cannon and thunder.
Verbal descriptions infusing sublime horror are such as convey lively ideas,
of the objects of superstition, as ghosts and enchantments; or of the
thoughts that haunt the imaginations of the guilty; or of those external
things, which are pleasingly terrible, as storms, conflagrations, and the like.

It may seem strange, that horror of any kind should give pleasure. But
the fact is certain. Why do people run to see battles, executions, and shipwrecks? Is it, as an Epicurean would say, to compare themselves with
others, and exult in their own security while they see the distress of those
who suffer? No, surely: good minds are swayed by different motives. Is it,
that they may be at hand, to give every assistance in their power to their
unhappy brethren? This would draw the benevolent, and even the tender-
hearted, to a shipwreck; but to a battle, or to an execution, could not bring
spectators, because there the humanity of individuals is of no use. – It must
be, because a sort of gloomy satisfaction, or terrifick pleasure, accompanies
the gratification of that curiosity which events of this nature are apt to raise
in minds of a certain frame.

No parts of Tasso are read with greater relish, than where he describes
the darkness, silence, and other horrors, of the enchanted forest: and the
poet himself is so sensible of the captivating influence of such ideas over the
human imagination, that he makes the catastrophe of the poem in some
measure depend upon them. Milton is not less enamoured 'of forests and
enchantments drear;' as appears from the use to which he applies them in
Comus: the scenery whereof charms us the more, because it affects our
minds, as it did the bewildered lady, and causes 'a thousand fantasies' –

> – to throng into the memory,
> Of calling shapes, and beckoning shadows dire,
> And aery tongues, that syllable mens names
> On sands, and shoes, and desert wildernesses.

Forests in every age must have had attractive horrors: otherwise so many nations would not have resorted thither, to celebrate the rites of superstition. And the inventors of what is called the Gothick, but perhaps should rather be called the Saracen, architecture, must have been enraptured with the same imagery, when, in forming and arranging the pillars and ai[s]les of their churches, they were so careful to imitate the rows of lofty trees in a deep grove.

Observe a few children assembled about a fire, and listening to tales of apparitions and witchcraft. You may see them grow pale, and croud [*sic*] closer through fear: while he who is snug in the chimney corner, and at the greatest distance from the door, considers himself as peculiarly fortunate; because he thinks that, if the ghost should enter, he has a better chance to escape, than if he were in a more exposed situation. And yet, notwithstanding their present, and their apprehension of future, fears, you could not perhaps propose any amusement that would at this time be more acceptable. The same love of such horrors as are not attended with sensible inconvenience continues with us through life: and Aristotle has affirmed, that the end of tragedy is to purify the soul by the operations of pity and terror.

The Banished Man (1794)*

CHARLOTTE SMITH (1749–1806)

Charlotte Smith's biography is a Dickensian tale of calamities. Her husband's wealthy father died in 1776, leaving a complex and confusing will, whose trustees acted so slowly (and fraudulently) that her children (there would be a total of 12) could derive no benefit from their legacies, and the family sank into appalling poverty as she persevered in Chancery, making many enemies and detractors. Her husband, a mad spendthrift, was declared bankrupt, and she spent seven months living with him in debtors' prison, while her brother looked after the children. It was during this period of voluntary imprisonment that she began to write in order to earn money for the release of her husband; her Elegiac Sonnets *(1784; see p. 228) was very well received by the public and the critics. Her husband was released and their property was sold, but he quickly found himself in debt again and fled to France to evade his creditors. Mrs Smith reluctantly followed, and lived in an unheated château near*

---

* Charlotte Smith, *The Banished Man*, 4 vols (London: T. Cadell, Jun. and W. Davies, 1794), vol. 2, pp. iii–vi, x–xi.

Dieppe for one winter, but eventually separated from her foolish husband in 1787. She wrote one novel a year for the next ten years (plus translations), to support her children and send occasional payments to her husband. As the years progressed, one son had his leg amputated, one daughter died, arthritis crippled her fingers. At the time of writing The Banished Man *(1794) she said that 'long anxiety has ruined my health, and long oppression broken my spirits'. The bequests due under her children's grandfather's will were finally paid six months after her death.*

Charlotte Smith may be entitled to rank as co-creator of the School of Radcliffe. Her early novel Emmeline, or the Orphan of the Castle, *published early in 1788, was enormously successful and widely imitated, and firmly established the tradition that the heroine must be an orphan. The technique of introducing poems into the narrative also may have derived from* Emmeline, *which includes an 'Ode to Despair' and a Sonnet addressed to Night. Though primarily a novel of domestic sensibility, the heroine finds herself alone in a castle, hears hollow sounds, footsteps and whispers; her candle is almost extinguished as the lock to her door slowly turns; there is a flight through winding passages and galleries.* Emmeline *and* Ethelinde; or, the Recluse of the Lake *(1789) influenced Radcliffe, though in turn Radcliffe influenced Smith's* The Old Manor House *(1793), which in turn influenced Radcliffe's* Udolpho, *which in turn influenced Smith's later novels, which became more decidedly Gothic; there is a vampire in* Marchmont *(1796), a gang of banditti in* Montalbert *(1795), and the spectre of a dead mother haunts 'The Story of Edouardo' in* The Letters of a Solitary Wanderer *(1799). Smith's novels are generally less elegant and less evocative of terror and unease, and she was more clearly interested in social and political issues related to her treatment by men.*

Avis au lecteur

'There was, an please your honor,' said Corporal Trim, 'There was a certain king of Bohemia, who had seven castles.'

A modern Novelist, who, to write 'in the immediate taste,' has so great a demand for these structures, cannot but regret, that not one of the seven castles was sketched by the light and forcible pencil of Sterne: for if it be true that books are made, as he asserts, only as apothecaries make medicines, how much might have been obtained from the king of Bohemia's seven castles, towards the castles which frown in almost every modern novel?

For my part, who can now no longer build chateaux even en Espagne, I find that Mowbray Castle, Grasmere Abbey, the castle of Roch-March, the castle of Hauteville, and Rayland Hall, have taken so many of my materials to construct, that I have hardly a watch tower, a Gothic arch, a cedar parlour, or a long gallery, an illuminated window, or a ruined chapel, left to help myself. Yet some of these are indispensibly necessary; and I have already built and burnt down one of these venerable edifices in this work, yet must seek wherewithal to raise another.

But my ingenious contemporaries have fully possessed themselves of every bastion and buttress – of every tower and turret – of every gallery and gateway, together with all their furniture of ivy mantles, and mossy battlements; tapestry, and old pictures; owls, bats, and ravens – that I had some doubts whether, to avoid the charge of plagiarism, it would not have been better to have *earthed* my hero, and have sent him for adventures to the subterraneous town on the Chatelet mountain in Champagne, or even to Herculaneum, or Pompeii, where I think no scenes have yet been laid, and where I should have been in less danger of being again accused of borrowing, than I may perhaps be, while I only visit

> The glympses of the moon.

On giving the first volume however to a friend to peruse, and hinting at the difficulty I was sensible of in finding novelty for my dark drawings, he bade me remember the maxim so universally allowed –

> 'Qui rien n'est beau que le vrai.'
> ['Nothing is as beautiful as truth.']

I asked him how it were possible to adhere to *le vrai*, in a work like this. But I believe I shall be better understood if I re-relate our conversation in the way of dialogue.

Friend. – 'I do not mean to say that you can adhere to truth in a book which is avowedly a fiction; but as you have laid much of the scene in France, and at the distance of only a few months, I think you can be at no loss for *real* horrors, if a novel must abound in horrors; your imagination, however fertile, can suggest nothing of individual calamity, that has not there been exceeded. Keep therefore as nearly as you can to circumstances you have heard related, or to such as might have occurred in a country where murder stalks abroad, and calls itself patriotism; where the establishment of liberty serves as a pretence for the violation of humanity; and I am persuaded, though there may be less of the miraculous in your work; though it may resemble less

> A woman's story at a winter's fire
> Authoriz'd by her granddam,
> SHAKESPEARE.

yet it will have the advantage of bearing such a resemblance to truth as may best become fiction, and that you will be in less danger of having it said, that

> Fancy still cruises, when poor Sense is tired.
> YOUNG.

. . .

[Friend.] But on some future occasion I may give you more fully my opinion of English novels. I speak not of the trifles which issue everyday from the press to satisfy the idlest readers of a circulating library, but such as deserve to be read by persons who have other purposes in reading than to pass a vacant hour, or to escape for a few moments from the insipid monotony of prosperity, by engaging their minds in the detail of impossible adventures; of fables, that only a distempered imagination can produce, or a vitiated taste enjoy.

Author. – I shall be extremely obliged to you for your opinion, which cannot fail to entertain and edify me; though I believe, as far as relates to the business of novel writing, I shall never have occasion to avail myself of your judgment.

Friend. – Why so?

Author. – Because I think I have taken my leave for ever of that species of writing.

Friend. – Your imagination then is exhausted?

Author. – Perhaps not. – In the various combinations of human life – in the various shades of human character, there are almost inexhaustible sources, from whence observation may draw materials, that very slender talents may weave into connected narratives: but in this as in every other species of composition, there is a sort of fashion of the day. *Le vrai*, which you so properly recommend, or even *le vrai semblance*, seems not to be the present fashion. I have no pleasure in drawing figures which interest me no more than the allegoric personages of Spencer: besides, it is time to resign the field of fiction before there remains for me only the gleanings, or before I am compelled by the caprice of fashion to go for materials for my novels, as the authors of some popular dramas have lately done, to children's story books, or rather the collection which one sees in farm houses; the book of apparitions; or a dismal tale of an haunted house, shewing how the inhabitants were forced to leave the same by reason of a bloody and barbarous murder committed there twenty years before, which was fully brought to light.

Friend. – Well! but if you should change your mind, I can furnish you with *such* a ghost story.

Author. – I thank you – but I have no talents that way; and will rather endeavour, in whatever I may hereafter produce, (if I am still urged by the same necessity as has hitherto made me produce so much,) to remember, whenever it can be remembered with advantage,

Qui rien n'est beau que le vrai.

Review of Radcliffe's *Mysteries of Udolpho* (1794)★

The Mysteries of Udolpho, a Romance; interspersed with some Pieces of Poetry. By Ann Radcliffe, Author of the *Romance of the Forest*, &c. 4 Vols. Robinsons, 1794.

> Thine too these golden keys, immortal boy!
> This can unlock the gates of joy,
> Of horror, that and thrilling fears,
> Or ope the sacred source of sympathetic tears.

Such were the presents of the Muse to the infant Shakespeare, and though perhaps to no other mortal has she been so lavish of her gifts, the keys referring to the third line Mrs. Radcliffe must be allowed to be completely in possession of. This, all who have read the *Romance of the Forest* will willingly bear witness to. Nor does the present production require the name of its author to ascertain that it comes from the same hand. The same powers of description are displayed, the same predilection is discovered for the wonderful and the gloomy – the same mysterious terrors are continually exciting in the mind the idea of a supernatural appearance, keeping us, as it were, upon the very edge and confines of the world of spirits, and yet are ingeniously explained by familiar causes; curiosity is kept upon the stretch from page to page, and from volume to volume, and the secret, which the reader thinks himself every instant on the point of penetrating, flies like a phantom before him, and eludes his eagerness till the very last moment of protracted expectation. This art of escaping the guesses of the reader has been improved and brought to perfection along with the reader's sagacity; just as the various inventions of locks, bolts, and private drawers, in order to secure, fasten, and hide, have always kept pace with the ingenuity of the pickpocket and housebreaker, whose profession is to unlock, unfasten, and lay open what you have taken so much pains to conceal. In this contest of curiosity on one side, and invention on the other, Mrs. Radcliffe has certainly the advantage. She delights in concealing her plan with the most artificial contrivance, and seems to amuse herself with saying, at every turn and doubling of the story, 'Now you think you have me, but I shall take care to disappoint you.' This method is, however, liable to the following inconvenience, that in the search of what is new, an author is apt to forget what is natural; and, in rejecting the more obvious conclusions, to take those which are less satisfactory. The trite and the extravagant are the Scylla and Charybdis of writers who deal in fiction. With regard to the work before us, while we acknowledge the extraordinary powers of Mrs. Radcliffe, some readers will be inclined to doubt whether they have been exerted in the present work with equal effect as in

---

★ *Critical Review*, **11** (August 1794), pp. 361–3.

the *Romance of the Forest*. – Four volumes cannot depend entirely on terrific incidents and intricacy of story. They require character, unity of design, a delineation of the scenes of real life, and the variety of well supported contrast. The *Mysteries of Udolpho* are indeed relieved by much elegant description and picturesque scenery; but in the descriptions there is too much of sameness: the pine and the larch tree wave, and the full moon pours its lustre through almost every chapter. Curiosity is raised oftener than it is gratified; or rather, it is raised so high that no adequate gratification can be given it; the interest is completely dissolved when once the adventure is finished, and the reader, when he is got to the end of the work, looks about in vain for the spell which had bound him so strongly to it. There are other little defects, which impartiality obliges us to notice. The manners do not sufficiently correspond with the æra the author has chosen; which is the latter end of the sixteenth century. There is, perhaps, no direct anachronism, but the style of accomplishments given to the heroine, a country young lady, brought up on the banks of the Garonne; the mention of botany; of little circles of infidelity, &c. give so much the air of modern manners, as is not counterbalanced by Gothic arches and antique furniture. It is possible that the manners of different ages may not differ so much as we are apt to imagine, and more than probable that we are generally wrong when we attempt to delineate any but our own; but there is at least a style of manners which our imagination has appropriated to each period, and which, like the costume of theatrical dress, is not departed from without hurting the feelings. – The character of Annette, a talkative waiting-maid, is much worn, and that of the aunt, madame Cheron, is too low and selfish to excite any degree of interest, or justify the dangers her niece exposes herself to for her sake. We must likewise observe, that the adventures do not sufficiently point to one centre: we do not, however, attempt to analyse the story; as it would have no other effect than destroying the pleasure of the reader . . .

The Mysterious Warning (1796)*

Eliza Parsons (d. 1811)

Gothic novels by women were sometimes dedicated to royal and aristocratic patrons. For example, Anna Maria Mackenzie's Mysteries Elucidated *was dedicated to Her Royal Highness Caroline, Princess of Wales, in 1795, and Ann Radcliffe dedicated the fourth edition of* Romance of the Forest *to the Duchess of Leeds in 1794. Such dedications were sometimes graciously allowed in order to ensure a large subscription, perhaps to help a widowed novelist care for a large family. Regina Maria*

---

* Eliza Parsons, *The Mysterious Warning, A German Tale*, 4 vols (London: Printed for William Lane, at the Minerva Press, 1796), pp. 1–4; 1–2 (new sequence).

Roche's Contrast *(1828) was published by subscription to relieve her destitution, and dedicated to HRH the Princess Augusta Sophia. Such dedications might also be used to establish the unimpeachable respectability of the novelists, despite the horrific content of their work. Eliza Parsons uses the opportunity of her dedication to* The Mysterious Warning *(one of the seven 'horrid' novels listed in Austen's* Northanger Abbey; *see also pp. 46ff.) to defend the morality of her work.*

Dedication
To
HER ROYAL HIGHNESS
THE PRINCESS OF WALES.

MADAM,

That respect, which High Birth, exalted Station, and personal Charms, exacts, is generally paid without discrimination, because they are adventitious circumstances from whence no merit can be derived to the possessor: But when added to these, we see the most brilliant accomplishments, a graciousness of manners, a condescending sweetness, that implies a wish to be distinguished more by goodness than greatness; then, indeed, we cheerfully tender the homage of our *hearts*, and feel the highest gratification when uniting admiration with respect, we love and reverence the same object.

To this voluntary homage your Royal Highness is more peculiarly entitled; the dignified features in your character are affability, and that condescension, which, from the pre-eminence of your situation, have irresistible claims upon the mind, confirms the fascination of the eye, and has insured to you, Madam, the affection of a grateful and admiring people.

The suffrage or praise of an obscure individual can be no ways interesting to your Royal Highness; happily your virtues and graces speak for themselves, and require no officious herald to blazon them to the world.

Under this conviction I repress my own feelings, and have only to acknowledge, with equal pride and gratitude, the lively sense I entertain of the distinguished honour conferred on me, in being permitted to inscribe the following Work to your Royal Highness; though I have not the presumption to hope you can derive much amusement from the perusal. The few pretensions I have to merit are merely negative ones: I have never written a line tending to corrupt the heart, sully the imagination, or mislead the judgment of my young Readers.

With the most profound respect, and every sentiment that admiration and gratitude can inspire, I have the honour to remain,

Madam,
Your Royal Highness's
Most obliged,
And most devoted,

Leicester-Square, No. 22,   Humble servant,
Nov. 15, 1795.   ELIZA PARSONS.

The Author of the following Work feels herself under the necessity of apologiz[i]ng to her numerous Friends, for the too frequent demands she makes on their indulgence. – Conscious of her deficiency in talents, inclination has no share in her feeble attempts to entertain the Public: She obtrudes neither from vanity or confidence, and shrinks from the severity of criticism, in the hope that her insignificance may protect her from the pointed darts of ridicule. – To wit and humour, the effervescence of a lively imagination and a happy turn of mind, she can make no pretensions; her former works have been thought to dwell too much on scenes of horror, and melancholy events; she cannot refute the charge: Perhaps her writings take their colouring from her mind; – when the heart is not at ease, it is incapable of communicating cheerful ideas to the descriptive pen; therefore she wisely declines an attempt she is unequal to, of *diverting* her Readers.

Dulness is a defect of the head, and is pardonable. – Wit, and spirited talents, are too often apt to run riot; their redundancy may sometimes draw vicious characters, and describe profligacy of manners in such seducing glowing colours, as to affect the imagination, to catch the attention of young people, into whose hands works of this kind frequently fall, and may have the dangerous tendency to lessen the horror they ought to feel at vice, and the detestation such characters should inspire.

The Author of this Work is a *Parent*; as such, she has been strictly observant that her writings should never offend against delicacy or common sense. – She has never dictated one page, or suggested one idea inimical to the precepts of virtue, or that should suffuse the cheek of innocence with a blush. – Here rests her merit; she has no other claims, and throws herself on the mercy of liberal and candid minds.

The Pursuits of Literature
or, What You Will (1794–7)*

THOMAS JAMES MATHIAS (1754?–1835)

But there is one publication of the time too peculiar and too important to be passed over in a general reprehension. There is nothing with which it may be compared. A legislator in our own parliament, a member of the House of Commons of Great Britain, an elected guardian and defender of the laws, the religion, and the good manners of the country, has neither scrupled nor blushed to depict and to publish to the world the arts of lewd and systematic seduction, and to thrust upon the nation the most open and

---

* Thomas Mathias, *The Pursuits of Literature*, Fourth Part, 3rd edn (London: T. Becket, 1797), pp. ii–v.

unqualified blasphemy against the very code and volume of our religion. And all this, with his name, style, and title, prefixed to the novel or romance called 'THE MONK.' And one of our public theatres has allured the public attention *still more* to this novel, by a scenic representation of an Episode in it, not wholly uninteresting. '*O Proceres, Censore opus est, an Haruspice nobis?*' ['O ancestors! Do we have need of a moral reformer, or a soothsayer?' Juvenal, *Satire* 2] I consider this a new species of legislative or state-parricide. What is it to the kingdom at large, or what is it to all those whose office it is to maintain truth, and to instruct the rising abilities and hope of England, that the author of it is *a very young man*? That forsooth he is a man of genius and fancy? So much the worse. That there are very poetical descriptions of castles and abbies in this novel? So much the worse again, the novel is *more alluring* on that account. Is this a time to poison the waters of our land in their springs and fountains? Are we to add incitement to incitement, and corruption to corruption, till there neither is, nor can be, a return to virtuous action and to regulated life? Who knows *the age* of this author? I presume, very few. *Who does not know*, that he is a Member of Parliament? He has told us all so himself. I pretend not to know, . . . whether this be an object of parliamentary animadversion. Prudence may possibly forbid it. But we can feel that it is an object of moral and national reprehension, when a Senator openly and daringly violates his first duty to his country. There are wounds and obstructions and diseases in the polit- ical, as well as in the natural, body, for which the removal of the part affected is alone efficacious. At an hour like this, are we to stand in consult- ation on the remedy, when not only the disease is ascertained, but the very stage of the disease, and its specific symptoms? Are we to spare the sharpest instruments of authority and of censure, when public establishments are gangrened in the life-organs? . . . But men, however dignified in their political station, or gifted with genius and fortune and accomplishments, may at least be made ashamed, or alarmed, or convicted before the tribunal of public opinion. Before that tribunal, and to the law of reputation, and every abiding and powerful sanction by which that law is enforced, is Mr. LEWIS this day called to answer.

NOTE.

'THE MONK, a Romance in three volumes by M. LEWIS, Esq. M.P.' printed for Bell, Oxford Street. At first I thought that the name and title of the author were fictitious, and some of the *public* papers hinted it. But I have been solemnly and repeatedly assured, that it is the writing and publi- cation of M. LEWIS, Esq. *Member of Parliament*. It is sufficient for me to point out Chap. 7. of Vol. 2. As a composition, the work would have been better, if the offensive and scandalous passages had been omitted, and it is disgraced by a *diablerie* and nonsense fitted only to frighten children in the

nursery. I believe this 7th Chap. of Vol. 2. *is actionable at Common Law.*
Edmund Curl in the first year of George II. was prosecuted by the Attorney
General (Sir Philip Yorke afterwards Lord Hardwicke) for printing two
obscene books. The Attorney General set forth several obscene passages,
and concluded, that *it was an offence against the King's peace.* The defendant
was found guilty and set in the pillory. . . . We know the proceedings
against the book, entitled 'Memoirs of a Woman of Pleasure,' by John
Cleland. To the passages of obscenity, (which certainly I shall not copy in
this place) Mr. Lewis has added blasphemy against the Scriptures; *if* the following passage may be considered as such.

> 'He (the Monk) examined the book which she (Antonia) had been
> reading, and had now placed upon the table. *It was* THE BIBLE.
> "How," said the Prior to himself, "Antonia reads the Bible, and is still so
> ignorant?" But upon further inspection he found that Elvira (the
> mother of Antonia) had made exactly the same remark. That *prudent*
> mother, while she admired *the beauties* of THE SACRED WRITINGS, was
> convinced, that *unrestricted, no reading more improper could be permitted a*
> *young woman.* Many of the narratives *can only tend to excite ideas the worst*
> *calculated for a female breast*; every thing is called roundly and plainly by
> it's own name; and *the annals of a brothel would scarcely furnish a greater*
> *choice of indecent expressions.* Yet this is the book which young women are
> recommended to study, which is put into the hands of children, able to
> comprehend little more than those passages *of which they had better remain*
> *ignorant,* and *which but too frequently inculcate the first rudiments of vice, and*
> *give the first alarm to the still sleeping passions.* Of this Elvira was so fully
> convinced, that she would have *preferred* putting into her daughter's
> hands Amadis de Gaul, or the Valiant Champion Tirante the White;
> and *would sooner have authorised her studying the lewd exploits* of Don
> Galaor, *or the lascivious jokes of the* Damzel Plazer de mi vida.' (p. 247,
> 248.) &c.

I state only what is printed. It is for others to read it and to judge. The falsehood of this passage is not more gross than it's impiety. In the case of
Thomas Woolston, in the 2d. of George II. for blasphemous discourses
against our Saviour's miracles, when arrest of judgment was moved, Lord
Raymond and the whole Court declared they would not suffer it to be
debated, *whether* to write against Christianity *in general* (not concerning
controverted points between the learned, but *in general*) was not an offence
punishable in the temporal Courts of Common Law. Woolston was
imprisoned one year, and entered into a large recognizance *for his good*
behaviour during life. Sir Philip Yorke, afterwards Lord Hardwicke, was
Attorney General at the time. The case of the King against Annet, when
the Hon. Charles Yorke was Attorney General, (3d of Geo. III.) for a blas-

phemous book entitled 'The Free Inquirer,' *tending,* among other points, to ridicule, *traduce and discredit the* HOLY SCRIPTURES, is well known to the profession. The punishment was *uncommonly* severe. Whether the passage I have quoted in a *popular* novel, has not a *tendency* to corrupt the minds of the people, and of the younger unsuspecting part of the female sex, by *traducing and discrediting* THE HOLY SCRIPTURES, is a matter of public consideration. – '*This book goes all over the kingdom*;' are the words of Judge Reynolds, in the case of E. Curl. What Mr. LEWIS has printed *publicly with his name,* that I state publicly to the nation. Few will dissent from the opinion of Lord Raymond and the Court, in the case of Curl above stated, as reported by Strange and Barnardiston to this effect; 'Religion is *part of the common law,* and therefore *whatever is an offence* against that, is an offence *against* THE COMMON LAW.' With this *opinion,* I conclude the note.

Review of Lewis's *The Monk* (1797)*

SAMUEL TAYLOR COLERIDGE (1772–1834)

Coleridge wrote to his friend William Lisle Bowles on 16 March 1797 that 'indeed I am almost weary of the Terrible, having been an hireling in the Critical Review for these last six or eight months – I have been lately reviewing the Monk, the Italian, Hubert de Sevrac [by Mary Robinson] &c &c & &c – in all of which dungeons, and old castles, & solitary Houses by the Sea Side, & Caverns, & Woods, & extraordinary characters, & all the tribe of Horror & Mystery, have crowded on me – even to surfeiting.' However, only his review of The Monk *was published; when he read passages from the others to Dorothy Wordsworth, she criticized his cleverness at the expense of others, and he committed them to the fire. The other reviews (plus the review of Radcliffe's* Mysteries of Udolpho *included in this collection, pp. 289ff.) are regularly misattributed to Coleridge, despite much evidence to the contrary.*

The Monk: A Romance. By M. G. Lewis, Esq. M.P. 3 Vols. 12mo. 9s. sewed. Bell. 1796.

The horrible and the preternatural have usually seized on the popular taste, at the rise and decline of literature. Most powerful stimulants, they can never be required except by the torpor of an unawakened, or the languor of an exhausted, appetite. The same phænomenon, therefore, which we hail as a favourable omen in the belles lettres of Germany, impresses a degree of gloom in the compositions of our countrymen. We trust,

---

* 'Lewis's Romance of the Monk', *Critical Review,* **19** (February 1797), pp. 194–8.

however, that satiety will banish what good sense should have prevented; and that, wearied with fiends, incomprehensible characters, with shrieks, murders, and subterraneous dungeons, the public will learn, by the multitude of the manufacturers, with how little expense of thought or imagination this species of composition is manufactured. But, cheaply as we estimate romances in general, we acknowledge, in the work before us, the offspring of no common genius. The tale is similar to that of *Santon Barsista* in the *Guardian*. Ambrosio, a monk, surnamed the Man of Holiness, proud of his own undeviating rectitude, and severe to the faults of others, is successfully assailed by the tempter of mankind, and seduced to the perpetration of rape and murder, and finally precipitated into a contract in which he consigns his soul to everlasting perdition.

The larger part of the three volumes is occupied by the under plot, which, however, is skilfully and closely connected with the main story, and is subservient to its development. The tale of the bleeding nun is truly terrific; and we could not easily recollect a bolder or more happy conception than that of the burning cross on the forehead of the wandering Jew (a mysterious character, which, though copied as to its more prominent features from Schiller's incomprehensible Armenian [in *The Ghost-Seer*], does, nevertheless, display great vigour of fancy). But the character of Matilda, the chief agent in the seduction of Antonio [*sic*: Ambrosio], appears to us to be the author's master-piece. It is, indeed, exquisitely imagined, and as exquisitely supported. The whole work is distinguished by the variety and impressiveness of its incidents; and the author everywhere discovers an imagination rich, powerful, and fervid. Such are the excellencies; – the errors and defects are more numerous, and (we are sorry to add) of greater importance.

All events are levelled into one common mass, and become almost equally probable, where the order of nature may be changed wherever the author's purposes demand it. No address is requisite to the accomplishment of any design; and no pleasure therefore can be received from the perception of *difficulty surmounted*. The writer may make us wonder, but he cannot surprise us. For the same reasons a romance is incapable of exemplifying a moral truth. No proud man, for instance, will be made less proud by being told that Lucifer once seduced a presumptuous monk. *Incredulus odit.* Or even if, believing the story, he should deem his virtue less secure, he would yet acquire no lessons of prudence, no feelings of humility. Human prudence can oppose no sufficient shield to the power and cunning of supernatural beings; and the privilege of being proud might be fairly conceded to him who could rise superior to all earthly temptations, and whom the strength of the spiritual world alone would be adequate to overwhelm. So falling, he would fall with glory, and might reasonably welcome his defeat with the haughty emotions of a conqueror. As far, therefore, as the story is concerned, the praise which a romance can claim, is simply that of having given pleasure during its perusal; and so many are the calamities of life, that he who has done this, has not written uselessly. The children of sickness and of solitude shall thank him. To this praise, however, our author has not entitled himself. The sufferings which he describes are so frightful and intolerable, that we break with abruptness from the delusion, and indignantly suspect the man of a species of brutality, who could find a pleasure in wantonly imagining them; and the abominations which he pourtrays with no hurrying pencil, are such as the observation of character by no means demanded, such as 'no observation of character can justify, because no good man would willingly suffer them to pass, however transiently, through his own mind.' The merit of a novellist [*sic*] is in proportion (not simply to the effect, but) to the *pleasurable* effect which he produces. Situations of torment, and images of naked horror, are easily conceived; and a writer in whose works they abound, deserves our gratitude almost equally with him who should drag us by way of sport through a military hospital, or force us to sit at the dissecting-table of a natural philosopher. To trace the nice boundaries, beyond which terror and sympathy are deserted by the pleasurable emotions, – to reach those limits, yet never to pass them, *hic labor, hoc opus est* [this is the labour, this the task]. Figures that shock the imagination, and narratives that mangle the feelings, rarely discover *genius,* and always betray a low and vulgar *taste*. Nor has our author indicated less ignorance of the human heart in the management of the principal character. The wisdom and goodness of providence have ordered that the tendency of vicious actions to deprave the heart of the perpetrator, should diminish in proportion to the greatness of his temptations. Now, in addition to constitutional warmth and irresistible opportunity, the monk is impelled to incontinence by friendship, by compassion, by gratitude, by all that is amiable, and all that is estimable; yet in a few weeks after his first frailty, the man who had been described as possessing much general humanity, a keen and vigorous understanding, with habits of the most exalted piety, degenerates into an uglier fiend than the gloomy imagination of Dante would have ventured to picture. Again, the monk is described as feeling and acting under the influence of an appetite which could not co-exist with his other emotions. The romance-writer possesses an unlimited power over situations; but he must scrupulously make his characters act in congruity with them. Let him work *physical* wonders only, and we will be content to *dream* with him for a while; but the first *moral* miracle which he attempts, he disgusts and awakens us. Thus our judgment remains unoffended, when, announced by thunders and earthquakes, the spirit appears to Ambrosio involved in blue fires that increase the cold of the cavern; and we acquiesce in the power of the silver myrtle which made gates and doors fly open at its touch, and charmed every eye into sleep. But when a mortal, fresh from the impression of that terrible appearance, and in the act of evincing for the first time the witching force of this myrtle, is represented as being at the same moment agitated by so fleeting an appetite as that of lust, our own feelings convince us that this is not improbable, but impossible; not preternatural, but contrary to nature. The extent of the powers that may exist, we can never ascertain; and therefore we feel no great difficulty in yielding a temporary belief to any, the strangest, situation of *things*. But that situation once conceived, how beings like ourselves would feel and act in it, our own feelings sufficiently instruct us; and we instantly reject the clumsy fiction that does not harmonise with them. These are the two *principal* mistakes in *judgment,* which the author has fallen into; but we cannot wholly pass over the frequent incongruity of his style with his subjects. It is gaudy where it should have been severely simple; and too often the mind is offended by phrases the most trite and colloquial, where it demands and had expected a sternness and solemnity of diction.

A more grievous fault remains, a fault for which no literary excellence can atone, a fault which all other excellence does but aggravate, as adding subtlety to a poison by the elegance of its preparation. Mildness of censure would here be criminally misplaced, and silence would make us accomplices. Not without reluctance then, but in full conviction that we are performing a duty, we declare it to be our opinion, that the *Monk* is a romance, which if a parent saw in the hands of a son or daughter, he might reasonably turn pale. The temptations of Ambrosio are described with a libidinous minuteness, which, we sincerely hope, will receive its best and only adequate censure from the offended conscience of the author himself. The shameless harlotry of Matilda, and the trembling innocence of Antonia, are seized with equal avidity, as vehicles of the most voluptuous images; and though the tale is indeed a tale of horror, yet the most painful impression which the work left on our minds was that of great acquirements and splendid genius employed to furnish a *mormo* [monster] for children, a poison for youth, and a provocative for the debauchee. Tales of enchantments and witchcraft can never be *useful*: our author has contrived to make them *pernicious,* by blending, with an irreverent negligence, all that is most awfully true in religion with all that is most ridiculously absurd in superstition. He takes frequent occasion, indeed, to manifest his sovereign contempt for the latter, both in his own person, and (most incongruously) in that of his principal characters; and that his respect for the *former* is not excessive, we are forced to conclude from the treatment which its inspired writings receive from him. Ambrosio discovers Antonia reading – [here Coleridge quotes the long blasphemous passage about the Bible – '*the annals of a brothel would scarcely furnish a greater choice of indecent expressions*' – that Mathias had quoted; see p. 294].

The impiety of this falsehood can be equalled only by its impudence. This is indeed as if a Corinthian harlot, clad from head to foot in the transparent thinness of the Cöan vest, should affect to view with prudish horror the naked knee of a Spartan matron! If it be possible that the author of these blasphemies is a Christian, should he not have reflected that the only passage in the scriptures (Ezekiel, chap. xxiii), which could give a *shadow* of plausibility to the *weakest* of these expressions, is represented as being spoken by the Almighty himself? But if he be an infidel, he has acted consistently enough with that character, in his endeavours first to influence the fleshly appetites, and then to pour contempt on the only book which would be adequate to the task of recalming them. We believe it not absolutely impossible that a mind may be so deeply depraved by the habit of reading lewd and voluptuous tales, as to use even the Bible in conjuring up the spirit of uncleanness. The most innocent expressions might become the first link in the chain of association, when a man's soul had been so poisoned; and we believe it not absolutely impossible that he might extract pollution from the word of purity, and, in a literal sense, *turn the grace of God into wantonness.*

We have been induced to pay particular attention to this work, from the unusual success which it has experienced. It certainly possesses much real merit in addition to its meretricious attractions. Nor must it be forgotten that the author is a man of rank and fortune. – Yes! the author of the *Monk* signs himself a LEGISLATOR! – We stare and tremble.

The poetry interspersed through the volumes is, in general, far above mediocrity. We shall present our readers with the following exquisitely tender elegy ['The Exile', omitted], which, we may venture to prophesy, will melt and delight the heart, when ghosts and hobgoblins shall be found only in the lumber-garret of a circulating library.

'The Terrorist System of Novel-Writing' (1797)*

SIR,

ALBEIT you may wish to avoid the dryness and dullness of political discussion in your Magazine, yet you must be sensible that in an age of *quidnunkery* like the present, it is not always possible to disregard the passing events of Europe. It has long, for example, been the fashion to advert to the horrid massacres which disgraced France during the tyranny of Robespierre; and, whatever a good and loyal subject happens to write, whether a history, a life, a sermon, or a posting bill, he thinks it his duty to introduce a due portion of his abhorrence and indignation against all such bloody proceedings. Happy, sir, would it be, if we could contemplate barbarity without adopting it; if we could meditate upon cruelty without learning it; and if we could paint a man without a head, without supposing what would be the case if some of our friends were without their heads. But, alas! so

---

* 'Letter to the Editor', *Monthly Magazine*, **4**, 21 (August 1797), pp. 102–4.

prone are we to imitation, that we have exactly and faithfully copied the SYSTEM OF TERROR, if not in our streets, and in our fields, at least in our circulating libraries, and in our closets. Need I say that I am adverting to the wonderful revolution that has taken place in the *art* of novel-writing, in which the only exercise for the fancy is now upon the most frightful subjects, and in which we reverse the petition in the litany, and riot upon 'battle, murder, and sudden death.'

Good, indeed, it must be confessed, arises out of evil. If, by this revolution, we have attained the art of frightening young people, and reviving the age of ghosts, hobgoblins, and spirits, we have, at the same time, simplified genius, and shown by what easy process a writer may attain great celebrity in circulating libraries, boarding schools, and watering places. What has he to do but build a castle in the air, and furnish it with dead bodies and departed spirits, and he obtains the character of a man of a most 'wonderful imagination, rich in imagery, and who has the wonderful talent of conducting his reader in a cold sweat through five or six volumes.'

Perhaps necessity, the plea for all revolutions, may have occasioned the present. A novel used to be a description of human life and manners; but human life and manners *always* described, must become tiresome; all the difficulties attending upon the tender passion have been exhausted; maiden aunts have become stale; gallent colonels are so common, that we meet with them in every volunteer *corps*. There are but few ways of running away with a lady, and not many more of breaking the hearts of her parents. Clumsy citizens are no longer to be seen in one horse-chaises, and their *villas* are removed from the bottom of Gray's Inn Lane, to the most delightful and picturesque situations, twelve or fifteen miles from London. Footmen and ladies' maids are no longer trusted with intrigues, and letters are conveyed with care, expedition, and secrecy, by the mail coach, and the penny-post. In a word, the affairs and business of common life are so perfectly understood, that elopments are practised by girls almost before they have learned to read; and all the incidents which have decorated our *old* novels, come easy and natural to the parties, without the assistance of a circulating library, or the least occasion to draw upon the invention of a writer of novels.

It was high time, therefore, to contrive some other way of interesting these numerous readers, to whom the stationers and trunk-makers are so deeply indebted, and just at the time when we were threatened with a stagnation of fancy, arose Maximilian Robespierre, with his system of terror, and taught our novelists that *fear* is the only passion they ought to cultivate, that to frighten and instruct were one and the same thing, and that none of the productions of genius could be compared to the production of an ague. From that time we have never ceased to 'believe and tremble;' our genius has become hysterical, and our taste epileptic.

Good, I have observed, arises out of evil, or apparent evil: it is now much easier to write a novel adapted to the prevailing taste than it was. The manners and customs of common life being no longer an object for curiosity or description, we have nothing to do but launch out on the main ocean of improbability and extravagant romance, and we acquire a high reputation. It having fallen to my lot to peruse many of these wonderful publications, previously to my daughters reading them (who, by the bye, would read them whether I pleased or not) I think I can lay down a few plain and simple rules, by observing which any man or maid, I mean, ladies' maid, may be able to compose from four to six uncommonly interesting volumes, that shall claim the admiration of all true believers in the marvellous.

In the first place, then, trembling reader, I would advise you to construct an *old* castle, *formerly* of great magnitude and extent, built in the Gothic manner, with a great number of hanging towers, turrets, and pinnacles. One half, at least, of it must be in ruins; dreadful chasms and gaping crevices must be hid only by the clinging ivy; the doors must be so old, and so little used to open, as to grate tremendously on the hinges; and there must be in every passage an echo, and as many reverberations as there are partitions. As to the furniture, it is absolutely necessary that it should be nearly as old as the house, and in a more decayed state, if a more decayed state be possible. The principal rooms must be hung with pictures, of which the damps have very nearly effaced the colours; only you must preserve such a degree of likeness in one or two of them, as to incline your heroine to be very much affected by the sight of them, and to imagine that she has seen a face, or faces, very like them, or very like something else, but where, or when, she cannot *just now* remember. It will be necessary, also, that one of those very old and very decayed portraits shall seem to frown most cruelly, while another seems to smile most lovingly.

Great attention must be paid to the tapestry hangings. They are to be very old, and tattered, and blown about with the wind. There is a great deal in the wind. Indeed, it is one of the principal objects of terror, for it may be taken for almost any terrific object, from a banditti of cut-throats to a single ghost. The tapestry, therefore, must give signs of moving, so as to make the heroine believe, there is something behind it, although, not being *at that time* very desirous to examine, she concludes very naturally and logically, that it can be nothing but the wind. This same wind is of infinite service to our modern castle-builders. Sometimes it *whistles*, and then it shows how sound may be conveyed through the crevices of a Baron's castle. Sometimes it *rushes*, and then there is reason to believe the Baron's great grandfather does not lie quiet in his grave; and sometimes it *howls*, and, if accompanied with rain, generally induces some weary traveller, perhaps a robber, and perhaps a lover, or both, to take up their residence in this *very same castle* where virgins, and virtuous wives, were locked up before the invention of a *habeas corpus*. It is, indeed, not wonderful, that so much use is made of the wind, for it is the principal ingredient in that sentimentality of constitution, to which romances are admirabl[y] adapted.

Having thus provided such a decayed stock of furniture as may be easily affected by the wind, you must take care that the battlements and towers are remarkably *populous* in *owls* and *bats*. The *hooting* of the one, and the *flitting* of the other, are excellent engines in the system of terror, particularly if the candle goes out, which is very often the case in damp caverns.

And the mention of caverns brings me to the essential qualities inherent in a castle. The rooms *upstairs* may be just habitable, and no more; but the principal incidents must be carried on in *subterraneous* passages. These, in general, wind round the whole extent of the building; but that is not very material, as the heroine never goes through above half without meeting with a door, which she has neither strength nor resolution to open, although she has found a rusty key, very happily fitted to as rusty a lock, and would give the world to know what it leads to, and yet she can give no reason for her curiosity.

The building now being completely finished, and furnished with all desirable imperfections, the next and only requisite is a heroine, with all the weakness of body and mind that appertains to her sex; but, endowed with all the curiosity of a spy, and all the courage of a troop of horse. Whatever she hears, sees, or thinks of, that is horrible and terrible, she must enquire into it again and again. All alone, for she cannot prevail on the timid *Janetta* to go with her *a second time*; all alone she sets out, in the dead of the night, when nothing but the aforesaid owls and bats are *hooting* and *flitting*, to resolve the horrid mystery of the moving tapestry, which threw her into a swoon the preceding night, and in which she knows her fate is awfully involved, though she cannot tell why. With cautious tread, and glimmering taper, she proceeds to descend a long flight of steps, which bring her to a door she had not observed before. It is opened with great difficulty; but alas! a rush of wind puts out the glimmering taper, and while Matilda, Gloriana, Rosalba, or any other name, is deliberating whether she shall proceed or return, without knowing how to do either, a groan is heard, a second groan, and a fearful crash. A dimness now comes over her eyes (which in the *dark* must be terrible) and she swoons away. How long she may have remained in this swoon, no one can tell; but when she awakes, the sun peeps through the crevices, for all subterraneous passages must have crevices, and shows her such a collection of sculls and bones as would do credit to a parish burying-ground.

She now finds her way back, determined to make a farther search next night, which she accomplishes by means of a better light, and behold! having gained the fatal spot where the mystery is concealed, the tapestry moves again! Assuming courage, she boldly lifts up a corner, but immediately lets it drop, a cold sweat pervades her whole body, and she sinks to the ground; after having discovered behind this dreadful tapestry, the tremendous solution of all her difficulties, the awful word

HONORIFICABILITATUDINIBUSQUE!!!

Mr. Editor, if thy soul is not harrowed up, *I* am glad to escape from this scene of horror, and am,

Your humble servant,

A JACOBIN NOVELIST.

Greenwich, Aug. 19, 1797.

'On the Titles of Modern Novels' (1797)[★]

. . . in education, it was some years ago an established maxim, that '*Novels* were *bad* things for young people.' The name novel was at this time given to productions very different from those which it at present comprehends. The objections to stories of intrigues, improbable adventures, and all the trash of a circulating library, are undoubtedly just; but surely it is not wise to extend the same censure to a class of books, which, though they bear the name of novels, have nothing in common with those pernicious productions. Is it not an inaccuracy in language to class the moral works of Fielding, and Richardson, and Moore, and Burney, &c. &c. and wretched performances, which disgrace our public libraries, under the same general denomination of novels?

Those who are not guided merely by names judge for themselves of the merit of a book, whether it be called a novel, a history, or a sermon; but there are many who think it virtuous to abstain from novel reading. No matter how much good sense, wit, reasoning, or morality, a work may claim which bears this proscribed title, and who repeat, with self-complacent emphasis, '*I* never read novels. – I dare say the book may have a vast deal of merit; but it's a novel, and I make it a rule never to read novels.' – With the same sagacious antipathy, they consider the whole race of *novel-writers*. If you were to ask one of these liberal critics, whether they did not think Dr. [Thomas] Moore a fine writer? they would probably answer your question by another question: Is not he a novel-writer?

Those who know how far it is in the power of the weak to work upon the strongest minds, those who know how much the self-approbation of individuals is at the mercy of combined numbers, will not be surprised, that this absurd prejudice has operated to deter men of superior abilities from this species of writing, merely by the dread of an opprobrious epithet. Women, who are far more dependent upon the opinion of others than men either are, or ought to be, have doubtless been still more restrained from the exertion of their talents by this harsh, indiscriminate prejudice against the writer of a novel. A woman who has sense enough to make a fair

---

★ *Monthly Magazine*, **4** (November 1797), pp. 347–8. Signed 'E.'

estimate of her own interests and happiness, will be prudently inclined to sacrifice the hope of fame, to avoid the possibility of odium.

To obviate these difficulties, we must evade, without attempting to conquer the prepossessions of those who will not, or who cannot, reason. Instead of wearying ourselves with attempting to demonstrate to those who have the *novellophobia*, that their antipathy is not rational, we had better change the name which excites their horror.

The ingenious critic, who had reviewed *Camilla*, in the *Monthly Review* for October, 1796, hints at a classification of novels into the humorous – the pathetic – and the romantic. There are many more varieties, and a few more distinct species; – the historic romance, in which there is a mixture of truth and fable, of novel and history, is a distinct species. We need not, at present, investigate the merits of these compositions; but we may remark that their ambiguous pretensions seem to arise from some faint hope, that, by their mixture of historical names and facts, they may escape the ignominy of being classed amongst mere novels.

The *hobgoblin-romance*, is a name, which might, perhaps properly distinguish those terrible stories with which the public have lately been entertained, where we have sorcerers, and magical delusions, and skeletons, and apparitions of all sorts and sizes, and midnight voices, and *petits talons*, and echoing footsteps, and haunted castles, and long passages, that lead to nothing. The innumerable imitations of writers of genius, who have succeeded in the terrible, are fair game for ridicule; but we do not mean to exclude some German romances – the fragment of *Sir Bertram*, was, perhaps, in England the first and best in this style – some parts of Mrs Radcliffe's romances, and the late romance called the *Monk* [by M. G. Lewis], which stands high upon this list.

We only hope that the high stimulus of terror may not be used so much as to exhaust the sensibility of the public mind; and that this 'second childishness' of taste will no longer be indulged by writers of superior talents, who would probably excel in a much higher style of composition.

The highest species of romance is surely that which, at once, exhibits just views of human nature and of real life, which mingles reasoning and philosophy, with strokes of humour, that play upon the fancy, and with pathos, which touches the heart. Who can with-hold applause from [Moore's] *Zelucco*, which Gibbon justly calls, '*the first philosophical romance of the present age?*' . . .

'Vindication of *The Monk*' (1798)*

From this I turn to another subject – his [i.e. Mathias's] attack upon Mr. Lewis, the Author of the Romance called the *Monk*; and if I dwell on this a little longer than usual, it is because the Author of the *Pursuits of Literature* has not been more copious in his observations than profuse in the invective and misrepresentation with which he has overwhelmed that Gentleman.

There is no book perhaps of modern production that has excited a greater share of curiosity, or been more the subject of public opinion, and public conversation, than the Romance of the *Monk*.

The Author of the *Pursuits of Literature* in particular has branded this work with the charge of obscenity and impiety, and accused Mr. Lewis of neither scrupling nor blushing to depict and publish to the world the arts of lewd and systematic seduction, and to thrust upon the nation the most open and unqualified blasphemy against the very code and volume of our religion. In the accusation of indecency the public opinion, under which the author of the *Pursuits of Literature* has artfully endeavoured to shelter and support his own, does certainly in a great measure coincide with him; but it must be recollected, that *assertion*, although founded on the *popular opinion*, does not always amount to incontrovertible proof. . . .

I must confess, I never perused a book with so much surprise and astonishment as I did that of the *Monk*. Led to expect, from general report, a compound of licentious indecency, when I took it up to read, which was not till very lately, it was with all the prejudice that it was possible for my mind to entertain against it. How much was I astonished then to find the impressions it made on me so widely different from those I was taught to look for: I was ashamed to perceive that I had so long been the dupe to a prejudice which appeared to me to be without foundation; and that, without any reason to authorise my forming an opinion at all, which I certainly could have no right to do till I had read the book, I had imperceptibly given way to the popular stream.

I am well aware of the difficulties I shall have now to encounter. I hear an immediate outcry raised against me – What! defend a bad book – a work of licentiousness and blasphemy? – Have patience a little, gentle critics, and I will answer you. I do not pretend to defend a bad book – I join issue with you in your opinion. I do not believe this to be such – I do not view it as a licentious or blasphemous work – I do not think it will either contaminate your morals, or bring your religion into contempt.

With regard to the charge of licentiousness, the *Monk* exhibits, it is true, a picture of vice unequalled hitherto by the pen of description. But I would

---

* *Impartial Strictures on the poem called 'The Pursuits of Literature:' and particularly a Vindication of the romance of 'The Monk'* (London: J. Bell, 1798), pp. 31–40.

ask this short and simple question – *Is the picture of vice, held up in its own native deformity*, a dangerous sight? I will add another – *Is it not attended with good effects, by acting as a beacon to mankind?* Vice in itself is even disgusting to its most zealous votaries, when it entirely abandons the semblance of virtue. Would you allure mankind to the path of vice, you must not terrify them with a prospect of the rocks and precipices which intersect the way; you must strew the path over with the flowers of virtue – you must make the surface smooth, to conceal the pits below. Vice must always wear a mask, or she will never gain converts to her principles: it is only when she arrays herself in the specious garb of virtue that she is to be feared. . . .

A book which boldly traces the progress of vice, accompanying her in her first deviation from the path of virtue, through all her subsequent transitions to the different stages of guilt, and at length exhibits her suffering the punishment due to her crimes, cannot be justly styled a bad book. I consider the Romance of the *Monk* as a work of this nature – I see a good and useful moral to be drawn from it. I see that the first abandonment to vice leads on imperceptibly to an accumulation of wickedness. But I also see that such a conduct infallibly brings on the wretched victim the punishment due to his crimes. I view it as a beautiful allegory, wherein is depicted the snares and delusions by which vice accomplishes her triumph over virtue. The character of Matilda, for example, I consider as so palpably allegorical, that when I am reading it, it is with difficulty I can bring my mind to favour the deceit sufficiently enough to look upon her as a woman.

From the language made use of in the *Pursuits of Literature*, a person unacquainted with the *Monk* would be induced to suppose that it was a character recommended as a model for imitation, rather than designed as an object of abhorrence. He would be surprised to find that his example was intended to inculcate the necessity of a proper distrust of ourselves, and the danger of placing too great a confidence in our own virtues, and above all to teach us that the suppression of our passions from their right and natural course, is too frequently the means of diverting them into a much more dangerous channel.

But, granting all this to be true, still it will be objected, why the necessity to introduce such licentiousness and obscenity, according to the Author of the *Pursuits of Literature*, into the work? Might not the indecent passages, it will be said, have been as well omitted? In the first place then I must declare, that I do not see these *licentious*, these *obscene*, or these *indecent* passages, as they are called, in the same point of view that the Author of the *Pursuits of Literature* represents them in. I cannot deny that the description of some of the scenes between Matilda and Ambrosio are painted in very strong colours. But, in my opinion, there was no remedy for it. Without these descriptions, the work, it is true, would have been chaster; but then it would have been incomplete as a work. It is to be considered that the Monk was *no common man*; therefore the common temptations of the world would have been lost upon him. – Not only from his habits of life were his religious principles tinctured with a shade of a deeper cast than those of other men, but also from keeping his passions under command he had acquired a self-denial unknown to men in general. With such a man, therefore, whatever ideas the attractions of the other sex might excite, they would make a much slighter impression on him than on the rest of mankind. No common blandishments would prevail over him. Had his temptations been of an inferior nature, they never would have had effect. The usual artifices of women would have been exerted in vain. He was not to be prevailed on in the first instance to debauch others, but it is necessary he should be debauched himself. This Matilda effects by a conduct adapted to such an intent – She practises every refinement in the art of seduction, and allures his passions by temptations too strong for mortality to resist. If he had fallen a victim to less subtile snares, or yielded to less tempting allurements, his character had been at once ill drawn and incomplete.

Whence then the danger to be apprehended from the perusal of this work? – The horror excited in the breast of the reader at the incantations and preternatural interferences by the aid of which the Monk is enabled to execute his infernal plans, is of itself a sufficient antidote to any emotions which the luscious description of some of the scenes could occasion, though I will not admit that they can produce any such. With weak minds, in particular, this cannot fail of having a very strong effect. Is it possible for any one to regard Matilda, after he has been a witness to her mysterious and unaccountable behaviour, without a suspicion bordering on disgust? Even the beauty of her person, and her blandishments, cease to affect the reader when he beholds her an agent in diabolical arts. And to the strong mind, capable of discrimination and of forming an opinion for itself, it can by no means be prejudicial. By such it will be considered as a perfect allegory, wherein is depicted the triumph of vice over virtue – and will be admired as a moral work, the effect of much ability and invention. . . .

Were it possible for me to suppose for a moment that the perusal of the *Monk* could induce a person, by the incitement of ideas he never before experienced, to attempt the execution of any plan of seduction, or even the gratification in any manner of a sensual passion, in consequence of what he had read therein, I would cease to vindicate it from that moment. But I beg to ask whether it is rational to suppose, that, if the mind could divest itself of all the horror occasioned by the manner in which the designs of the Monk are carried into execution, and even experience those sensations of incitement which I defy the book to inspire – whether, I say, the head could for a moment become so much the dupe of the passions as to attempt, from the example of Ambrosio, to do what it must perceive, without the same preternatural assistance, it never could achieve.

For, if it is impossible for any, the most ignorant and uninformed reader, to place the slightest belief in the reality of the facts that are related therein, which I apprehend must be answered in the affirmative, how can a person receive any bad impressions from the perusal of facts which he is convinced never did nor can take place? Do you say it is a bad example for him? I answer, that cannot operate as an example which he is sensible he cannot follow if he were even so inclined.

Ancient Records
or, The Abbey of Saint Oswythe (1801)*

T. J. HORSLEY CURTIES

Preface

The succeeding pages, like the [author's earlier novel, *Ethelwina, or the*] HOUSE OF FITZ-AUBURN, owe all their story to the imagery of, perhaps, a too heated imagination. Its mysteries – its terrific illusions – its very errors must be attributed to a love of Romance, caught from an enthusiastic admiration of *Udolpho's* unrivalled Foundress. – He follows her through all the venerable gloom of horrors, not as a kindred spirit, but contented, as a shadow, in attending her footsteps.

As this species of writing has of late been feebly attacked, I will venture a few observations on the subject. – Authors of Novels are nearly allied to those of Romance – are twin-sisters, and should be equally allied in affection; but as sisters will sometimes envy and disagree when the one has been more admired than the other, so the Writers of Novels, jealous of us humble architects, will not suffer us to build our airy castles, or mine our subterranean caverns unmolested.

Let me enlarge a little further on this theme. – Ought the female Novelist, in order to display a *complete* knowledge of human nature, to degrade that delicate timidity, that shrinking innocence which is the loveliest boast of womanhood in drawing characters which would ruin her reputation to be acquainted with? – Ought she to describe scenes which bashful modesty would blush to conceive an idea, much less avow a knowledge of? – Oh no! let the chaste pen of female delicacy disdain such unworthy subjects; – leave to the other sex a description of grovelling incidents, debased characters, and low pursuits: – there is still a range wide and vast enough for fanciful imagination; but when female invention will employ itself in images of the grosser sort, it is a fatal prediction of relaxed morals, and a species of – at least – LITERARY PROSTITUTION.

---

* T. J. Horsley Curties, *Ancient Records, or, The Abbey of Saint Oswythe. A Romance*, 4 vols (London: Minerva Press, William Lane, 1801), vol. 1, pp. vi–viii.

PLATE 9

Gondemar plunges the dagger into the heart of his brother Constantine, as Constantine's wife Rosaline rushes in. 'In that moment of horrible outrage, a soul-piercing shriek, that might have called to earth the forms of the long-buried dead, rang echoing through the chambers of death.' Note the Gothick table. Frontispiece to T. J. Horsley Curties's *Ancient Records, or, The Abbey of Saint Oswythe* (1801). By permission of the British Library 1578/3545.

'Novels and Romances' (1802)*

'RIMELLI'

MR. EDITOR,

It has been proposed as a question, whether the reading of romances and novels *only* (to the exclusion of all *other* books) or whether no reading of any kind whatever would be productive of the worst consequences. I have considered this question over and over again, and maturely weighed every pro and con that occurred to me on the subject. It is urged by the 'ante-novelists' that romances and novels serve only to estrange the minds of youth (specially of females) from their own affairs, and transmit them to those of which they read: so that, while totally absorbed in lamenting and

---

* Rimelli, 'Novels and Romances', *Monthly Mirror*, **14** (August 1802), pp. 81–2.

condoling with the melancholy situation of a Julia, an Emily, or a Matilda, or lost in the admiration of the glorious deeds of some *all-perfect* novel hero, they neglect both their own interests, and the several duties which they owe to parent, friend, or brother. That such is but too often the case, I am sorry to be obliged to confess. Yet, though a great part of our modern novels are flimsy productions, without either good writing or good sense, others mere catchpenny trash, and *some* immoral and even impious; though the press teems with *Midnight Bells, Black Castles*, and *Haunted Towers, Mysterious Monks*, &c. &c. with a long train of ghosts, phantoms, &c. yet I am inclined to think that many excellent precepts and morals are inculcated in by far the greatest part of them; and that the rest are to be censured rather as being *absurd, improbable, and ill-written*, than tending to corrupt the mind. (I except some few, such as the *Monk*, by Mr. Lewis, which is not only immoral, but blasphemous, *cum paucis aliis*.) For example those written by the ingenious and amiable Mrs. Anne [*sic*] Radcliffe, and Dr. Moore's *Edward, Zeluco*, &c. which are not only commendable, but thank-worthy; possess, in my opinion, the powers of pleasing and instructing at the same time: a rare coalition! The latter *particularly* paints life in accurate colours, and from the various actions and opinions of the characters, deduces morals the most wholesome and unexceptionable. I might mention several others of hardly inferior merits, but let these suffice. Such productions as these are doubly excellent; because, while they inculcate the best morals, they give the readers an accurate knowledge of life and manners; of which it is highly proper young people should have a correct idea. For a young unsophisticated person just entering upon life, imbibes with eagerness whatever principles he first becomes acquainted with; and if these should happen to have a bad tendency, what would become of him, if his mind had not been guarded against them, by some previous insight into the sophistry and fallacy of the world, which are duly exposed in the works before mentioned? But if we consider the other side of the question, and suppose a person, who, having never looked into a book, consequently can have no taste for reading, what a plodding, insensible, and worldly-minded mortal do we behold! Such a person may, possibly, make his way through the world with tolerable success, but can never have any pretensions to the character of a *gentleman*. He may meet with the applause of those of his own stamp (among the 'common herd;') but by the sensible and discerning his education will be considered as an everlasting monument to his own and his parents' folly. I am, Mr. Editor, yours, as I hope I ever shall be, with all due respect.

RIMELLI

'On the Supernatural in Poetry' (*c.* 1802/1826)*

ANN RADCLIFFE (1764–1823)

The following critical essay was found among Ann Radcliffe's papers after her death. It was written in the winter of 1802/3, and possibly revised between 1811 and 1815, as it contains passages copied verbatim from her travel journals describing visits to Warwick Castle in 1802, Penshurst in 1811 and Windsor Castle between 1812 and 1815. Ostensibly designed to form part of the Introduction to her post humously published novel Gaston de Blondeville, *it nevertheless reads like a carefully composed formal essay, summing up and defending her technique. The essay is in the form of a dialogue between the romantic enthusiast Willoughton (Mr. W——) and the debunking philistine Simpson (Mr. S——), who have stopped to examine the ruins of Kenilworth on their way from Coventry to Warwick – just as did Mrs Radcliffe and her husband. Radcliffe systematically develops a theory of 'correspondent scenery' or 'accordant circumstances', the eighteenth-century critical terms characterizing writing that parallels a psychological mood (or 'corresponding feeling') without directly describing it. Although, in actual practice, Radcliffe uses the words 'terror' and 'horror' interchangeably in her novels, she has considered the subject in the light of the public reaction to such novels, and seems to be defending sensibility and the sublime 'terror' of the Radcliffe School from sensationalism and the obscene 'horror' of the Lewis School. She defends Gilpin's principle that obscurity is necessary for the achievement of terror and the sublime. She does not mention Richard Payne Knight or Uvedale Price, but she does refer to 'the new school', so it is probable that she has kept up with contemporary aesthetic discussion of 'the picturesque'.*

One of our travellers began a grave dissertation on the illusions of the imagination. 'And not only on frivolous occasions,' said he, 'but in the most important pursuits of life, an object often flatters and charms at a distance, which vanishes into nothing as we approach it; and 'tis well if it leave only disappointment in our hearts. Sometimes a severer monitor is left there.'

These truisms, delivered with an air of discovery by Mr. S——, who seldom troubled himself to think upon any subject except that of a good dinner, were lost upon his companion, who, pursuing the airy conjectures which the present scene, however humbled, had called up, was following Shakspeare [*sic*] into unknown regions. 'Where is now the undying spirit,' said he, 'that could so exquisitely perceive and feel? – that could inspire itself with the various characters of this world, and create worlds of its own; to which the grand and the beautiful, the gloomy and the sublime of visible

* Ann Radcliffe, 'On the Supernatural in Poetry', *New Monthly Magazine*, **16** (1826), pp. 145–52.

Nature, up-called not only corresponding feelings, but passions; which seemed to perceive a soul in every thing: and thus, in the secret workings of its own characters, and in the combinations of its incidents, kept the elements and local scenery always in unison with them, heightening their effect. So the conspirators at Rome pass under the fiery showers and sheeted lightning of the thunder-storm, to meet, at midnight, in the porch of Pompey's theatre [*Julius Caesar*, I.iii]. The streets being then deserted by the affrighted multitude, that place, open as it was, was convenient for their council; and, as to the storm, they felt it not; it was not more terrible to them than their own passions, nor so terrible to others as the dauntless spirit that makes them, almost unconsciously, brave its fury. These appalling circumstances with others of supernatural import, attended the fall of the conqueror of the world – a man, whose power Cassius represents to be dreadful as this night, when the sheeted dead were seen in the lightning to glide along the streets of Rome. How much does the sublimity of these attendant circumstances heighten our idea of the power of Cæsar, of the terrific grandeur of his character, and prepare and interest us for his fate. The whole soul is roused and fixed, in the full energy of attention, upon the progress of the conspiracy against him; and, had not Shakspeare wisely withdrawn him from our view, there would have been no balance of our passions.' – 'Cæsar was a tyrant,' said Mr S——. W—— looked at him for a moment, and smiled, and then silently resumed the course of his own thoughts. In Cymbeline [IV.ii], for instance, how finely such circumstances are made use of, to awaken, at once, solemn expectation and tenderness, and, by recalling the softened remembrance of a sorrow long past, to prepare the mind to melt at one that was approaching, mingling at the same time, by means of a mysterious occurrence, a slight tremour of awe with our pity. Thus, when Belarius and Arviragus return to the cave where they had left the unhappy and worn-out Immogen to repose, while they are yet standing before it, and Arviragus, speaking of her with tenderest pity, as 'the poor sick Fidele,' goes out to enquire for her, – solemn music is heard from the cave, sounded by that harp which Guiderius says, '*Since the death of my dearest mother, it did not speak before.* All solemn things should answer solemn accidents.' Immediately Arviragus enters with Fidele senseless in his arms: . . .

Tears alone can speak the touching simplicity of the whole scene. Macbeth shows, by many instances, how much Shakspeare delighted to heighten the effect of his characters and his story by correspondent scenery: there the desolate heath, the troubled elements, assist the mischief of his malignant beings. But who, after hearing Macbeth's thrilling question –

> – 'What are these,
> So withered and so wild in their attire,
> That look not like the inhabitants o' the earth,
> And yet are on't?' –

who would have thought of reducing them to mere human beings, by attiring them not only like the inhabitants of the earth, but in the dress of a particular country, and making them downright Scotch-women? thus not only contradicting the very words of Macbeth, but withdrawing from these cruel agents of the passions all that strange and supernatural air which had made them so affecting to the imagination, and which was entirely suitable to the solemn and important events they were foretelling and accomplishing. Another *improvement* on Shakspeare is the introducing a crowd of witches thus arrayed, instead of the three beings 'so withered and so wild in their attire.'

About the latter part of this sentence, W——, as he was apt to do, thought aloud, and Mr. S—— said, '*I*, now, have sometimes considered, that it was quite suitable to make Scotch witches on the stage, appear like Scotch women. You must recollect that, in the superstition concerning witches, they lived familiarly upon the earth, mortal sorcerers, and were not always known from mere old women; consequently they must have appeared in the dress of the country where they happened to live, or they would have been more than suspected of witchcraft, which we find was not always the case.'

'You are speaking of old women, and not of witches,' said W—— laughing, 'and I must more than suspect you of crediting that obsolete superstition which destroyed so many wretched, yet guiltless persons, if I allow your argument to have any force. I am speaking of the only real witch – the witch of the poet; and all our notions and feelings connected with terror accord with his. The wild attire, the look *not of this earth*, are essential traits of supernatural agents, working evil in the darkness of mystery. Whenever the poet's witch condescends, according to the vulgar notion, to mingle mere ordinary mischief with her malignity, and to become familiar, she is ludicrous, and loses her power over the imagination; the illusion vanishes. So vexatious is the effect of the stage-witches upon my mind, that I should probably have left the theatre when they appeared, had not the fascination of Mrs. Siddons's influence so spread itself over the whole play, as to overcome my disgust, and to make me forget even Shakspeare himself; while all consciousness of fiction was lost, and his thoughts lived and breathed before me in the very form of truth. Mrs. Siddons, like Shakspeare, always disappears in the character she represents, and throws an illusion over the whole scene around her, that conceals many defects in the arrangements of the theatre. I should suppose she would be the finest Hamlet that ever appeared, excelling even her own brother in that character; she would more fully preserve the tender and refined melancholy, the deep sensibility, which are the peculiar charm of Hamlet, and which appear not only in the ardour, but in the occasional irresolution and weakness of his character – the secret spring that reconciles all his inconsistencies. A sensibility so profound can with difficulty be justly imagined, and therefore can very rarely be assumed. Her brother's firmness, incapable of being always subdued, does not so fully enhance, as her tenderness would, this part of the character. The strong light which shows the mountains of a landscape in all their greatness, and with all their rugged sharpnesses gives them nothing of the interest with which a more gloomy tint would invest their grandeur; dignifying, though it softens, and magnifying, while it obscures.'

'I still think,' said Mr. S——, without attending to these remarks, 'that, in a popular superstition, it is right to go with the popular notions, and dress your witches like the old women of the place where they are supposed to have appeared.'

'As far as these notions prepare us for the awe which the poet designs to excite, I agree with you that he is right in availing himself of them; but, for this purpose, every thing familiar and common should be carefully avoided. In nothing has Shakspeare been more successful than in this; and in another case somewhat more difficult – that of selecting circumstances of manners and appearance for his supernatural beings, which, though wild and remote, in the highest degree, from common apprehension, never shock the understanding by incompatibility with themselves – never compel us, for an instant, to recollect that he has a licence for extravagance. Above every ideal being is the ghost of Hamlet, with all its attendant incidents of time and place. The dark watch upon the remote platform, the dreary aspect of the night, the very expression of the officer on guard, 'the air bites shrewdly; it is very cold;' the recollection of a star, an unknown world, are all circumstances which excite forlorn, melancholy and solemn feelings, and dispose us to welcome, with trembling curiosity, the awful being that draws near; and to indulge in that strange mixture of horror, pity, and indignation, produced by the tale it reveals. Every minute circumstance of the scene between those watching on the platform, and of that between them and Horatio preceding the entrance of the apparition, contributes to excite some feeling of dreariness, or melancholy, or solemnity, or expectation, in unison with and leading on toward that high curiosity and thrilling awe with which we witness the conclusion of the scene.'. . .

'How happens it then,' said Mr. S——, 'that objects of terror sometimes strike us very forcibly, when introduced into scenes of gaiety and splendour, as, for instance, in the Banquet scene in Macbeth?'

'They strike, then, chiefly by the force of contrast,' replied W——; 'but the effect, though sudden and strong, is also transient; it is the thrill of horror and surprise, which they then communicate rather than the deep and solemn feelings excited under more accordant circumstances and left long upon the mind. Who ever suffered for the ghost of Banquo, the gloomy and sublime kind of terror, which that of Hamlet calls forth? though the appearance of Banquo, at the high festival of Macbeth, not only tells us that he is murdered, but recalls to our minds the fate of the gracious

Duncan, laid in silence and death by those who, in this very scene, are rev-
elling in his spoils. There, though deep pity mingles with our surprise and
horror, we experience a far less degree of interest, and that interest too of an
inferior kind. The union of grandeur and obscurity, which Mr. Burke
describes as a sort of tranquillity tinged with terror, and which causes the
sublime, is to be found only in Hamlet; or in scenes where circumstances of
the same kind prevail.'

'That may be,' said Mr. S——, 'and I perceive you are not one of those
who contend that obscurity does not make any part of the sublime.' 'They
must be men of very cold imaginations,' said W——, 'with whom cer-
tainty is more terrible than surmise. Terror and horror are so far opposite,
that the first expands the soul, and awakens the faculties to a high degree of
life; the other contracts, freezes, and nearly annihilates them. I apprehend,
that neither Shakspeare nor Milton by their fictions, nor Mr. Burke by his
reasoning, anywhere looked to positive horror as a source of the sublime,
though they all agree that terror is a very high one; and where lies the great
difference between horror and terror but in the uncertainty and obscurity,
that accompany the first [error for 'the latter'], respecting the dreaded evil?'

'But what say you to Milton's image –

"On his brow sat horror plumed."'

'As an image, it certainly is sublime; it fills the mind with an idea of
power, but it does not follow that Milton intended to declare the feeling of
horror to be sublime; and after all, his image imparts more of terror than of
horror; for it is not distinctly pictured forth, but is seen in glimpses through
obscuring shades, the great outlines only appearing, which excite the imagination to complete the rest; he only says, "sat horror plumed;" you will
observe, that the look of horror and the other characteristics are left to the
imagination of the reader; and according to the strength of that, he will feel
Milton's image to be either sublime or otherwise. Milton, when he
sketched it, probably felt, that not even his art could fill up the outline, and
present to other eyes the countenance which his "mind's eye" gave to him.
Now, if obscurity has so much effect on fiction, what must it have in real
life, when to ascertain the object of our terror, is frequently to acquire the
means of escaping it. You will observe, that this image though indistinct or
obscure, is not confused.'

'How can any thing be indistinct and not confused?' said Mr. S——.

'Ay, that question is from the new school,' replied W——; 'but recollect, that obscurity, or indistinctness, is only a negative, which leaves the
imagination to act upon the few hints that truth reveals to it; confusion is a
thing as positive as distinctness, though not necessarily so palpable; and it
may, by mingling and confounding one image with another, absolutely
counteract the imagination, instead of exciting it. Obscurity leaves

something for the imagination to exaggerate; confusion, by blurring one image into another, leaves only a chaos in which the mind can find nothing to be magnificent, nothing to nourish its fears or doubts, or to act upon in any way; yet confusion and obscurity are terms used indiscriminately by those, who would prove, that Shakspeare and Milton were wrong when they employed obscurity as a cause of the sublime, that Mr. Burke was equally mistaken in his reasoning upon the subject, and that mankind have been equally in error, as to the nature of their own feelings, when they were acted upon by the illusions of those great masters of the imagination, at whose so potent bidding, the passions have been awakened from their sleep, and by whose magic a crowded Theatre has been changed to a lonely shore, to a witch's cave, to an enchanted island, to a murderer's castle, to the ramparts of an usurper, to the battle, to the midnight carousal of the camp or the tavern, to every various scene of the living world.' . . .

Flowers of Literature (1803–6)

REV. F. PREVOST AND F. BLAGDON (Eds)

Introduction*

With respect to the NOVELS of our day, those imported from abroad, and chiefly those translated from the German, have lately presented nothing but an incongruous and cumbrous mass of fair captives, enchanted castles, or dreadful and mysterious apparitions, fit only to captivate or alarm weak imaginations. French novels, too, although a more faithful picture of modern manners, have been found to contain licentious and seductive descriptions of unbridled passions and abandoned profligacy. . . .

Our domestic Novelists, absurdly imitating the German literati, have long dealt in the marvellous; and, though they seem for the present to have abandoned the idle and frightful dreams of a distorted imagination, they are nevertheless to be deprecated for teaching youth to mistake loose sentiments for liberal opinions, heedless profligacy for benevolent disposition, and impiety for strength of mind. Happy would it be, for the welfare of the present generation, if those ridiculous fabrications, of weak minds and often depraved hearts, which constitute the enchantment of circulating libraries, could be entirely annihilated.

---

* Rev. F. Prevost and F. Blagdon (eds), *Flowers of Literature; for 1801 & 1802* (London: B. Crosby, 1803), n.p.n.

Invective against Novelist Goblin-Mongers★

O ye goblin-mongers! ye wholesale dealers in the frightful! is it not cruel to present to the imagination of a lovely female such horrid images, as skulls with the worms crawling in and out of their eyeless sockets? Is it not cruel to conjure up ghosts, murderers, magicians, faries [*sic*], devils, all those things invented to murder sleep, the innocent sleep of your poor terrified readers? To conjure up haunted castles, amid thunder, lightning, and all the other dreadful operations of nature? To make a man ride with a ghost in a post-chaise and four with, doubtless, two devils as postillions, over every hedge, and ditch, and quagmire, to be found or imagined? To depict the great devil himself taking a man up in the air by the crown of his head, as an eagle would a tortoise, to precipitate him on a rock, that he might the more expeditiously become possessed of his prey! And, lastly, to bring him to conclude the scene, as he is brought into a puppet-show, by flying away with the hero and heroine? Avaunt, ye enemies to sleep! Do not keep your fair readers tremblingly alive throughout the night, to make them look haggardly the next morning, for want of balmy rest. Does not Cicero call sleep the sweetest of the gods; and Seneca *pars humanæ melior vitæ*, the better part of human life? O ye goblin-mongers, cease then to disturb it, by the introduction of haunted castles, magic wands, murderous daggers, or poisonous bowls! (It is the continual influx of those wretched novel-writings, and the rare appearance of the good, that has brought this branch of literature in such merited disrepute. The generality of people hold them, with reason, in great contempt; and, perhaps, few deride them more than those who read them most. – This is strange; but there is one thing yet more strange, and that is, that those, who have for a series of years constantly and avowedly despised this species of composition, should in the end sit down to the very work. Such was the case with Jean Jacques Rousseau, and with Lord Bolingbroke the same, who wrote a romance in folio, called *Parthenissa*. It is reported in a life of his lordship, that he was sick all the time: whoever will read it, will *not doubt it*.)

Novelists†

It is a remarkable circumstance, that the most obscene dramatist, whose writings ever polluted the English stage, was a *woman* [i.e. Aphra Behn]; and it is a circumstance as remarkable, and as much to be regretted, that, with the exception of a certain *monkish* author [i.e. M. G. Lewis], the most

---

★ Rev. F. Prevost and F. Blagdon (eds), *Flowers of Literature; for 1801 & 1802* (London: B. Crosby, 1803), pp. 393–4.

† Francis William Blagdon (ed.), *Flowers of Literature; for 1806* (London: B. Crosby, 1807), pp. lxxiv–lxxv.

indecent playwright, and the *grossest* and *most immoral* novelists of the present day, are *women*!

The *fair* author of *Zofloya* [i.e. Charlotte Dacre] had before *distinguished* herself, in the annals of literary libertinism; and she has now *treated* HER admirers with the development of such scenes, as, we had hoped, no female hand could be found to trace.

But, as we wish not to initiate our readers in the mysteries of brothels, or in the more secret vices of the cloister, we dismiss the ungrateful subject.

Review of Maturin's *Fatal Revenge* (1810)★

SIR WALTER SCOTT (attrib.) (1771–1832)

The elegant and fascinating productions which honoured the name of novel, those which Richardson, Mackenzie, and Burney gave to the public; of which it was the object to exalt virtue and degrade vice; to which no fault could be objected unless that they unfitted here and there a romantic mind for the common intercourse of life, while they refined perhaps a thousand whose faculties could better bear the fair ideal which they presented – these have entirely vanished from the shelves of the circulating library. It may indeed be fairly alleged in defence of those who decline attempting this higher and more refined species of composition, that the soil was in some degree exhausted by over-cropping – that the multitude of base and tawdry imitations obscured the merit of the few which are tolerable, as the overwhelming blaze of blue, red, green, and yellow, at the Exhibition [i.e. the Royal Academy], vitiates our taste for the few good paintings which show their modest hues upon its walls. The public was indeed weary of the protracted embarrassments of lords and ladies who spoke such language as was never spoken, and still more so of the see-saw correspondence between the sentimental Lady Lucretia and the witty Miss Caroline, who battledored it in the pathetic and the lively, like Morton and Reynolds on the stage. But let us be just to dead and to living merit. In some of the novels of the late Charlotte Smith we found no ordinary portion of that fascinating power which leads us through every various scene of happiness or distress at the will of the author; which places the passions of the wise and grave for a time at the command of ideal personages; and perhaps has more attraction for the public at large than any other species of literary composition, the drama not excepted. Nor do we owe less to Miss Edgeworth, whose true and vivid pictures of modern life

---

★ Review of Maturin's *Fatal Revenge; or, the Family of Montorio*, *Quarterly Review*, **3** (May 1810), pp. 339–47.

contain the only sketches reminding us of the human beings, whom, secluded as we are, we have actually seen and conversed with in various parts of this great metropolis. . . .

'Plunging from depth to depth a vast profound,' we at length imagined ourselves arrived at the Limbus Patrum [place of the righteous] in good earnest. The imitators of Mrs. Radcliffe and Mr. Lewis were before us; personages, who to all the faults and extravagancies of their originals, added that of dulness, with which they can seldom be charged. We strolled through a variety of castles, each of which was regularly called Il Castello; met with as many captains of condottieri; heard various ejaculations of Santa Maria and Diavolo; read by a decaying lamp, and in a tapestried chamber, dozens of legends as stupid as the main history; examined such suites of deserted apartments as might fit up a reasonable barrack; and saw as many glimmering lights as would make a respectable illumination – Amid these flat imitations of the *Castle of Udolpho* we lighted unexpectedly upon the work which is the subject of the present article, and, in defiance of the very bad taste in which it is composed, we found ourselves insensibly involved in the perusal, and at times impressed with no common degree of respect for the powers of the author. We have at no time more earnestly desired to extend our voice to a bewildered traveller, than towards this young man, whose taste is so inferior to his powers of imagination and expression, that we never saw a more remarkable instance of genius degraded by the labour in which it is employed. It is the resentment and regret which we experience at witnessing the abuse of these qualities, as well as the wish to hazard a few remarks upon the romantic novel in general, which has induced us (though we are obliged to go back a little) to offer our criticism on the *Fatal Revenge, or the House of Montorio* [pub. 1807].

It is scarcely possible to abridge the narrative, nor would the attempt be edifying or entertaining. A short abstract of the story is all for which we can afford room. . . .

The history of these mysterious brethren is told by the officer who had recognized them, and runs briefly thus: Orazio, Count of Montorio – for we begin our story with the explanation, which in the original concludes it – possessed of wealth, honours, and ancestry, is married to a beautiful woman, whom he loves doatingly, but of whose affections he is not possessed. A villainous brother instils into his mind jealousy of a cavalier to whom the Countess had formerly been attached. Orazio causes the supposed paramour to be murdered in the presence of the lady, who also dies: he then flies from his country with the feelings of desperation thus forcibly described:

> 'My reason was not suspended, it was totally *changed*. I had become a
> kind of intellectual savage; a being that, with the malignity and deprav-
> ation of inferior natures, still retains the reason of a man, and retains it

only for his curse. Oh! that midnight darkness of the soul, in which it seeks for something whose loss has carried away every sense but one of utter and desolate privation; in which it traverses leagues in motion and worlds in thought, without consciousness of relief, yet with a dread of pausing. I had nothing to seek, nothing to recover; the whole world could not restore me an atom, could not shew me again a glimpse of what I had been or lost; yet I rushed on as if the next step would reach shelter and peace.' Vol. iii. p. 380.

In this manic state he reaches an uninhabited islet in the Grecian archipelago, where, from a conversation accidentally overheard between two assassins sent by his brother to murder him, the wretched Orazio learns the innocence of his victims, and the full extent of his misery. He contrives to murder the murderers, and the effect of the subsequent discovery upon his feelings is described in a strain of language which we were alternately tempted to admire as sublime and to reprobate as bombastic.

Orazio determines on revenge, and his plan is diabolically horrid. He resolved to accomplish the murder of his treacherous brother, who in consequence of his supposed death had now assumed the honours of the family; and he farther determined that this act of vengeance should be perpetrated by the hands of that very brother's own sons, two amiable youths, who had no cloud upon their character excepting an attachment to mysterious studies, and a strong propensity to superstition.

We do not mean to trace this agent of vengeance through the various devices and stratagems by which he involved in his toils his unsuspecting nephews, assumed in their apprehension the character of an infernal agent, and decoyed them first to meditate upon, and at length actually to perpetrate, the parricide which was the crown and summit of his wishes. The doctrine of fatalism, on which he principally relied for reconciling his victims to his purpose, is in various passages detailed with much gloomy and terrific eloquence. The rest of his machinery is composed of banditti, caverns, dungeons, inquisitors, trap-doors, ruins, secret passages, soothsayers, and all the usual accoutrements from the property-room of Mrs. Radcliffe. The horror of the piece is completed by the murderer discovering that the youths whom he has taken such pains to involve in parricide are not the sons of his brother, but his own offspring by his unfortunate wife. We do not dwell upon any of these particulars, because the observations which we have to hazard upon his neglected novel apply to a numerous class of the same kind, and because the incidents are such as are to be found in most of them.

In the first place, then, we disapprove of the mode introduced by Mrs. Radcliffe, and followed by Mr. Murphy [Maturin used the pseudonym Dennis Jasper Murphy] and her other imitators, of winding up their story with a solution by which all the incidents appearing to partake of the mystic and marvellous are resolved by very simple and natural causes. This seems, to us, to savour of the precaution of Snug the Joiner [in Shakespeare's *Midsummer Night's Dream*]; or, rather, it is as if the machinist, when the pantomime was over, should turn his scenes 'the seamy side without,' and expose the mechanical aids by which the delusions were accomplished. In one respect, indeed, it is worse management; because the understanding spectator might be in some degree gratified by the view of engines which, however rude, were well adapted to produce the effects which he had witnessed. But the machinery of the castle of Montorio, when exhibited, is wholly inadequate to the gigantic operations ascribed to it. There is a total and absolute disproportion between the cause and effect, which must disgust every reader much more than if he were left under the delusion of ascribing the whole to supernatural agency. This latter resource has indeed many disadvantages; some of which we shall briefly notice. But it is an admitted expedient; appeals to the belief of all ages but our own; and still produces, when well managed, some effect even upon those who are most disposed to contemn its influence. We can therefore allow of supernatural agency to a certain extent and for an appropriate purpose, but we never can consent that the effect of such agency shall be finally attributed to natural causes totally inadequate to its production. We can believe, for example, in Macbeth's witches, and tremble at their spells; but had we been informed, at the conclusion of the piece, that they were only three of his wife's chambermaids disguised for the purpose of imposing on the Thane's credulity, it would have added little to the credibility of the story, and entirely deprived it of the interest. In like manner we fling back upon the Radcliffe school their flat and ridiculous explanations, and plainly tell them that they must either confine themselves to ordinary and natural events, or find adequate causes for those horrors and mysteries in which they love to involve us. Yet another word on this subject. We know not if a novel writer of the present day expects or desires his labours to be perused oftener than once; but as there may be here and there a maiden aunt in a family, for whose advantage it must be again read over by the young lady who has already devoured it in secret, we advise them to consider how much they suffer from their adherence to this unfortunate system. We will instance the incident of the black veil in the castle of Udolpho. Attention is excited, and afterwards recalled, by a hundred indirect artifices, to the dreadful and unexplained mystery which the heroine had seen beneath it; and which, after all, proves to be neither more nor less than a waxen doll. This trick may indeed for once answer the writer's purpose; and has, we suppose, cost many an extra walk to the circulating library, and many a curse upon the malicious concurrent who always has the fourth volume in hand. But it is as impossible to reperuse the book without feeling the contempt awakened by so pitiful a contrivance as it is for a child to regain his original respect for King Solomon after he has seen the monarch disrobed of all his glory, and deposited in the same box with Punch and his wife. And, in fact, we feel inclined to abuse the author in such a case as the watch do Harlequin, when they find out his trick of frightening them by mimicking the report of a pistol.

> Faquin, maraud, pendard, impudent, temeraire,
> Vous osez nous faire peur!

In the second place, we are of opinion that the terrors of this class of novel writers are too accumulated and unremitting. The influence of fear – and here we extend our observations as well to those romances which actually ground it upon supernatural prodigy as to those which attempt a subsequent explanation – is indeed a faithful and legitimate key to unlock every source of fancy and of feeling. Mr. Murphy's introduction is expressed with the spirit and animation which, though often misdirected, pervade his whole work.

> 'I question whether there be a source of emotion in the whole mental frame so powerful or universal as *the fear arising from objects of invisible terror*. Perhaps there is no other that has been, at some period or other of life the predominant and indelible sensation of every mind, of every class, and under every circumstance. Love, supposed to be the most general of passions, has certainly been felt in its purity by very few, and by some not at all, even in its most indefinite and simple state.
>
> 'The same might be said, *à fortiori,* of other passions. But who is there that has never feared: Who is there that has not involuntarily remembered the gossip's tale in solitude or in darkness? Who is there that has not sometimes shivered under an influence he would scarce acknowledge to himself? I might trace this passion to a high and obvious source.
>
> 'It is enough for my purpose to assert its existence and prevalancy, which will scarcely be disputed by those who remember it. It is absurd to depreciate this passion, and deride its influence. It is *not* the weak and trivial impulse of the nursery, to be forgotten and scorned by manhood. It is the aspiration of a spirit; "it is the passion of immortals," that dread and desire of their final habitation.' Pref. pp. 4 & 5.

We grant there is much truth in this proposition taken generally. But the finest and deepest feelings are those which are most easily exhausted. The chord which vibrates and sounds at a touch, remains in silent tension under continued pressure. Besides, terror, as Bob Acres says of its counterpart, courage, will come and go; and few people can afford timidity enough for the writer's purpose who is determined on 'horrifying' them through three thick volumes. The vivacity of the emotion also depends greatly upon surprize, and surprize cannot be repeatedly excited during the perusal of the same work. It is said, respecting the cruel punishment of breaking alive upon the wheel, the sufferer's nerves are so much jarred by the first blow, that he feels comparatively little pain from those which follow. There is something of this in moral feeling; nor do we see a better remedy for it than to recommend the cessation of these experiments upon the public, until their sensibility shall have recovered its original tone. The taste for the marvellous has been indeed compared to the habit of drinking ardent liquors. But it fortunately differs in having its limits: he upon whom one dram does not produce the effect, can attain the desired degree of inebriation by doubling the dose. But when we have ceased to start at one ghost, we are callous to the exhibition of a whole Pandemonium. In short, the sensation is generally as transient as it is powerful, and commonly depends upon some slight circumstances which cannot be repeated.

> The time has been our senses would have cool'd
> To hear a night-shriek, and our fell of hair
> Would at a dismal treatise rise and stir
> As life were in't. We have supped full with horrors;
> And direness, now familiar to our thoughts,
> Cannot once start us.

These appear to us the great disadvantages under which any author must at present struggle, who chuses supernatural terror for his engine of moving the passions. We dare not call them insurmountable, for how shall we dare to limit the efforts of genius, or shut against its possessor any avenue to the human heart, or its passions? Mr. Murphy himself, for aught we know, may be destined to shew us the prudence of this qualification. He possesses a strong and vigorous fancy, with great command of language. He has indeed regulated his incidents upon those of others, and therefore added to the imperfections which we have pointed out, the want of originality. But his feeling and conception of character are his own, and from these we judge of his powers. In truth we rose from his strange chaotic novel romance as from a confused and feverish dream, unrefreshed, and unamused, yet strongly impressed by many of the ideas which had been so vaguely and wildly presented to our imagination.

Walpole's *Castle of Otranto* (1811)★

Sir Walter Scott (attrib.) (1771–1832)

It is doing injustice to Mr Walpole's memory to allege, that all which he aimed at in the *Castle of Otranto* was 'the art of exciting surprise and horror;'

★ 'Introduction', Horace Walpole, *The Castle of Otranto* (Edinburgh: James Ballantyne, 1811), pp. xvii–xxxvi.

or, in other words, the appeal to that secret and reserved feeling of love for the marvellous and supernatural, which occupies a hidden corner in almost every one's bosom. Were this all which he had attempted, the means by which he sought to attain his purpose might, with justice, be termed both clumsy and puerile. But Mr Walpole's purpose was both more difficult of attainment, and more important when attained. It was his object to draw such a picture of domestic life and manners, during the feudal times, as might actually have existed, and to paint it chequered and agitated by the action of supernatural machinery, such as the superstition of the period received as a matter of devout credulity. The natural parts of the narrative are so contrived, that they associate themselves with the marvellous occurrences; and, by the force of that association, render those *speciosa miracula* striking and impressive, though our cooler reason admits their impossibility. Indeed to produce, in a well-cultivated mind, any portion of that surprise and fear which is founded on supernatural events, the frame and tenor of the whole story must be adjusted in perfect harmony with this main-spring of the interest. He who, in early youth, has happened to pass a solitary night in one of the few ancient mansions which the fashion of more modern times has left undespoiled of their original furniture, has probably experienced, that the gigantic and preposterous figures dimly visible in the defaced tapestry, the remote clang of the distant doors which divide him from living society, the deep darkness which involves the high and fretted roof of the apartment, the dimly-seen pictures of ancient knights, renowned for their valour, and perhaps for their crimes, the varied and indistinct sounds which disturb the silent desolation of a half-deserted mansion; and, to crown all, the feeling that carries us back to ages of feudal power and papal superstition, join together to excite a corresponding sensation of supernatural awe, if not of terror. It is in such situations, when superstition becomes contagious, that we listen with respect, and even with dread, to the legends which are our sport in the garish light of sun-shine, and amid the dissipating sights and sounds of every-day life. Now it seems to have been Walpole's object to attain, by the minute accuracy of a fable, sketched with singular attention to the costume of the period in which the scene was laid, that same association which might prepare his reader's mind for the reception of prodigies congenial to the creed and feelings of the actors. His feudal tyrant, his distressed damsel, his resigned, yet dignified, churchman, – the Castle itself, with its feudal arrangement of dungeons, trap-doors, oratories, and galleries, the incidents of the trial, the chivalrous procession, and the combat; – in short, the scene, the performers, and action, so far as it is natural, form the accompaniments of his spectres and his miracles, and have the same effect on the mind of the reader that the appearance and drapery of such a chamber as we have described may produce upon that of a temporary inmate. This was a task which required no little learning, no ordinary degree of fancy, no common portion of genius, to execute. The association of which we have spoken is of a nature peculiarly delicate, and subject to be broken and disarranged. It is, for instance, almost impossible to build such a modern Gothic structure as shall impress us with the feelings we have endeavoured to describe. It may be grand, or it may be gloomy; it may excite magnificent or melancholy ideas; but it must fail in bringing forth the sensation of supernatural awe, connected with halls that have echoed to the sounds of remote generations, and have been pressed by the footsteps of those who have long since passed away. Yet Horace Walpole has attained in composition, what, as an architect, he must have felt beyond the power of his art. The remote and superstitious period in which his scene is laid, the art with which he has furnished forth its Gothic decorations, the sustained, and, in general, the dignified tone of feudal manners, prepare us gradually for the favourable reception of prodigies which, though they could not really have happened at any period, were consistent with the belief of all mankind at that in which the action is placed. It was, therefore, the author's object, not merely to excite surprise and terror, by the introduction of supernatural agency, but to wind up the feelings of his reader till they became for a moment identified with those of a ruder age, which

Held each strange tale devoutly true.

The difficulty of attaining this nice accuracy of delineation may be best estimated by comparing the *Castle of Otranto* with the less successful efforts of later writers; where, amid all their attempts to assume the tone of antique chivalry, something occurs in every chapter so decidedly incongruous, as at once reminds us of an ill-sustained masquerade, in which ghosts, knights-errant, magicians, and damsels gent, are all equipped in hired dresses from the same warehouse in Tavistock-street.

There is a remarkable particular in which Mr Walpole's steps have been departed from by the most distinguished of his followers.

Romantic narrative is of two kinds, – that which, being in itself possible, may be matter of belief at any period; and that which, though held impossible by more enlightened ages, was yet consonant with the faith of earlier times. The subject of the *Castle of Otranto* is of the latter class. Mrs Radcliffe, a name not to be mentioned without the respect due to genius, has endeavoured to effect a compromise between those different styles of narrative, by referring her prodigies to an explanation, founded on natural causes, in the latter chapters of her romances. To this improvement upon the Gothic romance there are so many objections, that we own ourselves inclined to prefer, as more simple and impressive, the narrative of Walpole, which details supernatural incidents as they would have been readily believed and received in the eleventh or twelfth century. In the first place, the reader feels indignant at discovering he has been cheated into a sympathy with terrors which are finally explained as having proceeded from some very simple cause; and the interest of a second reading is entirely destroyed by his having been admitted behind the scenes at the conclusion of the first. Secondly, The precaution of relieving our spirits from the influence of supposed supernatural terror, seems as unnecessary in a work of professed fiction, as that of the prudent Bottom [in Shakespeare's *Midsummer Night's Dream*], who proposed that the human face of the representative of his lion should appear from under his masque, and acquaint the audience plainly that he was a man as other men, and nothing more than Snug the joiner. Lastly, These substitutes for supernatural agency are frequently to the full as improbable as the machinery which they are introduced to explain away and to supplant. The reader, who is required to admit the belief of supernatural interference, understands precisely what is demanded of him; and, if he be a gentle reader, throws his mind into the attitude best adapted to humour the deceit which is presented for his entertainment, and grants, for the time of perusal, the premises on which the fable depends. But if the author voluntarily binds himself to account for all the wondrous occurrences which he introduced, we are entitled to exact that the explanation shall be natural, easy, ingenious, and complete. Every reader of such works must remember instances in which the explanation of mysterious circumstances in the narrative has proved equally, nay, even more incredible, than if they had been accounted for by the agency of supernatural beings. For the most incredulous must allow, that the interference of such agency is more possible than that an effect resembling it should be produced by an inadequate cause. But it is unnecessary to enlarge further on a part of the subject, which we have only mentioned to exculpate our author from the charge of using machinery more clumsy than his tale from its nature required. The bold assertion of the actual existence of phantoms and apparitions seems to us to harmonise much more naturally with the manners of feudal times, and to produce a more powerful effect upon the reader's mind, than any attempt to reconcile the superstitious credulosity of feudal ages with the philosophic scepticism of our own, by referring those prodigies to the operation of fulminating powder, combined mirrors, magic lanthorns, trap-doors, speaking trumpets, and such like apparatus of German phantasmagoria.

It cannot, however, be denied, that the character of the supernatural machinery in the *Castle of Otranto* is liable to objections. Its action and interference is rather too frequent, and presses too hard and constantly upon the same feelings in the reader's mind, to the hazard of diminishing the elasticity of the spring upon which it should operate. The fund of fearful sympathy which can be afforded by a modern reader to a tale of wonder, is much diminished by the present habits of life and mode of education. Our ancestors could wonder and thrill through all the mazes of an interminable metrical romance of fairy land, and of enchantment, the work perhaps of some

> Prevailing poet, whose undoubting mind
> Believed the magic wonders which he sung.

But our habits and feelings and belief are different, and a transient, though vivid, impression is all that can be excited by a tale of wonder even in the most fanciful mind of the present day. By the too frequent recurrence of his prodigies, Mr Walpole ran, perhaps, his greatest risk of awakening *la raison froide*, that cold common sense, which he justly deemed the greatest enemy of the effect which he hoped to produce. It may be added also, that the supernatural occurrences of the *Castle of Otranto* are brought forward into too strong daylight, and marked by an over degree of distinctness and accuracy of outline. A mysterious obscurity seems congenial at least, if not essential, to our ideas of disembodied spirits, and the gigantic limbs of the ghost of Alphonso, as described by the terrified domestics, are somewhat too distinct and corporeal to produce the feelings which their appearance is intended to excite. This fault, however, if it be one, is more than compensated by the high merit of many of the marvellous incidents in the romance. . . .

We have only to add, in conclusion to these desultory remarks, that if Horace Walpole, who led the way in this new species of literary composition, has been surpassed by some of his followers in diffuse brilliancy of description, and perhaps in the art of detaining the mind of the reader in a state of feverish and anxious suspence, through a protracted and complicated narrative, more will yet remain with him than the single merit of originality and invention. The applause due to chastity and precision of style, to a happy combination of supernatural agency with human interest, to a tone of feudal manners and language, sustained by characters strongly drawn and well discriminated, and to unity of action producing scenes alternately of interest and of grandeur; – the applause, in fine, which cannot be denied to him who can excite the passions of fear and of pity, must be awarded to the author of the *Castle of Otranto*.

'The Preternatural in Works of Fiction' (1818)*

Some have thought that, in modern works of fiction, there should be no gratuitous introduction of the preternatural, and that superstitious tales are only to be tolerated when they form a part of some picture of past ages, during which such things were universally believed. But, even in the most enlightened age, so desirous is the human mind of an outlet by which to escape from the narrow circle of visible things into the unknown and

---

* 'Some Remarks on the Use of the Preternatural in Works of Fiction', *Blackwood's Edinburgh Magazine*, **3**(18) (September 1818), pp. 648–50.

unlimited world, that surely poets should be permitted to feign all wonders which cannot be proved to be impossible, and which are not contradictory to the spirit of our religion.

To this class belong the re-appearance of the dead, and the struggle of evil beings for an ascendancy over human nature. The eastern talismanic theory of sorcery supposed that super-human powers were acquired by discovering and taking advantage of the occult laws of nature to compel the service of spirits; but the notion of a voluntary assistance lent by wicked angels to wicked men is much more sublime, and agrees better with the spirit of modern thought. The one is a childish idea founded on the mechanical operation of causes which have never been proved to exist; but the other has a moral interest, being conformable to our knowledge of character and passion.

That there exists in this country that strength of imagination which delights in the feeling of superstitious horror, is proved by the practice of our ancient dramatists; and of all those authors who wrote in the original English spirit down to the end of last century, when, partly from the revival of old ballads, and partly from the importation of German books, there sprung up an immense number of romances and fictions, the interest of which was founded almost entirely upon apparitions and the mysteries of haunted castles, or prophecies, dreams, and presentments [*sic*].

Every sort of machinery of this kind was put in requisition; till, by the unskilfulness of the artists, and the unsparing manner in which their resources were employed, the superstitious branch of romance writing fell gradually into disrepute; and probably among the immense number of novels published, there are now six that represent modern manners, for one that resorts to the old machinery of spectres and mysteries. The greatest poets of the present time, however, have not disdained to continue the use of it; and indeed some of Scott's works excite the feelings of superstitious fear and traditional awe in a degree that has never been surpassed. Wordsworth's fictions in this line have exquisite beauty, and may be said to represent the spontaneous and creative superstition of the human mind, when acted upon by impressive circumstances. The poems of the Thorn, Lucy Gray, and Hartleap Well, are instances of this. The poem of the Danish Boy is a beautiful superfluity of fancy, but is too entirely poetical to please common readers. Lord Byron's strength lies in a different direction; and the spectres which appear in his poetry are not the product of imagination working upon what is unknown and invisible, but are created by the passions of the heart striving to embody their own objects. The world of spirits is not an object of interest to him for its own sake, and when he resorts to it, he does so only for the images of what he loved or hated on earth. Mr Coleridge has perhaps the finest superstitious vein of any person alive. The poem of Christabel is the best model extant of the language fit to be employed for such subjects. It was the greatest attempt, before Walter

Scott's poems, to turn the language of our ancient ballads to account in a modern composition, and is perhaps more successful in that respect than the Lay of the Last Minstrel itself. Indeed Christabel may be considered as a test by which to try men's feeling of superstition, and whoever does not perceive the beauty of it, may rest assured that the world of spectres is shut against him, and that he will never see 'any thing worse than himself.'

To make the marvellous a means of producing the ludicrous; that is to say, to arrive at new and diverting situations, by feigning a suspension of the laws of nature, has not been much attempted in English literature, and is perhaps rather a cheap species of wit, since it supposes more fancy than knowledge or penetration. At the same time it has its attractions; for it gives the mind a pleasing respite from the inexorable tyranny of facts, and flatters us for a time with the appearance of vivid and immoveable nature relaxing from its severity, and ceasing to present the usual barriers to our wishes. The tale of Vathek [by Beckford], in which these things are well exemplified, has never been very popular in this country. It would appear that such painted air-bubbles are too childish for our taste, and that the marvellous is only relished here when linked to the higher and more serious feelings. . . .

Upon the whole, romance writers ought to look jealously after their privileges, and prevent the use of apparitions from incurring proscription in these latter days of the scoffers, who think it no great matter to take the bread out of the mouths of an hundred industrious persons in Grub Street, for the sake of shewing themselves above vulgar prejudices. Surely romance writers are far more numerous than philosophers, and might be well able to mob any prating son of Epicurus who attempted to undermine the credit of their machinery.

'William Godwin's Novels' (1819)*

William Hazlitt (1778–1830)

Whoever else it is, it is pretty clear that the author of *Caleb Williams* [1794] and *St. Leon* [1799] [i.e. William Godwin] is not the author of *Waverley* [1814; i.e. Sir Walter Scott]. Nothing can be more distinct or excellent in their several ways than these two writers. If the one owes almost every thing to external observation and traditional character, the other owes every thing to internal conception and contemplation of the possible workings of the human mind. There is little knowledge of the world, little variety, neither an eye for the picturesque, nor a talent for the humorous in *Caleb Williams*, for instance, but you cannot doubt for a moment of the

---

* William Hazlitt, *Lectures on the English Comic Writers* (London: Taylor and Hessey, 1819), pp. 259–65.

originality of the work and the force of the conception. The impression made upon the reader is the exact measure of the strength of the author's genius. For the effect, both in *Caleb Williams* and *St. Leon*, is entirely made out, neither by facts, nor dates, by black-letter or magazine learning, by transcript nor record, but by intense and patient study of the human heart, and by an imagination projecting itself into certain situations, and capable of working up its imaginary feelings to the height of reality. The author launches into the ideal world, and must sustain himself and the reader there by the mere force of imagination. The sense of power in the writer thus adds to the interest of the subject. – The character of Falkland is a sort of apotheosis of the love of fame. The gay, the gallant Falkland lives only in the good opinion of good men; for this he adorns his soul with virtue, and tarnishes it with crime; he lives only for this, and dies as he loses it. He is a lover of virtue, but a worshipper of fame. Stung to madness by a brutal insult, he avenges himself by a crime of the deepest die, and the remorse of his conscience and the stain upon his honour prey upon his peace and reason ever after. It was into the mouth of such a character that a modern poet has well put the words,

> '– Action is momentary,
> The motion of a muscle, this way or that;
> Suffering is long, obscure, and infinite.'

In the conflict of his feelings, he is worn to a skeleton, wasted to a shadow. But he endures this living death to watch over his undying reputation, and to preserve his name unsullied and free from suspicion. But he is at last disappointed in this his darling object, by the very means he takes to secure it, and by harassing and goading Caleb Williams (whose insatiable, incessant curiosity had wormed itself into his confidence) to a state of desperation, by employing every sort of persecution, and by trying to hunt him from society like an infection, makes him turn upon him, and betray the inmost secret of his soul. The last moments of Falkland are indeed sublime: the spark of life and the hope of imperishable renown are extinguished in him together; and bending his last look of forgiveness on his victim and destroyer, he dies a martyr to fame, but a confessor at the shrine of virtue! The re-action and play of these two characters into each other's hands (like Othello and Iago) is inimitably well managed, and on a par with any thing in the dramatic art; but Falkland is the hero of the story, Caleb Williams is only the instrument of it. This novel is utterly unlike any thing else that ever was written, and is one of the most original as well as powerful productions in the English language. – *St. Leon* is not equal to it in the plot and groundwork, though perhaps superior in the execution. In the one Mr. Godwin has hit upon the extreme point of the perfectly natural and perfectly new; in the other he ventures into the preternatural world, and comes nearer to the world of common place. Still the character is of the same exalted intellectual kind. As the ruling passion of the one was the love of fame, so in the other the sole business of life is thought. Raised by the fatal discovery of the philosopher's stone above mortality, he is cut off from all participation with its pleasures. He is a limb torn from society. In possession of eternal youth and beauty, he can feel no love; surrounded, tantalized, tormented with riches, he can do no good. The faces of men pass before him as in a *speculum*; but he is attached to them by no common tie of sympathy or suffering. He is thrown back into himself and his own thoughts. He lives in the solitude of his own breast, – without wife or child, or friend, or enemy in the world. His is the solitude of the soul, – not of woods, or seas, or mountains, – but the desart [*sic*] of society, the waste and desolation of the heart. He is himself alone. His existence is purely contemplative, and is therefore intolerable to one who has felt the rapture of affection or the anguish of woe. The contrast between the enthusiastic eagerness of human pursuits and their blank disappointment, was never, perhaps, more finely pourtrayed than in this novel. Marguerite, the wife of St. Leon, is an instance of pure and disinterested affection in one of the noblest of her sex. It is not improbable that the author found the model of this character in nature. – Of *Mandeville* [1817], I shall say only one word. It appears to me to be a falling off in the subject, not in the ability. The style and declamation are even more powerful than ever. But unless an author surpasses himself, and surprises the public as much the fourth or fifth time as he did the first, he is said to fall off, because there is not the same stimulus of novelty. A great deal is here made out of nothing, or out of a very disagreeable subject. I cannot agree that the story is out of nature. The feeling is very common indeed; though carried to an unusual and improbable excess, or to one with which from the individuality and minuteness of the circumstances, we cannot readily sympathise.

It is rare that a philosopher is a writer of romances. The union of the two characters in this author is a sort of phenomenon in the history of letters; for I cannot but consider the author of *Political Justice* [1793] as a philosophical reasoner of no ordinary stamp or pretentions. That work, whatever its defects may be, is distinguished by the most acute and severe logic, and by the utmost boldness of thinking, founded on a love and conviction of truth. It is a system of ethics, and one that, though I think it erroneous myself, is built on following up into its fair consequences, a very common and acknowledged principle, that abstract reason and general utility are the only test and standard of moral rectitude. If this principle is true, then the system is true: but I think that Mr. Godwin's book has done more than any thing else to overturn the sufficiency of this principle by abstracting, in a strict metaphysical process, the influence of reason or the understanding in moral questions and relations from that of habit, sense, association, local and personal attachment, natural affection, &c.; and by thus making it appear how necessary the latter are to our limited, imperfect, and mixed being, how impossible the former as an exclusive guide of action, unless man were, or were capable of becoming, a purely intellectual being. Reason is no doubt one faculty of the human mind, and the chief gift of Providence to man; but it must itself be subject to and modified by other instincts and principles, because it is not the only one. This work then, even supposing it to be false, is invaluable as demonstrating an important truth by the *reductio ad absurdum*; or it is an *experimentum crucis* [crucial test] in one of the grand and trying questions of moral philosophy. – In delineating the character and feelings of the hermetic philosopher St. Leon, perhaps the author had not far to go from those of a speculative philosophical Recluse. He who deals in the secrets of magic, or in the secrets of the human mind, is too often looked upon with jealous eyes by the world, which is no great conjuror; he who pours out his intellectual wealth into the lap of the public, is hated by those who cannot understand how he came by it; he who thinks beyond his age, cannot expect the feelings of his contemporaries to go along with him; he whose mind is of no age or country, is seldom properly recognised during his life-time, and must wait, in order to have justice done him, for the late but lasting award of posterity: – 'Where his treasure is, there his heart is also.'

Review of Maturin's *Melmoth the Wanderer* (1821)*

Melmoth the Wanderer: a Tale. By the Author of 'Bertram,' &c. 12mo. 4 Vols. 1l. 8s. Boards. Hurst and Co. 1820.

The taste for horrors, or for tales abounding in supernatural events and characters, compacts with the devil, and mysterious prolongations of human life, has for some years past been on the decline in England. The necromancers of the Rhine, the Italian assassins of Mrs. Radcliffe, the St. Leons of Mr. Godwin, &c. &c., had indeed begun to disappear, overwhelmed by their own extravagance, previously to any positive symptom of a returning relish for sense and nature: but when, in addition to the satiety which a repetition of this highly-peppered diet had engendered, plain and substantial food was also administered to the novel-reader, in the exquisitely true and national descriptions of Maria Edgeworth and Walter Scott, there was no excuse even for the most devoted slave of a diseased imagination, who could boast any pretensions to cultivated intellect, to continue exclusively his unwholesome recreations; and, consequently, the

---

* Review of Maturin's *Melmoth the Wanderer, Monthly Review*, N.S. **44** (January 1821), pp. 81–3, 84–5.

works in question (even the most meritorious of them) have partially descended from the shelves of fashionable repositories of light reading, to make room for worthier occupants; yet still retaining, with soiled leaves and second-hand honours, their station in the first rank of the provincial circulating library. There, while they receive the faded garlands and spiritless incense of unrefined adulation, they cast a vain retrospect on their brighter days; when the boudoir of the lady, instead of the closet of the housekeeper, enshrined their volumes; and when the *real* Captain of the guard, instead of the yeomanry-serjeant, used them as the happiest of time-killers, during the intervals of active service, and considered them as the perfection of English literature.

Still, however, it is confessedly *possible* for a man of decided genius to revive, for a while, this exploded predilection for *impossibility*, even among better readers; and if, in this uphill work, he should even for one season gain his point, we might be disposed to ascribe to him nearly the same honours as to the inventor of gas or galvanism; inasmuch as he also would illuminate one of the darkest and most hopeless corners of literature, and might even be said to have recalled, for one apparent instant, the spirit of the dead. Besides, it must be acknowledged that the fluctuations of fashion are not more rapid than they are diametrically opposed to each other; and that to the taste for works of amusement, especially, we may apply the remark of Horace on the vicissitudes of language:

> '*Multa renascentur quæ jam cecidere, cadentque/Quæ nunc sunt in honore.*'
> [Many forgotten words will be restored to honour, while others will fall into disuse; Horace, *Ars Poetica*]

Influenced by these considerations, perhaps, and still more by the passion for the violent, the ferocious, and the dreadful in poetry, which our contemporaries have so eminently displayed; – a passion that would seem to promise equal favour to kindred flights in prose; – or, which is most likely, hurried along by the unreflecting impulse of his own fancy, Mr. Maturin has again appeared before the public as the author of a most extravagant work, in the true St. Leon tone and character. The hero, Melmoth, is a personage of a most enduring vitality, making large inroads on centuries of time in his duration; and the only novelty which we have discovered in the plan of the book (to which novelty, however, we are disposed to allow considerable praise,) is the idea of this miraculously gifted being, of bright eyes and black disposition, attempting to gain proselytes to his friend the Devil with indefatigable zeal, but, throughout his lengthened existence, *attempting in vain*. Not that he entirely fails in his amiable pursuits, but that he finds no single individual, in his varied and protracted 'wanderings,' (in which, by the way, it is odd enough that he should never encounter his old friend 'the Wandering Jew,') whom he can induce, however misled and rendered miserable by his temptations, to barter the hopes of eternity for the super-human longevity and magical locomotivity which he has himself gained in exchange for his own soul. This idea, Mr. Maturin quaintly enough informs us, was borrowed from one of his sermons! and he quotes the passage in his preface. At the close of that preface we find a statement, which will occasion us double regret at any severity of censure that we may be compelled to inflict on portions of the work before us: but which will add largely to the pleasure that we always feel in being able to accord the meed of praise to a writer of merit. Mr. Maturin himself '*regrets the necessity*' that compels him to appear again before the public, 'in so unseemly a character as that of a writer of romances;' adding, 'did my profession furnish me with the means of sub-sistence, I should hold myself culpable indeed in having recourse to any other, but – am I allowed the choice?'

In explanation of this allusion, we are obliged to notice a rumour that Mr. Maturin has lost his ecclesiastical employment, in consequence of his having written the play of *Bertram*. Of that tragedy we spoke fully in a former article, and certainly we have not changed our opinion on the subject: – but it is a very different question, indeed, whether a clergyman should be deprived of the means of subsistence in his profession for a literary offence of that nature, or whether he should be condemned for it in a critical journal. We are not sufficiently informed to speak farther: but we must, at present, consider Mr. Maturin as very harshly treated; and we are bound to remind his judges, whoever they may be, of the merciful injunc-tion of the heathen satirist:

> '*Ne scuticá dignum, horribili sectére flagello.*' [Don't inflict the fearful scourge on someone deserving only the strap; Horace, *Satires* I. 3]

. . .

To come now to the story, or rather stories, of 'Melmoth.' The con-necting link is very slight; merely that of a descendant of the family of Melmoth witnessing, at the beginning and the end of the four volumes, some impressive instances of the supernatural powers of his ancestor 'the Wanderer;' and, during the greater part of those volumes, hearing tales from a Spaniard who is shipwrecked on the Irish coast, which carry to the highest pitch the curiosity of young Melmoth concerning the wonder-working wickednesses of his great progenitor. From these tales we shall select one or two detached passages: but, as the principal merit and attrac-tion of the work depend on the variety of the incidents scattered throughout the four volumes, we should ill perform our duty to the author or the reader by offering any thing like an abstract of their contents.

We are bound, however, to record the great fertility of invention which Mr. Maturin has exhibited in these incidents; and also the strong graphic power to which he lays claim in the delineation and contrast of character. – 'Walberg and his Wife' (although the author, as is too frequently the case, *out-horrorizes* horror in this story,) are indeed powerfully described; and if the original of the lady be living, as Mr. M. intimates, we can only say that he who is acquainted with her is so far happy. The tale of 'John Sandal and Elinor Mortimer' is said to have foundation in fact. At all events it is very interesting, and displays (perhaps *displays* rather too much) a very amusing knowledge of English historical anecdote, during a long period. The parts of the work which depicture the crimes and miseries of conventual life; which lead us from the dungeons of a monastery into those of the Inquisition, and through false doors under the floorings of rooms, down sloping passages, into subterraneous apartments, where old conjurors sit by candle-light surrounded with sculls; those parts, we say, in which the author seems lost in a kind of wearisome climax of the surprizingly wretched, and where the toiling reader yawns after him in vain, have in our opinion by far the least originality. They are, 'in good truth,' (to use a comfit-maker's phrase,) nothing but ten-times repeated copies of the *Radcliffe-romance*; of which, as Mr. Maturin tells us, he was warned by a judicious friend. His distinction between his own convents and those of old is rather fanciful than real. He imagines that he has made the sufferings of an unwilling monk novel in their appearance, by dwelling more on that 'irritating series of petty torments,' which 'solitude gives its inmates leisure to invent, and power combined with malignity the full disposition to practise, than on the startling adventures one meets with in romances.' Many of these 'petty torments,' however, are most serious inflictions, and strange events (we should hope) even in a convent; while, with regard to 'startling horrors,' we should think that few romances could boast any thing equal to the nocturnal visits of Melmoth, unchecked by the bolts and bars of the most *perfect* of human prisons. . . .

'Monk Lewis and His Coterie' (1851)★

DAVID MACBETH MOIR (1798–1851)

To the artistic artificial school of Darwin, Seward, Hayley, and the Della Cruscans, may be said to have succeeded the purely romantic one – of which Matthew Gregory Lewis ought to be set down as the leader, and John Leyden, Walter Scott, Coleridge, Southey, James Hogg, Mrs

---

★ David Macbeth Moir, *Sketches of the Poetical Literature of the Past Half-Century* (Edinburgh and London: William Blackwood and Sons, 1851), pp. 17–22.

Radcliffe, Anna Maria Porter, and Anne Bannerman, as the chief disciples. The germ of their tenets must be traced back to the North, rather than to the ballads and romances of Percy, Ritson, and Ellis; and their demonology throughout savours much more of the Teutonic than either the Saxon or Celtic. The unsettling of men's minds by the writings of Voltaire and Rousseau, among the French – and the new order of things created by the dangerous philosophising of the Academicians, and by Kant, Schelling, and the German transcendentalists – combined to bring about a new era, in which were rekindled all the magical and mystic reminiscences of the dark ages. Horace Walpole had written his *Castle of Otranto* merely as a burlesque; but hitting the tone of the day, it had been read and relished as an admirable transcript of feudal times and Gothic manners; and his success taught Mrs Radcliffe and others to harp – and far from unpleasantly – on the same string. *Clarissa Harlowe* and *Pamela* quietly located on the book-shelves, had for a while their 'virtue unrewarded,' even by a reading; and nothing went down but *Udolphos* and *Romances of the Forest, Sicilian Bravos*, and *Legends of the Hartz Mountains*; corridors and daggers, moonlight and murdering, ruined castles and sheeted spectres, gauntleted knights and imprisoned damsels.

Three men of peculiar, two of them, indeed, of great imaginative strength at this time started up – Godwin, Coleridge, and Lewis; but it is with the last of them only that I have at present to do. As a man of truly original powers, M. G. Lewis was far behind either Godwin or Coleridge, and stood much on the level of his successor Maturin; but what his imagination lacked in grandeur, was made up by energy: he was a high-priest of the intense school. Monstrous and absurd, in many things, as were the writings of Lewis, no one could say that they were deficient in interest. Truth and nature, to be sure, he held utterly at arm's-length; but, instead, he had a life-in-death vigour, a spasmodic energy, which answered well for all purposes of astonishment. He wrote of demons, ghouls, ghosts, vampires, and disembodied spirits of every kind, as if they were the common machinery of society. A skeleton 'in complete steel,' or the spectre of 'a bleeding nun,' was ever at hand, on emergencies; and wood-demons, fire-kings, and water-sprites, gave a filip to the external scenery. His *Monk*, that strange and extramundane production, made the reader 'sup so full of horrors,' that mothers were obliged to lock it up from their sickly and sentimental daughters – more especially as its morale was not of the choicest; and when Lewis took a leap from the closet to the stage, his power was equally felt. I yet remember, when a boy, trembling in the very theatre at the scene in *The Castle Spectre* which brings the murdered maiden on the stage; and if productions are to be judged by their effect, that drama, like *The Robbers* of Schiller, has left on facile imaginations traces never to be obliterated. The *Tales of Wonder*, and the *Tales of Terror*, succeeded; some of them stories of amazing vigour – wild, extravagant, unnatural – but withal highly readable, nay, occasionally of enchaining interest. In spirit Lewis was a thorough convert to the raw-head-and-bloody-bones and the trap-door German school; and his thoughts were ever away amid the Hartz Mountains, seeing 'more spirits than vast hell could hold.' His every night was Hallowe'en, or a Walpurgis Night; and he is said to have become, in his later years, the dupe of his own early over-excited feelings, and as sincere a convert to a frequent infringement of the established laws of physics, as Mrs Crowe in her *Night Side of Nature*, or the Baron von Reichenbach himself, with his Odylie light. He conjured up ghosts to affright others, and came to be haunted by them himself – a most natural retribution.

Most of the writers of the *Tales of Wonder* were young men of enthusiastic temperament, panting for distinction; and in their contributions they gave vivid indications of what, in maturer years, was to accomplish greater and better things. Lewis himself had an exquisite ear for versification, as demonstrated in his 'Durandarte,' and 'Alonzo the Brave,' – of which latter, 'The Fire-King' of Smith, in *The Rejected Addresses*, was a legitimate and scarcely extravagant burlesque. In 'The Eve of St John,' and 'Glenfinlas,' Walter Scott exhibited the glorious dawn of that day, whose transcendant meridian was to irradiate the world in 'The Lay of the Last Minstrel,' in 'Marmion,' and in 'The Lady of the Lake.' Leyden poured out his whole rough strength in 'Lord Soulis' and 'The Mermaid of Coryvreckan.' Southey forestalled his 'Madoc' and 'Roderick' in 'Mary, the Maid of the Inn,' 'Donica,' 'Rudiger,' 'The Old Woman of Berkeley,' and 'Lord William,' – The last thoroughly exquisite. While, although published elsewhere, Coleridge displayed wild and wondrous fruits from the same Hesperides in 'The Rime of the Ancient Mariner,' and 'Tales of the Dark Ladie,' 'Christabel,' and 'Kubla Khan.'

I repeat, however, that Lewis was a man rather of enthusiastic temperament than of high and sustained imagination. He could not face the sunlight and the clear blue sky; he required clouds and tempest, a howling wind and a troubled sea. He was what the vulture is to the eagle, what the leopard is to the lion, what the scene-painter is to the artist. His plays are what melodramas are to tragedy; and the terrors of his poetry trench as much on the burlesque as on the sublime; yet so great were the effects he produced, more especially in his prose romances, and so unbounded was their popularity, that the mighty Minstrel [i.e. Walter Scott], then a young man, confessed to have looked up to him with an admiration bordering on awe, and even deferentially submitted to be schooled by him in the art of versification.

Like the school of Darwin, that of Lewis was destined to have a day fully as remarkable for its brevity as its brightness. The readers of *The Feudal Tyrants*, *The Monk*, *The Tales of Terror*, *The Isle of Devils*, and *The Castle Spectre*, became surfeited with perpetually dining on high-spiced curries, and began to long for a little 'plain potato and salt.' His spirit-world was neither the spirit-world of Milton in his *Paradise Lost* and his *Comus*; nor of

Shakespeare in his *Hamlet* and *Macbeth*; nor of Spenser in his *Faery Queen*. It was not the spirit-world of the Greek drama, which Æschylus and Euripides never ventured into, save in search of an avenging Nemesis, worthy of some awful occasion – transcendent misery, or transcendent guilt. On the contrary, the exceptions, with Lewis, were all on the other side, and were made the rule. Every one is bamboozled about the nature of every thing he either hears or sees. What we take for a knight, may be the foul fiend in *incognito*. Every third house is haunted; every second old woman is a witch; each tree has an owl; the moon is in conspiracy with the stars to blight the earth, on which they shed a malign influence; and thunder is ever at hand, with copious streams of blue zig-zag lightning. The noises on the wind are the howling of spirits; the skeleton of a murderer dangles in chains at every cross-road; very many chambers are particularly dark, grotesquely wainscotted, have secret doors, and are disturbed by the death-tick; while all the ponderous mail-studded gates hideously creak on their rusty hinges. In short, man, instead of being a prosaic payer of poor-rates and property-tax, is made to inhabit a land of enchantments; where ogres tyrannise in castles, and dragons spout fire in caves; and where all the accredited Aristotelian elements – fire, air, earth, and water – are continually reverberating to each other –

> 'Black spirits and white,
>   Blue spirits and grey –
> Mingle, mingle, mingle,
>   Ye that mingle may!'

The hideousness, the monstrosity, the exaggeration of this style of writing, combining and amalgamating with the perturbed temper of the times, gave it an acceptability and a fascination which it probably would not have otherwise acquired. At its acme it caught hold also of our most powerful contemporary prose, in the *St Leon* of Godwin; it was reflected in the *Canterbury Tales* of Sophia and Harriet Lee, in the *Frankenstein* of Mrs Shelley, and the *Melmoth* of Maturin, and died away into a gentler and more graceful spirituality in the *Rip Van Winkle* and *Headless Hessian* of Washington Irving, the *Vanderdecken's Message Home* of John Howison, and *The Metempsychosis* of Robert Macnish. As the sacrifices of the high-priest ceased to ascend, the worshippers gradually deserted the mouldy shrine: the younger devotees – Scott, Southey, Coleridge, and Leyden – took, in the maturity of intellect, to higher and more legitimate courses – forsook the melodrama for veritable tragedy and comedy, and, doffing the masquers' robes, endeavoured 'to look melancholy like gentlemen.' To accelerate their flight from this debateable land, the bow of ridicule was also bent against them. Jeffrey let fly a few sharp arrows; and the *Water Fiends* of George Colman the younger, as well as the burlesques of Horace Smith, will long be remembered as exquisite pleasantries.

— 8 —

Readers' Responses

MANY PEOPLE DURING the late eighteenth and early nineteenth centuries kept literary journals or diaries, listing the books they read and commenting upon them, thereby constructing an image of themselves as 'lovers of literature'. Both literary amateurs and professional writers such as Anna Seward in the provinces of Staffordshire kept up with current literature and shared their views with their literary friends, sometimes in extensive literary correspondence. It is interesting to see how these honest interchanges between literary friends differ from the official critical reviews. Such personal documents also provide information about literary fashions, and about reading practices. For example, many people read books aloud to one another (including 'horrid' novels); many people enjoyed sharing ghost stories with one another; and readers seldom regarded multi-volumed Gothic novels as being too taxing – Mary Russell Mitford read two dozen books a month. Such private responses were generally more favourable to Gothic novels than the increasingly carping critical reviews.

Whereas literary journals record the professional context of literature, these private sources often touch upon the emotional context in which such books were read. Many were read in a secluded chimney corner as a kind of consolation as well as for shivers of excitement. Fanny Burney wrote to her husband M. D'Arblay that she believed that Radcliffe's writings 'are all best calculated for lonely hours & depressed spirits. I should probably have done more justice to Udolpho if I had read it in one of my solitary intervals' (1 August 1797). Scott felt that the Radcliffe School had a particularly strong appeal to sequestered invalids and spinsters and bachelors, bewitching them away from their world of secret sorrow, while many critics felt that the Lewis School stirred up the libidinous passions of young men.

Many of the responses in this section come from people who were young at the turn of the century, and were responding to a 'modern' fashion created by equally young writers – Lewis was 19 when he wrote *The Monk* and Radcliffe wrote four novels by the age of 30. But even later in life, people nostalgically remembered the books of their youth, and enjoyed rereading them. Scott's claim that once you know the riddle of *Udolpho* you can no longer reread the novel is not true: Charles Bucke, for example, read it *nine times* with pleasure. A critic of Radcliffe's post-humously published novel *Gaston de Blondeville* observed in 1826 that even though the works of novelists such as Jane Austen and Sir Walter Scott had supplanted the earlier taste for the Gothic, some of the best Gothic novels 'have continued to excite the girl's first wonder, and to supply the last solace to her grandame's age, thumbed over, begged, borrowed, and thought of as often as ever!'

'Beckford's Favourite Propensity' (1791)*

HESTER LYNCH THRALE PIOZZI (1741–1821)

I have been reading Vathek, 'tis a mad Book to be sure, and written by a mad Author, yet there is a Sublimity about it – particularly towards the Conclusion.

Mr Beckford's *favourite Propensity* is all along visible I think; particularly in the luscious Descriptions given of Gulchenrouz: but his Quarantine seems to be performed, & I am told he is return'd quietly to Fonthill. When we were at Milan Mr Bisset brought over the news how he was hooted from Society by my Lord Loughborough, who threatened corporal or legal Punishment for Mr Beckford's Violation of young Courtenay – Brother to Lady Loughborough [Beckford's aunt]. at Lausanne no Englishman would exchange a Word with the Creature; & charming Doctor Fisher's charitable Heart pitied his wretched exclusion from the World.

But since Courtenay came to his Estate and Title, and I suppose treated the whole Business as a Joke, or common Occurrence, all is over; and I hear nothing said of Mr Beckford but as an *Authour*. what a World it is!!!!

Letter to Sophy Ruxton (14 August 1792)†

MARIA EDGEWORTH (1767–1849)

Has my aunt [Mrs Ruxton] seen the *Romance of the Forest*? It has been the fashionable novel here, everybody read and talked of it; we were much interested in some parts of it. It is something in the style of the *Castle of Otranto*, and the horrible parts are we thought well worked up, but it is very difficult to keep Horror breathless with his mouth wide open through three volumes.

★ *Thraliana: The Diary of Mrs. Hester Lynch Thrale*, 2 vols, 2nd edn, ed. Katharine C. Balderston (Oxford: Clarendon Press, 1951), 3 January 1791, vol. 2, p. 799.

† Maria Edgeworth, *Chosen Letters*, ed. F. V. Barry (London: Jonathan Cape, 1931), p. 58.

Letter to Mr Walker (8 March 1794)*

JOSEPH RITSON (1752–1803)

Novel-writing is certainly in high estimation. Mrs Radcliffe, author of 'The Romance of the Forest,' has one at present in the hands of Robinsons for which she asks five hundred pounds, though it is but to consist of four volumes. Godwin also, and I believe, Holcroft, have each one in the press. In short, one would suppose all the world to be novel readers, though, for my part, I must with shame confess I never look into one.

A Literary Journal (1796–9)†

HENRY FRANCIS CARY (1772–1844)

The literary journals of the Rev. Henry Francis Cary, translator of Dante, reveal how easily Gothic novels were intermixed with the classics and foreign works in the reading of a literary gentleman. He began writing for the Gentleman's Magazine and caught the attention of Anna Seward, who befriended him in the late 1780s, and with whom he corresponded for many years, discussing the latest literary productions. He took orders in 1796 and settled as the priest of Abbots Bromley, Staffordshire, where he began a regular system of keeping a literary journal. He became Assistant Librarian at the British Museum in 1826, and had many literary friends later in life, such as Lamb and Coleridge. When he died in 1844 he was buried beside Samuel Johnson in Westminster Abbey.

1796

June 20 to 22. At Cannock. Read Maximes, &c. du Duc de la Rochefoucauld. They contain much unpleasant truth, some useful and some, perhaps, dangerous instruction. Read Montalbert, a novel, by Charlotte Smith, in three volumes.

24. Continued Valerius Flaccus, books iv. and v. The Argonauts proceed on their voyage, and Amycus, king of the Bebricians, who cruelly sacrificed all who came on his coast, is killed by Pollux. . . .

1797

January 5 and 6. Read Hayley's Life of Milton. A warm but injudicious vindication of the poet's character from the violent and illiberal aspersions of Johnson. . . .

---

* *The Letters of Joseph Ritson* (London: William Pickering, 1833).

† *Memoir of the Rev. Henry Francis Cary*, 2 vols (London: Edward Moxon, 1847).

11 to 13. Read the Lives of Rafaelle and Michelagnolo in Vasari.

14. Read Thomson's Castle of Indolence, with Jane [his wife].

15. Proceeded in the Voyage du Jeune Anacharsis, with Jane, and read to vol. ii., p. 21.

16. Translated Dante, Purgatorio, part of the first canto. Continued Anacharsis to p. 41, with Jane. . . .

26. Began Burke on the Sublime and Beautiful, and read to Part ii., with Jane.

27. Continued Burke to Part iii., with Jane.

28. Proceeded in Dante, Purgatorio, canto iii.

30. Proceeded in Dante, Purgatorio, canto iii. Continued Burke to Part v., with Jane.

31. Continued and finished Burke on the Sublime and Beautiful, and read Miss Seward's Monody on Major André, with Jane. – The system of Burke appears to be founded in nature and truth, though erroneous in some of its details, and defective even in its general view. The Platonic idea of mental beauty is too entirely excluded. Perhaps Burke, in his wonderful range of knowledge, has never visited the writings of Plato. . . .

February

5. Read the first canto of Falconer's Shipwreck.

6. Finished the Shipwreck, a little epic poem, rendered pleasing by the truth of its narrative, its brevity, and language generally animated and sometimes poetical, though too much disfigured by sea-terms. Its unfortunate author was lost twenty-seven years ago in a voyage to the East Indies. The *Aurora* frigate, in which he sailed, it is feared, perished by fire, with all her crew. Continued Anacharsis to p. 350, with Jane. Proceeded in Dante, Purgatorio, canto iii. . . .

23. Finished the third part of Henry VI., and began Richard the Third, with Jane. . . .

March

5 to 9. At Lichfield with Miss Seward. Read Sappho, and Curan and Argentile, two dramatic pieces, with some other new poems lately published by Mason.

10. Began Southey's Joan of Arc, and read the two first books, with Jane. . . .

13. Concluded Joan of Arc with Jane. About four hundred lines in the second book on 'preternatural agency,' by Coleridge, are in the Lucretian manner, and much superior to the rest. The poem on the whole is spirited, and keeps alive the attention, though it contains few passages admirable either for sublimity or beauty. The writer I remember sometimes to have met in company at Oxford. . . .

May
15 to *June* 3. At Cannock. Concluded Travels of Cyrus. Read Ward's Origin and History of the Law of Nations, from the time of the Greeks and Romans to the Age of Grotius. The author endeavours to confute the notion of a moral principle existing in the human mind, and founds the basis of the law of nations on the influence of Christianity. The work is chiefly estimable for information it contains of curious customs in the middle ages. Read Wood's Life of Homer; an attempt to assign the reasons of Homer's superiority over all other poets, in which much learning and ingenuity are displayed, though some of the arguments appear fanciful. The style is quaint and affected. Read The Italian, a new novel by Mrs. Radcliffe, and Julie de Roubigné. These two tales are of a very different cast. The former raises an unmixed sensation of horror, the latter affects the mind with pity and terror. Taste must give the preference to Julie de Roubigné. . . .

June 28 to *December* 20. – Read Klopstock's Messiah, and Schiller's Ghost-Seer in English, and Disobedience, a new novel, with Jane and Mrs. Ormsby. Read Favole di Pignotti; Rabaut de St. Etienne's Account of the French Revolution; . . .

1798
November 1798 to *January* 10, 1799. Read Roscoe's Life of Lorenzo de' Medici; two volumes of Canterbury Tales by Harriet and Sophia Lee, very amusing, of which Lothaire, the Ghost Story, is the best. Reynolds' Works; Cowper's translation of the Odyssey, the twelve last books with Jane, and the twelve first of the Iliad; and concluded Ariosto's Orlando Furioso and the five supplementary Cantos.

1799
January. Began Montesquieu, L'Esprit des Loix.
   23. Read Lewis's Castle Spectre, a new play. Continued Montesquieu. Began Smollett's Count Fathom.
   24, 25. Finished Count Fathom. Continued Montesquieu. . . .

July 28 to *December* 24. In Wales and Dublin. Read the second volume of Southey's Poems, Barrington's History of Henry the Second, Memoires du Chevalier de Grieux. The Midnight Bell, a novel, Hayley's Triumphs of Temper, most of the Critical Works of Dionysius Halicarnassensis, the Hecuba of Euripides, in Porson's new edition, the first book of Hobbes's Leviathan, some of Filicaja's Poems, Bishop Taylor on the Liberty of Prophesying, &c., &c. . . .

Letters*

ANNA SEWARD (1747–1809)

Anna Seward was the daughter of the Canon of Lichfield, Staffordshire, where she lived most of her life in the Bishop's Palace. Dubbed 'the Swan of Lichfield', she was a poet of the old school, writing mostly sentimental and melancholic works. She found the provinces to be a firm foundation for her literary reputation and cultivated a wide circle of literary correspondents. Most critics were too polite to point out that Miss Seward was a self-important busybody, though Mary Russell Mitford was prompted to describe her as 'the Venus and Muse of a provincial city; the one-eyed monarch of the blind at Lichfield, who thought nobody could see elsewhere' (letter, 31 October 1814). She corresponded frequently with 'the Ladies of Llangollyn': Miss Sarah Ponsonby, companion to Lady Eleanor Butler, sent Seward a copy of Walpole's The Mysterious Mother, *and they often discussed Radcliffe, Baillie, Lewis and others. Seward, like many others, was under the mistaken impression that Joanna Baillie's* Plays on the Passions *were written by Ann Radcliffe, a subject which she discusses with her friend Whalley, whose play* The Castle de Montval *was a recent success. She encouraged Sir Walter Scott's early work, and left her literary remains to him.*

To C. Smyth (3 August 1794)

I read not, neither doubtless do you, the Novel trash of the day. Hours are too precious for such frivolous waste, where the mind has in itself any valuable resources; yet are there a few pens which possess the power so to inspirit those fond fancies of the brain, as to render them gratifying to an imagination which demands more to please it than amorous story. Mrs Radcliffe's pen is of this number. Though she aims not at the highly important morality of the great Richardson, nor possesses scarce a portion of his ample, his matchless ability, in discriminating characters,

> 'Yet does she mount, and keep her distant way
> Above the limits of the vulgar page.'

Her Mysteries of Udolpho is a much superior work to her Romance of the Forest. The first volume of that is fine, the rest heavy, uninteresting, and contains very affected writing. Udolpho contains enough to awaken and interest attention in every volume. I was, however, frequently wearied in the perusal, since, though her powers of scenic description are very

---

* *Letters of Anna Seward*, 6 vols (Edinburgh, 1811), vol. 3, pp. 389–90; vol. 4, pp. 151–2; vol. 5, pp. 241–4, 253, 256–7.

considerable, she wants judgment to be aware that the incessant and laboured exertion of those powers counteracts their influence, weakening it by degrees, till attention sinks in languid satiety. Her style is fine, and her poetic mottos admirably chosen, nor are the interspersed verses without beauty; but her great fort [*sic*] is in displaying terrific images. The object behind the mysterious veil, described at first only by saying what it is not, and the long deserted bed-chamber of the late Marchioness, form a very august exhibition of the terrible graces, who never frown with effect but when they are led by the hand of Genius.

To The Right Hon. Lady Eleanor Butler (4 February 1796)

There is more fascination for my fancy and my feelings, in Mrs Brookes's Lady Catesby, Excursion, and Emily Montague, in Sidney Biddulph, in Caroline de Litchfield, in Julie de Roubigné, in the Simple Story, and even in the wild extravagancies of the Mysteries of Udolpho, than in the mild Evelina, or the rigid Cecilia.

To Rev. Thomas Sedgwick Whalley (7 June 1799)

Never, till yesterday, have I seen or heard the celebrated, though not yet acted dramas on the passions; and of them only the Count de Montford, which Mr White read me last night very finely. I like the style, it is often Shakespearean, without servile imitation. Many of the reflections and observations in the earlier scenes of that play, evince a discriminating insight into human feeling and character. The situations in the close are of soul-harrowing strength and horror. It appears indubitable that the sublime, though exceptionable novel, Caleb Williams, was the origin of Mrs Radcliffe's design of writing plays illustrative of the passions, and the mischiefs that result from the absorbing dominion of any one of them; but the character of Falkland, in Caleb Williams, is a much more masterly comment on that text than the Count de Montford. Hatred, indulged to excess, must demonize any man; but when we perceive an high and delicate sense of honour the domineering idol of the soul, and find, as in Falkland, that a boundless devotion to its sway is capable of leading the human mind from great elevant [*sic*] of moral virtue to the last excesses of vice, naturally, and step by step, we find a nobler and more useful lesson of morality engraven on the heart. Greatly horrible effects are produced in the play of the Count de Montford, but nature and probability are grossly outraged in the incompetency of the causes which produce them. The native vices of the brutal Tyrrel are blended with the native virtues of Falkland; extremes which nature decreed should never meet. Falkland, it is true, becomes a demon, who was long an angel; but then the outrageous violence with which the vile Tyrrel persecutes and provokes, and, at length, by personal disgraceful insult, after every other abuse had been borne with the calmest sweetness, urges the stab of revenge from the greatly injured, preserves that apostasy from appearing unnatural! Those circumstances make the subsequent degeneracy of Falkland, extreme as it proves, not incredible. The object of De Montford's deadly hatred is amiable, gentle, sportive; – he repays it with a sweetness and magnanimity, to which De Montford is twice indebted for his life; – he even seeks the monster's friendship, and is guilty of no offence but that of having tried to jest him out of his surly aversion. It is not only out of probability, but of possibility, that such a nothing of a provocation could urge a man, whose disposition was originally generous, brave, and merciful, to the darkest, foulest, and most deliberate murder. It violates all unity of character, the only dramatic unity which ought to be kept sacred. In the ever, and on all occasions, dark, violent, and envious Tyrrel, such love of hatred is natural, from the eclipsing graces, and talents, and consequent influence of Falkland disarming the despotism which Tyrrel's large fortune had long enabled him to exert in his neighbourhood. In the gallant and liberal Montford, it is monstrous and inconceivable. If he had been represented as implacable, though brave – if the pride and arrogance of his disposition had been heightened, and heightened also the gay contempt of Rezenvelt – and if Rezenvelt had not twice, or even once, given Montford his life, the grandly horrible effects of the close might have been preserved in this play, without such total revolt of our credulity; but it is most true what Mrs Jackson observes, that, in all Mrs Radcliffe's writings, attentive only to terrific effects, she bestows no care upon their causes, and rashly cuts the knot of probability which she seems to want patience to untie. One has heard of a labouring mountain bringing forth a mouse: In Mrs R.'s writings mice bring forth mountains.

To Rev. Thomas Sedgwick Whalley (7 October 1799)

I am glad we agree so well on the subject of the Plays on the Passions. My literary friends now assert that they are not Mrs Radcliffe's; and, indeed, though the defects and merits of the plans and characters are each of her complexion, yet I always thought the masterly nature of several of the single speeches above her powers, as comparing them with her novels. There is one line poetically great and original as anything in our language. Where De Montford, shuddering at the newly conceived idea of an impending marriage between his darling sister and hated rival, exclaims:

'The morning-star mix'd with infernal fire!'

Montford's soliloquy in the wood, is, as you observe, noble writing. It is in the same spirit with that of Narbonne [in Robert Jephson's *The Count of Narbonne*, 1781], roaming through the aisles of the church at midnight, previous to the commission of that murder which proves parricidal. We find it hard to say which passage is the most sublime.

To Mrs M. Powys (17 October 1799)

The literary world now asserts that the Plays on the Passions are not Mrs Radcliffe's. I should have been incredulous to the report that they are, had not the error, as to responsibility of causes to their effects, and the atoning excellence, resulting from the horrible grandeur of those effects in themselves, been of the same complexion with the faults and beauties in her novels. Otherwise the occasionally rich vein of poetry, which we find in the single passages, together with a degree of deep insight into the human mind, are above the level of talent which produced her romances. When I spoke of my sentiments to you of the plays, I had not read their introductory dissertation. Now, after perusal, I confess it is far from pleasing me. The ideas in that tract are confused and abortive, and the language has no felicity. Abounding in Scoticisms, that, at least, cannot have been written by an Englishwoman – and Mrs R is an English woman. They now tell us this work is from the other side of the Tweed [i.e. by a Scotswoman].

'A Lover of Literature' (1797–1800)*

Thomas Green (1769–1825)

MARCH the 25th. [1797]
    Finished the Italian. This work will maintain, but not extend, Mrs. Radcliffe's fame as a novelist. It has the same excellencies and defects as her former compositions. In the vivid exhibition of the picturesque of nature, in the delineation of strong and dark character, in the excitation of horror by physical and moral agency, I know not that Mrs. R. has any equal: but she languishes in spinning the thread of the narrative on which these excellencies are strung; natural characters and incidents are feebly represented; probability is often strained without sufficient compensation; and the developement of those mysteries which have kept us stretched so long on the rack of terror and impatience (an unthankful task at best) is lame and impotent. Eleanor and Vivaldi, either in their separate character or mutual attachment (a wire-drawn theme), touched me but little; but I confess myself to have been deeply and violently impressed, by the midnight examination of the corpse of Bianchi; by the atrocious conference of

---

* Thomas Green, *Extracts from The Diary of a Lover of Literature* (Ipswich: John Raw; London: Longman, Hurst, Rees, and Orme, 1810), pp. 28, 43, 44, 209.

Schedoni and the Marquesa, in the dim twilight of the Church of San Nicolo; and, above all, by what passed in Spalatro's solitary dwelling on the sea shore. If Mrs. Radcliffe justly consulted her fame, she would confine herself to fragments. – She and Miss Burney might compose a capital piece between them – Mrs. R. furnishing the landscape, and Miss B. the figures.

SEPTEMBER the 3rd. . . . Read Sir Horace Walpole's Mysterious Mother. There is a gusto of antiquity, and peculiar raciness in this piece, which is quite to my taste: the terrible graces are finely maintained, and the passion of horror is ably prepared, and successfully excited; but the catastrophe is at last worked up to a crisis of distraction, for which no power of thought or language can find adequate expression.

SEP. the 8th. . . . There is a very happy ridicule of the prevailing system of terror in certain modern novels, by a 'Jacobin Novelist,' in the last Monthly Magazine [see pp. 299ff.]. It seems hard, but it is true, that original excellence in any department of writing, by provoking scurvy imitation, has a natural tendency to bring disgrace upon itself.

MARCH the 25th. [*1800*]

Read Godwin's St. Leon. In the Preface, he explicitly abjures the doctrine of extinguishing the private affections, which he had inculcated in his Political Justice; and the subsequent pages bear repeated testimony to the sincerity and completeness of his conversion: – yet he professes to see no cause to change the fundamental principle of that Work! I flatter myself with having been instrumental in a little humanizing him; but the volcanic and blasphemous spirit still peeps, occasionally, through a flimsy disguise. His sentiments and expressions are often borrowed; and the account of the interrogatories at the Inquisition, with the decoy employed there, are directly and impudently stolen from Mrs. Radcliffe. In his struggles to be sublime, there is something inexpressibly hideous and revolting: – they are not the exertions of mighty power, but the convulsive throes and ghastly agonies of a distempered sensibility. – After all, too, though one may be amused with the adventures of St. Leon, what impression do they leave upon the mind? They do not *indoctrinate* the unsatisfactory nature of boundless opulence and immortal youth, as Nourjahad does, – for St. Leon seems rather persecuted by his ill fortune, than by the natural consequences of his supernatural acquisitions. What, then, do they inculcate? – I am quite unable to tell.

'A Solitary Life' (1797)*

MARY HARTLEY (c. 1738–1803)

Mary Hartley was the unmarried daughter of Dr David Hartley, philosopher and physician, friend of Joseph Priestley. She lived at Belvedere, Bath, with her brother, the Liberal MP for Hull, who worked in the cause against slavery and was a good friend of Benjamin Franklin. Mary Hartley was acquainted with Fanny Burney, Mrs Ord and other Bluestockings, and the Dowdlers.

Letter to Sir William Weller Pepys (4 November 1797)

I have no family round me, no companion, with whom I can interchange my thoughts, except when my brother is at home, and even then I have very little society with him. He is always employed with his books and papers. Of course therefore I lead a very solitary life. I find company very disagreeable to him, (for he flies out of the room the minute he hears a rap) and it is now grown tiresome to me; for I have not the spirits I used to have; and therefore I am generally denied; at least whenever my brother is at Bath. . . .

I told you I had few companions; but I converse very much with books: yet I am not eager to seek for new ones. There are so many valuable old books, which I have not yet read, and which I am eager to read, as soon as I can find time, that I have already a large field before me. I read however, with great eagerness, the memoirs and letters of Gibbon, when that book came out, and was much entertained with it, but his criticisms on his studies were rather too learned for me, and spoke of many books which I have not read. . . . I read too with the greatest avidity, Roscoe's *Life of Lorenzo di Medici*; a most admirable performance on a most entertaining subject. . . . As I cannot afford to buy books of value, and only hire them from a library, I cou'd not keep a book so much in request, as long as I cou'd have wished to study it; but I was much delighted with many of Lorenzo's poems, in which I thought there was much imagination and beautiful diction. But I am talking of an old subject – last year's news. I have since read a lighter work; but of beautiful imagination, interesting scenes, and true genius, *The Italian, or the Confessional of the black Penitents*. I hope you like it and that you read it with as much eagerness as I do; Mrs. Radcliffe's works, seem to me more like Epic poems, than ordinary romances. She equals any author that I ever read, in fertility of imagination, intricacy of plot, and consistency of character.

---

* *A Later Pepys. The Correspondence of Sir William Weller Pepys, Bart.*, ed. Alice C. C. Gaussen, 2 vols (London and New York: John Lane: The Bodley Head, 1904), vol. 2, pp. 132–3.

'An Introduction to Ann Radcliffe'

ELIZABETH CARTER (1717–1806)

Elizabeth Carter, famous for her brilliant translation of Epictetus, friend of Dr Johnson, Hannah More, Elizabeth Montagu and many notables in the literary and intellectual world, was the archetypal Bluestocking. But like many of the late Augustans, she was sensitive to the appeal of romantic melancholy and sublime scenery, and visited the gloomy ruins of Fountains Abbey and the solemn shades of Ripon Minster in the 1780s. She became an avid reader of novels in the 1790s, and made a special effort to become acquainted with Mrs Radcliffe, by an introduction through Henrietta Maria (Harriet) Bowdler, the sister of the man who 'bowdlerized' Shakespeare's plays to make them less dangerous for young readers.

Mrs Carter to Mrs Montagu (11 December 1759)★

I have not read the *History of the Penitents*, except a little extract, with which I was greatly pleased. It is much to be wished indeed that the general fashion of novel reading did not render such antidotes very necessary. Various kinds of antidotes perhaps are necessary to the various kinds of poison imbibed in the study of these wretched books★, by which the understanding, the taste, and the heart are equally in danger of being vitiated. Those which are writ in the most specious manner, with great appearance of delicacy, and high pretensions to virtue, are of all others the most destructive; they form a jumble of right and wrong, so entangled together, that it requires exactness of judgment to separate them, which seldom or never belongs to young people, who take all together; and thus their heads become a mere chaos of confused ideas, and their hearts are cheated out of every fixed principle of action.

[★*Note by Mrs Carter's Nephew:* It will be obvious to the reader, how great has been the improvement which has taken place in writing novels, since the date of this letter. Mrs. Carter highly approved of many that have since been written by authors of considerable genius, as well as of strict morals, such as Mrs. West and Mrs. Radcliffe, and others who might be named; and she found the reading of such works a very pleasing relaxation from her severer studies.]

★ *Letters from Mrs. Elizabeth Carter to Mrs. Montague*, ed. Rev. Montagu Pennington, 3 vols (London: F. C. and J. Rivington, 1817), vol. 1, pp. 69–70.

Mrs Carter to Mrs Montagu (15 December 1790)⋆

I have been reading with much pleasure the *Sicilian Romance*. The language is elegant, the scenery exquisitely painted, the moral good, and the conduct and conclusion of the fable, I think, original. Have you read it? And do you know the name of the authoress? I do not.

Joseph Farington's Diary (15 September 1794)†

Lady B[eaumont] recd. a letter to-day from Mrs Carter, who expresses herself in a very strong manner in favour of the *Mysteries of Udolpho* and of the talents of Mrs Radcliffe, the author.

Comments by Mrs Carter's Nephew‡

After the publication of the third edition of her Poems, in which some were added which had not appeared before, she [i.e. Mrs Carter] wrote nothing for the press. Her head-aches were very frequent and violent, and often prevented her from reading or writing any thing which required much attention. At such times, when she was able to sit up, she was glad to have recourse to any novel, or modern romance, provided the tendency, or moral, of it was good. These she read with much pleasure, especially if removed from real life, from the delineations of which she did not derive much satisfaction. The novels of Mrs. D'Arblay [i.e. Fanny Burney] are indeed exceptions to this rule; for she thought very highly of them, especially of Evelina, the first published; she had them all, and read them with increasing approbation more than once.

But of Mrs. Charlotte Smith's works in general she highly disapproved; and was indeed hardly willing to give her credit for the genius which she was generally allowed to possess; the reason of which was, that she thought their morality at least very defective, and in some of them positively bad. Upon the same principles she was very partial to all Mrs. West's publications, both in prose and verse, as not only displaying a very considerable, and indeed very remarkable, share of genius, under so many disadvantages, and as having the morality of them founded upon the only unerring basis, that of religion. [Mrs West dedicated her *Tales of the Times* to Mrs Carter.]

But of all authors of this class, Mrs Carter thought most highly of Mrs Radcliffe, and was most delighted with the perusal of her Romances. The good tendency of all her works, the virtues of her principal characters,

---

⋆ *Ibid.*, vol. 3, pp. 323–4.

† *The Farington Diary* (1922), vol. 1, p. 71.

‡ Montagu Pennington, *Memoirs of the Life of Mrs Elizabeth Carter* (London: F. C. and J. Rivington, 1807), pp. 298–301.

supported on the solid foundation of religion, the elegance of her style, and her accurate, as well as vivid, delineations of the beauties of nature, appeared to her such as to raise Mrs Radcliffe to a degree of eminence far superior to any writer of romance of the present day. Of her, however, she had no personal knowledge, any more than of Mrs. Smith; but she was well acquainted with Mrs. D'Arblay, whose worthy and respectable father, Dr. Burney, she had long known, and slightly with Mrs. West, of whose character she thought as highly as she did of her works.

Few ages have probably been more fruitful than the present, in literary performances of various kinds, and often of great merit, by female writers; but a few years since the world was surprized by a work from a young lady, in the very highest rank of genius, and that in which, perhaps, of all others, women have least succeeded. Their attempts in the tragic line of the drama have generally failed, and it was reserved for the present age to see more of the genuine spirit of Shakespeare revive in the tragedies of Miss Joanna Baillie, than has inspired any other author since his time. This was also Mrs. Carter's opinion, when the first volume of her Plays was published without her name; and her judgment must therefore be free from prejudice. No one then supposed it was written by a woman; but when she found it was by a female author, a young one too, and hitherto unknown to the literary world, she felt a triumph, which those who know her partiality to her own sex will easily believe. She was previously acquainted with Miss Baillie a little, and much better since, and had a great regard for her person, as well as respect for her extraordinary talents.

Mrs Carter to Mrs Radcliffe (April 1799)★

If Mrs Radcliffe is not engaged, Mrs Carter will have the pleasure of calling upon her about twelve o'clock tomorrow morning.

Henrietta Maria Bowdler to Mrs Radcliffe (18 April 1799)

Dear Madam,

I venture to give you this trouble, at the request of Mrs Carter, whose admirable talents, and far more admirable virtues, are too well known to need any introduction from me. She very much wishes to have the pleasure of knowing you; and will deliver this letter, if she has the good fortune of finding you at home. As I am persuaded the acquaintance must afford mutual satisfaction, I could not refuse the request with which Mrs Carter honoured me; though it is made on the supposition of my having some degree of interest with you, to which I have no claim, except from the very

---

★ *Annual Biography and Obituary*, for the Year 1824, vol. 8, pp. 103–4.

sincere admiration I have ever felt for your talents, and the regard and esteem with which I am, dear Madam,

Your obliged and affectionate humble servant,

H. M. Bowdler

P.S. If Mrs Carter does not deliver this letter herself, she will, I believe, take an early opportunity of waiting on you, with a very amiable friend of mine, Miss Shipley, who has promised to carry her in her carriage.

Mrs Radcliffe to Mrs Carter (April 1799)

Mrs Radcliffe is extremely sorry that an engagement to go into the country to-morrow, for some time, on account of Mr R's state of health, which is very critical, will deprive her of the honour intended her by Mrs Carter; for which she requests Mrs C. to believe that she has a full and proper respect.

Letter to Miss E. Belsham (1800)★

Anna Laetitia Barbauld (1743–1825)

I have received . . . great pleasure lately from the representation of *De Montfort*, a tragedy which you probably read a year and half ago, in a volume entitled *A Series of Plays on the Passions*. I admired it then, but little dreamed I was indebted for my entertainment to a young lady of Hampstead [i.e. Joanna Baillie] whom I visited, and who came to Mr. Barbauld's meeting all the while with as innocent a face as if she had never written a line. The play is admirably acted by Mrs. Siddons and Kemble, and is finely written, with great purity of sentiment, beauty of diction, strength and originality of character; but it is open to criticism, – I cannot believe such a hatred natural. The affection between the brother and sister is most beautifully touched, and, as far as I know, quite new. The play is somewhat too good for our present taste.

★ *The Works of Anna Lætitia Barbauld*, with a Memoir by Lucy Aikin, 2 vols (London: Longman, Hurst, Rees, Orme, Brown, and Green, 1825), vol. 2, pp. 67–8.

Letter to Miss Robinson (27 December 1802)*

SAMUEL TAYLOR COLERIDGE (1772–1834)

Coleridge objected not only to Gothic novels in general, but to the unmanly per-
versity of some of their writers. For example, he said that Walpole's 'Mysterious
Mother is the most disgusting, detestable, vile composition that ever came from the
hand of a man. No one with one spark of true manliness, of which Horace Walpole
had none, could have written it.' Mary Robinson's mother (Mary Robinson, author
of Hubert de Sevrac*) had included Coleridge's poem 'The Mad Monk' (see pp.*
243ff.) in her collection Wild Wreath *(1804), and his poem 'A Stranger Minstrel'*
was included in her posthumous Memoirs *(1801). Coleridge objected to this, and*
wrote to her daughter, a good friend of his, in a manner which seems intemperate.

Your Mother had indeed a good, a very good, heart – and in *my* eyes, and in
my belief, was in her latter life – a blameless Woman – Her memoirs I have not
seen – I understood that an excessively silly copy of Verses, which I had
absolutely forgotten the very writing of, disgraced one of the volumes – This
publication of a private letter (an act so wholly unjustifiable, and in its nature
subversive of all Social Confidence) I attributed altogether to the man, at
whose shop the volumes were published –. . . . But, my dear Miss Robinson!
(I pray you, do not be wounded – rather consider what I am about to say as a
pledge of my esteem, and confidence in your honour and prudence, a confidence beyond the dictates of worldly caution) – but I have a wife, I have
sons, I have an infant Daughter – what excuse could I offer to my conscience
if by suffering my own name to be connected with those of Mr. Lewis, or Mr.
Moore, I was the *occasion* of their reading the Monk, or the wanton poems of
Thomas Little [Moore's pseud.] Esqre? Should I not be an infamous Pander to
the Devil in the Seduction of my own offspring? My head turns giddy, my
heart sickens, at the very thought of seeing such books in the hands of a child
of mine – I neither have or profess an excess of religious Faith or Feeling – I
write altogether from the common feelings of common Honesty – The
mischief of these misery-making writings *laughs* at all calculations – On my
own account therefore I must in the most emphatic manner decline all such
connection. . . . O dear Miss Robinson! Exert your own Talents – do you
plant the night violets of your own Genius and Goodness on the Grave of
your dear Parent – not Hensbane, not Hemlock! Do not mistake me! I do not
suspect, that the Poems, you mean to publish, have themselves aught in the
least degree morally objectionable; but the *names* are those of men, who have
sold provocatives to vulgar Debauchees, and vicious schoolboys – in no other
Light can many of their writings be regarded by a Husband and a Father.

★ *Unpublished Letters of Samuel Taylor Coleridge*, ed. Earl Leslie Griggs (London: Constable,
1932), vol. 1, pp. 233–5.

'Percy Bysshe Shelley's Reading' (1803)*

Thomas Medwin (1788–1869)

He was very fond of reading, and greedily devoured all the books which were brought to school after the holidays; these were mostly *blue* books. Who does not know what blue books mean? but if there should be any one ignorant enough not to know what those dear darling volumes, so designated from their covers, contain, be it known, that they are or were to be bought for sixpence, and embodied stories of haunted castles, bandits, murderers, and other grim personages – a most exciting and interesting sort of food for boys' minds; among those of a larger calibre was one which I have never seen since, but which I still remember with a *recouchè* delight. It was *Peter Wilkins*. How much Shelley wished for a winged wife and little winged cherubs of children!

But this stock was very soon exhausted. As there was no school library [at Sion House school, where Shelley and Medwin were schoolmates], we soon resorted, 'under the rose,' to a low circulating one in the town (Brentford), and here the treasures at first seemed inexhaustible. Novels at this time, (I speak of 1803) in three goodly volumes, such as we owe to the great Wizard of the North [i.e. Sir Walter Scott], were unknown. Richardson, Fielding, and Smollett, formed the staple of the collection. But these authors were little to Shelley's taste. Anne Ratcliffe's works pleased him most, particularly the *Italian*, but the Rosa-Matilda school, especially a strange, wild romance, entitled *Zofloya, or the Moor*, a Monk-Lewisy production, where his Satanic Majesty, as in Faust, plays the chief part, enraptured him. The two novels he afterwards wrote, entitled *Zastrozzi* and *[St Irvyne, or] The Rosicrucian*, were modelled after this ghastly production, all of which I now remember, is, that the principal character is an incarnation of the devil, but who, unlike the *Monk*, (then a prohibited book, but afterwards an especial favourite with Shelley) instead of tempting a man and turning him into a likeness of himself, enters into a woman called Olympia, who poisons her husband homœopathically, and ends by being carried off very melodramatically in blue flames to the place of dolor.

'Accursed,' said Schiller, 'the folly of our nurses, who distort the imagination with frightful ghost stories, and impress ghastly pictures of executions on our weak brains, so that involuntary shudderings seize the limbs of a man, making them rattle in frosty agony.' &c. 'But who knows,' he adds, 'if these traces of early education be ineffaceable in us?' Schiller was, however, himself much addicted to this sort of reading. It is said of Collins that he employed his mind chiefly upon works of fiction and

---

★ Thomas Medwin, *The Life of Percy Bysshe Shelley*, 2 vols (London: Thomas Cautley Newby, 1847), vol. 1, pp. 29–34.

subjects of fancy, and by indulging some peculiar habits of thought, was universally delighted with those flights of imagination which pass the bounds of nature, and to which the mind is reconciled only by a passive acquiescence in popular tradition. He loved fairies, genii, giants, and monsters; he delighted to rove through the meanders of enchantment, to gaze on the magnificence of golden palaces, to repose by the waterfalls of Elysian gardens. Milton, too, in early life, lived in a similar dream-land, was fond of high romance and gothic diableries; and it would seem that such contemplations furnish a fit *pabulum* for the development of poetical genius.

This constant dwelling on the marvellous, had considerable influence on Shelley's imagination, nor is it to be wondered, that at that age he entertained a belief in apparitions, and the power of evoking them, to which he alludes frequently in his afterworks, as in *Alastor*:

> By forcing some lone ghost,
> My messenger, to render up the tale
> Of what we are;

and in an earlier effusion:

> Oh, there are genii of the air,
> And genii of the evening breeze,
> And gentle ghosts, with eyes as fair
> As star-beams among twilight trees;

and again in the *Hymn to Intellectual Beauty*:

> While yet a boy I sought for ghosts, and sped
> Through many a listening chamber, cave and ruin,
> And starlight wood, with fearful steps pursuing
> Hopes of high talk with the departed dead,
> I called on poisonous names with which our youth is fed –
> I was not heard – I saw them not.

After supping on the horrors of the Minerva press, he was subject to strange, and sometimes frightful dreams, and was haunted by apparitions that bore all the semblance of reality. We did not sleep in the same dormitory, but I shall never forget one moonlight night seeing Shelley walk into my room. He was in a state of somnambulism. His eyes were open, and he advanced with slow steps to the window, which, it being the height of summer, was open. I got out of bed, seized him with my arm, and waked him – I was not then aware of the danger of suddenly rousing the sleep-walker. He was excessively agitated, and after leading him back with some difficulty to his couch, I sat by him for some time, a witness to the severe erethism of his nerves, which the sudden shock produced.

This was the only occasion, however, to my knowledge, that a similar event occurred at school, but I remember that he was severely punished for his involuntary transgression. If, however, he ceased at that time to somnambulize, he was given to waking dreams, a sort of lethargy and abstraction that became habitual to him, and after the *accès* was over, his eyes flashed, his lips quivered, his voice was tremulous with emotion, a sort of ecstacy came over him, and he talked more like a spirit or an angel than a human being.

Passages of a Working Life (1805)*

CHARLES KNIGHT

Charles Knight was a young provincial journalist on a literary newspaper in Windsor. In 1810 he formed a dozen young men into a Reading Society, a precursor to the many Literary and Scientific Institutions that swept across England in the early Victorian period. Here he recalls his early reading.

And now began to be developed the peculiar temptations of my position – the opportunity for desultory reading to the neglect of all systematic acquirement; the tendency to day-dreams and morbid fancies, in the utter want of any improving companionship with those of my own age. From fourteen to seventeen I was learning the printer's trade, more, as it were, for recreation than for use; set no task-work, but occasionally working with irregular industry at some self-appointed tasks. The indulgence of my father was meant, I may believe, to compensate me for his opposition to my desire for a higher occupation than that which he pursued. Thus I was often galloping my pony along the glades of the forest; or watching my float, hour after hour, from the Thames bank at Datchet or at Clewer; or wandering, book in hand, by the river-side in the early morning; or plunging into 'the shade of melancholy boughs' on some 'sunshine holiday.' I read the old novels and the old poems again and again. Miss Porter and Mrs. Opie gave me fresh excitement when I was tired of Mrs. Radcliffe. *The Pleasures of Hope* and Beattie's *Minstrel* had long been my familiar favourites. At this time there were published charming little volumes of verse and prose, as 'Walker's Classics,' one of which was generally in my pocket. But in 1805 a new world of romance was opened to me by *The Lay of the Last*

---

* Charles Knight, *Passages of a Working Life During Half a Century*, 3 vols (London: Bradbury & Evans, 1864), vol. 1, pp. 69–70.

Minstrel. The old didactic form of poetry now seemed tedious compared with the adventures of William of Deloraine, and the tricks of the Goblin Page. Meanwhile my small Latin and less Greek were vanishing away. The newspaper, too, occupied much of my reading time. It was a period of tremendous interest, even to the apprehension of a boy. What an autumn and what a winter were those of 1805, in which I was enabled, day by day, to read the narratives of such deeds as stirred the heart of England in the days of the great Armada! Napoleon had broken up the camp at Boulogne, and was marching to the Rhine. Nelson had gone on board the *Victory* at Portsmouth, and had joined the fleet before Cadiz. On the 3rd of November came the news of the surrender of the Austrian army to the French Emperor at Ulm. On the 7th we were huzzaing for the final naval glory of Trafalgar, and weeping for the death of Nelson. Pitt rejoiced and wept when he was called up in the night to receive this news, as the humblest in the land rejoiced and wept.

Books and Their Writers (1816–29)*

Henry Crabb Robinson (1775–1867)

March 3rd [1816]. . . . Read till near one the beginning of *Vathek*.

March 4th. . . . Continued till near one *Caliph Vathek*, a book which is quite original in its style. It is marvellous without surfeiting and, without falling into the ridiculous, is humorous. I know not when I have been so amused.

March 5th. . . . Read *Vathek* till past one – the tale increases in horror, perhaps it becomes disgusting as it advances. It is a powerful production. . . .

March 10th. . . . Finished *Vathek*. As I advanced in this book it pleased me less. There is a strange want of keeping in the style, Johnsonian parade being blended with colloquial familiarities, and an unsuccessful attempt to unite the description of horrid situations and incidents with strokes of humour. The finest part is the description of hell at the close. The immense and gorgeous hall surrounded by objects of magnificence and wealth, full of wretches each tormented by an incessantly burning heart and each bearing his torment in mournful seclusion from others, all crowded together and each bearing his own suffering and further tormented by his hatred of his former friends – this is a very fine picture certainly. But the philosophy of the tale is not better than the philosophy of other like tales. If all the sufferers like Vathek have been wrought on by the agency of the necromancer and Giaour who wrought the Caliph's downfall, the same

---

* Henry Crabb Robinson, *Henry Crabb Robinson on Books and Their Writers*, ed. Edith J. Morley, 3 vols (London: J. M. Dent, 1938), vol. 1, pp. 180–1, 202, 366.

objection will apply to all. Either such an agent was not wanted to effect the perdition of the individual, and then he is an impertinent intruder; or he was, and then why was he permitted to ruin those who otherwise would have remained innocent?

How glad I should be if such an objection never occurred to me but on the perusal of a fairy tale! . . .

JANUARY 13th [1817] . . . I called at the library and coffee-house. From the former I stole the *Sicilian Romance*, and at the latter I was pained to see a subscription set on foot for *The Farmer's Boy*, R. Bloomfield, who is in poverty. I desired Thomas to put my name down for a guinea. . . . I read the *Sicilian Romance* with interest and curiosity, though I read it some twenty years ago. . . . At the inn I enjoyed myself in my room . . . reading the *Sicilian Romance*. . . .

JUNE 23rd & 27th [1829] . . . In my room at night [during a visit to Frankfurt] I read *The Mysteries of Udolpho*, which occupies time that might be better employed. But though not so strongly as in youth, this romance even now is capable of diverting my attention from objects that would seem to be irresistible in their demands. . . . Finished *Udolpho*, in which I ought not to have begun. Yet towards the end it indisposed me to any other occupation. But, after all, the interest is merely that of the worry of finding out a riddle. The poetry and much of the descriptions I skipped. Yet thirty years ago these were much admired. . . .

MARY RUSSELL MITFORD (1787–1855)

Mary Russell Mitford at the age of ten won £20,000 on the sweepstake, but her father, an unemployed physician, quickly gambled this away and reduced his family to penury. In 1820 they moved to a simple cottage in Berkshire, where she began writing essays on rural life, published under the title Our Village *(1824–32), which became an enormous success. She also wrote poetry and several plays, and numerous letters to literary friends.*

List of Books Read (January 1806)★

	Vols.
St. Margaret's Cave	4
St. Clair of the Isles	4
Scourge of Conscience	4
Emma Corbett	4

★ *The Life of Mary Russell Mitford, Related in a Selection from Her Letters to Her Friends*, 3 vols, ed. A. G. L'Estrange (London: Richard Bentley, 1870), vol. 1, p. 30.

Poetical Miscellany	1
Vicenza	2
A Sailor's Friendship and a Soldier's Love	2
The Castles of Athlin and Dunbayne	1
Polycratia	2
Travels in Africa	1
Novice of St. Dominick	4
Clarentina	3
Leonora (Miss Edgeworth's)	2
Count de Valmont	3
Letters of a Hindoo Rajah	2
Fourth Volume of Canterbury Tales	1
The Citizen's Daughter	1
Amazement	3
Midnight Weddings	3
Robert and Adela	3
The Three Spaniards	3
De Clifford	4

[55 volumes in 31 days]

Letter to Mrs Hofland (7 February 1821)★

Yes, I have read *Melmoth* all through; I never read much by Mr. Maturin before, – for *Woman* I could not bear, and, I believe, never finished, and *Bertram* was not at all to my taste; and *Montorio* and the rest I never saw. I don't think I shall want to look at *Melmoth* again in a hurry, and yet it is a most extraordinary book, full of power – terrible power – but with some most splendid painting and touches, that go quite to the heart, particularly in – I forget the name – the starving story. It is very painful too, but not, I think, on the whole so painful as *Kenilworth*, which is the most complete anatomy of the bad human heart that I have ever met with.

Letter to Mrs Hofland (4 March 1842)†

After finishing my last letter, I finished Lewis's *Memoirs*. It is grievous to think how – by the publication of a book (*The Monk*) that never ought to have been written or thought, far less printed – he stamped himself with an evil fame; for really he seems to have been one of the most benevolent, kind persons that ever lived. I think you would like his *Memoirs*, and the

---

★ *Letters of Mary Russell Mitford*, ed. Henry Chorley, 2 vols (London: Richard Bentley and Son, 1872), vol. 1, p. 101.
† *Ibid.*, pp. 198–9.

West Indian Journal. The ballad, 'Bill Jones,' of which Scott gave him the story, and which is versified in the plainest manner, and almost verbatim, is very striking. I remember, too, being much pleased, years ago, with the 'Anacreon.' Poor Lewis! I can't get him out of my head. – And yet the book is wretchedly done. It's the man's own character that forces itself upon one, in spite of the biographer; and the more strongly, of course, from the reaction – having before thought so ill of him. He died as early as Byron; and I am much more certain (humanly speaking) that he, if he had been spared, would have redeemed himself nobly, than I can feel about the other. There was in the one so much self-denial and care for others; – precisely what *Childe Harold* wanted.

'A Meeting with Mrs Radcliffe' (*c.* 1822)*

CHARLES BUCKE (1781–1846)

For this criticism [Bucke had praised Ann Radcliffe very highly in the 1821 edition of his book] Mrs Ratcliffe was pleased to send me her thanks. Sometime after, I was invited to supper. Her conversation was delightful! She sung *Adeste Fideles* with a voice mellow and melodious, but somewhat tremulous. Her countenance indicated melancholy. She had been, doubtless, in her youth, beautiful. She was a great admirer of Schiller's *Robbers*. Her favourite tragedy was *Macbeth*. Her favourite painters were, Salvator, Claude, and Gaspar Poussin: her favourite poets, after Shakespeare, Tasso, Spenser, and Milton.

There was, for many years, a report that this accomplished lady was afflicted with insanity. How the report came to be raised I know not; but, I believe, it never was the case. She had not only an elegant taste, but a comprehensive understanding. She died in 1823; and was buried in the chapel of ease, (belonging to the parish of St. George, Hanover Square,) at Bayswater.

I have read her *Romance of the Forest* four times; her *Italian* five times; her *Mysteries of Udolpho* nine times; and my imagination is, even now, always charmed whenever I think of either.

---

* Charles Bucke, *On the Beauties, Harmonies, and Sublimities of Nature*, New Edition, 3 vols (London: Thomas Tegg and Son, 1837), vol. 2, p. 123.

'Reminiscences' (*c.* 1823)

WILLIAM MAKEPEACE THACKERAY (1811–63)

The Victorian novelist Thackeray stayed with his mother and step-father in Tunbridge Wells in the summer of 1823, when he read many Gothic novels. He loved drawing, and used to cover the margins of his schoolbooks with caricatures from The Italian, The Castle of Otranto *and other novels. His childhood is described in the autobiographical excerpt from his novel* The Newcomes *and in his recollections published in the* Cornhill *magazine during 1860–2.*

The Newcomes (1853–5)★

There is a kind lady in the neighbourhood, who . . . has a stock of novels for the ladies of the upper servants' table. Next to Miss Cann, Miss Flinders is John James's greatest friend and benefactor. She has remarked him when he was quite a little man, and used to bring his father's beer of a Sunday. Out of her novels he has taught himself to read, dull boy at the day-school though he was, and always the last in his class there. Hours, happy hours, has he spent cowering behind her counter, or hugging her books under his pinafore when he had leave to carry them home. The whole library has passed through his hands, his long, lean, tremulous hands, and under his eager eyes. He has made illustrations to every one of those books, and been frightened at his own pictures of Manfroni or the One-handed Monk, Abellino the Terrific Bravo of Venice, and Rinaldo Rinaldino Captain of Robbers. How he has blistered Thaddeus of Warsaw with his tears, and drawn him in his Polish cap, and tights, and Hessians.

A Shabby Genteel Story (1840)†

I think it may be laid down as a pretty general rule, that most romantic little girls of Caroline's age have such a budding sentiment as this young person entertained; quite innocent, of course; nourished and talked of in delicious secrecy to the *confidante* of the hour. Or else what are novels made for? Had Caroline read of Valancourt and Emily for nothing, or gathered no good example from those five tear-fraught volumes which describe the loves of Miss Helen Mar and Sir William Wallace? Many a time had she depicted

---

★ William Makepeace Thackeray, *The Newcomes. Memoirs of a Most Respectable Family*, 2 vols (London: Bradbury and Evans, 1854), vol. 1, p. 117.

† William Makepeace Thackeray, *A Shabby Genteel Story* (1840) (London: Sidgwick & Jackson, 1971; facsimile of the 1879 edition), p. 49.

Brandon in a fancy costume such as the fascinating Valancourt wore; or painted herself as Helen, tying a sash round her knight's cuirass, and watching him forth to battle. Silly fancies, no doubt; but consider, madam, the poor girl's age and education; the only instruction she had ever received was from these tender, kind-hearted, silly books: the only happiness which Fate had allowed her was in this little silent world of fancy.

Roundabout Papers (1860–2)★

Yonder comes a footman with a bundle of novels from the library. Are they as good as *our* novels? Oh! how delightful they were! Shades of Valancour[t], awful ghost of Manfroni, how I shudder at your appearance! Sweet image of [Jane Porter's] Thaddeus of Warsaw, how often has this almost infantile hand tried to depict you in a Polish cap and richly embroidered tights! . . . Who knows? They *may* have kept those very books at the library still – at the well-remembered library on the Pantiles, where they sell that delightful, useful Tunbridge ware. I shall go and see. . . . As for the library, its window is full of pictures of burly theologians, and their works, sermons, apologues, and so forth. Can I go in and ask the young ladies at the counter for [Mary Anne Radcliffe's] *Manfroni, or the One-Handed Monk*, and [Pierce Egan's] *Life in London, or the Adventures of Corinthian Tom, Jeremiah Hawthorn, Esq., and their friend Bob Logic?* – absurd. I turn away abashed from the casement – from the Pantiles – no longer Pantiles, but Parade. . . . [My eyes] are looking backwards, back into forty years off, into a dark room, into a little house hard by on the Common here, in the Bartlemy-tide holidays. The parents have gone to town for two days: the house is all his own, his own and a grim old maid-servant's, and a little boy is seated at night in the lonely drawing-room, poring over *Manfroni, or the One-Handed Monk*, so frightened that he scarcely dares to turn round. . . .

For our amusements, besides the games in vogue, which were pretty much in old times as they are now (except cricket, *par exemple* – and I wish the present youth joy of their bowling, and suppose Armstrong and Whitworth will bowl at them with light field-pieces next), there were novels – ah! I trouble you to find such novels in the present day! O Scottish Chiefs, didn't we weep over you! O Mysteries of Udolpho, didn't I and Briggs minor draw pictures out of you, as I have said? This was the sort of thing; this was the fashion in *our* day: – Efforts, feeble indeed, but still giving pleasure to us and our friends. 'I say, old boy, draw us Vivaldi tortured in the Inquisition,' or, 'Draw us Don Quixote and the windmills, you know,' amateurs would say, to boys who had a love of drawing. . . .

'Valancourt, and who was he?' cry the young people. Valancourt, my

---

★ William Makepeace Thackeray, *Roundabout Papers*, ed. John Edwin Wells (New York: Harcourt, Brace, 1925), pp. 69–70, 80–1, 255.

dears was the hero of one of the most famous romances which ever was published in this country. The beauty and elegance of Valancourt made your young grandmammas' gentle hearts to beat with respectful sympathy. He and his glory have passed away. Ah, woe is me that the glory of novels should ever decay; that dust should gather round them on the shelves; that the annual cheques from Messieurs the publishers should dwindle, dwindle! Inquire at Mudie's, or the London Library, who asks for the *Mysteries of Udolpho* now? Have not even the *Mysteries of Paris* ceased to frighten? Alas, our novels are but for a season; and I know characters whom a painful modesty forbids me to mention, who shall go to limbo along with *Valancourt* and *Doricourt*, and *Thaddeus of Warsaw*.

Fifty Years' Recollections

Cyrus Redding (1785–1870)

A Visit to William Beckford (*c.* 1834)★

The door of Mr. Beckford's house [at Lansdowne Terrace, Bath] was opened by the porter, a dwarf, named Pero. I took leave of my companion, Mr. Goodrich, the architect [of Beckford's Lansdowne Tower further up the hill], to whose kindness I felt indebted for the pleasure I had experienced, and that I was about to receive. I have said I had seen Mr. Beckford on horseback, with the Duke of Hamilton, but I had no idea of ever approaching the presence of a man so retiring, proud, and inaccessible. It was, in fact, the most difficult thing possible to get acquainted with him – all but impracticable for any one not connected with literature or art. He had great resources for the employment of his time; he had none to spare for 'dawdling,' so he called it, for he told me subsequently, he never had a moment's *ennui* in his life. Byron, he said, had defied the world, and been beaten. He had never defied the world, but could live out of it; he cared nothing about it, and it could not beat him; he had seen all he could see of it, and knew how little it was worth.

An acquaintance once made, Mr. Beckford was unreserved, kind, and of a feeling disposition; but evidently quick to anger. But I forget that his dark-complexioned dwarf porter, Pero, as broad as he was long, had opened the door of his house to me – my companions had disappeared, and I was alone. A second servant led the way up to the library, the prolongation of which was over the arch [thrown over a driveway to connect two

★ Cyrus Redding, *Fifty Years' Recollections*, 3 vols (London: Charles J. Skeet, 1858), vol. 3, pp. 91–4.

houses] already mentioned. This the people of Bath gave out was the habitation of the mysterious dwarf. They knew, as I have said, as little of Mr. Beckford as if he dwelt fifty miles away. The servant announced my name, and retired.

The author of *Vathek* was sitting before a table covered with books and engravings. He rose, and, bowing with all the ease of a gentleman of the old school, began conversation without further ceremony. He was then in his seventy-fourth year, but did not look anything like as old. His temperance and activity, no doubt, contributed to this less senile appearance. Rather of a slender and delicate, than an athletic frame, he appeared a trifle above the middle height, dressed in a green coat, with cloth-covered buttons, a buff-coloured waistcoat, breeches of the same colour as his coat, and brown-topped boots, the fine cotton stocking appearing just over them. His eyes were small, acute, and grey, but expressive; his features in other respects not remarkable. On the whole, he appeared much as well-bred gentlemen did about thirty years before. . . .

'*Vathek*,' I observed, 'made a great sensation when it appeared?'

'You will hardly credit how closely I could apply myself to study when young. I wrote *Vathek* in the French, as it now stands, at twenty-two years of age. It cost me three days and two nights of labour. I never took off my clothes the whole time. It made me ill.'

'Your mind must have been deeply imbued with a love for Eastern literature?'

'I revelled day and night, for a time, in that sort of reading. It was a relief from the dryness of the old classical writers. The Greek and Latin were always tasks; the Persian I began to teach myself.'

'Byron praises the description of the "Hall of Eblis" for its sublimity. It is simply described.'

'That is a great point; all grand descriptions must be simple. Byron complimented me on my *Vathek* more than once.'

'I never read any description like that of the "Hall of Eblis" in any of the Eastern writings.'

'I took it from the "Hall of Old Fonthill," [the mansion built by his father] which was remarkably large – perhaps the largest in a private house in the kingdom – but I made mine larger still. There were numerous places of exit from it into other parts of the house, by long, winding passages. It was from that hall I worked, magnifying and colouring it with Eastern character. All the females were portraits drawn from the domestic establishment of Old Fonthill – their good or evil qualities ideally exaggerated to suit my purpose.'

Fashions in Novel Writing★

There have been as many different fashions in novel writing as in the shape of a coat, in the same duration of time. The novels of the Minerva Press were the rage in my youth. Many works appeared too openly licentious to be tolerated now; yet it is a question whether that insidious immorality which prevails in some works of imagination, with too fair an outside, is not really more prejudicial than where vice is at once apparent.

Monk Lewis's works fell early into my hands, but they operated in a different mode from that the author intended. I set Lewis down for a bigot in faith, as well as a man of loose morality. I had known some Catholic sisters of exemplary character; and I had early become acquainted with several excellent persons, members of their faith. There are many excellent people who will believe chalk is cheese, if they are told they must believe it, their fault being a belief in anything but the dictates of good sense – are they to be maligned rather than pitied? Lewis hated the men, the creed was of less moment. He described vice too well not to have been familiar with it. I read his *Monk* at fifteen; he borrowed that tale, I have no doubt, from *l'Année Littéraire*, for 1772, and the article *Le Diable Amoureux*. The *Tales of Wonder* I well recollect appearing. The first edition of his *Monk* shamed even its author into the suppression of some of its pruriences on its reaching a second. I heard of his *Castle Spectre* in the country; but I did not see it performed until I arrived in town. It produced no effect on my mind – I was an infidel as to ghostly appearances even then; but it drew crowds to the theatre. London was full of the praises of the productions of Lewis. His lubricity was tolerated in compliment to the service it rendered to intolerance. In those days, numberless stories were told and credited of the fleshless gentry, who appear to visit the earth on very silly errands, and hobgoblin Lewis found superstition and intolerance towers of strength in support of his popularity. Lewis was a pale, small man, no wizard in manners nor appearance, to be possessed of the talent with which he was unquestionably endowed. It was in 1807, when he was getting ready his *Romantic Tales* that I last saw him. . . .

The youth of the present day is fortunate in not having to contend with the tales of spectres and apparitions, which once made children so miserable, imbibed among other mischiefs in the nursery, the invention of superstition to overawe mind for the worst purposes. What, for example, would our forefathers not have said of the electric telegraph, but to prove that we dealt with the devil?

Moore's *Poems* under the name of Thomas Little, published after his *Anacreon*, I read by stealth soon after their appearance. It was not a feather in

---

★ Cyrus Redding, *Fifty Years' Recollections*, 3 vols (London: Charles J. Skeet, 1858), vol. 1, pp. 58–63.

his poetical renown, that he should, in youth, treat love no better than harlotry. It did not speak a pure spirit. I doubt whether Moore ever felt real love. The language of artifice and warmth beyond delicacy, coloured the passion after the mode in which rakes would depict it, but in more elegant language. It was the love of the lip, not the heart. . . .

The Children of the Abbey, by Maria Roche, Surr's *Splendid Misery*, and Mrs. Opie's *Mother and Daughter*, I remember successively taking to my place of reading in fine weather. This was a dense wood, seldom intruded upon, where I could enjoy reading undisturbed. I carried thither a piece of white-painted board for a seat, on which I had pencilled, in an idle mood, Pope's line:

> Divine oblivion of low-thoughted care.

I never knew, for certain, what fair footsteps had followed me unob-served, but I had been followed, and by one who was familiar with Pope, for I found the line written under mine in a lady's hand:

> For God, not man, absolves our frailties here.

I must state that Charlotte Smith's beautiful *Sonnets* were among my early reading, and that I read them still with great pleasure. Her novels, too, were popular, and rank with the best of those days. She had a far-spread reputation. Miss Owenson's [Lady Morgan's] *St. Clair*, and *Novice of St. Dominick*, I read about the same time as I perused Surr. Clara Reeve's *Old English Baron* followed. Godwin was too profound for my youth. Bage's *Hermsprong* I well remember, and Moore's *Zeluco*. The last was the first novel I ever called my own property. The fault of many of the novelists of that time, was that they relied too much upon imagination, leaving prob-ability out of sight. What a history, by no means honourable to the popular taste, would that of novel-writing be, with its lights and shadows, for sixty years past!

Shirley (1849)*

CHARLOTTE BRONTË (1816–55)

Caroline advanced to the mighty matron with some sense of diffidence: she knew little of Mrs. Yorke; and, as a parson's niece, was doubtful what sort of a reception she might get. She got a very cool one, and was glad to hide her discomfiture by turning away to take off her bonnet. Nor, upon sitting

---

* Charlotte Brontë, *Shirley. A Tale.* By Currer Bell, 3 vols (London: Smith, Elder, 1849), vol. 2, pp. 281–4.

down, was she displeased to be immediately accosted by a little personage in a blue frock and sash, who started up like some fairy from the side of the great dame's chair, where she had been sitting on a footstool, screened from view by the folds of the wide red gown, and running to Miss Helstone, unceremoniously threw her arms round her neck and demanded a kiss.

'My mother is not civil to you,' said the petitioner, as she received and repaid a smiling salute; 'and Rose, there, takes no notice of you: it is their way. If, instead of you, a white angel, with a crown of stars, had come into the room, mother would nod stiffly, and Rose never lift her head at all: but I will be your friend: I have always liked you!'

'Jessy, curb that tongue of yours, and repress your forwardness!' said Mrs. Yorke.

'But, mother, you are so frozen!' expostulated Jessy. 'Miss Helstone has never done you any harm: why can't you be kind to her? You sit so stiff, and look so cold, and speak so dry, – what for? That's just the fashion in which you treat Miss Shirley Keeldar, and every other young lady who comes to our house. And Rose, there, is such an aut— aut— – I have forgotten the word, but it means a machine in the shape of a human being. However, between you, you will drive every soul away from Briarmains, – Martin often says so!'

'I am an automaton? Good! Let me alone then,' said Rose, speaking from a corner where she was sitting on the carpet at the foot of a bookcase, with a volume spread open on her knee. 'Miss Helstone – how do you do?' she added, directing a brief glance to the person addressed, and then again casting down her grey, remarkable eyes on the book, and returning to the study of its pages.

Caroline stole a quiet gaze towards her, dwelling on her young, absorbed countenance, and observing a certain unconscious movement of the mouth as she read, – a movement full of character. Caroline had tact, and she had fine instinct: she felt that Rose Yorke was a peculiar child, – one of the unique; she knew how to treat her. Approaching quietly, she knelt on the carpet at her side, and looked over her little shoulder at her book. It was a romance of Mrs. Radcliffe's – *The Italian.*

Caroline read on with her, making no remark: presently Rose showed her the attention of asking, ere she turned a leaf, – 'Are you ready?'

Caroline only nodded.

'Do you like it?' inquired Rose, ere long.

'Long since, when I read it as a child, I was wonderfully taken with it.'

'Why?'

'It seemed to open with such promise, – such foreboding of a most strange tale to be unfolded.'

'And in reading it, you feel as if you were far away from England – really in Italy, – under another sort of sky – that blue sky of the south which travellers describe.'

'You are sensible of that, Rose?'

'It makes me long to travel, Miss Helstone.'

'When you are a woman, perhaps, you may be able to gratify your wish.'

'I mean to make a way to do so, if one is not made for me. I cannot live always in Briarfield. The whole world is not very large compared with creation: I must see the outside of our own round planet at least.'

'How much of its outside?'

'First this hemisphere where we live; then the other. I am resolved that my life shall be a life: not a black trance like the toad's, buried in marble; nor a long, slow death like yours in Briarfield Rectory.'

'Like mine! What can you mean, child?'

'Might you not as well be tediously dying, as for ever shut up in that glebe-house, – a place that, when I pass it, always reminds me of a windowed grave? I never see any movement about the door: I never hear a sound from the wall: I believe smoke never issues from the chimneys. What do you do there?'

'I sew, I read, I learn lessons.'

'Are you happy?'

'Should I be happier wandering alone in strange countries as you wish to do?'

'Much happier, even if you did nothing but wander. Remember, however, that I shall have an object in view: but if you only went on and on, like some enchanted lady in a fairy tale, you might be happier than now. In a day's wandering, you would pass many a hill, wood, and water-course, each perpetually altering in aspect as the sun shone out or was overcast; as the weather was wet or fair, dark or bright. Nothing changes in Briarfield Rectory: the plaster of the parlour-ceilings, the paper on the walls, the curtains, carpets, chairs, are still the same.'

'Is change necessary to happiness?'

'Yes.'

'Is it synonymous with it?'

'I don't know; but I feel monotony and death to be almost the same.'

Here Jessy spoke.

'Isn't she mad?' she asked.

'But, Rose,' pursued Caroline, 'I fear a wanderer's life, for me at least, would end like that tale you are reading, – in disappointment, vanity, and vexation of spirit.'

'Does *The Italian* so end?'

'I thought so when I read it.'

'Better to try all things and find all empty, than to try nothing and leave your life a blank.'

Author Index